PCs All in One Desk Reference For Dummies

D1238480

Microsoft Office 2000 Shortcuts

The following table lists toolbar buttons and keyboard shortcuts that work in all (or at least most) of the Office 2000 applications.

Button	Shortcut	Action
	Ctrl+N	Opens a new document
	Ctrl+O	Opens an existing document
	Ctrl+S	Saves the open document
	Ctrl+P	Prints the open document
	(none)	Previews the open document
	F7	Checks spelling
	Ctrl+X	Cuts a selection
	Ctrl+C	Copies a selection

Button	Shortcut	Action
	Ctrl+V	Pastes a selection
	Ctrl+Shift+C	Copies formatting for you to apply elsewhere
	Ctrl+Z	Undoes most recent action
	Ctrl+Y	Redoes an Undo operation
	Ctrl+K	Inserts a hyperlink
	F1	Starts the Office Assistant
B	Ctrl+B	Bold
I	Ctrl+I	Italic
U	Ctrl+U	Underline

Photography Resources

You can find information about photographers, graphic design, using digital cameras, tips for selling your photos, and lots of other stuff at these sites:

- ✔ `http://mavicausers.org/NYIphotoCover.html`: Take a basic photography course in digital photography.
- ✔ `www.askme.com`: Ask the experts, for free, about any digital photography topic.
- ✔ `www.kodak.com`: Kodak has online photography courses that cover everything from composition to lighting.
- ✔ `www.photo-seminars.com`: Choose from a selection of online classes.

PCs All in One Desk Reference For Dummies®

Cheat Sheet

E-Mail Abbreviations and Emoticons

Abbreviation	What It Means
AFAIK	As far as I know
AFK	Away from keyboard
BAK	Back at keyboard
BRB	Be right back
BTW	By the way
CYA	See ya!
FWIW	For what it's worth
GMTA	Great minds think alike
IMHO	In my humble opinion
L8R	Later
LOL	Laughing out loud
OIC	Oh, I see
OTOH	On the other hand
ROFL	Rolling on floor, laughing
SO	Significant other
TTFN	Ta-ta for now
WTG	Way to go!

Emoticon	What It Means
:) or :-)	Smile
:(or :-(	Frown
;) or ;-)	Wink
:D or :-D	Big smile (or laugh)
8-) or B-)	Sunglasses
:-o	Uh-oh!
:-#	Lips are sealed
>:-(	Mad
o:-)	Angel
:-\	Undecided
\o/	Praise the Lord!
{}	Hug
:-*	Kiss
{*}	Hug and a kiss
<g> or <grin>	Same as :-)
<sigh>	Sigh!

Search Engines and Directories

If you can't find the Internet site you're looking for, try these helpful search engines and directories:

AltaVista

www.altavista.com
Sophisticated Internet searching

Deja

www.deja.com
Directory of Usenet newsgroups

Excite

www.excite.com
News, directories, searching, reviews

Google

www.google.com
Simple design, lightning-fast search results

HotBot

hotbot.lycos.com
State-of-the-cool Net searching

LookSmart

www.looksmart.com
Internet directory with a useful design

Yahoo!

www.yahoo.com
The granddaddy of Internet directories

Yahooligans!

www.yahooligans.com
Kid-safe Internet directory

For Dummies: Bestselling Book Series for Beginners

PCs

ALL IN ONE DESK REFERENCE

FOR

DUMMIES®

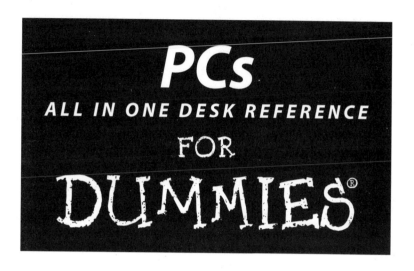

PCs
ALL IN ONE DESK REFERENCE
FOR
DUMMIES®

**by Dan Gookin, Sandra Hardin Gookin,
Greg Harvey, Lee Musick, John Levine,
Arnold Reinhold, Margaret Levine Young,
Doug Lowe, Viraf Mohta, Kelly Ewing,
Jennifer Kaufeld, John Kaufeld, David D. Busch,
Jim McCarter, Brian McCarter, and Sue Plumley**

Edited by Joyce J. Nielsen

WILEY

Wiley Publishing, Inc.

PCs All in One Desk Reference For Dummies®

Published by
Wiley Publishing, Inc.
909 Third Avenue
New York, NY 10022
www.wiley.com

For general information on our other products and services or to obtain technical support, please contact our Customer Care Department within the U.S. at 800-762-2974, outside the U.S. at 317-572-3993, or fax 317-572-4002.

Wiley also publishes its books in a variety of electronic formats. Some content that appears in print may not be available in electronic books.

Library of Congress Cataloging-in-Publication Data:

Library of Congress Control Number: 00-109320
ISBN: 0-7645-0791-5

Manufactured in the United States of America
10 9 8 7 6 5

1B/QV/QS/QT/IN

Hungry Minds, Inc., gratefully acknowledges the contributions of these authors and contributing writers: Dan Gookin, Sandra Hardin Gookin, Greg Harvey, Lee Musick, John Levine, Arnold Reinhold, Margaret Levine Young, Doug Lowe, Viraf Mohta, Kelly Ewing, Jennifer Kaufeld, John Kaufeld, David D. Busch, Jim McCarter, Brian McCarter, and Sue Plumley. Joyce J. Nielsen's developmental and editorial expertise and her keen awareness of our readers served to help make this book an invaluable resource. Thanks also to Bill Helling, Jodi Jensen, and Constance Carlisle for breathing life into this new series of books.

Publisher's Acknowledgments

We're proud of this book; please send us your comments through our online registration form located at www.dummies.com/register/.

Some of the people who helped bring this book to market include the following:

Acquisitions, Editorial, and Media Development

Senior Project Editor: Nicole Haims

Senior Acquisitions Editor: Steve Hayes

Copy Editor: Beth Parlon

Proof Editor: Seth Kerney

Technical Editor: Lee Musick

Media Development Coordinator: Marisa Pearman

Editorial Manager: Leah Cameron

Media Development Manager: Laura Carpenter

Media Development Supervisor: Richard Graves

Editorial Assistant: Candace Nicholson

Production

Project Coordinator: Maridee V. Ennis

Layout and Graphics: Barry Offringa, Jill Piscitelli, Jacque Schneider, Brian Torwelle, Julie Trippetti, Erin Zeltner

Proofreaders: Laura Albert, Joel K. Draper, David Faust, Susan Moritz, Angel Perez, Carl Pierce

Indexer: Maro Riofrancos

Special Help: Kim Darosett, Rebecca Senninger

Publishing and Editorial for Technology Dummies
Richard Swadley, Vice President and Executive Group Publisher
Andy Cummings, Vice President and Publisher
Mary C. Corder, Editorial Director

Publishing for Consumer Dummies
Diane Graves Steele, Vice President and Publisher
Joyce Pepple, Acquisitions Director

Composition Services
Gerry Fahey, Vice President of Production Services
Debbie Stailey, Director of Composition Services

Contents at a Glance

Cartoons at a Glance

By Rich Tennant

"I think the cursor's not moving, Mr. Dunt, because you've got your hand on the chalk board eraser and not the mouse."

page 5

"QUICK, KIDS! YOUR MOTHER'S FLAMING SOMEONE ON THE INTERNET!"

page 121

WIRED HOME OF THE FUTURE

"I'm setting preferences—do you want Oriental or Persian carpets in the living room?"

page 621

"It's a ten-step word processing program. It comes with a spell-checker, grammar-checker, cliché-checker, whine-checker, passive/aggressive-checker, politically correct-checker, hissy-fit-checker, pretentious pontificating-checker, boring anecdote-checker, and a Freudian reference-checker."

page 311

"Can't I just give you riches or something?"

page 239

WANDA HAD THE DISTINCT FEELING HER HUSBAND'S NEW SOFTWARE PROGRAM WAS ABOUT TO BECOME INTERACTIVE.

page 61

"Well, well! Guess who just lost 9 pixels?"

page 515

"Ronnie made the body from what he learned in Metal Shop, Sissy and Darlene's Home Ec. class helped them in fixing up the inside, and then all that anti-gravity stuff we picked up off the Web."

page 565

It started as a wasp around porch, and then Stuart found information on medieval architecture on AOL.

page 425

Cartoon Information:
Fax: 978-546-7747

E-Mail: richtennant@the5thwave.com
World Wide Web: www.the5thwave.com

Table of Contents

· ·

Introduction

*P*Cs All in One Desk Reference For Dummies is intended to be a reference for all the great things (and maybe a few not-so-great things) that you need to know when you're getting started with (or upgrading) your PC, browsing the Internet, writing e-mail, using America Online, working with Microsoft Works or Microsoft Office applications, composing pictures with a digital camera, setting up a home network, and so forth. Of course, you could go out and buy a book on each of these topics, but why would you want to when they're all conveniently packaged for you in this handy reference? *PCs All in One Desk Reference For Dummies* doesn't pretend to be a comprehensive reference for every detail of these topics. Instead, this book shows you how to get up and running fast so that you have more time to do the things that you really want to do. Designed using the easy-to-follow *For Dummies* format, this book helps you get the information you need quickly.

About This Book

PCs All in One Desk Reference For Dummies is a big book made up of several smaller books — minibooks, so to speak. Whenever one big thing is made up of several smaller things, confusion is always a possibility, right? That's why *PCs All in One Desk Reference For Dummies* is designed to have multiple access points (should we call them MAPs?) to help you find what you want. Each minibook begins with a parts page that tells you what chapters are included in that minibook. Useful running heads (the text you can find at the very top of a page) point out the current topic being discussed on that page. And who can overlook those handy thumb tabs that run down the side of the page and show the minibook number and chapter number and title? Finally, a small index is located at the end of each minibook, in addition to the regular full-length index at the end of the entire book.

How to Use This Book

This book acts like a reference so that you can locate what you want to know and get something done as quickly as possible. In this book, you can find concise descriptions introducing important concepts, task-oriented topics to help you identify what you need to do, and step-by-step instructions, where necessary, to show you the way.

At times, this book presents you with specific ways of performing certain actions. For example, when you must use a menu command, you see a command sequence that looks like this:

File➪Print

This command simply means to click the File menu with your mouse and then click the Print option.

Sometimes, we tell you about keyboard shortcuts. These shortcuts are key combinations such as

Ctrl+C

When you see this shortcut, it means to press and hold down the Ctrl key as you press the C key. Then release both keys together. (Don't attempt to type the plus sign!)

Throughout the book, information that you need to type appears in **boldface**. If what you're being asked to type appears within a bolded step, however, it appears in regular (nonbold) type.

This book also capitalizes the first letters of the names of dialog boxes, menu commands, and options, even though those letters may not be capitalized on your screen. This format makes sentences filled with long option names easier for you to read. (Haven't we thought of *everything?*)

When you're asked to click or double-click something, this book assumes that you're using the default mouse settings. So when you're told to *click,* use the left mouse button. When you need to use the right mouse button (to display a shortcut menu, for example), you're specifically told to *right-click.* So be sure to make the mental adjustments to these instructions if, for example, you're left-handed and have reversed your mouse buttons.

How This Book Is Organized

Each of the minibooks contained in *PCs All in One Desk Reference For Dummies* can stand alone — each has its own table of contents and index. The first minibook covers the PC basics that you should know to help you understand the rest of the stuff in this book. Of course, if you've been using a PC for a while now, you can probably skip Book I and surf on over to the minibook that truly interests you.

The remaining minibooks cover a variety of topics and software that you would normally find in multiple books. Refer to the table of contents for a detailed list of topics covered in each of these minibooks. The books are

- ✦ PC Basics
- ✦ Microsoft Windows
- ✦ The Internet
- ✦ Microsoft Works 6
- ✦ Microsoft Office 2000
- ✦ America Online 6.0
- ✦ Digital Photography
- ✦ Upgrading and Fixing a PC
- ✦ Home Networking

Icon Alert!

As you flip through this book, funny-looking pictures, called *icons,* in the margins draw your attention to important information. You'll find the following icons in this book:

This icon points out tidbits of information that may come in handy as you're performing a task.

Watch out! This icon warns you of things that can go wrong, such as data loss or unexpected events.

Just a reminder . . . this information may be worth remembering.

This icon indicates a quick alternative for accomplishing a task.

This icon appears beside guru-type stuff that you may want to skip over or read later.

This icon points out a nifty program feature, helpful shortcut, or insider tip.

This icon highlights a feature or procedure that may not work as you would expect.

You see this icon when we reference another book that provides additional details on the topic at hand.

When we talk about Microsoft Windows, we are referring to Microsoft Windows Millennium Edition. If you're using an older version of Windows, look for this icon to show you what's different between the two versions.

Book I

PC Basics

The 5th Wave   By Rich Tennant

"I think the cursor's not moving, Mr. Dimt., because you've got your hand on the chalk board eraser and not the mouse."

Contents at a Glance

Chapter 1: The Personal Computer

*I*n a way, a computer is just another electronic gadget. But unlike your toaster, a personal computer can be *programmed* to do a number of interesting tasks. It's up to you to tell the computer what you want it to do, making a computer's potential limitless. This chapter describes the components of a PC, including peripherals — the extras that you can add to a PC to make it more useful (or more fun!).

What Is a PC?

Technically, a personal computer is a large calculator. Of course, the display is better, and it has a ton more buttons. PCs are as proficient at working with words as they are with numbers. And even though laptop and notebook computers are lighter and more portable, they are still considered PCs.

You can use a PC for a number of different tasks; in the process, you can solve an infinite number of problems in a number of creative ways. Just about anything you can do with words, numbers, information, or communication, you can do with a PC. Remember these important things about PCs:

✦ You don't have to be a programmer to use a computer. Someone else does the programming; then you buy the program (the software) to get your work done.

✦ Your job, as the computer operator, is to tell the software what to do, which then tells the computer what to do.

Hardware

Two separate things make up a computer: hardware and software. They go hand in hand. You cannot have one without the other.

Hardware is the physical part of a computer (including peripherals), or any-thing you can touch and anything you can see. Yet, hardware is nothing unless it has software to control it. In a way, hardware alone is like a car without a driver or a saw without a carpenter; you need both to make some-thing happen.

Software

Software is the brains of the computer. It tells the hardware what to do. Without software, hardware just sits around bored and unappreciated. You must have software to make a computer go. In fact, software determines your computer's personality. Remember these important points about software:

✦ Computer software is nothing more than instructions that tell the hardware what to do, how to act, or when to lose your data. Without the proper software, your computer is merely an expensive doorstop.

✦ Although computer software comes on disks (CDs or floppy disks), the *disks* themselves aren't the software. Software is stored on disks just as music is stored on cassettes and CDs.

The operating system

The *operating system* is the most important piece of software. The operating system rules the computer, controlling all the individual computer compo-nents and making sure that everything gets along well. It's the actual brains of the operation, telling the nitwitted hardware what to do next.

The operating system typically comes with the computer when you buy it. You never need to add a second operating system, although operating sys-tems do get updated and improved from time to time. Your PC probably includes some version of Microsoft Windows as its operating system, such as Windows 95, Windows 98, Windows NT, Windows 2000 Professional, or Windows Millennium Edition. (See Book II, "Microsoft Windows," for more on Windows.)

Application programs

By itself, an operating system doesn't really do much for you. To get work done, you need an *application program*. Application programs do the work. Whatever you do on your computer, you do using an application program. These programs include word processors, spreadsheets, databases, utili-ties, games, and educational and programming software. And then you have all the Internet applications: Web browsers, e-mail programs, and software of that ilk.

Types and Models of PCs

For the first ten years or so after the PC came into existence, the desktop model was the most popular. Now, mini towers are more common. But you can choose from plenty of other models, each with an orientation, size, and enough blinking lights to please just about anyone.

The following list describes the various types and models of PCs:

✦ **Mini tower:** This type is currently the most popular PC configuration. The console sits upright on a desktop or beneath the desk.

✦ **Desktop:** Formerly the most popular PC configuration, this model has a console that lies flat on the tabletop with the monitor placed on top.

✦ **Notebook or laptop:** This type of computer folds into a portable, light-weight package, ideal for lugging around airports.

✦ **Towers:** This model is essentially a full-sized desktop model standing on its side, making it tall, like a tower. Manufacturers are phasing out this model in favor of the mini tower.

Identifying Peripherals

A computer peripheral is any accessory or auxiliary piece of equipment you buy that is outside the main computer system, such as scanners, tape drives, CD-RWs, digital cameras, video cameras, and external modems. The most popular PC peripherals today are the scanner and the digital camera. These accessories have dropped in price over the past few years, making them even more accessible. Common peripherals are described below:

✦ **DVDs:** DVDs are fast becoming the standard for computer hardware. DVD discs can store up to 17GB of information on a two-sided disc. If you have a DVD drive, you can access CD-ROMs and watch the movies that are available in DVD format. (See Book I, Chapter 4 for more information.)

✦ **CD-RWs:** You use rewritable CDs to store information, just as you would store information on a floppy disk. Like a floppy disk, you can also erase the information on a CD-RW and write new information to the disc. To take advantage of this technology, you need a CD-RW drive, and you have to buy special CD-RW discs. (For more details, see Book I, Chapter 4.)

✦ **Tape backup units:** A tape backup unit is a device that you can use to store backups (copies) of all the information on your PC's hard drive. Most PCs don't come with a tape backup unit. (See Book I, Chapter 7 for more information on backing up your data. Refer to Book VIII, Chapter 4 for information on how to install a tape backup unit.)

✦ **Zip drives:** Zip drives are popular for exchanging large amounts of information. Zip disks come in two different capacities: 100MB and 250MB. You can buy internal or external Zip drives. (See Book I, Chapter 4 for details on using a Zip drive. Book VIII, Chapter 4 explains how to install a Zip drive.)

✦ **Modems:** A modem is what connects your computer to the Internet. Many computers manufactured today have built-in modems, but if your computer is an older model, you may need to purchase one. (See Book III, Chapter 1 for information on choosing a modem. Refer to Book VIII, Chapter 6 for help on upgrading and troubleshooting modems.)

✦ **Sound cards:** A sound card enables your computer to play the recorded sounds you hear when you turn on the computer, run a program, or play a game. In addition, you need a sound card to play music (such as from a music CD or from a MIDI file) or to record your own voice — if you have a microphone and the proper software. (See Book VIII, Chapter 4.)

✦ **Microphones:** Speech recognition software and Internet telephone setups require a microphone, but other than that, you can probably live without one. You can purchase most microphones for under $20. People who use the computer for professional tasks, like music mixing, use a higher-end microphone with professional-level sound quality.

✦ **Scanners:** Scanners work like photocopiers except the image is translated into a graphics image in your computer rather than copied onto paper. After you scan an image, you can modify the image, save it to disk, add it to a document, or send it as an e-mail attachment. (See Book VIII, Chapter 7 for information on installing a scanner.)

✦ **Digital cameras:** The digital camera is *the* hip toy to have. The images they take are often excellent, and their plunging prices make them much more affordable. They range in price from a few hundred to several thousand dollars. Book VII provides a wealth of information on selecting and using a digital camera as well as tips on composing great pictures.

✦ **Video cameras:** You can use video cameras to record movies or single images and to send live images over the Internet. What you can do with the video camera depends on the software that comes with it. A Web cam is a video camera that is connected directly to a computer and sends pictures to the Web.

Plugging Stuff In

The back of your computer has a host of plug-in places. That side of your PC probably faces the wall because it's a ghastly sight. Yet this ugly sight of holes and plugs help you expand your PC system, as well as connect important items to the main console unit. Officially, these holes are known as *jacks* or *ports*. (Refer to Book VIII, "Upgrading and Fixing a PC," for additional details.)

Jacks and audio connectors

Located on the back of your PC are several *jacks,* which are the same thing as connectors. You can plug into a jack any one of a variety of external devices with which your computer can communicate. Some jacks, known as *ports,* can connect to a variety of things. Others are dedicated to particular devices.

Figure 1-1 illustrates a panel you would see on the backs of many PCs. You find all the common jacks in this panel. More jacks can be found on various expansion cards, but most can be found in one place. You should find the following items:

1. Keyboard connector

2. Mouse connector

3. USB port connector (usually two of them)

4. Serial port connector (usually two of them)

5. Printer (parallel) port connector

6. Joystick port connector

7. Audio connectors (three of them)

Figure 1-1:
Typical
jacks you
find on the
back of
a PC.

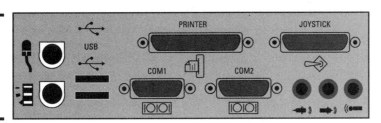

Most PCs are sold with audio jacks. These audio jacks enable you to connect fun stuff, such as a microphone or external speakers. More ports can be added to any PC through an expansion card. For example, for the price of an expansion card (the going rate is around $60 to $70), you can add a USB port to your computer.

 You connect the PC's speakers at the line-out or speaker jack. Some speakers are hooked up to the PC's monitor.

 You plug a microphone into the microphone jack. Doing so enables you to record your voice.

Any other external sound-producing device that you may want to connect to your PC is done through the line-in jack.

The keyboard and the mouse

The keyboard and mouse jacks look identical on most PCs, so look for the little keyboard and mouse pictures above or below the jacks to guide you in plugging in these devices.

If you have a serial mouse, you have to plug it into the computer's serial port. Plug it into COM1; COM2 is often used as the modem port, and plugging the mouse into COM2 can cause problems. If your PC has a COM3 port, you may plug your serial mouse into it instead of COM1. If your PC uses a USB mouse, plug it into the USB port. Many PCs have a spare USB port on the keyboard.

The printer port

You plug your printer into (surprise, surprise) the printer port. Generally, the port displays a little picture of a printer so that you know that you have the right port. The printer cable has two ends: one that plugs into the printer and one that plugs into the computer. If you look carefully, you'll notice that the connectors are different, making it somewhat impossible to plug a printer cable in backwards. The printer port can also be used as a link to certain external devices, such as CD-ROMs, DVDs, or external tape drives.

 You won't see this on your printer box, but you have to buy the printer cables that your printer requires. You won't find them hidden in your printer box anywhere.

The SCSI port

The SCSI (Small Computer System Interface) port, often pronounced *scuzzy*, is typically the fastest port available on many PCs. The SCSI port gives you the capability to connect multiple devices by using a *daisy chain* configuration in which devices are chained to one another, with the final device being connected to the SCSI port. This connection method enables one circuit board or card to handle all the devices instead of requiring a separate card for each device. SCSI technology is continually evolving, so the number of devices that you connect to a single port depends on the type of SCSI port available in your computer.

You can connect the following kinds of devices to a SCSI port:

✦ CD-ROM, CD-R (recordable CD-ROM), and CD-RW (rewritable CD-ROM) drives

✦ Hard drive

✦ Removable hard drive or magneto-optical disk drive

✦ Scanner

✦ Tape backup drive

SCSI ports are great for PC users who don't mind tinkering with their equipment. The SCSI port can be a challenge to configure because each SCSI device must have its own ID number, and you have to attach a gadget called a *terminator* to the device at the end of the daisy chain.

Serial (or COM) ports

You can plug just about anything that requires two-way communication into a serial port. Because of this fact, serial ports are also called COM ports, which stands for *communication*. Computers can have up to four serial ports but typically come with two: COM1 and COM2. An external modem is the most common device plugged into this port. Other typical uses for serial ports include a mouse, serial printer, scanner, and digital camera.

The USB port

Unlike most other ports, the USB (Universal Serial Bus) port was designed to host a number of different and interesting devices, making it possible to replace just about every other connector on the back of the PC. Microsoft incorporated USB drivers in its Windows 98 operating system, and most new computers and peripheral devices include USB technology. One of the biggest advantages of the USB port is that it requires no configuration. In true *plug-and-play* fashion, you simply plug in a USB device and begin using it. You don't even have to turn off your computer before plugging in the device; your computer recognizes it without rebooting. One additional bonus: unlike your printer and some other peripherals, USB devices all come with their own cables.

 Before you can use a USB device, make sure that your PC has one or more USB connectors. Check the back of your PC for a rectangular port with the USB symbol.

 The USB interface is not the solution for all peripherals. The USB port's speed is still too slow to work with fast hard disk drives. This problem may be solved in the future, however.

Chapter 2: Getting Started with Your PC

In This Chapter

- ✔ Turning the computer on
- ✔ The Windows desktop
- ✔ Setting the date and time
- ✔ Shutting down the computer

*C*hapter 1 introduces you to the basic parts of the PC, peripherals that can be attached to your PC, and how to plug stuff in. This chapter takes you a bit further and helps you actually start putting your computer to good use! We cover how to safely turn your computer on, change the date and time, and shut down the computer. In addition, this chapter helps you understand the layout and function of the Windows desktop.

Turning On the Computer

To turn on the computer, just make sure your computer is plugged in and push the on/off button or switch. Finding the computer switch is really the toughest part of turning on the computer. Most PCs put the switch on the front of the console, but on others, you may find the switch on the side or even on the back.

Most of the things connected to your PC have an on/off switch. You should turn on these basic components in this order:

1. **Turn on the *monitor* first so that it can warm up.**

2. **Turn on any *peripherals* — external devices that you plan to use, such as a printer, scanner, external disk drives, and digital camera — so that the computer will "see" them after it's up and running.**

3. **Turn on the *console* last.**

    After your computer completes its startup procedure (which may take a minute or two), you see the Windows desktop on your screen.

The Windows Desktop

Windows, the operating system on your PC, is basically full of pictures (otherwise known as *graphics* or *icons*) that you click when you want to select something. All these graphics are on what is called the *desktop*. What you see on the desktop are icons that represent programs in your computer. Double-click one of these icons, and you start that program. You can change the way your desktop looks, and you can decide (somewhat) what goes on your desktop. This section provides a brief overview of the Start button and the taskbar. For much more information on these and other Windows features and procedures, see Book II, "Microsoft Windows."

The Start button

The Start button is the door to all the programs and games that lurk in your computer. Click the Start button once (located at the bottom-left of your screen), and you open a *menu*. Hover your mouse over one of the words on the menu that has an arrow next to it, and a *submenu* appears. Keep hovering your mouse over more words with more arrows, and more submenus appear. If you find a particular program name that interests you, simply click it to start the program.

The Taskbar

The taskbar is that gray strip at the bottom of your screen that acts as a calling card to the programs that are currently running. Open a program, and you see an icon and a button on the taskbar. Close the program, and the icon and button go away. Want to switch to another program? Just click the icon on the taskbar.

Also nestled on the taskbar are the Start button, the Quick Launch bar, and the system tray. Check out Figure 2-1 to see all these goodies and to help you spot your taskbar, too. See Book II, "Microsoft Windows" for more details.

Figure 2-1: The Windows taskbar provides quick access to your applications.

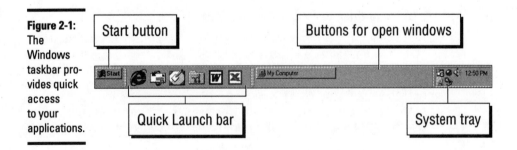

Start button

Buttons for open windows

Quick Launch bar

System tray

Setting the Date and Time

Most computers come with an internal, battery-operated clock. The battery enables your computer to keep track of the time, even when your computer is off. The current time is located at the far-right side of the Windows taskbar. If you point the mouse at the time, Windows displays the current date.

Computers don't really do a good job of keeping accurate time. No one knows why, but they don't. So, you may need to set or change the date on your computer periodically. Follow these steps to change the time or date:

1. **Double-click the time on the right end of the taskbar.**

This displays the Date/Time Properties dialog box, shown in Figure 2-2. (You can also right-click the time, and then choose Adjust Date/Time.)

Figure 2-2:
Change the
current date
or time
using the
Date/Time
Properties
dialog box.

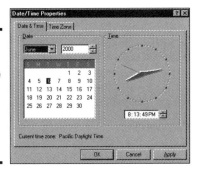

2. **Highlight the time displayed, and type the new time. Make any neces-sary changes to the current day, month, and year.**

3. **Click the Apply button to set the new date and/or time instantly.**

4. **Click OK after you finish.**

Shutting Down the Computer

When you're ready to turn off your computer, you should always exit your programs first, and then shut down Windows properly. *Never* turn off a com-puter when you're in the middle of something! The only time you should turn off your PC is when the screen tells you that it's *safe* to do so. Otherwise, you may lose unsaved information and eventually mess up your computer.

Follow these steps to shut down Windows the correct way:

1. **Click the Start button.**

The Start button is in the bottom-left corner of the taskbar.

2. **Click Shut Down.**

The Shut Down Windows dialog box appears, offering you additional options for shutting down your PC (see Figure 2-3).

Figure 2-3:
The Shut
Down
Windows
dialog box.

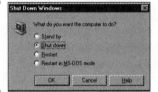

3. **Click the Shut Down option button.**

4. **Click the OK button.**

Windows is outta here! If you haven't saved the information in any open programs, Windows tells you about it. Go ahead and save everything.

5. **Flip the Off switch on your computer.**

Click. You're done.

Newer PCs may actually go into Sleep mode or shut themselves off automatically. If that's the case, you don't have to do Step 5 of the preceding list. You may still have to switch off your monitor, printer, and other peripheral devices, however.

Resetting your computer

You may need to reset your computer if it starts acting strange, or freezes up, and nothing seems to work. Follow these steps to reset your computer:

1. **Click the Start button.**

2. **Choose Shut Down.**

3. **Click the Restart option button.**

4. **Click the OK button.**

If your computer freezes and you can't get to the Start button, you may need to press the reset button on your computer or press the Ctrl+Alt+Delete keys at the same time (that means the Control key plus the Alt key plus the Delete key). This option should only be a last resort!

Never reset your computer to get out of an application (unless your program is frozen and you can't get out of it any other way). Never reset when the disk drive light is on. Also, don't forget to remove any floppy disks from your floppy drive before you reset.

Putting your monitor to sleep

Putting your monitor to sleep shuts it off and saves power after a period of inactivity. The PC simply stops sending a signal to the monitor, and the monitor goes blank — as if it weren't working. (For more information on maintaining monitors and installing a new monitor, see Book VIII, Chapter 5.)

Follow these steps to put your monitor to sleep:

1. **Click the Start button.**

2. **Choose Settings⇨Control Panel.**

3. **Double-click the Power Management icon.**

 The Power Management Properties dialog box opens.

4. **Choose a time to shut down the monitor.**

 You choose the time near the bottom of the dialog box next to Turn Off Monitor. Click the drop-down arrow for more time options.

5. **Click OK to close the dialog box.**

6. **Close the Control Panel by clicking the X (the Close button) in the upper-right corner.**

Now your monitor will sleep after a given period of inactivity. So when you're away from the computer for a while, the monitor will stop displaying an image. This doesn't turn the monitor off; you still need to push the monitor's Off button to turn it off. (To waken a sleeping monitor, just move the mouse or press a key.)

Suspending your PC

Suspending your computer is putting your whole computer to sleep without turning it off. This energy-saving mode supplies just enough power to keep memory going so that your computer remembers what you just did. But it doesn't keep all the lights and sounds alive, thus saving power.

Follow these steps to suspend your computer:

1. **Click the Start button.**

2. **If you have Windows 95, click the Suspend option. (For Windows 98, Windows Me, or Windows 2000) Choose Shut Down; then choose the Stand By option.**

3. **Click OK.**

    Your PC looks like it was just switched off, but it's not really off. It's just suspended.

When you're tired of watching your computer do nothing, press any key on the keyboard (the Enter and spacebar keys are our favorites) or jiggle the mouse. Either one of these actions revives your computer.

If, for some bizarre reason, your computer enters this suspend mode and won't come out of it (which has been known to happen), just reset your computer.

Chapter 3: Working with the Keyboard and Mouse

In This Chapter

✔ Getting acquainted with the keyboard keys

✔ Performing actions with the mouse

✔ Tweaking the mouse settings in Windows

*U*nless you have a keyboard and mouse, your computer isn't going to do much other than just sit there. The keyboard and mouse are the tools you use to make things happen in programs. You type something by using the keyboard, and click something by using the mouse. Your computer is useless without them.

Keyboard Basics

The typical PC keyboard is shown in Figure 3-1, although what is considered "typical" is quickly changing. What you see here is called the Enhanced 104-key keyboard. You also can purchase a keyboard that is designed to provide better support to your wrists when you type (commonly called an ergonomic keyboard). See Book VIII, Chapter 5 for information on upgrading and installing a new keyboard.

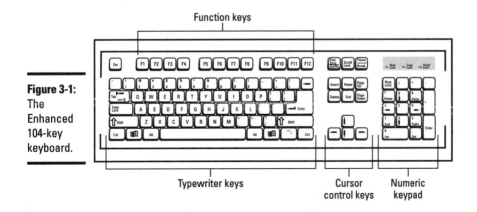

Figure 3-1:
The
Enhanced
104-key
keyboard.

Keyboard layout

Keyboards include the following four main areas:

✦ **Function keys:** These keys are located on the top row of the keyboard and are labeled from F1 through F12.

✦ **Typewriter keys:** With a few exceptions, such as Alt, Ctrl, and (on some keyboards) a couple of special Windows keys, these keys are the same keys that you find on a typewriter: letters, numbers, and punctuation symbols.

✦ **Cursor-control keys:** These four keys are commonly referred to as *arrow keys*. You can use them to move the cursor in the direction that the arrow is pointing: up, down, left, or right. Above the arrow keys are the Insert, Delete, Home, End, PgUp (page up), and PgDn (page down) keys.

✦ **Numeric keypad:** The numeric keypad contains additional number keys laid out as they appear on a calculator keypad. The following math symbols are available on the numeric keypad:

> \+ is for addition
>
> – is for subtraction
>
> * is for multiplication
>
> / is for division

You can also use the numeric keypad to act as a cursor control device. Press the Num Lock key (on many keyboards, a light appears above or near the Num Lock key) to make the numbers work. Press the Num Lock key again to turn off the numeric keypad so that you can use the arrow keys (as labeled) to move the cursor around.

The screen says, `Press any key to continue.` Hmmm. Any key? Where is the Any key? Any key refers to, literally, any key on your keyboard. To be safe, however, press the spacebar or the Enter key when your screen says to press "any key."

The Windows key

If you're using Windows 95 or later, your keyboard probably has a few additional keys, such as the Windows key. The Windows key sits between the Alt and Ctrl keys on either side of the spacebar and serves the same purpose as pressing Ctrl+Esc — it pops up the Start menu.

When pressed with other keys, the Windows key provides a shortcut to various functions. The following table shows what these key combinations do.

Key Combo	Function
Win+D	Displays the desktop (this may not work for Windows 95)
Win+E	Starts Windows Explorer
Win+F	Displays the Find Files dialog box
Win+R	Displays the Run dialog box

The Shortcut Menu key

 The Shortcut Menu key, located between the Windows key and the Ctrl key on the right side of your keyboard, displays the shortcut menu for whatever item is currently selected on the screen. This key works the same as if you had right-clicked an item.

The Enter key

Your PC sports not one, but two, Enter keys. The first one is located just to the right of the quotation mark/apostrophe key. The second Enter key is placed to the right of the numeric keypad for speedy entry of numbers. You use the Enter key to select the highlighted option in a dialog box, to end a paragraph in a word processing program, and when you're instructed to "press any key."

 Don't press Enter after filling in a text box inside a dialog box. In some cases, pressing Enter closes the dialog box. Use the Tab key to move between fields.

The Tab key

Tabs are considered single, separate characters. When you backspace over a tab in a word processing program, the tab disappears in one chunk — not space by space. The Tab key can be used to space evenly across a page to make spacing consistent and to move between fields or areas in a dialog box. On the Internet, use Tab rather than Enter to fill in a form.

The Escape key

The Windows Escape key (shown as Esc on your keyboard) acts the same as clicking Cancel when you're in a dialog box. It also closes some windows.

Editing keys

You can always edit typed text in a Windows document. Windows provides special editing keys to make changing text fast and easy. Table 3-1 lists the common keys and key combinations that you can use for editing text.

Table 3-1	Keyboard Shortcuts for Editing
Key/Key Combo	*Function*
←	Moves the text cursor left (back) one character.
→	Moves the text cursor right (forward) one character.
↑	Moves the text cursor up one line.
↓	Moves the text cursor down one line.
Ctrl+←	Moves the text cursor left one word.
Ctrl+→	Moves the text cursor right one word.
Home	Moves the text cursor to the start of the line.
End	Moves the text cursor to the end of the line.
Delete	Deletes the character immediately to the right of the text cursor.
Backspace	Deletes the character immediately preceding the text cursor.
PgUp	Moves the text cursor up one screen page.
PgDn	Moves the text cursor down one screen page.
Ctrl+↑	Moves the text cursor to the preceding paragraph.
Ctrl+↓	Moves the text cursor to the next paragraph.
Ctrl+Delete	Deletes characters from the cursor's position to the end of the word. (**Note:** Ctrl+Delete may not work for Windows 95 computers.)
Ctrl+End	Moves the text cursor to the end of the document.
Ctrl+Home	Moves the text cursor to the beginning of the document.

Other keyboard keys

The following keys affect the way the keyboard functions. Often, these keys are used in conjunction with other keys:

✦ **Caps Lock:** The Caps Lock key enables you to type all capital letters without having to hold down the Shift key. Press the Caps Lock key once, and all your letters appear in uppercase; press it again, and the letters you type return to their normal lowercase state.

✦ **Num Lock:** Num Lock makes the numeric keypad on the right side of the keyboard produce numbers. Press this key again, and you can use the arrow keys in the numeric keypad to move the text cursor.

✦ **Shift:** Hold down the Shift key before you press a letter key to make a capital letter. You also can insert %, @, #, ^, and so on, by typing the number keys while pressing the Shift key.

✦ **Ctrl:** The Control key, labeled Ctrl, is used in combination with one or two additional keys to carry out specific commands. For example, in many applications you can press the Ctrl key along with the *S* key (Ctrl+S) to save a file.

✦ **Alt:** Use the Alt key in combination with other keys to carry out commands. For example, press the Alt key and the F4 key (Alt+F4) to close a window on the desktop.

Mouse Basics

Many of the commands you use to get things done involve the mouse. If you need to replace or upgrade your mouse (or install another type of pointing device, such as a trackball or touchpad), see Book VIII, Chapter 5.

You can perform the following actions with the mouse:

✦ **Click:** Press and release the mouse's main button, which is the one on the left.

✦ **Double-click:** Two quick clicks in a row, both pointing at the same spot.

✦ **Right-click:** Press and release the right button on the mouse.

✦ **Drag:** Move the mouse around while pressing and holding down the main mouse button. In Windows, this technique is often used to select text or move objects around on the screen.

✦ **Point:** Move the mouse pointer on the screen so that it's hovering over some object, such as a button.

✦ **Select:** Point to something on the screen and then click to highlight it. Sometimes, you drag the mouse around one or more items to select them.

Clicking and double-clicking

A *click* is a single press of the mouse button. You are likely to read things that say something like "Click the OK button." This instruction means that some type of graphic appears on-screen with the word *OK* on it. Move your mouse (which moves the pointer on the screen) until the pointer is over the word *OK*. Then with your index finger, click the left mouse button. If you need to click the right mouse button instead of the main (left) button, the instructions tell you to "right-click" or to "click the right mouse button." These same instructions are true for the wheel button, if you happen to have an IntelliMouse that includes a little wheel between the other two regular buttons. (See "Using the IntelliMouse," later in this chapter.)

A *double-click* is two rapid clicks in a row. You typically do this in Windows to open a file or a folder. Don't move the mouse around between the clicks — both clicks have to be on the same spot.

If you double-click your mouse and nothing happens, you may not be clicking fast enough. Try clicking the mouse button a bit faster.

Dragging the mouse

You drag the mouse when you want to select a group of items on the screen or when you want to move something around on the screen. For example, you can drag the mouse to move your desktop icons to more convenient locations. You can also draw a rectangle around a group of items to select them all.

Follow these steps to drag something with the mouse:

1. **Point the mouse cursor at what you want to drag.**

2. **Press and hold down the left mouse button as you move the mouse to a new location.**

   The drag operation is really a *move* — you start at one point on the screen and move (drag) the item to another location.

3. **Lift your finger to release the mouse button.**

   You're done dragging. When you release the mouse button, you let go of what you were dragging.

Pointing the mouse

When you're told to "point the mouse," it means that you use the mouse pointer to point at something on the screen. The pointer may change to a different shape.

Selecting with the mouse

Selecting is often the same as clicking. When you are told to select that doohickey over there, you move the mouse pointer and click the doohickey. Simple. To deselect something, such as when you click the wrong thing or change your mind, just click somewhere else — the desktop, for example.

Tweaking the mouse in Windows

The Mouse Properties dialog box is where you play with all the mouse settings. You can adjust your mouse to accommodate left-handers, change the speed of the double-clicking process, or even change the way your mouse pointer looks.

Follow these steps to open the Mouse Properties dialog box:

1. **Click the Start button and choose Settings⊅Control Panel.**

   The Control Panel's main window appears.

 2. **Double-click the Mouse icon.**

   The Mouse Properties dialog box opens, as shown in Figure 3-2. Click each tab at the top of the dialog box to check out each section.

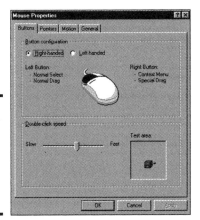

Figure 3-2:
Change
mouse set-
tings in the
Mouse
Properties
dialog box.

3. **If you want to make a change to a setting, do so and click OK.**

   If you're left-handed, for example, you can reverse the operations of the
   mouse buttons by selecting the Left-handed option on the Buttons tab.
   Otherwise, if you don't want to mess with anything, and you're happy
   with the way your mouse works, click Cancel and move on.

You see a different dialog box if you have the Microsoft IntelliMouse (see the
next section) installed on your computer. The dialog box associated with
the IntelliMouse has more options and goodies.

Using the IntelliMouse

Microsoft's *IntelliMouse,* shown in Figure 3-3, is also known as a *wheel mouse*
and has a wheel inserted between the two mouse buttons, which enables you
to do some neat tricks:

✦ You can roll the wheel up and down to scroll a document (although not
  all programs respond to the IntelliMouse, so it doesn't always work).

✦ You can press and hold the wheel button to pan the document up,
  down, left, or right. Quite handy, really.

Figure 3-3:
The
Microsoft
IntelliMouse
provides
additional
mouse
functions.

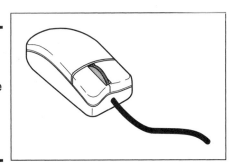

Chapter 4: Dealing with Disk Drives

In This Chapter

✓ Understanding your computer's storage drives

✓ Finding your disk drives

✓ Floppy disk drive basics

✓ Inserting a CD-ROM or DVD

✓ Using a Zip drive

*Y*ou may accumulate tons of documents and images in your computer. Disk drives are used for storing stuff — the operating system, programs, and all the wonderful things you create on your PC. When you finish creating something, you can save your work by making a permanent copy on a disk (either your hard drive or a floppy disk — it doesn't really matter).

Many PCs are sold with 64, 128, or more megabytes of RAM *(random access memory)*. That seems to be enough, so why even bother with this disk storage stuff? The reason you should bother with disk storage is that disk drives are for long-term storage. RAM is temporary storage because that memory is erased each time you turn off the computer's power. But if you save your information to a disk, it's available the next time you turn on your computer. This chapter tells you how to work with disk drives in Windows. For information on how to install or replace disk drives, refer to Book VIII, Chapter 4.

A *megabyte* is a million bytes, or enough storage space to hold roughly one million characters, one thousand pages of information, or several hundred graphics files. That's a lot of space.

Understanding Your Computer's Storage Drives

No matter what types of drives your computer has, all drives function in essentially the same way. Drives store your words and pictures in bunches of 0s and 1s. Unlike RAM (discussed in Book VIII, Chapter 2), the information that you store on your computer's drives doesn't disappear after you turn off the computer. The information remains stored on your drive until you choose to delete it. This section takes a brief look at the various types of storage drives.

Floppy drive

The floppy drive is the oldest and slowest of the drives found on today's computers. The *floppy drive* uses a 3 ½-inch removable disk that can hold up to 1.44MB of information. In the ancient days of computing, computers had 5 ¼-inch floppy drives that held even less information — up to 1.2MB. If you think you have a problem with a floppy drive, most of the time the problem is that the disk is defective, but the drive itself is fine. If your floppy drive does go on the blink, you can buy a replacement for about $25. Floppy drives are handy for storing and exchanging small files.

Hard drive

The *hard drive* is a non-removable device hidden away in your computer's nether regions. Hard drives are very fast and can store thousands of times more information than floppy disks can. The smallest hard drives available today hold about 3.2GB of information and cost about $125. The largest hard drives can store 50GB of information and cost about $1,500. Hard drives are the main storage devices for personal computers. They hold your operating system and application programs as well as your data.

CD-ROM drive

CD-ROM drives — or *Compact Disk Read-Only Memory* drives — are read-only devices. *Read-only* means that the CD-ROM drive can read information that has been placed on a CD-ROM, but the drive cannot change or delete the information. In other words, you can't save information onto a typical CD-ROM, but you can use your CD-ROM drive to read a lot of information (about 650MB-worth). The CDs look just like the ones that you play in your stereo's CD player. In fact, most computer CD-ROM drives are capable of playing music CDs. You can buy a CD-ROM drive for as little as $50 but take a look at the following paragraph first. Most new computer programs are sold on CD-ROMs.

CD-R and CD-RW drives

CD-R — or *CD Recordable* drives — and *CD-RW* — or *CD ReWriteable* drives — can not only read CD-ROMs like their simpler CD-ROM drive cousins, but can also write information to special CDs.

CD-R drives can write to a CD only one time. After that, the CD effectively becomes a CD-ROM, meaning that the information on it is read-only and can't be modified. CD-R drives are available starting at about $200. Also, you can't record to just any CD-ROM. You have to buy special CDs labeled CD-R. CD-R drives are great for making permanent copies of large amounts of information. After they're created, they can't be overwritten.

On the other hand, CD-RW drives can write to a CD many times over, just as floppy disks can be used again and again. CD-RW drives are available starting at about $300. CD-RW drives can read from both regular CDs as well as CD-Rs, but require special CD-RW discs for actual rewriting. CD-RW drives are handy for making copies of large amounts of information that changes frequently. A CD-RW disc can be overwritten up to 1,000 times.

DVD-ROM drive

The *DVD-ROM* — or *Digital Versatile Disk Read-Only Memory* — is the newest type of compact disc drive available. It can hold up to 5.2GB of information on a disk that looks just like a CD-ROM but isn't. DVD-ROM drives can also read regular CD-ROMs. The most popular use of DVD-ROM drives is watching feature movies. DVD-ROM drives are available for as little as $100.

DVD-RAM drive

The DVD-RAM drive is the rewriteable version of the DVD-ROM drive. Like its read-only sibling, the DVD-RAM drive can hold up to 5.2GB of information. DVD-RAM drive prices start at about $500.

Zip drive

Zip disks look like floppy disks on steroids. *Zip* disks come in two different capacities: 100MB and 250MB. The 250MB model is capable of reading from and writing to 100MB Zip disks. The 100MB model can only read and write to 100MB Zip disks. You can buy internal or external Zip drives. The external models usually connect to your computer's parallel printer port, but *USB — Universal Serial Bus* — and *SCSI — Small Computer Systems Interface* — models are available. Many computer manufacturers offer internal Zip drives as an option. Prices for Zip drives start at about $100. Zip drives are popular for exchanging large amounts of information.

Tape backup drive

As the name implies, *tape backup drives* are useful for making backup copies of your computer files. Tape backup drives come in various sizes and capacities, from a low end of a couple of hundred megabytes to a high end of up to 70GB. Prices range from about $100 for a low-capacity tape backup drive to thousands of dollars for the high-capacity systems.

Finding Your Disk Drives

Windows keeps a representation of all your PC's disk drives in the My Computer window. When you double-click the My Computer icon on the desktop, the My Computer window pops up and lists all the disk drives in your computer system. You should be able to locate the following disk drives in this window:

✦ **Drive A:** Your PC's main floppy disk drive. You manually insert and remove the floppy disk here.

✦ **Drive C:** Your PC's main hard disk drive. You may also have a hard drive D and possibly even a hard drive E. (See Chapter 7 for more information on using and maintaining hard drives.)

✦ **CD-ROM drive:** On most PCs, the CD-ROM or DVD drive is usually given the letter following the last hard drive, which is usually drive D. Even if it's a different letter on your PC, it uses the same icon.

✦ **Other drives:** Other drives may exist in your system, such as a Zip drive. A Zip disk is similar to a floppy disk drive but provides more storage capacity. A Zip disk is also physically thicker than a floppy disk, which is why it needs its own drive.

In the My Computer window, each disk drive has an icon, a letter, and an optional name. The icon indicates which type of disk drive it is: hard disk, floppy disk, or CD-ROM/DVD. My Computer even offers a generic looking icon for removable disks (such as a Zip disk or Magneto Optical disk), RAM drives, network drives, and other interesting storage devices. All CD and DVD drives use the same CD-ROM drive icon, but you can change the optional name. See "Naming your disk drives," later in this chapter, to find out how to change the optional name.

Understanding drive letters

To Windows and to your software, disk drives are known by letters, from A (skipping B), C, D, and up to Z. Drive A is the first floppy drive — meaning the main floppy drive. Drive C is the first hard drive.

Drive B is reserved for the second floppy drive. Back in the early days when hard drives were outrageously expensive, most PCs were sold without them. The second floppy drive served as a cheap form of extra storage. Today, it's not needed, but letter B is still set aside just in case.

Drive letters are up for grabs after drive C. For example, no hard and fast rule says that drive D must be the CD-ROM drive. If you have any extra hard drives in your PC, they're given drive letters D and up. After the last hard drive letter comes your CD-ROM or DVD drive, which could be drive D or E or up to Z.

Naming your disk drives

The hard drives in your PC can each be given a name. You don't have to do this unless you want to see the name displayed in the My Computer window (and other places in Windows). But if you're curious, or if you want to change the name from MICRON or PRESSARIO to something more personal, you can do so.

Follow these steps to change the name of your hard drive:

1. **Double-click the My Computer icon located on the desktop.**

2. **Right-click the disk drive's icon.**

A shortcut menu appears.

3. **Choose the Properties command from the shortcut menu.**

4. **In the General tab of the Properties dialog box, type the new name for your hard drive in the Label text box.**

5. **Click OK.**

Floppy Disk Drive Basics

Many programs still come on 3 ½-inch floppy disks. For example, driver files for new hardware that you can add to your PC often come on floppy disks. You can also use floppy disks to move files between two computers. (You can't move very large files, but most document files fit on a floppy disk.)

Inserting and removing floppy disks

To properly insert a floppy disk into your PC's floppy drive, stick it into the drive, label side up, round metal circle on the bottom, with the shiny metal piece going in first. The disk makes a *thunk* noise when it's in place. To remove the floppy disk, push the button near the floppy drive slot. Doing so ejects the disk out of the drive about an inch or so. Grab the disk and put it away.

Always make sure that the computer is not "writing to" the floppy disk before you eject it (the blinking access light on the floppy drive should be off). Also, make sure that you're not currently using any files on the floppy drive; before you eject the disk, close any files that you may have accessed. If you don't, Windows asks you to reinsert the floppy disk so that it can finish writing information.

Don't use sticky notes as disk labels! They fall off when you're not looking and can sometimes get stuck inside your disk drives.

Formatting floppies

A floppy disk must be formatted before you can use it. Unless you were smart enough to buy preformatted floppy disks, you have to format them at some point. Most computer stores, however, stock preformatted disks. Read the labels carefully to find them — it'll save you some time and effort.

If the disk isn't formatted and you try to access it, Windows displays the error message shown in Figure 4-1. If you get this error message, click the Yes button to begin formatting the disk.

Figure 4-1:
You receive this error message when you try to access an unformatted disk.

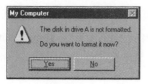

Follow these steps to format a floppy disk:

1. **Insert an unformatted disk in drive A.**

   You can insert a brand new disk or a disk you've used before into the drive. If you use an old disk, however, be aware that formatting erases everything on the disk. This act could be devastating, so be careful!

2. **Double-click the My Computer icon.**

3. **Right-click the icon for drive A and choose Format from the shortcut menu.**

   The Format dialog box appears, as shown in Figure 4-2.

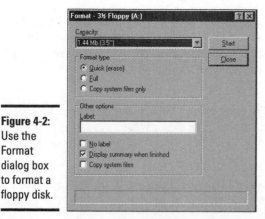

Figure 4-2:
Use the Format dialog box to format a floppy disk.

4. **Click the Start button.**

Windows takes a few minutes to finish formatting. When it finishes, you may or may not see a summary screen. Press Esc to close the dialog box, and you're ready to use the freshly formatted disk.

Sending files to a floppy disk

You can send a file to a floppy disk in two ways (remember to put a format-ted floppy disk into drive A before you do this):

✦ Choose drive A from any Save As dialog box.

✦ In Windows Explorer, find and select the file(s) that you want to save to drive A. Choose File⇨Send To⇨3 ½ Floppy (A) from the menu.

How Much Space Is on the Disk Drive?

Disk drives fill up, and at some point, you may want to see how much space is available on the disk drive. Follow these steps:

1. **Double-click the My Computer icon on the desktop.**

2. **Right-click a disk drive.**

A disk must be in the floppy drive or CD-ROM drive before you right-click those icons. A shortcut menu appears.

3. **Choose Properties to display the Properties dialog box.**

4. **Read the information on the General tab.**

The amounts of space *used* and *free* for that disk are listed here.

5. **Click OK to close the dialog box.**

Don't be surprised if disks such as CD-ROMs and DVDs are always full. These disks can only be read from, not written to.

(See Chapter 7 for information on maintaining your computer.)

Inserting a CD-ROM or DVD

Computer CDs go into CD-ROM drives in one of two ways: slide-in or tray. (A DVD drive looks and acts just like a CD-ROM drive. But in addition to reading computer CDs and music CDs, the DVD drive accesses computer DVD and video DVD disks.) The following list explains how each type works:

✦ **Slide-in:** Slide the CD into the CD-ROM drive — just as you would slide a CD into your car's CD player.

✦ **Tray:** Press the CD-ROM drive's eject button to pop the tray out of the drive. Drop the CD into the tray, with the label up. Press the CD-ROM drive's eject button again, and the tray slides back into the computer.

Using a Zip Drive

Zip drives are becoming popular alternatives and supplements to the traditional PC floppy disk, because they are a great way to transfer massive files from one computer to another. Zip drives come with many new PCs and are available as options on others. You can add a Zip drive to your PC at any time. Some models are installed internally, whereas others can be attached to your PC with a cable.

Inserting a Zip disk

You insert a Zip disk into a Zip drive just as you would insert a floppy disk into a floppy drive — label up with the shiny metal part stuck in first. When you insert a Zip disk, don't force it into the drive. If it doesn't fit, you are probably trying to put the disk in the wrong drive. Instead of forcing the Zip disk into the drive, carefully push the disk all the way into it. After a certain point, the disk locks into place.

Accessing the Zip menu

After a Zip disk is inserted into the drive, right-click the Zip disk icon in My Computer or Windows Explorer to display a detailed menu with special Zip menu options. Special commands that are unique for Zip disks are preceded with the I logo (for Iomega, the Zip drive's manufacturer). These are Zip-drive only commands. For example, the Format command is particular to Zip drives. Also notice the Eject command, which you can use to eject a Zip disk automatically. Other commands on the menu are explained in the Zip drive manual.

Chapter 5: Printing Your Work

A printer is a device that produces an image on paper. The image can be text or graphics, and it can be printed in black ink or in full color. Using a printer is often your last step in creating something on the PC, so you want that final image to be as professional looking as possible. (For information on installing and troubleshooting printers, see Book VIII, Chapter 7.)

Types of Printers

Printers are judged by the quality of the images they produce and by their price. Generally, you can pay anywhere from $100 to thousands of dollars for a printer. The two types of printers that are most popular today are inkjet and laser printers, which are reviewed in this section.

Inkjet printers

Inkjet printers are the most popular types of computer printer sold today. They're primarily color printers, and they produce high-quality text or graphics on just about any type of paper. Many inkjet printers are even capable of photographic quality output.

Figure 5-1 illustrates a typical inkjet printer. Most inkjet printers print with both color and black inks; the printer literally sprays tiny balls of ink onto paper from multiple, tiny jets (thus, the name inkjet). These tiny ink balls stick to the paper, so inkjets don't need a ribbon or a toner cartridge.

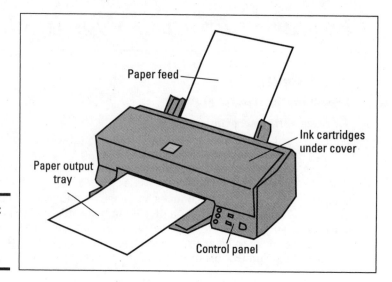

Paper feed

Ink cartridges under cover

Paper output tray

Control panel

Figure 5-1:
A typical inkjet printer.

Some low-end inkjet printers can be purchased for only about $100 to $300, and you may find that their quality and speed (from about 3 to 12 pages per minute) are fine for your needs. Higher-end models produce a better image, faster, but they can cost from $500 to $1,000. However, the broad price range of the inkjet printer makes it one of the best-suited printers for any PC.

You don't always have to print in color with an inkjet printer! You can also just print in black ink, which saves the pricey color cartridge from running low.

Laser printers

Laser printers are for heavy workloads and are primarily used in the office. Laser printers are great for producing both text and graphics, but usually only in black and white. Color laser printers are available, but they're outrageously expensive — especially when a low-cost inkjet printer can do most color jobs.

As you can see in Figure 5-2, a laser printer often resembles a squat copy machine. Generally, you place the paper into a tray, which then slides into the printer. The paper scrolls through the printer, and the final result slides out on top.

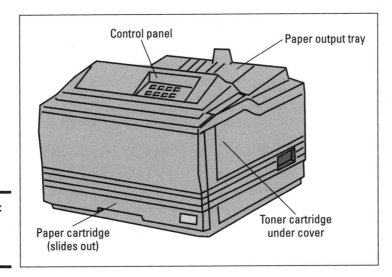

Figure 5-2:
A typical laser printer.

Control panel

Paper output tray

Paper cartridge (slides out)

Toner cartridge under cover

Laser printers are generally more expensive than inkjet printers because they are faster and produce higher-quality output. Most personal (home-based) black and white laser printers cost between $300 and $1,500 and can print anywhere from 6 to 16 pages per minute. Workgroup (office) laser printers can cost several thousand dollars and print up to 40 pages per minute. Color laser printers are quite expensive (about $2,500 up to $10,000 or more), but their color quality is usually better than inkjets' color quality.

Be careful when comparing laser printers' speed ratings. The speed is measured in pages per minute (ppm), and it can be deceptive. Laser printers print faster when they print the same image over and over, which is how they are measured for the ppm rating. Actual output under normal circumstances is slower.

Laser printers require drop-in toner cartridges. They are easy to install and come with their own instructions. Some manufacturers sell their cartridges with return envelopes so that you can send the old cartridge back to the factory for recycling or proper disposal.

Working with Your Printer

All you need to do to get your printer to work (after everything is hooked up and the software is installed) is to flip the switch on. Most printers can be left on all the time. But you may want to turn off your laser printer because it uses a lot of energy. Energy Star laser printers can be left on all the time, however, because these printers run in a low-power mode when they're not working. You can leave an inkjet printer on all the time because they don't use much energy, or you can turn it off when you finish printing.

Printing data

All Windows applications support the same basic print command, so the following steps work the same, regardless of the program you use:

1. **Choose File⇨Print or press Ctrl+P.**

    The Print dialog box opens.

2. **Select the printer next to Name if you have more than one printer to choose from (which is the case if you have a separate color printer or if you are on a network).**

3. **Choose the pages you want to print.**

    Sometimes you may want to print only a certain page or a range of pages, instead of the whole document.

4. **Choose the number of copies you want to print.**

5. **Click OK.**

Printing sideways

Printing on a sheet of paper sideways is called printing in *landscape* mode. Your text goes from left to right — the long way on the page. This mode is especially good for information that requires lots of columns, such as a spreadsheet.

Follow these steps to use landscape mode to print sideways:

1. **Choose File⇨Print or press Ctrl+P.**

2. **Click the Properties button.**

3. **Click the Paper tab.**

4. **Select the Landscape option.**

5. **Click OK to return to the Print dialog box.**

6. **Click OK to begin printing.**

Printing the screen

Printing the screen means printing a copy of exactly what is on your screen. This capability can come in handy when you need a hard copy of your screen to refer to later. Follow these steps to print a copy of your Windows desktop or the active window on the screen:

1. **Arrange the screen so that it looks the way that you want to see it printed.**

2. **If you want a snapshot of the whole screen, press the Print Scrn key on your keyboard. If you want a snapshot of only the active window on the screen, press Alt+Print Scrn.**

The image of the screen is now stored on the Windows Clipboard.

3. **Next, click the Start button and then choose Programs⇨Accessories⇨Paint.**

The Paint program opens.

4. **From the Paint menu bar, choose Edit⇨Paste.**

This takes the screen image you just placed on the Clipboard and pastes it into the Paint program. If a warning box tells you that the image is too big, click Yes. This tells Paint that you would like the bitmap enlarged.

5. **To print the image, choose File⇨Print from the Paint menu bar.**

6. **Click OK.**

The image from your screen prints to your printer.

General Printing Tips

The following tips can help make printing as painless as possible:

+ **Ink:** Ink is obviously an important part of printing, so keep these points in mind:

  • Keep a spare printer cartridge on hand. You don't want to be in the middle of printing a big report when you find that you're out of ink with no extras available.

  • Never let your printer toner get too low, and don't let ink cartridges go dry. You may think that squeezing out every last drop of ink saves money, but it's not good for the printer.

  • Many laser printers have a "toner low" light or warning message. When you first see it, you can take the toner out of the printer and rock it from side to side. This redistributes the toner and gets more mileage from it — but you can do this only once! Replace the old toner as soon as you see the "toner low" light again.

+ **Location:** Place your printer within arm's reach of your PC, if possible. You may find that you like to frequently print a single page as you work, and you want to be close enough to easily grab the page from the printer.

✦ **Paper:** You can't print without paper, so remember the following points:

- Stock up on the proper paper for your printer. Go to a discount paper warehouse and buy a few boxes to keep on hand.

- Keep all your paper and envelope supplies near your printer for easy access.

- If you see an arrow on one side of the outside paper wrapping, it usually indicates whether the top side of the paper is up or down.

✦ **Plugging in:** You have to properly connect everything before you print:

- If your PC has more than one printer port, plug your printer into LPT1, which is the first printer port.

- Printers generally don't come with cables! You must buy the cable separately from the printer.

- The printer cable can be no more than 20 feet long. After 20 feet, the transfer of information isn't always reliable.

✦ **Print Preview:** It's a good idea to preview your work before you start printing so that you're sure to print exactly what you want to print. Many Windows programs have a File⇨Print Preview command that lets you review the page before you print it.

✦ **Print toolbar icon:** Many applications sport a Print toolbar icon. If that's the case in the application you're using, you can click that button to quickly print your document. Be forewarned though: Clicking the Print toolbar icon will use the last printer you chose to use, provided you have more than one printer you can use.

✦ **Saving:** Always save your stuff before you print — it's a good habit to get into. That way, if you run into any problems during printing that cause you to reboot, all your hard work is safe.

Chapter 6: Software Guide

In This Chapter

✔ **Software for home and office**

✔ **Buying and installing software**

✔ **Uninstalling software**

✔ **Updating software**

Software is power. You can punch all kinds of key combinations and press all kinds of buttons, but the software makes things happen. Software entertains you, balances your checkbook, and makes you an artist. This chapter describes the major categories of software that are currently available and provides helpful information on how to buy, install, and update software.

Software for Home and Office

If you ever visit one of those huge computer superstores, you're sure to find the enormous amount of software overwhelming. How do you choose what to get? Not to worry. We're here to help.

Word processing

Word processing is all about writing, and that's why most people want to use the computer. Word processing programs simplify the writing process and make producing professional-looking documents easier.

The following types of word-processing software are available:

✦ **Text editors:** Text editors are word processors that do nothing but record the characters you type. They typically have little or no text formatting or few fonts. Text editors are fast and easy to use, so they are great for keeping lists and jotting notes. Windows Notepad is an example of a text editor. It saves documents as plain text or ASCII files.

✦ **Word processors:** The word processor makes writing easy. You can edit, rewrite, spell-check, and format to make your text look professional. Word processors, such as Microsoft Word, work with text just like text editors, but they add formatting, styles, proofing, and a bunch of features that make working fun, in addition to putting together a dynamite-looking document.

✦ **Desktop publishers:** Desktop publishing programs merge text and graphics into one document. (See "Desktop publishing," later in this chapter.)

Spreadsheet

Like a paper ledger, a spreadsheet provides a large grid of rows and columns for entering text, numbers, and formulas. The spreadsheet's job is to take the numbers and formulas that you enter into individual *cells,* process the information, and perform the calculations. The formula part is what makes the spreadsheet so powerful: You can add numbers in columns, compare values, and perform any number of mathematical operations. The entire spreadsheet is instantly updated, too. You change one value, and all related information is also updated.

Spreadsheets, such as Microsoft Excel, are great for organizing any information that can fit into a grid — anything that requires columns or scheduling. And you can also use spreadsheets for charting and data analysis.

Database

Databases help you to organize, sort, and report any type of information. Most people don't need databases, although they are handy in organizing information, such as client lists. Database programs come in three flavors:

✦ **Free-form database:** This type works best when you're organizing a big file that's full of random information. For example, if you search for the word *tomato,* the database retrieves every paragraph mentioning *tomato,* which may bring up a grocery list or a favorite recipe.

✦ **Flat file database:** This database retrieves information that's been organized into fields, records, and files so that you can request information about people named Dan who drive Hummers and vote Libertarian. This database requires the information to be organized in specific ways.

✦ **Relational database:** This is the most powerful type of database. The data is organized in tables that are "related" by a common field or column. Microsoft Access is an example of a relational database program.

Some database programs have all the forms ready, and you need only fill in the blanks. Other databases require you to make the forms and design how everything looks. More complex databases make you do *everything,* which includes writing the program that runs the database.

Before you go hunting for a database, see if your computer has Microsoft Works. It contains a pretty decent database that should fit most needs.

Desktop publishing

You can use a desktop publishing program to merge text and graphics for a professional-looking document. However, desktop publishing software is expensive. Cheaper, "home" versions are available, but expect to pay quite a bit for the programs that the professionals use.

Microsoft Publisher is often installed on many computers. It can be found by clicking Start⇨Programs⇨Microsoft Publisher. The many Wizards in Microsoft Publisher make this program simple to use. However, you don't have a lot of room to be truly creative. Professional desktop publishers generally prefer to use such desktop publishing software as PageMaker, In Design, and Quark.

Personal finance

Personal finance software is designed to help with those tedious financial tasks that you must perform, such as balancing your checkbook, keeping track of your receipts, and calculating interest on your savings account. Quicken and Microsoft Money are popular finance packages today for both home and small businesses. Additional tasks you can perform with Quicken or Money include writing and printing checks, keeping track of credit card expenses, tracking stocks, and managing a portfolio.

Education

Educational software programs are not just for kids. Lots of fun software is available to teach the basics of identifying shapes or learning ABCs, but you can also find educational software that can teach you a new language, how to type, how to read music, or about human anatomy.

Educational software comes in different types. Mavis Beacon teaches typing through a series of drills cleverly disguised as games. Dr. Seuss's ABCs is a read-along computer "book" that educates as it entertains. Encarta is a great encyclopedia program with samples of classical music and African poetry.

The best way to find respectable educational software is to ask people who already use the software (your friends, family, and coworkers). You can also check family and computer magazines as well as the Internet for reviews of the software. Make sure that you find an actual review and not just a report of what the software does.

Games

Don't fool yourself. Games are time wasters. In fact, you should limit the amount of time children spend playing computer games. You can find fun and educational games, but some games are violent and inappropriate for kids. Pay attention to the rating system on the software package, and monitor the games your kids use. Several categories of games are available:

♦ **Arcade:** These games are the classic games — the kind where you shoot something, work puzzles, or maneuver through a maze.

♦ **Simulation:** The flight-simulator games tend to be the most popular. Other types of simulators include golf, war, battle simulations, sporting games, and the popular SimCity-like simulations in which you create and manage an artificial world.

♦ **Virtual reality:** Virtual reality games are where *you* become the person on the computer. You control yourself as you walk through a new world, see your enemies coming after you, and experience all the good and scary stuff. Games like Doom, Duke Nukem, Descent, Quake, Myst, and a host of Star Wars games are popular. Be warned: These games can get violent!

Buying Software

Buying software is part of the computer-buying process. You decide what software you want to run *first,* and then you choose the hardware that can run it.

Here are some software-buying tips to help you make educated choices:

♦ See what other people are using. Are they happy with the software? Are they getting their tasks done?

♦ Make sure that you buy software that fits your needs, not just what's cheap and popular.

♦ Ask if you can try the software before you buy it. You may be able to download a demo of the software program from the Internet.

♦ Have someone at the store demonstrate the software for you.

♦ Always check out a store's return policy on software.

♦ Check the software's requirements. You don't want to buy Macintosh software if you're running Microsoft Windows.

If you're serious about making smart software investments (you can waste a lot of money on useless software), check out *Buying a Computer For Dummies* by Dan Gookin (published by IDG Books Worldwide, Inc.).

Installing Software

You automatically have some software on your new computer when you buy it. But this software may not be enough for you. So head off to your local computer store, check out the rows and rows of software products, pick out what you want, bring it home, open the box, and then the fun begins — you get to install it!

Your new software should come with specific instructions for installing the program. Each software package is a little different and may require different steps. Be sure to check the disk or CD for a Read Me file, which may include more recent information than the program's documentation. If you can't find a Read Me file, look on the cover of the CD case where this information is usually stored. Also remember to register your software so that you receive support information and updates that may not otherwise be available.

If the instructions for installing a software program aren't available, you can generally install the software by following these basic steps:

1. **Insert the software disk or CD-ROM into the drive.**

2. **Click the Start button, and choose Settings⇨Control Panel.**

3. **Double-click the Add/Remove Programs icon.**

4. **Click the Install/Uninstall tab to bring it forward.**

5. **Click the Install button.**

6. **Follow the remaining steps provided with the installation wizard.**

These steps vary depending on the program you are installing.

Keep the information that comes in the software box. The quick reference card is sometimes more helpful than the manual. You may also need the card with the serial number on it. Some software companies won't let you upgrade if you don't have the serial number of your current version.

Uninstalling Software

Many programs come with their own uninstall feature. Typically, you can find the uninstall program if you click the Start button and choose Programs. Some programs that you installed previously may display a right-pointing arrow on the right side of their Programs menu. When you click that arrow, a submenu opens that often offers an Uninstall option.

If your software lacks an uninstall program, you can use the Windows Add/Remove Program feature. Follow these steps to uninstall a program:

1. **Click the Start button and choose Settings⇨Control Panel.**

2. **Double-click the Add/Remove Programs icon.**

3. **Click the Install/Uninstall tab to bring it forward.**

4. **In the list box, click the program that you want to uninstall.**

5. **Click the Add/Remove button.**

   A warning dialog box appears, asking you if you're sure that you want to remove the selected program.

6. **Click Yes.**

For the best results, *never* try to uninstall *any* software by deleting it from your hard drive. Also, *never* delete any file that you did not create yourself. The file may be a key program in running some software you use all the time.

Updating Software

You may notice that most software has a number after the name, such as Word 2000. This number tells you which version — or update — of the software you have. Some computer users are obsessed with updating software. Is it necessary? You should order the update to your software only if it has features or makes modifications that you desperately need. Otherwise, if the current version is doing the job, don't bother.

Think carefully about each upgrade offer. Will you use the new features? Do you share files with someone who continually upgrades so that your lower version of the software is making it difficult to work together? After a while, newer versions of programs become incompatible with the older models. At that point, you may not have any choice but to upgrade.

Chapter 7: Maintaining Your Computer

In This Chapter

- ✔ Scheduling disk maintenance
- ✔ Deleting temporary files
- ✔ Defragmenting your hard drive
- ✔ Running ScanDisk
- ✔ Scanning for viruses
- ✔ Backing up your hard drive

*M*uch of what you do in Windows deals with disks, so they are central to your PC's operation. If you have a speedy computer, maintaining the disk drive keeps it speedy. Ignoring your disk drive slows your computer to a painfully slow crawl. Therefore, keeping drives happy and healthy is important. In this chapter, we tell you what you can do to minimize your risk of PC problems. For more computer maintenance information and tips, refer to Book VIII, "Upgrading and Fixing a PC."

Tech support people want to know information, such as the make and model of your computer, how much memory you have, and what kind of hardware you have. You can find all this information by clicking the Start button and choosing Programs➪Accessories➪System Tools➪System Information.

Scheduling Disk Maintenance

Using all the Windows disk maintenance tools is necessary to keep your computer operating at the best possible level of performance. The Scheduled Tasks utility program automatically starts various routine disk operations so that you don't have to remember to do them yourself.

Follow these steps to schedule disk maintenance:

1. **Click the Start button.**

2. **Choose Programs➪Accessories➪System Tools➪Scheduled Tasks.**

   The Scheduled Tasks dialog box appears.

3. **Double-click Add Scheduled Task.**

   The Scheduled Task Wizard starts. The next steps walk you through the tasks that you want to run and the times you want to run them.

4. **Click Next and select an appropriate task from the Application column. Or click Browse to find the program you want to schedule.**

   For example, you can choose Disk Defragmenter from the application list.

5. **Click Next. Then select the option that represents how frequently you want the task to run. Click Next again.**

6. **Choose the month(s), days, and/or times you want to run this task.**

   Pick a time when you're not using the computer to run scheduled tasks. Just remember that you have to leave your computer on for this application to work.

7. **Click Next.**

   Review the summary of your scheduled task. If you want to change anything, click the Back button and make your changes.

8. **Click Finish.**

   An icon is listed, along with the scheduled time of the task.

Deleting Temporary Files

Disk drives don't exactly get dirty, but they do accumulate lots of junk files. You accumulate all sorts of temporary files when you browse the Web, and all that junk takes up space. You need to run the Disk Cleanup tool every month or so to get back all that precious hard drive space.

Follow these steps to run Disk Cleanup:

1. **Click the Start button.**

2. **Choose Programs⇨Accessories⇨System Tools⇨Disk Cleanup.**

3. **Select the drive that you want to clean and click OK.**

   The Disk Cleanup for your disk drive shows you how much disk space you can clean up by running this program.

4. **Select the files that you want to delete and click OK.**

   The files you marked are deleted.

Defragmenting Your Hard Drive

To make room for all your files, Windows often takes advantage of empty spaces on the hard drive. Windows takes a file and splits it up — fragmenting the file into pieces that can fit into smaller, empty spaces on the hard drive. When you want to access a fragmented file, remember that the reassembling takes time, which results in a sluggish computer. The Disk Defragmenter utility puts fragmented files back together. You should run this utility about once a month.

Follow these steps to run Disk Defragmenter:

1. **Close all open documents and programs.**

2. **Double-click the My Computer icon on the desktop.**

3. **Right-click drive C: or whatever drive you want to defragment.**

4. **Choose Properties to display the Properties dialog box.**

5. **Click the Tools tab. Then click the Defragment Now button.**

Windows starts working to defragment your drive. A dialog box appears when the defragmentation is complete.

6. **Click View Report, if you want to review the results; then click Print, Save As, or Close.**

You don't have to save or print this report, but you can if you want to compare your reports.

7. **Click the Close button.**

The defragmentation process can take an hour or longer to complete. Don't start this process if you don't have the time to wait for it to finish.

Running ScanDisk

For some reason, files get lost or bits and pieces of them disappear, which seems to happen randomly and at unpredictable times. Fortunately, ScanDisk, a tool in Windows, lets you fix these minor file boo-boos. You should run ScanDisk at least once a week — more often if your hard drives are particularly fussy (that is, they tend to freeze often or take a while to open your documents).

Follow these steps to run ScanDisk:

1. **Double-click the My Computer icon on the desktop.**

2. **Right-click drive C: or whatever drive you want to scan.**

3. **Choose Properties to display the Properties dialog box.**

4. **Click the Tools tab. Then click the Check Now button.**

5. **In the dialog box that appears, choose the type of test that you want to run: Standard or Thorough.**

   The Standard scan checks for corrupt files, while the Thorough test checks for both corrupt files and physical problems on the disk.

6. **Click the Start button.**

   ScanDisk fires up. A progress bar shows you how long until the process is complete. When the disk check is complete, the ScanDisk Results window appears, providing the drive statistics.

7. **Click Close to make the Results dialog box disappear and then click Close to close the ScanDisk program.**

8. **Click Close again to close the Properties dialog box.**

Don't waste your time running ScanDisk on floppy disks — they are so inexpensive that you can toss them if they give you trouble.

Scanning for Viruses

A *virus* is a malicious, unauthorized computer program that is capable of replicating itself. While most viruses don't cause any real harm to your computer, some can delete files or even format your entire hard drive. Viruses can be very bad news, especially if you don't have a current backup of your files. Even if you do have a good backup, recovering from a virus can take a significant amount time and work.

Some common symptoms of a virus-infected computer are:

✦ Applications behaving erratically

✦ A system that slows down for no apparent reason

✦ Frequent system crashes

✦ Unexplained file size increases

With over 45,000 known viruses in existence, your chances of encountering one sooner or later are pretty high. If you have access to the Internet, you can find a lot of information about viruses at www.teamanti-virus.org.

What should you do if you suspect that your computer is infected with a virus? If you don't have a virus-scanning program, you definitely need to buy one. A couple of the more popular packages are McAfee VirusScan, found at www.mcafee.com and Norton Anti-Virus, which is located at www.symantec.com/avcenter/index.html.

Most antivirus software manufacturers offer periodic updates for a small fee. New viruses crop up all the time. Make sure that you update your virus scanning software at least every six months.

Virus scanning software offers many different features. The software that you purchase should:

✦ Automatically scan floppy disks after you access files from them

✦ Automatically scan your system periodically in the background

✦ Scan files downloaded from the Internet

✦ Scan files attached to the e-mail that you receive

Scan your system for viruses on a regular basis. If your software doesn't automatically scan your hard disk when you turn the computer on, remember to run the virus scanning software manually.

Backing Up Your Hard Drive

Backing up your hard drive is underrated. You need a backup copy in case something bad happens — for example, if a file is mangled or overwritten, if you lose a file that was there yesterday, a severe system failure, a hard drive crash that doesn't let you access your data, or worse yet — if someone reformats your hard drive.

You should have a backup schedule that works like this:

✦ **Back up your entire hard drive every week.** A full backup takes some time, but it keeps that valuable second copy of your information current.

✦ **Back up the work you do every day.** This incremental backup backs up only those files that have been changed or created since the last time you did a full backup.

How to back up

Whether it's a daily backup or a weekly backup, you follow the same steps. Because we don't know exactly what you're backing up, we give you a fairly generic procedure here. Also, the following steps are for those using a tape backup system, which we highly recommend. (For details on installing a tape backup unit or other high-capacity storage devices, refer to Book VIII, Chapter 4.) You can use a floppy disk or Zip drive to back up, but the tape backup systems have the room to accommodate all the information on your hard drive, without your needing to change disks.

Don't start your backup until you're ready to go to bed. Yes, your computer can work while you sleep. When you start your backup, you are locked out of your computer until it's finished. This backup process can take several hours!

Follow these steps to back up your computer:

1. **Close all open applications and then double-click the My Computer icon on the desktop.**

2. **Right-click a disk drive, such as drive C:.**

3. **Choose Properties to display the Properties dialog box.**

4. **Click the Tools tab and then click the Backup Now button.**

5. **At this point, your course takes one of two paths:**

   If you haven't performed a backup before: Make sure that the Create a New Backup Job option is selected. Click OK to start the Backup Wizard and go to Step 6.

   If you have performed a backup before and created a backup job: Choose Open an Existing Backup Job. Pick your weekly or daily backup regimen from the window and click OK. Move on to Step 12.

6. **In the Backup Wizard, choose Back Up My Computer. (Back up all files and folders on my local drives.)**

7. **Click Next.**

8. **Choose the All Selected Files option and click Next.**

9. **Choose your tape drive from the Where to Back Up drop-down list.**

   (You should have a tape drive if you choose the tape drive option. If you don't, Windows doesn't back up your computer.)

10. **Tell the Backup Wizard that you *do* want the backup system to compare the files to verify that the job was done successfully and that you *do* want the files compressed to save space; then click Next.**

11. **Name your backup job, because you're backing up the entire hard drive — a full backup — call it Weekly or Monthly or however often you plan to do this.**

    Review the information that appears in the box in the middle of your screen; this information confirms what you have selected. If there's something there that you don't like, click the Back button and do it over.

12. **Click the Start button.**

Your computer is now being backed up.

13. **Switch tapes as necessary.**

Switching tapes isn't always necessary for every backup. So don't be surprised if you're never asked to do this. Then . . . you're done (eventually!).

14. **Remove your backup tape, label it, and keep it in a safe place.**

15. **Close the various windows to exit out of the Backup program.**

Restoring something that you backed up

Backing up is pretty much useless without its counterpart, Restore. You use Restore to take the files stored on backup tapes and recopy them to your hard drive. Backing up your computer literally takes the information on your hard drive, compresses the information, and stores it on the backup tape. Restoring is the process of taking this compressed information, uncompressing it, and putting it back on your computer.

Follow these steps to restore files from your backup tape or disk:

1. **Start the Backup program. (See the preceding section.)**

2. **Choose Restore Backed Up Files. Click OK.**

The Restore Wizard begins.

3. **Insert your first (or only) backup tape into the tape drive.**

4. **Choose the proper backup device from the Restore Wizard program, and click Next.**

The Restore program scans your backup tape for a catalog of files.

5. **Choose the *backup set* from which you want to restore files.**

It's probably the most recent set. If you're restoring only one file, you may need to choose a specific set. Click that set to put a check mark in its box.

6. **Click OK and wait while the catalog (a list of files stored on the backup tape) is created.**

If your backup used multiple tapes, you're asked to insert the next tape.

7. **The list of files appears in the Restore Wizard window so that you can select the ones you want to restore.**

Similar to when you're backing up, you choose the files by working through the collapsible tree structure and placing a check mark beside the files that you want to restore.

8. **Click Next and choose where you want to restore the files. You have two choices: the Original Location or an Alternative Location.**

For full backups or any time that you're recovering lost data, choose Original Location. For recovering older versions of files, you may want to choose Alternative Location.

9. **Click Next. You are asked whether you want to replace newer files with older ones on the backup tape.**

Choose Do Not Replace the File on My Computer (unless you are replacing a corrupt file, in which case you *may* want to overwrite the newer file with the older one).

10. **Click the Start Restore button.**

Windows asks you to insert the first backup tape (even if you haven't removed it). Do so if necessary.

11. **Click OK. Swap tapes if necessary.**

Windows restores the files from your backup copy to your hard drive.

12. **Close the various windows to exit out of the Backup program.**

Index

Book II

Microsoft Windows

The 5th Wave By Rich Tennant

Contents at a Glance

Chapter 1: Getting to Know the Windows Desktop

*I*f you've used Windows 95 or 98 before, welcome to a new look and somewhat of a new feel — with many new added features in Windows Me. If you're jumping up from an earlier version of Windows or if you're a complete novice, you're also in the right place. To get along in the world of Windows Me, you need to feel comfortable with the Windows desktop — the screen where you eventually end up after you start your computer. And what is the most common element that populates the desktop? Those pretty little pictures called icons.

This chapter introduces you to desktop basics and gets you started on working with icons.

Many features and procedures in Windows Me are similar or identical to those in Windows 98. In Book II, all references to just plain "Windows" refer to both versions — Windows 98 and Windows Me. Any features or tasks that relate specifically to either version are noted as such. In addition, text that applies only to Windows 98 is highlighted with an icon in the margin.

Windows Desktop

The Windows desktop is the background against which all the action takes place. The desktop contains the standard Windows icons such as My Computer, Recycle Bin, and the like (explained later in this chapter). In addition, the desktop area holds all the shortcut icons you may create (see Book II, Chapter 4, for the lowdown on shortcuts). Finally, the desktop also has the Windows taskbar (which you can read about in Book II, Chapter 2). Figure 1-1 shows a typical desktop.

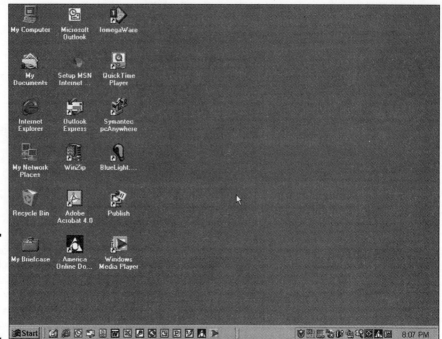

Although working with the Windows desktop isn't a high-maintenance routine, knowing how to manage your desktop and its icons can make your life
a little easier. (You can find an explanation of icons later in this chapter.)
The easiest way to manage your desktop is to use the desktop shortcut
menu. You open this menu by right-clicking any open area of the desktop
(off the taskbar and any icons), as shown in Figure 1-2. The shortcut menu
contains the following commands, which enable you to customize the look
and feel of the Windows desktop:

Figure 1-2:
Customizing
the look of
your desk-
top begins
with these
menu
options.

✦ **Active Desktop:** Turns the Active Desktop off and on with the View As Web Page command; opens the Display Properties dialog box with the Customize My Desktop command; or updates Active Desktop items with the Update Now command. See Book II, Chapter 5 for information on the Active Desktop.

✦ **Arrange Icons:** Enables you to arrange the desktop icons by Name, by Type, by Size, or by Date, or you can use Auto Arrange to let Windows decide how to arrange them.

✦ **Line Up Icons:** Arranges the icons in neat columns and rows on the desktop.

✦ **Refresh:** Updates icons and Active Desktop items on the desktop.

✦ **Paste:** Creates a shortcut to whatever document you're currently working on and pastes its icon onto the desktop. You can read about shortcuts in Book II, Chapter 4.

✦ **Paste Shortcut:** Pastes whatever shortcut you've cut or copied to the Clipboard.

✦ **New:** Creates an empty folder, a file of a particular type (such as an Excel file or Word document), or a new shortcut. You can read about all this stuff in Book II, Chapter 4.

✦ **Properties:** Opens the Display Properties dialog box, where you can change display stuff, like the video settings and Windows color combinations.

Icons on the Desktop

Icons are the small pictures identifying the type of object (be it a disk drive, folder, file, or some other such thing) that you're dealing with in Windows. You run into icons everywhere you turn — they're all over the desktop, and the Internet Explorer 5, My Computer, and Windows Explorer windows are loaded with them.

Windows gives you a number of new ways to modify the appearance of the icons as well as to determine the order in which they appear on the desktop or within their window (a job that Windows usually does all by itself). See Book II, Chapter 2, for details.

Types of icons

The icons that you encounter in Windows fall into one of the following types:

✦ **Disk icons:** Represent the various drives on your computer or drives that are currently connected to your computer

✦ **File icons:** Represent the different types of documents used by Windows and produced by the programs that you run on your computer

✦ **Folder icons:** Represent the various directories that you have on your computer

✦ **Windows component icons:** Represent the various modules that are running on your computer, such as the desktop, My Computer, Internet Explorer, and the Recycle Bin

✦ **Program icons:** Represent the various executable programs that you have installed on your computer

✦ **Shortcut icons:** Point to files, folders, Windows components, or executable programs that are located elsewhere on the computer

Clicking techniques

All the icons that you meet in Windows are made for clicking with the *mouse* — you know, that little white handheld gizmo that came with your computer. Table 1-1 shows the various mouse-click techniques that you employ on the icons you encounter in Windows.

Table 1-1	Clicking Techniques
Name	*Mouse Action*
Click	Point the mouse pointer at the object and then press and quickly release the primary mouse button. The primary mouse button, whether you're right-handed or left-handed, is the one closest to your thumb.
Double-click	Press and release the primary mouse button two times in rapid succession.
Right-click	Also known as a secondary mouse click, right-click means to press and release the button that is not designated as your primary mouse button. This action often brings up shortcut menus and other goodies.
Drag and drop	First point to an object with the mouse pointer; then click and hold down the primary mouse button as you move the mouse to drag the object to a new position on-screen. Finally, let go of the mouse button to drop the object into its new position. This action is quite useful when rearranging icons or moving files to the Recycle Bin.

Selecting and Opening Icons

Traditionally, *graphical user interfaces* (known affectionately as GUIs), such as Windows, use the following mouse-click scheme to differentiate between selecting and opening an icon:

✦ Single-click the icon to *select* it (indicated on the screen by highlighting the icon).

✦ Double-click the icon to *open* its object. (See "Types of icons," earlier in this chapter for details on the different types of Windows objects.)

Pages on the World Wide Web, however, typically use a slightly different mouse-click scheme to differentiate between selecting and following (the equivalent of opening) hyperlinks, which can be attached to graphics or text on the page:

✦ Move the mouse pointer over the hyperlink to select it (indicated by the mouse pointer changing to the hand icon).

✦ Click (don't double-click) the hyperlink to follow the link. (Normally, following the link means to jump to another section of the page or to open a completely different Web page.)

The Active Desktop (see Book II, Chapter 5, for full details) enables you to choose between selecting and opening Windows icons the normal GUI way (single- and double-click) or the normal Web way (point and click). When Windows is first installed on your computer, the traditional GUI single- and double-click scheme is in effect. If you want to switch over and experiment with the Web point-and-click system, you can do so at any time by making a few simple modifications (see Book II, Chapter 5 for the fine points of putting this new system into effect).

Book II
Chapter 1

Getting to Know the Windows Desktop

Selecting More Than One Icon at a Time

The time may come when you need to select more than one icon at a time, especially when these icons represent files and folders. For example, you may want to drag a bunch of files from one folder to another or carry out a group delete without performing the same action for each icon.

First, you need to know which method you're using to select icons, as explained in the preceding section. Next, you need to know if the icons are *contiguous* or *noncontiguous,* which affects how you select more than one icon. So if you know which method you're using to select icons and whether these icons are contiguous or noncontiguous, the rest is simple!

Selecting contiguous icons

Contiguous simply means that the icons are listed next to each other. Actually seeing what icons are next to each other is a lot easier when you view the icons in a window in list form (see Book II, Chapter 2). Follow these steps to select contiguous icons:

1. **Select the first icon in a group (either at the top or bottom of the list).**

2. **Hold down the Shift key and select the last icon in your group.**

   All the icons in between the two files you have selected become your *selection,* as shown in Figure 1-3.

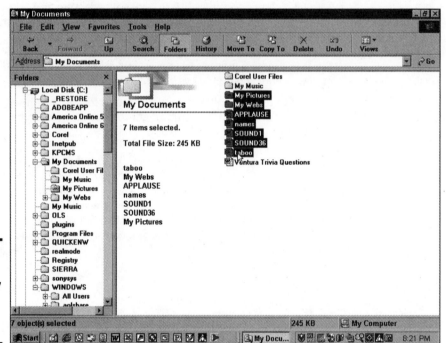

Figure 1-3: Hold down the Shift key to select contiguous icons.

Selecting noncontiguous icons

Noncontiguous simply means that the icons are *not* all listed next to each other. Follow these steps to select noncontiguous icons:

1. **Select the first icon (select any icon; you have to start somewhere!).**

2. **Hold down the Ctrl key and select each and every icon that you want.**

   All the icons that you select remain selected (as shown in Figure 1-4). If you slip up and select a file you don't want, simply deselect it — which is simply a matter of re-selecting it while still holding down the Ctrl key.

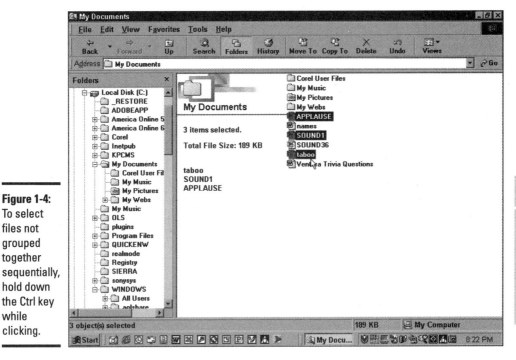

Figure 1-4:
To select
files not
grouped
together
sequentially,
hold down
the Ctrl key
while
clicking.

Standard Desktop Icons

After you install Windows, you notice that the desktop is littered with a few
icons that allow you to perform some essential tasks. This section gives a
brief overview of some standard desktop icons that every Windows user
deals with at some time or another. Double-clicking an icon (or single-clicking,
depending on your setup) opens the window, file, or folder (or whatever the
icon represents!). You can also right-click on an icon and choose Open from
the pop-up menu that appears.

My Computer

 My Computer gives you quick access to all the major *local* components of
your computer system. When you first open the My Computer window, it
displays all the local drives attached to your computer and the Control
Panel folder (which gives you options on installing software, configuring
your computer, and adding or maintaining your printers).

If you're using Windows 95 or 98, you see a couple more folders — Printers and Dial-Up Networking. The Printers folder gives you access to the printers installed on your computer as well as the option to add new printers. Dial-up Networking houses the different Internet access set-ups that you may have. If you haven't got an Internet account set up, you can double-click the Make a New Connection icon to guide you through the necessary steps.

My Documents

 If you're unsure where to store all those files you generate, Windows gives you a head start to file organization. Beginning with the My Documents folder, you can store your greatest works of fiction, poetry, reports, letters, and more. Depending on the version of Windows you're running and the software you have installed, you may find some other folders with the My Documents folder — My Pictures, My Webs, or My Music, for example.

My Network Places

 In Windows Me, My Network Places gives you an overview of all the work-groups, computers, and shared resources on your local area network (LAN). As a permanent resident on the desktop, whether you're on a LAN or not, you can open it and get a graphic view of the workgroups set up on your network and the resources that are networked together. Windows Me gives you all the tools except the network card and cable to set up your own home or small office network.

 In Windows 98, the network-related icon is named Network Neighborhood, but doesn't include the Home Networking Wizard.

Recycle Bin

 The Recycle Bin is the trash can for Windows. Don't be confused by the "recycle" name; you're not putting things in there to be reused. Anything you delete in Windows goes into the Recycle Bin and stays there until you either retrieve the deleted item or empty the Recycle Bin. The only thing that you gain when you empty the Recycle Bin is the space that the deleted items took up. (See Book II, Chapter 4, for more on how to use the Recycle Bin.)

My Briefcase

 My Briefcase enables you to synchronize versions of files from different computers or disks so that you don't drive yourself crazy trying to figure out which version of the file isn't as up-to-date as the other one.

Outlook Express

 Microsoft thinks of everything, don't they? With a strong focus of computer and Web integration, there has to be some way to communicate over the Internet. Enter Outlook Express, a combination e-mail and address book. If you're impressed with Outlook Express, you should look into using the full-blown version of Outlook. Not only do you get e-mail and address book features, but you also have a calendar to get organized, a to-do listing, little yellow sticky notes that you place throughout the program, and a journal.

Internet Explorer

 If browsing the World Wide Web is one of the main reasons you have a computer, you'll find an icon for Microsoft's Internet Explorer, one of the top Internet browsers available.

Windows Media Player

 With a major focus on multimedia, Windows Media Player has been redesigned and includes many expanded capabilities over the older version. And, Windows Me itself has been optimized for things like digital cameras, scanners, videos and sound. With Windows Media Player, you can manage and play your favorite CDs, movies, audio files, and more.

Chapter 2: Getting Started in Windows

In This Chapter

- ✓ Using and customizing the taskbar
- ✓ Launching and switching between programs
- ✓ Working with on-screen windows
- ✓ Using Windows Explorer
- ✓ Exploring Explorer bars
- ✓ Shutting down Windows

A journey of 1,000 miles begins with the first step, or so the saying goes, and one of the best first steps in Windows can usually be found at the bottom of the desktop screen. Customarily, this area is where the taskbar lurks, and from here, you can begin your computer journey. This chapter shows you how to get things going and how to make the taskbar fit your computing needs.

In addition, this chapter dispenses helpful information for the Windows newbie and seasoned pro alike. If you're just starting out with the Windows operating system or if you need a refresher on its fundamentals, you've come to the right place. A lot of this knowledge also applies to the programs that you use with Windows (which you can read about in the rest of this book).

Taskbar Basics

The taskbar forms the base of the Windows desktop. Running along the bottom of the screen, the taskbar is divided into three sections: the Start button with the accompanying Start pop-up menu at the far left; buttons for open toolbars and windows in the center area; and, at the far right, the status area with icons showing the current status of computer components, programs, and processes that are running in the background. Figure 2-1 shows you a typical taskbar.

Figure 2-1:
You'll spend
many hours
at the
Windows
taskbar.

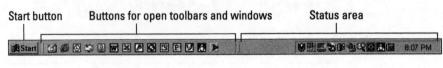

Start button   Buttons for open toolbars and windows   Status area

When you open a window or program on the Windows desktop, Windows adds a button representing that window or program to the center section of the taskbar. Clicking one of the window or program buttons brings the program's window to the front, so you can use the taskbar buttons to quickly switch between open programs. You can always tell which program is open because on the taskbar its button appears like it's pressed in.

The Start menu

The Start button, which opens the Start menu, always appears as the first button on the taskbar. The Start menu is the most basic pull-down menu in Windows, containing almost all the programs you'll ever need to use. To open the Start menu (shown in Figure 2-2), simply click the Start button in the lower-left corner of the taskbar or press Ctrl+Esc.

Nowadays, many keyboards come with a key that has the Windows logo, which you can press to get the Start menu. If you're still pounding away on an old keyboard, you can press Alt+S to open the Start menu.

Figure 2-2:
The Start
menu gives
you access
to almost
anything
you want
to do.

The following list describes some of the commands or options you encounter on the Start menu (running from bottom to top). To select a command on the Start menu, just navigate to it with the mouse pointer and click.

✦ **Shut Down:** See "Shutting Down Windows," later in this chapter.

✦ **Log Off:** On a local area network (LAN), this option enables you to log off the current user so that you can then log on yourself. If you're not on a network, you can set up multiple users, each with his or her own custom settings. To switch users, one logs off and the other logs in. When the new user logs in, his or her personal settings take effect — changing, among other things, the desktop background, screen savers, and desktop icon placement.

✦ **Run:** Opens the Run dialog box, where you enter the pathname of a file, folder, program, or Internet resource that you want Windows to locate and open.

✦ **Help:** Opens Windows Help, an online help database that also includes Web elements, so you can jump to the Internet for even more help.

✦ **Search:** Opens a submenu with the following options: For Files or Folders, which enables you to find particular files on local or networked disk drives; Computer, to find a particular computer on your network; On the Internet, which enables you to find a Web site on the Internet; On The Microsoft Network, which enables you to search for something or someone on The Microsoft Network (available only if you subscribe to MSN); or People, which enables you to find a particular person or business in one of the online directories. Other programs that you install may also add entries on this menu, so you may have even more options. In Windows 98, the Find command on the Start menu performs the same function as the Search command.

✦ **Settings:** Opens a submenu with the following options: Control Panel, which enables you to open the Control Panel window; Dial-up Networking (Windows Me only), for accessing your various Internet connection modem dialing configurations; Printers, which enables you to open the Printers window; and Taskbar and Start Menu, which opens the Taskbar Properties dialog box, where you can modify the appearance of the Start menu and the taskbar.

In Windows 98, you also have these options: Folder Options, to open the Folder Options dialog box; Active Desktop, for activating, customizing, and updating the Active Desktop; and Windows Update, which enables you to connect to a page on the Microsoft Web site to download updates to Windows 98.

+ **Documents:** Opens a submenu containing shortcuts to all your most recently opened files. You can purge this list from time to time by using the Taskbar Properties dialog box.

+ **Favorites:** In Windows 98, this option enables you to access the items designated as your favorite files, folders, Web channels, or Web pages.

+ **Programs:** Opens a submenu containing all the programs installed on your computer. You can control which programs appear on the Programs menu by adding folders to or removing folders from the Programs folder.

+ **Windows Update:** Connects you to the Microsoft Web site, which then checks your computer system to see if your version of Windows needs updating and, if you allow, automatically downloads and installs the new updated components.

+ **Open Office Document:** If you have Microsoft Office installed on your computer (and who doesn't?), you can use this command to display the Open Office Document dialog box, where you can search for the particular Office document (such as Word, Excel, PowerPoint, or Access) you want to open. See Book V, "Microsoft Office 2000," for more information.

+ **New Office Document:** If you have Microsoft Office installed on your computer, you can use this command to open a new Office document using one of many different types of templates available (Word, Web page, Excel, PowerPoint, Binder, or Access).

Taskbar toolbars

Windows enables you to add various toolbars, such as the Address, Quick Launch, and Desktop toolbars, to the center section of the taskbar. You can then use their buttons to accomplish routine tasks in Windows. See Book II, Chapter 3, for details on displaying and using these different toolbars.

The Status area

The status area (sometimes called the *system tray*) contains icons that indicate the current status of various physical components, such as a printer attached to a desktop computer, as well as the status of various programs or processes that run in the background, such as a virus-scanning program or the video display settings you're using.

To identify an icon that appears in the status area, position the mouse pointer over it until its ToolTip appears. To change the status of an icon, right-click it to display its pop-up menu, and then click the appropriate menu option.

Note: You can customize the taskbar so that it removes the clock, shows smaller icons, hides itself, and so on. You can also customize the Start menu. Choose Start⇨Settings⇨Taskbar and Start Menu to get started. See *Windows Me For Dummies* by Andy Rathbone (from IDG Books Worldwide, Inc.) for all the details.

Starting Programs

In Windows, you can open the programs that you've installed on your hard drive in any one of the following three ways:

✦ **Select the program on the Programs menu, which you open from the Start menu.** See "The Start menu," earlier in this chapter, for information about the Start menu.

✦ **Open a shortcut to the program or to a document you open regularly.** See Book II, Chapter 4, for information about creating shortcuts for opening a program or a file that in turn opens its associated program.

✦ **Open a file created with the program:** See Book II, Chapter 4, for information about opening a program by opening its file.

Switching Between Programs

The Windows taskbar makes switching between programs as easy as clicking the button representing the program. (Open folders and documents are also represented on the taskbar.) To activate a program (or access an open folder or document) and bring its window to the top of your screen display, click the appropriate button on the taskbar.

Working With On-Screen Windows

A *window,* whether it's the window you see when you open a system window such as My Computer or a window from a program such as Word, contains various combinations of controls and features that you use to navigate and modify the window. Figure 2-3 shows you a typical window.

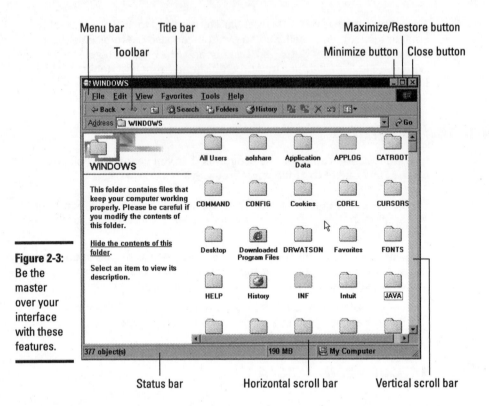

Figure 2-3:
Be the
master
over your
interface
with these
features.

The following list describes the features and controls found in all your typical windows:

✦ **Title bar:** Identifies the program or file in the opened window; also houses the Control menu, which appears when you click the program icon on the left side of the title bar.

✦ **Menu bar:** Contains the pull-down menus with commands specific to a program (see Book II, Chapter 3).

✦ **Minimize button:** Shrinks the window down to a button on the taskbar.

✦ **Maximize/Restore button:** The Maximize button zooms the window up to full size; When a window is maximized, this button's appearance changes. To restore a maximized window to its former size, click the Restore button.

✦ **Close button:** Closes the window and exits any program running in it.

✦ **Toolbars:** If the window is equipped with other toolbars, these extra toolbars are usually located below the menu bar.

✦ **Vertical scroll bar:** Enables you to vertically scroll new parts of the window into view with the up and down arrows or by dragging the scroll button.

✦ **Horizontal scroll bar:** Enables you to horizontally scroll unseen parts of the window into view with the right and left arrows or by dragging the scroll button.

✦ **Status bar:** Gives you different sorts of information about the current state of the program.

Moving and resizing windows

You can move windows around the desktop and resize them from full-screen (or *maximized*) view all the way down to buttons on the taskbar (or *minimized*) view at your convenience. To move a window, follow these steps:

1. **If necessary, restore the window to an in-between size, either by clicking the Restore button if the window is maximized or by clicking its taskbar button if the window is minimized.**

2. **Position the mouse pointer over the window's title bar.**

3. **Drag the outline of the window to its new location on the desktop, and release the mouse button.**

To maximize a window, you have three methods to choose from:

✦ Click the Maximize button on the window's title bar if the window is displayed at less than full size. (The Maximize button is located in the middle of the three buttons on the right side of the title bar.) Otherwise, click the window's taskbar button if the window is minimized.

✦ Choose Maximize from the window's Control menu (which you open by clicking the program's icon in the far left of the window's title bar or by right-clicking the window's icon on the taskbar).

✦ Double-click the title bar of the window to make the window expand to fill the screen.

Remember that after you maximize a window, you can restore the window to its original size by doing one of these three things:

✦ Click the Restore button on the window's title bar. (The Restore button is located in the middle of the three buttons on the right side of the title bar.)

✦ Choose Restore from the window's Control menu (which you open by clicking the program's icon in the far left of the window's title bar or right-clicking the window's icon in the taskbar).

✦ Double-click the title bar again to take the window back to its previous size.

Book II
Chapter 2

Getting Started in Windows

To minimize a window to just a button on the taskbar, you can do either of the following:

✦ Click the Minimize button on the window's title bar. (The Minimize button is the one with the minus sign, located on the left of the three buttons on the right side of the title bar.)

✦ Choose Minimize from the window's Control menu (which you open by clicking the program's icon on the far left of the window's title bar or by right-clicking the window's icon on the taskbar).

In addition to using the automatic sizing controls, you can manually resize a window (assuming that it's not currently minimized or maximized) by clicking and dragging any of its sides or corners. You can always tell when Windows allows you to move one or more of the sides of a window by dragging, because the mouse pointer changes from the standard pointer to a double-headed arrow when you move the mouse across the window.

Arranging and sizing icons in a window

When browsing local files in any browsing window, you can modify the size of the icons used to represent files and folders as well as determine how much (if any) information about them is displayed.

To change the way icons appear in any of these windows, choose from the following commands on the window's View pull-down menu. Note that the same menu options appear when you right-click the window:

✦ **Large Icons (the default):** Displays the largest version of the folder and file icons, with their names below.

✦ **Small Icons:** Displays a smaller version of the folder and file icons, with their names on the right side of the icons.

✦ **List:** Uses the same icons as the Small Icons option except that the icons with their folders and filenames are arranged in a single column along the left side of the window.

✦ **Details:** Adds columns of additional information (like a description, the file type, file size, and so on) to the arrangement used when you select the List option.

✦ **Thumbnails (new in Windows Me):** Displays graphic files as small images inside a box with the filename listed below it.

Switch to the Small Icons viewing option when you need to see as much of the window's contents as possible. Switch to the Details viewing option when you need to get as much information as possible about the files and folders in a window.

After you decide how file and folder icons appear in a window, you can also choose how they are arranged. Choose View⇨Arrange Icons and choose from the following options on the Arrange Icons submenu:

✦ **By Name:** Sort icons alphabetically by name.

✦ **By Type:** Sort icons by file type.

✦ **By Size:** Sort icons by size, from smallest to largest.

✦ **By Date:** Sort icons by date, from oldest to most recent.

✦ **Auto Arrange:** Let Windows sort icons by the default setting (which happens to be by filename).

Windows Explorer

Windows Explorer enables you to view the contents of any part of your computer system. As with the My Computer and Internet Explorer, you can then use Windows Explorer to open files (and their associated application programs), start programs, and even open Web pages on the Internet.

But Windows Explorer is most useful when you need to move or copy files and folders from one disk to another on your computer — or even between networked drives, if you're on a network. See Book II, Chapter 4, for details on how to do this.

To open Windows Explorer in Windows Me, choose Start⇨Programs⇨ Accessories⇨Windows Explorer; in Windows 98, choose Programs⇨Windows Explorer. You can also right-click any folder (or shortcut to a folder), My Computer, or the Start button and choose Explore from the shortcut menu. Windows opens a window (which you see in Figure 2-4) that is divided into these two panes:

✦ The Folders pane on the left shows an outline view of all the components on your computer system.

✦ The Contents area on the right displays the folders and files in whatever component is currently selected in the Folders pane (also shown on the Address bar at the top of the window).

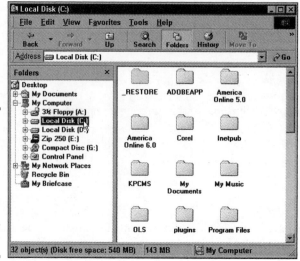

Figure 2-4:
The
Windows
Explorer
window
lets you see
different
parts of your
computer.

To select a new part of your system to view in the Contents area pane, click
the icon for that component in the Folders pane. An icon in the Folders
pane with a plus sign connected to it indicates a sublevel within that icon.

When you click a plus sign, Windows expands the outline, showing all the
subfolders within the next level. Note also that when you click the plus sign,
it changes to a minus sign, and the next level in the hierarchy is displayed.
Clicking the minus sign collapses the sublevel of the hierarchy, condensing
the outline. (See Figure 2-5.)

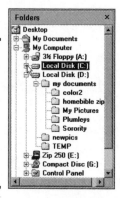

Figure 2-5:
Expand and
collapse
drives and
folders
using the
plus and
minus
buttons.

Sometimes, the expanded folder/subfolder outline in the Folders pane (or
the icon arrangements in the Contents pane) becomes too large to view in

its entirety. When this happens, vertical and horizontal scroll bars appear as needed, to help you navigate your way through the lists of folders and components.

Explorer Bars

Explorer bars are a nifty feature in Internet Explorer, My Computer, and Windows Explorer windows. When you open an Explorer bar in one of these windows, the Explorer bar splits the window into two panes, one on the left and one on the right. The Explorer bar appears in the left pane, and the object or objects that you decide to explore appear in the pane on the right (as suitably shown in Figure 2-6).

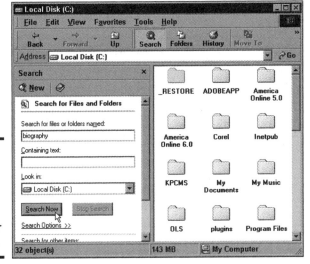

Figure 2-6: Search drives for misplaced files with the Explorer Search bar.

Windows offers several different types of Explorer bars (most of which are Internet related). To display a particular Explorer bar, choose View⇨ Explorer Bar on the window's pull-down menu and then select one of the following commands from the submenu that appears:

✦ **Search:** Opens or closes the Search Explorer bar, where you can select one of the available Web search engines (such as Yahoo!).

✦ **Favorites:** Opens or closes the Favorites Explorer bar, which contains a list of hyperlinks to your favorite Web sites, folders, and files.

✦ **History:** Opens or closes the History Explorer bar, which contains a chronological list of hyperlinks to Web sites you've recently visited and the folders and files that you've recently opened.

✦ **Folders:** Opens or closes the list of folders, leaving a context-sensitive area that displays thumbnails of graphics files, information on the folder or file that is selected, and links to other areas (which give you more options to explore Windows).

Shutting Down Windows

Windows includes a shut-down procedure that you should follow before you turn off your machine. To shut down Windows so that you can safely shut off your computer and get on with your life, follow these steps:

If you turn off your computer while a program is running and you have a file or other data open, you run the risk of corrupting that information or losing it altogether. Always shut down programs that you are running before shutting down Windows. Use the Shut Down option in the Start menu.

To shut down Windows:

1. **Click the Start button and then choose Shut Down.**

The Shut Down Windows dialog box opens.

2. **To completely shut down Windows and power down your computer, choose Shut Down from the drop-down menu and then click the OK button or press Enter. (In Windows 98, click the Shut Down option button and click OK.)**

In addition to the Shut Down option, you can select from these options in the Shut Down Windows dialog box:

✦ **Restart:** Choose this option when you need to restart the computer (which you often have to do after installing a new piece of hardware or software, for example).

✦ **Stand By:** Choose this option when you want to put your computer into a deep sleep. This mode powers down the computer but maintains the state of your desktop.

✦ **Hibernate:** Choose this option (Windows Me only) when you want to shut down your computer but want programs and windows to return to the state they're in when you shut down.

✦ **Restart in MS-DOS Mode:** Choose this option when you are inexplicably possessed by a need to type some DOS command or to take one last look at that old DOS prompt.

Chapter 3: Working with Toolbars, Menus, and Dialog Boxes

In This Chapter

✔ **Using toolbars**

✔ **Placing special toolbars on your taskbar**

✔ **Customizing your toolbars**

✔ **Managing pull-down menus**

✔ **Using shortcut and Control menus**

✔ **Working with dialog boxes**

*T*oolbars contain the buttons and menus that you love to click and pull at in Windows. Different types of toolbars (each with its own group of buttons) can appear within the various windows, such as My Computer, Windows Explorer, and Internet Explorer, on the taskbar on the Windows desktop, or they can simply float within or around an application window. No matter where you or the software places them, toolbars become a means to get things done *your* way.

If you enjoy checking off little boxes, filling in blanks, clicking buttons, and tugging on sliders, you'll certainly love dealing with the dialog boxes that Windows — and any Windows program — throws at you. In any event, dialog boxes give you some exercise in responsibility because *you* make the choices. And if you have a taste for reading little menus that precede even the most mundane action, you invested your money wisely. The Windows dialog boxes and menus are your gateway to getting productive.

Using the Toolbars

When you first display toolbars in a window, they appear docked one on top of the other in neat little rows at the top of the window. When you first display toolbars on the taskbar, they appear one after the other on the taskbar, often scrunching up the buttons representing the various windows open on the desktop.

To display a certain type of toolbar in a window like My Computer, Windows Explorer, or Internet Explorer, choose View⇨Toolbars and then select one of the following commands on the cascading menu that appears:

♦ **Standard Buttons:** Displays or hides the Standard Buttons toolbar. Which particular buttons that appear on this toolbar depends on whether you are browsing local files and folders or Web pages on the Internet or the corporate intranet.

♦ **Address Bar:** Displays or hides the Address toolbar. The Address toolbar contains a text box in which you can enter the URL of the Web page you want to visit or the pathname of the folders you want to browse.

♦ **Links:** Displays or hides the Links toolbar. The Links toolbar contains buttons with links to your favorite Web pages.

♦ **Radio:** Further enhancing integration of the Internet into the Windows interface, you can use the Radio toolbar for finding stations broadcasting over the Internet. This option is visible only if you opted to install the Windows Media Player.

The Standard Buttons Toolbar

The Standard Buttons toolbar is the main toolbar that appears in the My Computer, Windows Explorer, and Internet Explorer windows. It is also the most chameleon-like toolbar, because its buttons change to suit the particular type of browsing you are doing. When you browse local files and folders on your computer, the Standard Buttons toolbar contains the following buttons, as shown in Figure 3-1:

Figure 3-1:
Use the
Standard
Buttons
toolbar to
browse
files, fold-
ers, and
Web pages.

♦ **Back:** Returns to the previously browsed folder or Web page.

♦ **Forward:** Returns to the folder or Web page that you browsed right before using the Back button to return to the current page.

♦ **Up:** Moves up one level in the directory structure.

♦ **Search:** (Windows Me) Changes the left panel of the window to allow searching for files, folders, and text within a document. If you're online, you can also use this panel to search for people and Web sites. Network users can find other users logged on to the network.

✦ **Folders:** (Windows Me) Displays the folders in the drive you're currently browsing as well as your network resources, desktop, and frequently used default folders.

✦ **History:** (Windows Me) Shows you a record of past files or Internet sites visited in Microsoft Explorer. The files are displayed either by day or by week.

✦ **Move To:** (Windows Me) Moves the currently selected files or folders to a drive and folder you specify in the resulting dialog box.

✦ **Cut:** Moves the currently selected files or folders to the Clipboard.

✦ **Copy To:** (Windows Me) Copies the currently selected files or folders to a drive or folder you specify in the resulting dialog box.

✦ **Copy:** Copies the currently selected files or folders to the Clipboard.

✦ **Paste:** Places files or folders that have been moved or copied onto the Clipboard to the current folder.

✦ **Delete:** Gets rid of the files or folders you've selected. (See Book II, Chapter 4, for details.)

✦ **Undo:** Undoes your most recent change.

✦ **Properties:** Displays properties information about the disks, files, or folders you've selected. (See Book II, Chapter 5, for details.)

✦ **Views:** Click repeatedly to rotate through the icon view options or use the attached pull-down menu to select a different icon view for the current window.

When you browse a Web page, whether it's a local HTML document on your hard drive or one located on a Web server somewhere in cyberspace, the Back and Forward buttons that you see when browsing local folders and files are then joined by the following new buttons:

✦ **Stop:** Immediately halts the downloading of a Web page that is just taking far too long to display.

✦ **Refresh:** Refreshes the display of the current Web page (which sometimes helps when the contents of the page appear jumbled or incomplete).

✦ **Home:** Displays the Web page designated as the start page. This Web page appears each time you launch Internet Explorer and connect to the Internet.

✦ **Search:** Displays the Search Explorer bar for searching the Internet.

✦ **Favorites:** Displays the Favorites Explorer bar for revisiting favorite Web pages that you've bookmarked.

**Book II
Chapter 3**

Working with Toolbars, Menus, and Dialog Boxes

✦ **History:** Displays the History Explorer bar for revisiting Web pages that you've visited within the last few days or weeks.

✦ **Mail:** Displays a pop-up menu of e-mail options, including Read Mail, New Message, Send a Link, Send Page, and Read News.

✦ **Print:** Sends the current Web page to your printer.

✦ **Edit:** Opens the current Web page in the Notepad text editor (exposing the *raw* HTML tags).

✦ **Discuss:** Connects you to a discussion server through the Internet for chats with individuals that have similar interests as you.

Other buttons may be added to the toolbar when you install additional software. For example, Real Player, an audio and video player, and Microsoft Messenger populate the toolbar with their own button renditions.

Displaying Toolbars on the Taskbar

In addition to using toolbars with windows, you can also place toolbars on your Windows taskbar to customize — or complicate — your computing style. (Read all about the taskbar in Book II, Chapter 2.) To display a certain type of toolbar on the taskbar, right-click the taskbar (making sure that you don't click the Start button or any of the other buttons that currently appear on the taskbar), choose Toolbars from the shortcut menu, and choose Address, Links, Desktop, Quick Launch, or New Toolbar from the cascading menu that appears.

The Address bar

You can use the Address bar to search or browse Web pages on the Internet or your corporate intranet or to browse folders and files on local or networked disk drives. Just click the Address bar, type in the URL of the Web page or the pathname of the folder you want to browse (see Figure 3-2), and press Enter.

Figure 3-2:
Type an
Internet URL
into the
Address bar
to visit that
location.

The Links toolbar

The buttons on the Links toolbar (more often than not simply called the *Links bar*) are hyperlinks that open favorite Web pages. When you first start using Windows, the Links bar contains only buttons with links to Web pages on the Microsoft Web site. These buttons include Best of the Web, Microsoft, Product News, Today's Links, and Web Gallery.

You can add buttons to the Links toolbar. To add a button with a link to a preferred Web page, folder, or file, drag its icon to the place on the Links bar where you want the button to appear (this icon appears on the Address bar in front of the Web page URL or folder or file pathname).

To delete a button that you no longer want on the Links bar, right-click the button and then choose the Delete command from the button's shortcut menu.

The Desktop toolbar

The Desktop toolbar, shown in Figure 3-3, contains buttons for all the icons that appear on the Windows desktop. These buttons include ones for the standard Desktop icons, such as My Computer, Internet Explorer, and Recycle Bin, as well as those for the program, folder, and file shortcuts that you create. (See Book II, Chapter 4, for more information on shortcuts.)

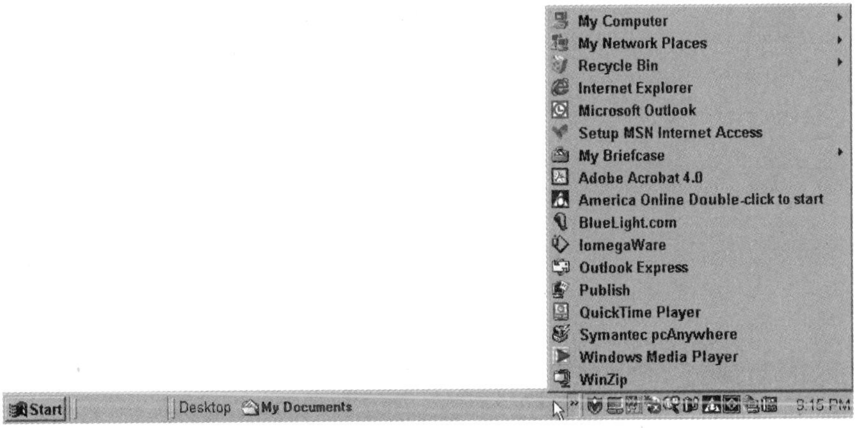

Figure 3-3:
Icons on the
desktop are
duplicated
on the
Desktop
toolbar.

My Computer
My Network Places
Recycle Bin
Internet Explorer
Microsoft Outlook
Setup MSN Internet Access
My Briefcase
Adobe Acrobat 4.0
America Online Double-click to start
BlueLight.com
IomegaWare
Outlook Express
Publish
QuickTime Player
Symantec pcAnywhere
Windows Media Player
WinZip

Start | Desktop My Documents | 8:15 PM

The Quick Launch toolbar

The Quick Launch toolbar adds a group of buttons you can use to start commonly used programs to the Windows taskbar. These buttons, shown in Figure 3-4, include:

Figure 3-4:
You can click once to activate any program on the Quick Launch bar.

+ **Launch Internet Explorer Browser:** Starts Internet Explorer so you can browse.

+ **Launch Outlook Express:** Starts Outlook Express so you can send and receive e-mail and messages from the newsgroups to which you have subscribed.

+ **Launch TV Viewer:** Starts the Microsoft TV channel guide so you can get the latest information on the current TV programming in your local area. Note that this button appears on the Quick Launch toolbar *only* if your computer is equipped with a TV tuner card *and* you have installed the Microsoft guide software.

+ **Show Desktop:** Minimizes all open windows enabling you to obtain immediate access to the Windows desktop and all the Windows icons and Active Desktop items it contains.

+ **MSN Messenger Service:** (Windows Me) Enables you to meet and chat with other users over the Internet. You can build a list of online friends and be alerted when they log on.

+ **Windows Media Player:** (Windows Me) Enables you to play audio and video files. Also, you can use Media Player as a CD or MP3 player. Check out the new version's ability to change its appearance with custom *skins*.

+ **View Channels:** Starts the Active Channel viewer so you can subscribe to, update, and browse particular Web channels.

You can also add your own custom buttons to the Quick Launch toolbar. Follow these steps:

1. **Open the folder that contains the executable file that starts the program or that contains a shortcut to this executable file.**

2. **Click and drag the program's file icon or shortcut icon to the desired position on the Quick Launch toolbar and then release the mouse button.**

   A button for the program appears at the position of the I-beam in the Quick Launch toolbar.

You can delete any of the buttons from the Quick Launch toolbar by right-clicking the button, choosing the Delete command on the shortcut menu, and then clicking the Yes button in the alert box that asks you to confirm the deletion.

Creating a New Toolbar

The New Toolbar option enables you to make buttons for the items in a particular folder and place those buttons on a new custom toolbar. Just follow these steps:

1. **Right-click the taskbar and choose Toolbars➪New Toolbar from the shortcut menu.**

   The New Toolbar dialog box appears.

2. **In the New Toolbar list box, open the folder whose contents will be used to create the new toolbar.**

3. **Close the New Toolbar dialog box.**

   Windows adds the new toolbar, with buttons for each shortcut and icon, to the taskbar. Note that Windows gives the new toolbar the same name as that of the folder you selected, which is automatically displayed along with the names of the buttons.

All custom toolbars that you create last only for the duration of your current work session. In other words, whenever you close a custom toolbar or restart your computer, the toolbar is automatically erased and you must re-create it.

Customizing the appearance of a toolbar

You can move or resize a toolbar, as well. To change the position or length of a toolbar, click and drag the toolbar by its sizing handle (the vertical bar that appears at the very beginning of the toolbar) as soon as the mouse pointer assumes the shape of a double-headed arrow. You can also click and drag a toolbar to move it around, just the way you move windows.

Managing Menus

Menus organize and display the command choices available at any given time, as well as enabling you to indicate your particular command choice. Windows relies mainly on three types of command menus (each of which is described in the following sections).

The following are a few general guidelines that apply when using menus:

✦ If you see a right-facing arrowhead (>) to the right of an option on a menu, another menu containing more options appears when you highlight (or select) that option.

✦ If you see an ellipsis (...) at the end of an option in a menu, a dialog box appears when you select that option. (See "Using Dialog Boxes," later in this chapter.)

✦ If you don't see any kind of symbol next to a menu option, the selected option is carried out immediately.

Displaying pull-down menus

Pull-down menus are the primary means for making your wishes known in Windows. Although most commands on pull-down menus live up to their names and appear below the menu, some (like the Start menu) actually display their options above the menu name when you open them. Within windows, the pull-down menus are located on their own menu bar right below the title bar (as shown in Figure 3-5).

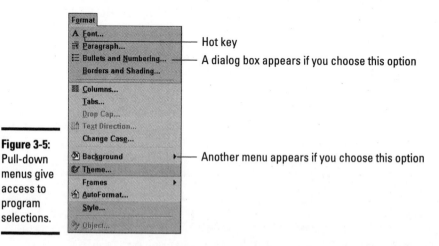

Figure 3-5:
Pull-down menus give access to program selections.

You have two main methods to open pull-down menus and select commands:

✦ **Using the mouse:** Click the menu name on the menu bar. Move the mouse pointer through the menu to highlight the desired command and then click to select that command.

✦ **Using the Alt key:** Hold down the Alt key as you type the *command letter* in the menu name (that is, the underlined letter) to open the pull-down menu (Refer to Figure 3-5.) Then type the command letter of the menu item to select that item. The underlined letter is sometimes known as the *hot key*.

Using shortcut menus

Shortcut menus (also known as *context*) are pull-down menus that are attached to particular objects in Windows, such as the desktop icons or even the desktop itself. These menus contain commands directly related to the object to which they are attached. To open a shortcut menu, simply right-click it.

In Figure 3-6, you see the shortcut menu associated with the hard drive icon in the My Computer window. To open this shortcut menu on the lower right of the hard drive (C:) icon, simply right-click the icon.

Book II
Chapter 3

**Working with
Toolbars, Menus,
and Dialog Boxes**

Figure 3-6:
When in doubt, right-click icons, selections, or just about anything in Windows to open the shortcut menu.

After you open a shortcut menu, you can use either of the pull-down menu methods described in the preceding section, "Displaying pull-down menus," to choose its commands.

Using the Control menu

The Control menu is a standard pull-down menu attached to all the windows that you open in Windows. To open the Control menu, click the little icon to the immediate left of the window's name on the title bar.

If you double-click this icon instead of single-clicking it, Windows closes the window and quits any application program that happens to be running in it. If you have an unsaved document open in the program whose window you just closed, Windows displays an alert dialog box that gives you a chance to save it before shutting down the shop.

Using Dialog Boxes

A *dialog box* is a special type of window that enables you to specify a bunch of settings at the same time. Most dialog boxes appear as a result of selecting a menu command from either a pull-down menu or a shortcut menu.

At the top of each dialog box, you find a title bar that contains the name of the dialog box. You can reposition the dialog box on the screen by dragging its title bar. You can't, however, resize a dialog box, which is the major difference between a dialog box and a window.

Dialog boxes also contain any number of buttons and boxes that you use to make selections in Windows or in the particular Windows program you have open.

Note that if the name on a command button is followed by an ellipsis (...), clicking the button displays another dialog box. For example, clicking the Options button in Figure 3-7 displays a new dialog box.

After you use these various buttons and boxes to make changes to the current settings controlled by the dialog box, you can close the dialog box and put the new settings into effect by clicking OK.

If you want to close the dialog box without making *any* changes to the current settings, press the Esc key or click the Close button of the dialog box.

Check box

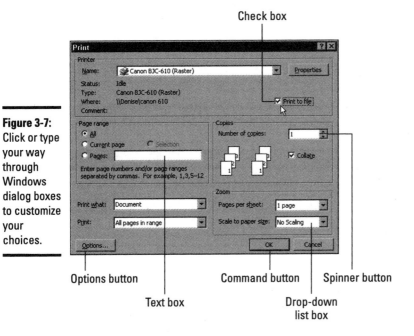

Figure 3-7:
Click or type
your way
through
Windows
dialog boxes
to customize
your
choices.

Options button

Text box

Command button

Drop-down
list box

Spinner button

Chapter 4: File and Folder Management

In This Chapter

✔ Working with files and folders

✔ Creating shortcuts to files and folders

✔ Selecting, copying, and moving files and folders

✔ Finding files and folders

✔ Renaming files and folders

✔ Deleting unwanted files and folders

*I*f you work with any Windows-based program (such as Word, Excel, and so on) for more than a few minutes, you're probably already starting a collection of files that you'll soon lose track of. This is not good. What if you need to finish your letter to the editor or you need to redo the presentation that you're giving the next morning? Without a little file-savvy, you could be in trouble.

This chapter introduces you to files and folders in general, and then shows you the best ways to create, select, move, copy, paste, find, rename, and delete files and folders.

Working with Files

Files contain all the precious data that you create with those sophisticated (and expensive) Windows-based programs. Files occupy a certain amount of space, measured by kilobytes (K) on a particular disk, be it your hard drive or a removable floppy disk. For example, if you write a letter to your brother in Microsoft Word and then save the document to your hard drive, you've just created a file.

Naming files

Each filename in Windows consists of two parts: a main filename and a file extension. The *file extension,* which identifies the type of file and what program created it, consists of a maximum of three characters that are automatically assigned by the creating program. Typically, these file extensions are not displayed in the lists of filenames that you see.

Although the creating program normally assigns the file extension, Windows enables you to call the main part of the filename whatever you want, up to a maximum of 255 characters (including spaces!). There are, however, some characters that are not allowed in filenames:

\ / : * ? " < > |

Versions of Windows earlier than Windows 95, and some programs that run on Windows 98 or Windows Me, do not support long filenames.

Identifying files by their icons

In Windows, files are assigned special icons along with their filenames. These icons help you quickly identify the type of file. Table 4-1 shows some examples of these icons. (See Book II, Chapter 1, for more on the care and feeding of icons.)

Table 4-1	Icons Associated with Certain Files
File Icon	*File Type and Program That Opens It*
	Special program file recognized by Windows as one that will install an application on your computer
	A different type of program file which will either run an application program or installation program
	Word document that will open in Microsoft Word or Word Pad
	Excel workbook that will open in Microsoft Excel
	Text file that will open in Notepad
	HTML document that will open in Internet Explorer
	Unidentified or generic file that will open the Open With dialog box, which asks you to identify a program that can open the file

Working with Folders

Folders are the data containers in Windows. You can recognize folder icons because they actually look like those nice manila folders that you never seem to have enough of. Well, don't worry. In Windows, you have access to an endless supply of folders. (And to prevent any confusion while increasing your boredom, folders in Windows always have the little tab on the left side.) Folders can contain files or other folders or a combination of files and folders (see Figure 4-1). Like files, folders occupy a certain amount of space (measured in kilobytes) on a particular disk, be it your hard drive or a removable floppy disk.

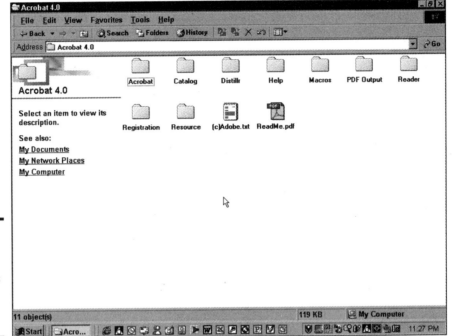

Figure 4-1:
Clicking drives and folders gets you more folders and files.

You can get lots of good information about a file — such as which program created it, how big it is, when it was created and last revised, and so on. Choose the Properties command on the file's shortcut menu. (Right-click an icon to bring up the shortcut menu.)

Windows 98 and Windows Me dramatically alter the way you view and navigate through folders on the desktop. The Folder Options feature enables you to configure folders with attributes normally found in a Web browser, like Internet Explorer. (See Book II, Chapter 5, for details.)

Opening Files and Folders

The most common way to open a file or folder is to open its icon in one of the three browsing windows (My Computer, Windows Explorer, or Internet Explorer). How you open the file or folder icon after you have it displayed in a browsing window depends on the Active Desktop setting that your computer uses. You can

+ Double-click the icon if you've set up the Active Desktop with the so-called *classic* setting.

+ Single-click the icon if you've set up the Active Desktop so that icons act and look like hyperlinks (so-called *Web style*). See Book II, Chapter 5, for information on changing between Web style and classic style.

Remember that you can also open a file or folder that Windows recognizes by right-clicking its icon and then choosing the Open command from its shortcut menu.

Using Shortcuts

Shortcuts make it possible to open a favorite document, folder, program, or Web page directly from the desktop of the computer — even when you have absolutely no idea how deep the object is buried on your computer or where it may be in cyberspace. The following list gives the basic lowdown on shortcuts:

+ Shortcuts can be located anywhere on your computer, but keep them right out in the open on the desktop so that you can get at them easily.

+ When you create a shortcut for an object, Windows creates an icon for it with a name like "Shortcut to *such and such.*" You can rename the shortcut to whatever name suits you, just as you can rename any file or folder in Windows.

+ You can always tell a shortcut icon from another kind of icon because the shortcut icon contains a little box with a curved arrow pointing up to the right.

To create a shortcut for a folder, file, or other type of local object on the Windows desktop, follow these steps:

1. **Select the icon for the object for which you want to create a shortcut.**

2. **Choose File⇨Create Shortcut or choose Create Shortcut from the object's shortcut menu.**

3. **If Windows displays the error message** Unable to create a shortcut here. Do you want the shortcut placed on the desktop?, **click Yes.**

If Windows doesn't give you this error message, it places the new shortcut in the currently open window. If you want the shortcut on the desktop, where you have constant access to it, click and drag the shortcut's icon to any place on the desktop and release the mouse button.

You mess up a shortcut if you move the object to which it refers to a new place on your computer, because Windows still looks for it (unsuccessfully) in the old location. If you do mess up a shortcut by moving the object it refers to, you have to trash the shortcut and then re-create it or move the original file back to its location.

If the shortcut's destination is the desktop, right-click the file and choose Send To⇨Desktop (create shortcut).

Creating New Files and Folders

You create empty folders to hold your files and empty files to hold new documents of a particular type, right within Windows. Create a new folder when you need to have a new place to store your files and other folders. Create an empty file in a particular folder before you put something in it.

To create an empty folder, follow these steps:

1. **Inside a browsing window, open the folder in which you want the new folder to appear.**

2. **Choose File⇨New⇨Folder from the menu bar or New⇨Folder on the window's shortcut menu (right-click anywhere inside the window).**

3. **Replace the temporary folder name *(New Folder)* by typing a name of your choosing and pressing Enter.**

To create an empty file of a certain type, follow these steps:

1. **Open the window and the folder where the new file is to appear.**

2. **Choose File⇨New from the menu bar.**

3. **Choose the type of file you want to create (such as Microsoft PowerPoint Presentation, Microsoft Excel Worksheet, Microsoft Word Document, Microsoft Access Database, Wave Sound, Text Document, Briefcase, and so on) from the New submenu.**

4. **Replace the temporary file name (such as New Microsoft Word Document) by typing a name of your choosing and pressing Enter.**

Copying and Moving Files and Folders

If you want to perform many actions on files and folders, you need to know how to select them. Because files and folders are represented by icons, jump back to Book II, Chapter 1, for all the details.

Copying and pasting

You can copy and move files and folders in Windows by using the two universal methods described in this section — *drag and drop* and *copy/cut and paste.*

The copy and paste commands, like many of the everyday tasks in Windows, can be performed either by selecting commands on the menu bar or by using keyboard-combination shortcuts. To copy and paste files using either method, follow these steps:

1. **Open a browsing window that holds the items you want to copy.**

2. **Select all the items you want to copy (see Book II, Chapter 1, for the details) and then choose Edit⇨Copy, or press Ctrl+C.**

   The files are temporarily copied to the Windows Clipboard.

3. **Open a browsing window that holds the folder or disk where you want the copied items to appear.**

4. **Open the folder or disk to hold the copied items and then choose Edit⇨Paste, or press Ctrl+V.**

The art of dragging and dropping is simplicity itself. To copy files by dragging and dropping, follow these steps:

1. **Open the window that contains the items you want to copy, as well as the window with the folder or disk to which you want to copy the items.**

2. **Select all the items you want to copy (see Book II, Chapter 1, for details on selecting).**

3. **Hold down the Ctrl key as you drag the selected items to the folder to which you want to copy them (you'll notice the appearance of a plus sign next to the pointer).**

4. **After the destination folder icon is selected (that is, highlighted), drop the selected items by releasing the mouse button.**

Use the drag-and-drop method to copy when both the folder with the items to be copied and the destination folder or disk are displayed on the desktop (as when using the Windows Explorer). Use the copy-and-paste method to copy when you can't easily display both the folder with the items to be copied and the destination folder or disk together on the desktop.

The Ctrl key enables you to copy the selected files or folders — meaning they also remain in their original location.

Moving files and folders

You can move files and folders in Windows Explorer by using either the drag-and-drop or the cut-and-paste method. To move an object using the drag-and-drop method, follow these steps:

1. **Open a browsing window that contains the folders and files that you want to move.**

If you're just moving some files in a folder, be sure to open that folder in the window.

2. **Open a browsing window that displays the icon for the folder or disk to which you want to move certain files and folders.**

3. **In the first window, select all the files and folders that you want to move.**

4. **Hold down the Shift key and drag the selected files and folders from the first window to the window that contains the destination folder or disk (the one where the files will be moved).**

Using the Shift key ensures that the folders or files are moved—they don't remain in their original location.

5. **As soon as you select the icon of the destination folder or disk (indicated by a highlighted name), release the mouse button and Shift key to move the files into that folder or disk.**

When you drag files or folders from one disk to another, Windows automatically copies the files and folders rather than moving them (meaning that you must still delete them from their original disk if you need the space).

If you can't remember whether to hold down the Shift or Ctrl key, drag with the right mouse button pressed instead of the left. When you release the right mouse button, you get a menu that lets you choose to copy the files, move the files, or cancel the operation.

Drag-and-drop moving from folder to folder is great because it's really fast. However, this method does have a major drawback: It's pretty easy to drop file icons into the wrong folder. Instead of having a cow when you open up what you thought was the destination folder and find that your files are gone, you can locate them by using the Find Files or Folders command (see "Finding Files and Folders," later in this chapter). Or, if you want, you can undo the move by pressing Ctrl+Z or choosing Edit⇨Undo to put the files back where they came from.

Moving files and folders via the cut-and-paste method ensures that the lost files scenario just described won't happen, though it's much clunkier than the elegant drag-and-drop method. To move files and folders by cutting and pasting, follow these steps:

1. **Open a window that displays all the files and folders you want to move.**

2. **Select all the files and folders you want to move (see Book II, Chapter 1, for info on selecting).**

3. **Choose Edit⇨Cut, or press Ctrl+X, to cut the selected files and place them on the Clipboard.**

4. **Open a window that contains the destination folder or disk (the one to which you want to move the selected files or folders).**

5. **Choose Edit⇨Paste in the window where the selected stuff should be moved, or press Ctrl+V, to insert the files into the folder or disk.**

Use the drag-and-drop method when you can see on the desktop both the files and folders to be moved and the folder to which you are moving them. Switch to the cut-and-paste method when you cannot see both.

Windows automatically moves files when you drag their file icons from one folder to another on the same disk and copies files (indicated by the appearance of a plus sign next to the pointer) when you drag their icons from one disk to another.

Finding Files and Folders

The Find feature enables you to quickly locate all those misplaced files and folders that you're just sure are hiding somewhere on your hard drive. To open the Find window to search for a file or folder, follow these steps:

1. **Choose Start⇨Search⇨For Files or Folders.**

This action opens the Search Results window.

2. **On the left side of the window, enter the search conditions in the Search for Files or Folders Named text box and choose where to look from the Look In drop-down menu.**

3. **Click the Search Now button to start the search.**

While Windows Me conducts the search, you see the files that meet your criteria on the right side of the window (as shown in Figure 4-2). This window shows the name, location, size, type, and the date the file was last modified.

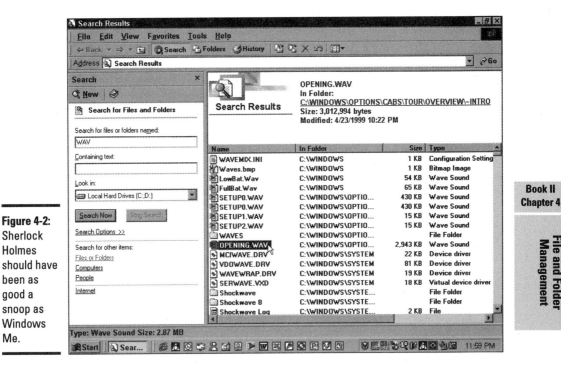

Figure 4-2:
Sherlock
Holmes
should have
been as
good a
snoop as
Windows
Me.

By clicking the Advanced Search Options hyperlink, you can also specify other criteria like the date the file was last modified, the type of file, or the size of the file, or choose the Advanced Options for even more possibilities.

Here are a couple more things you should know to get the most of the Search Results dialog box:

✦ To clear the information and start again, click the New button in the top of the left side of the window.

✦ On the right side of the window, where the search results are listed, you may sometimes need to see more of a long filename or the entire path of the file. Place your cursor on the line dividing the column headers and drag it to the left or right; this expands or reduces the width of the column, allowing you to view more or less of the information.

✦ You can click the column headers to sort the list by the date the files and folders were created or by file size. Click once for ascending order; click a second time for descending order. Remember that folders are listed before files.

✦ If you have an Internet connection active, you can search for People and Web sites by clicking the hyperlinks at the bottom of the left side of the window.

✦ If your PC is part of a network, you can look for resources to use (if they are made available to you by the network administrator) by using the Computers hyperlink.

✦ Don't forget to use the Look In drop-down list. This list enables you to narrow your search if you halfway know where the sought-after item is, or to expand your search to the outer limits of your computer's realm.

 Windows 98's routine for finding file works roughly the same way but with a different visual twist. Choose Start⇨Find⇨Files or Folders to open the Find All Files dialog box. Enter the phrase, file name, file extension, or whatever you want to search for in the Named text box. You can narrow the search by using the Look In option. Choose the drive you want to scan, and click the Find Now button. While Windows begins hunting for all the files that meet the criteria you specified, the Find All Files dialog box expands and lists the results.

Renaming Files and Folders

You can rename file and folder icons directly in Windows by typing over or editing the existing file or folder name, as outlined in these steps:

1. **Right-click the file or folder icon and choose Rename from its shortcut menu, or select the file and press F2.**

2. **Type the new name that you want to give the folder (up to 255 characters) or edit the existing name.**

   You can use the Delete key to remove characters and the ← or → key to move the cursor without deleting characters.

3. **After you finish editing the file or folder name, press the Enter key to complete the renaming procedure.**

Deleting Old Files and Folders

Because the whole purpose of working on computers is to create junk, you need to know how to get rid of unneeded files and folders to free up space on your hard drive. To delete files or folders, follow these steps:

1. **In one of the three browsing windows, open the folder that holds the files or folders to be deleted.**

2. **Select all the files and folders you want to delete (see Book II, Chapter 1, for the lowdown on selecting items).**

3. **Choose File⇨Delete from the menu bar or press the Delete key.**

   You may find dragging the selected items to the Recycle Bin easier. Use the method you prefer.

4. **Click the Yes button in the Confirm File Delete or Confirm Multiple File Delete dialog box that appears.**

Use the following tips to work efficiently with the Recycle Bin:

✦ **To retrieve stuff from the Recycle Bin:** Open the Recycle Bin and then drag the icons for the files and folders you want to save out of the Recycle Bin and drop them in the desired location. You can also choose File⇨Restore from the Recycle Bin window menu bar.

✦ **To permanently delete only a few items from the Recycle Bin:** Open the Recycle Bin and select the files or folders to be removed. Use the Shift key to select contiguous files or hold the Ctrl key to select noncontiguous files. After selecting the files, press the Delete key. The files that may have a fighting chance for survival are still safe in the Recycle Bin file list, but the files you deleted are gone for good.

✦ **To empty the Recycle Bin:** Open the Recycle Bin and choose File⇨Empty Recycle Bin from the Recycle Bin window menu bar. You can also empty it by right-clicking the Recycle Bin icon on the desktop and choosing Empty Recycle Bin from the icon's shortcut menu — and you can never retrieve these files again.

Chapter 5: Getting Involved with the Active Desktop

In This Chapter

- Taking charge of the Active Desktop
- Browsing folders the Windows way
- Changing the way you deal with folders

As Microsoft begets more generations of the Windows operating system, the World Wide Web gets further integrated into the Windows interface. If you have Internet access, the importance of the Windows interface woven seamlessly into the Internet will be very useful. It all begins with the Active Desktop.

What is the Active Desktop?

The Active Desktop is the amazing set of features that continues the Microsoft grand plan for building Web integration into the Windows operating environment. The Windows Me (and Windows 98) desktop consists of three layers, each of which lies on top of the others:

- ✦ The top layer contains the Windows desktop icons, including standard shortcuts to items such as My Computer and Network Neighborhood, as well as custom shortcuts to your favorite programs and folders.

- ✦ The middle layer contains all displayed Active Desktop items, such as the Internet Explorer Channel bar, along with other Active Desktop items that you subscribe to.

- ✦ The bottom layer contains the desktop wallpaper, which can be an HTML document or a graphics file format such as BMP, GIF, or JPEG.

You can turn the "active" aspect of the Windows desktop on and off at will by turning on and off the Web Content view. When you turn off the Web Content view, Windows hides the middle layer, which contains all the Active Desktop items. If you have made an HTML document into the desktop wallpaper, turning off the Active Desktop also hides the bottom layer. The result is that only the top layer, which has the Windows desktop icons, is visible.

Figure 5-1 shows the desktop of a computer with the Web Content view turned on. In this figure, you can see the whole shebang: the Windows desktop icons on the left, and the Active Desktop items (including the Hungry Minds and Windows Me Web sites).

In Windows 98, you'll find the terminology is a bit different, but the results are the same. Windows 98 calls Web Content view the Web Page view.

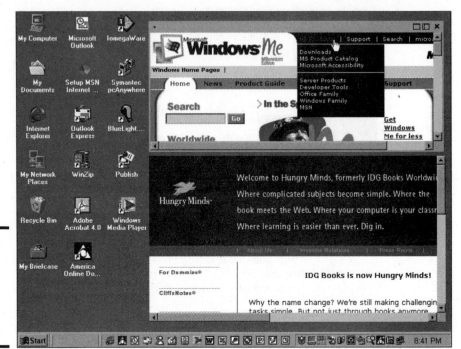

Figure 5-1:
You can view the Web from the Windows Desktop.

Turning the Desktop Web Content View On and Off

As is often the case, Microsoft gives you several ways to turn the desktop Web Content view on and off:

✦ In Windows Me, right-click somewhere on the desktop (outside of a desktop icon or an Active Desktop item) and choose Active Desktop⇨Show Web Content from the shortcut menu. In Windows 98, choose Active Desktop⇨View As Web Page.

✦ In Windows Me, choose Tools⇨Folder Options in any open browsing window like Windows Explorer or My Computer. On the General tab, select the Enable Web Content on My Desktop option in the Active Desktop section, and select the Enable Web Content in Folders option in the Web View section. In Windows 98, choose View⇨Folder Options⇨ Web Style.

✦ Right-click the desktop, choose Properties, and click the Web tab. Select the Show Web Content on My Active Desktop check box. (In Windows 98, select the View My Active Desktop as a Web Page check box.)

When you turn on the Web Content layer, you may not see a noticeable difference to the desktop. That's because you haven't chosen or created any of the various Web pages that may be viewed on the desktop. To have your current home page opened on your desktop, right-click any vacant area of the desktop and choose Properties. Click the Web tab and select the My Current Home Page check box. If there are no selections in the listing, click the New button and follow along with the Wizard to add one or more Web addresses to your desktop.

The Windows desktop is not the only Windows element that you can view as a Web page. In fact, any window in Windows (My Computer, Windows Explorer, the Control Panel, and so on) can be viewed as a Web page. (They didn't call it "Web integration" for nothing.) For more on working with Web Content views in the browsing windows, see "Browsing folders with Web Content view turned on," later in this chapter.

Browsing Folders on a Local Disk

You can use any of the three Windows browsing windows (My Computer, Windows Explorer, or Internet Explorer) to browse the contents of the drives attached to your computer. These can be local drives, such as your floppy drive (A:), hard drive (C:), or CD-ROM drive (whatever its drive designation is). If your computer is on a Local Area Network (LAN), these can be remote drives to which you have access, such as a network E:, F:, or G: drive. Browsing folders with My Computer and Windows Explorer is much more direct (because these windows both include icons for the drives attached to your computer).

Browsing folders with Web Content view turned on

Windows supports a folder view called Web Content view. When you turn on this view in one of the browsing windows, vital statistics appear in an info panel on the left side of the window each time you select a particular file or folder icon. These statistics include the folder name or filename, the last date modified, and, in the case of files, the file type and size in kilobytes. When you select a file, like a Microsoft Word or Excel document, the name of the person who created the document also appears in the info panel. Windows also displays a thumbnail of an image or document if it can decipher the graphics file or if the document is written in HTML.

Figure 5-2 shows Windows Explorer after selecting the My Documents folder in the Folders pane, turning on Web Content view, and selecting a file containing a TIF graphic image in the contents pane. In addition to vital statistics (filename, type, date last modified, and size), a thumbnail preview of the graphic appears in the info panel in the contents pane.

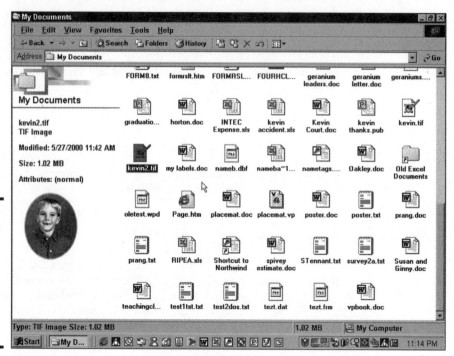

Figure 5-2: You can get more information and previews when viewing folders as Web pages.

Browsing folders with Thumbnail view turned on

When browsing folders that contain graphics or Web pages (such as the pages that you're developing for your own Web site on the Internet), you can use the Thumbnail view to see a larger representation of the image in the file listing.

If you're using Windows 98, you must first enable the Thumbnail view for a particular folder by adding the Thumbnail view to the folder's properties, as follows:

1. **Open one of the three browsing windows (My Computer, Windows Explorer, or Internet Explorer) and then open the drive and folder that contains the folder to which you want to add the Thumbnail view.**

2. **Right-click the folder's icon and choose Properties to open the Properties dialog box.**

3. **Select the Enable Thumbnail View check box on the General tab of the folder's Properties dialog box and then click OK.**

To display the Thumbnail view for a folder (in both Windows 98 and Windows Me), follow these steps:

1. **Open the folder you want to see in Thumbnail view in the My Computer, Windows Explorer, or Internet Explorer window.**

2. **Choose View⇨Thumbnails (or click the drop-down button attached to the Views button on the Standard Buttons bar and then choose Thumbnails from the pop-up menu).**

   Figure 5-3 shows you what a folder looks like in Thumbnail view.

To turn off the Thumbnail view for a folder, just select another view (such as Large Icons or List) from the View pull-down menu or the Views button.

Book II
Chapter 5

Getting Involved
with the Active
Desktop

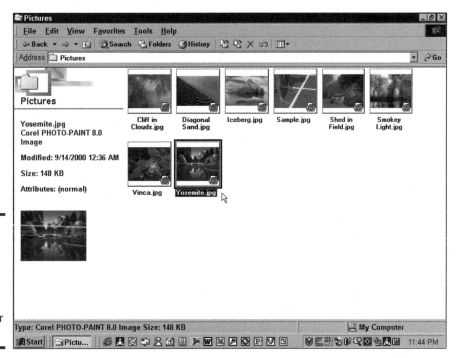

Figure 5-3: Thumbnail view gives you larger samples of the graphic files on your system.

Changing the Folder Options for Windows

You can use the Folder Options dialog box to modify the default Active Desktop and Web Content view setting. You can also change how you select and open folder and file icons, customize file information that appears in the browsing windows, and determine which programs are associated with which file types.

You can open the Folder Options dialog box in one of two ways:

✦ Choose Tools⟹Folder Options from the pull-down menus in any of the three browsing windows: My Computer, Windows Explorer, or Internet Explorer. (In Windows 98, Folder Options is located in the View menu.)

✦ Choose Start⟹Settings⟹Control Panel⟹Folder Options (Windows Me). In Windows 98, choose Settings⟹Folder Options.

If you don't see the Folder Options icon or any other icons that are supposed to appear in Control Panel, click the View All Control Panel Options link in the left pane.

Changing the Way You Select and Open Icons

Use the General tab of the Folder Options dialog box to change the Active Desktop and Web Content view default settings. Also use these tabs to change the way you select and open desktop and windows icons. The General tab contains the following options:

✦ **Active Desktop:** Enables or disables all Web-related content on the Active Desktop, such as Web sites that you have defined for the Active Desktop or live Web content that you have added. To add desktop content, right-click the desktop and choose Active Desktop⟹New Desktop Item. Browse the drive or the Internet, or click the Visit Gallery button to see what Microsoft has in its collection of Active Desktop Gallery items.

✦ **Web View:** Enables or disables all Web-related content in folders. The left window pane, that carries the filename, size, type, thumbnail preview (if one is available), and sometimes the file author's name disappears. Choosing the Use Windows Classic Folders option removes the information panel.

✦ **Browse Folders:** When opening folders within a browsing window, this command tells Windows whether to replace the current window with the one you click, or to open a new window with a view of the folders and files of the drive or folder you selected. Personally, we prefer to open each folder in the same window. If you need a second window open, just double-click the My Computer icon on the desktop.

✦ **Click Items as Follows:** You can cut down on the strain of the clicking finger by choosing to open items with a single click instead of a double-click. Simply pointing to an item selects it, and clicking it once opens it. Conversely, choosing the traditional Windows way, the Double-Click to Open an Item option, maintains your habit of single-clicking to select an item and double-clicking to open it.

To customize these settings in Windows 98, open any browsing window, such as My Computer or Windows Explorer. Select View➪Folder Options and choose the General tab. To customize your Windows desktop, choose the Custom, Based on Settings You Choose option and click the Settings button. All of the options outlined in the previous list are there for you to customize in the Custom Settings dialog box.

Book II
Chapter 5

Getting Involved
with the Active
Desktop

Index

Book III

The Internet

The 5th Wave   By Rich Tennant

"QUICK, KIDS! YOUR MOTHER'S FLAMING SOMEONE ON THE INTERNET!"

Contents at a Glance

Chapter 1: Getting Started with the Internet

In This Chapter

- ✔ Understanding the Internet
- ✔ Buying a computer for Internet access
- ✔ Upgrading an existing computer
- ✔ Gathering the software you need
- ✔ Getting connected to the Internet
- ✔ Safety and security issues

*G*etting on the Internet is much easier than it used to be, but the process still can be daunting to new users. We try to help you as you figure out the world of modems, Internet Service Providers, and communications software that you need to connect to the Net. It used to be that either your computer had a direct connection to the Internet at school or work, or you bought a modem and dialed in over an ordinary phone line. Today, you have many more choices, including cable and specialized telephone services, such as DSL and ISDN. This chapter also covers the basics of safety and security issues on the Net, including how to add security to your e-mail messages, and how to control your kids' access to the Internet.

For more detailed help on the Internet and getting connected, refer to *The Internet For Dummies,* 7th Edition, by John Levine, Carol Baroudi, and Margaret Levine Young (published by IDG Books Worldwide, Inc.).

What Is the Internet?

The *Internet* is a system that lets computers all over the world talk to each other. That's all you really need to know. If you have access to a computer, you can probably use "the Net." The U.S. Department of Defense Advanced Research Projects Agency originally sponsored Internet development because it wanted a military communications system that could survive a nuclear war. Later, the Internet was funded as a research support system by the National Science Foundation. That's all ancient history now, though, because support for the Internet comes almost entirely from commercial sources.

The term *Internet* is often used interchangeably with the *Web,* although this isn't really accurate. The *World Wide Web* (or just the *Web*) is actually one special area of the Internet (other areas include newsgroups, mailing lists, FTP, and chat). The Web is based on *hyperlinks,* (also called *links*), that enable Web surfers to travel quickly from one Web server to another. The Web allows pages with fancy graphic and multimedia elements to be constructed, while other areas of the Internet do not.

What makes the Internet great is that it brings together the best qualities of the communications systems that precede it while improving on their worst features:

✦ **Postal mail (known as *snail mail* on the Net):** Takes at least a day — often a week — to get to its destination, and you must have envelopes and stamps, and find a mailbox. E-mail is quicker to compose, arrives faster, and doesn't require a stamp.

✦ **The telephone:** The other person must be available to talk, and usually no record exists of what was said. You can read e-mail when you feel like it, and it doesn't interrupt you during dinner.

✦ **The fax machine:** It's a chore to incorporate a fax into another document or to pass it on to someone else. Faxes of faxes of faxes become illegible. E-mail stays readable no matter how many times it's forwarded.

✦ **The public library:** You have to go to the library to find information, and half the time, the book you want is checked out or missing. By the time information gets into the library, it is often out of date. The Internet is open 24 hours a day, 7 days a week, and you don't have to get in your car to go there.

✦ **The newspaper:** Most newspapers come out only once a day, and they decide what news you get to see and what spin to put on it. On the World Wide Web, news is updated continuously. (On the other hand, it's hard to line a litter box with a Web page.)

What Services Does the Internet Provide?

The Internet provides these basic services:

✦ Electronic mail, or *e-mail*

✦ Access to the World Wide Web — the information system of the twenty-first century

✦ Newsgroups

✦ Mailing lists

+ File transfers from other computers

+ The capability to log on to other computers

+ Discussions with other people using chat

The Internet also provides advanced services, including multimedia broadcasts, Internet radio, secure financial transactions, video conferencing, and wireless communication.

You can do an almost endless list of things with the Internet, from finding a job to finding a mate, from searching the card catalogs of the greatest libraries in the world to ordering a pizza. Most important, the Internet is the place to learn more about the Internet.

Buying a Computer for Internet Access

Almost any new computer you can buy today is ready for Internet use. Of course, computer salespeople will try to sell you the most expensive model possible. This section tells you what you really need to know when purchasing an Internet-ready computer.

For a lot more information about what to look for when you're getting ready to buy a computer, check out *Upgrading and Fixing PCs,* 5th Edition, by Andy Rathbone (published by IDG Books Worldwide, Inc.).

**Book III
Chapter 1**

Getting Started with the Internet

What should you do with your old computer? Give it to a charitable institution and take a tax deduction. Call your local school district, library, church, or other charity and offer the computer as a donation, or visit the following Web site, which lists computer recyclers by state and country: www.microweb. com/pepsite/Recycle/recycle_index.html. Be sure to get a written receipt that details everything you donated, including software. Tax laws are changing, so get up-to-date advice about how much you can deduct.

Using a set-top box

One new option for connection to the Internet is the *set-top box.* As its name implies, it's a box the size of a small VCR that sits on top of your television set. (The best-known brand is WebTV, from Microsoft.) You hook it up to your TV in much the same way that you hook up a VCR, and you also plug the set-top box into a telephone jack. *Voilà!* You're connected to the Internet — without a computer. These units are available for as little as $100 plus $20 per month for Internet service. Although set-top boxes do work, they have some drawbacks:

+ Because televisions can display only a half-dozen or so lines of text at a time, you tediously have to press Page Down repeatedly to read even a modest-size Internet page.

✦ You're usually limited to one Internet Service Provider. The monthly rate is about the same as for regular Internet service.

✦ You cannot use set-top boxes for much more than looking at World Wide Web pages, text chat, and e-mail.

Deciding between a desktop and a laptop PC

Although laptops are really cool, they cost much more for the same performance. Get a desktop model unless you plan to travel frequently with your computer.

Deciding if Linux is for you

Linux is a free version of the Unix operating system. It supports a full range of tools for Internet access and has a very loyal following. Indeed, many ISPs use Linux on their servers. Although Linux is very powerful, it is still complex to install and use; beginners may want to stick to Windows. You can find out more about Linux in *Linux For Dummies,* 2nd Edition, by Jon Hall (published by IDG Books Worldwide, Inc.).

Making sure that your computer is cable ready

Make sure that any computer you buy can be used with a cable or DSL modem — some new lower-priced PCs cannot! To be cable ready, your computer must have an *Ethernet port* or an available slot into which you can plug an Ethernet card. The slot may be called a PCI, ISA, NuBus, or PC card slot — just make sure that any computer you buy has one. In some cases, it is possible to run a cable modem through a USB port by using an adapter. (Check with your cable company to see if this option can work for you.)

Knowing about your PC's memory, hard drive, monitor, and printer

An adequate amount of memory (RAM) does more for your computer's performance than processor speed. These days, 32 megabytes (MB) of RAM is the absolute minimum. Get 64MB or more if you can afford it. Many new computer systems now come with 128MB or 256MB of RAM. (For information on upgrading memory, refer to Book VIII, Chapter 2.)

Most new desktop machines come with at least 4 *gigabytes* (GB) of hard drive (sometimes called *hard disk*) space — more than enough for Internet use. A gigabyte is about 1,000 megabytes.

Most computers come with an adequate monitor for Internet use. Step up one level if you feel rich. Anything beyond that level is overkill for the Net.

Most modern printers can print graphics. Any printer will do. You can even live without a printer while you're getting started, although having one is handy. (For more on printers, see Book I, Chapter 5 and Book VIII, Chapter 7.)

Preparing to back up

Hard drives are much more reliable these days, although they still crash sometimes. And they're just too big to back up to floppy disks. A removable cartridge tape or disk drive is cheap insurance against data loss. Remember to back up regularly, or you'll be sorry that you didn't. Refer to Book I, Chapter 7 for more information.

Determining Whether Your Computer Is Internet Ready

If you already have a computer, you may be in luck: You may be able to use it as is to access the Internet. If not, a few simple improvements may be all you need to make your computer ready for the Internet. The following sections show you how to determine what upgrades, if any, your computer needs to access the Internet. (For more specific information on upgrading your computer and installing components, refer to Book VIII, "Upgrading and Fixing a PC.")

To upgrade or not to upgrade

With the price of new Internet-ready computers at or below $1,000, your old computer may not be worth upgrading. In fact, you can easily spend more money upgrading an old computer than you would spend on a new computer. Here are some signs that you should buy a new computer instead of wasting time and money upgrading an old computer:

✦ The computer is more than a few years old.

✦ The computer runs Windows 3.1.

✦ The computer has vacuum tubes inside.

✦ The computer is only a year or two old, but you read through the rest of this section and found out that you need to upgrade everything.

The bare minimum

To access the Internet and enjoy it, your Windows computer should at least have the following components:

✦ **A Pentium-class processor:** The faster the better, but any Pentium computer can do the job.

✦ **At least 32MB of RAM:** More is better, of course, but 32MB is usually adequate and 64MB is preferable. (Technically, you can get by with as little as 16MB, but the performance is slow.)

✦ **At least 1GB of free drive space:** In most cases, your hard drive should have a total capacity of 2GB or more. If your computer does not have enough free drive space, you'll see `You have run out of space on Drive C` messages instead of the Web sites that you want to visit.

✦ **A modem:** Yep, you need one of those things — unless you have a high-speed connection, such as DSL. (For more information, see "Choosing a Modem," later in this chapter.)

Other goodies you don't need but could use

Besides an adequate Pentium or better processor, RAM, drive storage, and a modem (or high-speed connection), your Internet-ready computer should have the following:

✦ **Video card capable of displaying at least 800 x 600 resolution with 24-bit color:** Higher resolutions are nice, but most Web pages are designed to be viewed at 800 x 600. To find out if your video card is up to snuff, right-click a blank spot of your desktop, choose Properties, and click the Settings tab. Then see if you can set the Desktop Area or Screen Area control to 800 x 600 pixels. If you can't, you should purchase and install a better video card. (For the best viewing of Internet graphics and video, also make sure that you can set the Color control to True Color while the resolution is set to 800 x 600 pixels.)

✦ **Monitor large enough to prevent squinting when viewing an 800 x 600 screen:** If you have a small (13-inch or 14-inch) monitor, you may want to upgrade to a larger 17-inch or 19-inch monitor or invest in stronger glasses.

✦ **CD-ROM drive:** Although a CD-ROM drive is not an absolute necessity for accessing the Internet, most software is distributed via CD-ROM these days. So if you plan on purchasing and using any Internet software, you need a CD-ROM (or DVD-ROM) drive.

✦ **Sound card and speakers:** You don't have to worry too much about how good your sound card and speakers are unless you are an audiophile. Just about any sound card is capable of playing most of the sounds you listen to over the Internet; but if you aren't happy with the quality of what you hear, you can upgrade to a better sound card and speakers.

✦ **Microphone:** A microphone plugged into your sound card enables you to send your voice over the Internet.

✦ **Camera:** An inexpensive ($100 or so) Web cam lets you send video images over the Internet.

✦ **Scanner:** A scanner enables you to scan your family photographs and attach them to e-mail messages or post them on your Web pages. You can purchase a decent scanner for as little as $100.

Do it yourself?

If you're a bit of a techno-geek and enjoy opening up a computer and fiddling with its innards, you can perform hardware upgrades, such as adding more memory, installing a hard drive, or upgrading your sound or video card yourself. You can purchase any of these components at your local computer store or at one of the large office supply chain stores. You'll find step-by-step installation instructions inside the box. See Book VIII, "Upgrading and Fixing a PC" for additional information on upgrading your PC.

If you prefer, you can have the service department of your local computer store install the upgrade for you. You'll pay a fee, but you won't have to spend the time performing the upgrade yourself and you know that they'll do it right.

Choosing a Modem

Most new computers come with a modem as standard equipment. A *modem* is a device that enables your computer to connect to the Internet via a telephone line, also known as a *dial-up connection*. (An alternative to using a modem is a high-speed connection, such as DSL — see the next section, "High-Speed Connections.") This section discusses the differences between types of modems. Refer to Book VIII, Chapter 6 for modem installation information and troubleshooting tips.

Book III
Chapter 1

Getting Started with the Internet

You can find out if your computer has a modem installed by choosing Start⇨Settings⇨Control Panel and double-clicking the Modems icon to open the Modems Properties dialog box. This dialog box lists any modems installed on your computer.

You attach modems either internally or externally. *Internal* modems are cards placed in a slot within your computer's case. *External* modems are small boxes that live outside your computer and connect to your computer through a cable. Either type works well. Internal modems are a bit cheaper than external modems, but an internal modem requires that you take your computer apart to install the modem card. External modems are a bit more expensive but are easier to install. If you are unsure about which type of modem to buy, consult your computer's documentation or contact your computer's manufacturer.

If you have a laptop or notebook computer, you can still use an internal modem. Just be sure to buy a PCMCIA card modem.

Modems are rated by their speed, using a measurement called *bps* (which stands for *bits per second*). Although you can connect to the Internet with a 28,800 bps (28.8K) modem, your Internet experience is much more satisfying if you use a faster modem, such as 33.6K or 56K. You can purchase a 56K modem for well under $100. (Unfortunately, your phone line may not be able to handle connections faster than 28.8K. Even if you upgrade to the fastest modem available, your phone connection may limit your Internet speed.)

To connect to the Internet, the modem requires a telephone line. You don't need a special computer-type telephone line; your standard telephone line that you hold conversations on can work. However, be warned that when you connect your computer to the Internet, you can't use that telephone line for anything else. If you try calling home and the phone is busy for hours, don't automatically assume that your teenager is talking — it may be that your spouse is using the Internet. (For this reason, many people add a second phone line just for Internet access.)

High-Speed Connections

If you use the Internet a lot and aren't satisfied with the slow speeds of dial-up connections via a modem, consider a high-speed Internet access (also known as *broadband*) alternative such as ISDN, DSL, cable, or wireless. These services are not available in all areas.

Both cable and DSL connect to your computer via an Ethernet network card, which you must purchase and install in your computer. An inexpensive Ethernet card sets you back about $30. Alternatively, you may be able to connect your cable or DSL modem to your computer via your computer's USB port. Ask your cable company or DSL provider for more information.

Besides the speed, the biggest advantage of cable, DSL, and wireless connections is that you are always connected to the Internet, 24 hours a day. As a result, you can access the Internet instantly, without waiting for your modem to dial and establish a connection.

ISDN

An older digital telephone service, known as Integrated Services Digital Network (ISDN), lets you connect to the Internet at twice the speed of a standard dial-up connection and share the connection with a voice phone. The phone company uses digital lines and equipment to provide you with the service. Check with your telephone company for availability and pricing. ISDN connections require special ISDN modems, and you still need to pay for an ISP. As DSL becomes more popular, ISDN will soon fade into memory.

DSL

Digital Subscriber Line (DSL) is a high-speed digital phone line provided by your local telephone company. DSL offers speeds similar to cable modems but uses your existing phone line rather than your TV cable. DSL can even share its high-speed Internet connection with your telephone, so you can talk to your mother-in-law and access the Internet at the same time by using the same phone line. The bad news is that DSL is more expensive than cable. You can expect to pay $100 per month for good DSL service. (In some areas, you can get DSL for as little as $50 per month, but at that price the DSL connection is usually limited to speeds that are only about twice that of regular phone connections.) In addition to the monthly service fees, expect to pay $150 or more for installation. Contact your local phone company to find out if DSL service is available in your area. Current DSL technology requires you to be within three miles of your telephone company's central office. Most DSL connections require external modems.

Cable

A cable modem connection lets you connect to the Internet via your cable television provider. Cable modems aren't really modems at all. They are network devices that connect your network, usually consisting of your computer with an Ethernet card, to the cable television company's network. The device uses the same cable that brings television programming into your home to bring you access to the Internet. Cable modem connections are lightning fast — from 500 Kbps to 10 Mbps and cost about $50 per month. In addition, you must purchase a cable modem (about $300) and an Ethernet card (about $50). Installation usually costs $150 or more. The speed of your connection may vary depending on the number of other cable modem users in your neighborhood. Of course, just because you have cable television doesn't mean that you can get cable modem access to the Internet. Call your local cable company to find out if cable modem service is available in your area.

Book III
Chapter 1

**Getting Started with
the Internet**

Wireless

An alternative to high-speed cable and DSL connections is wireless Internet. For example, DirecPC is a satellite-based service that lets you access the Internet as much as eight times faster than with a standard phone connection. The main advantage of DirecPC over cable and DSL connections is that DirecPC is available almost anywhere (well, at least in the U.S.). In addition, companies such as Sprint and AT&T are currently testing fixed wireless service in limited markets across the U.S. This service employs towers (similar to those used for cellular phone service) that communicate with home-based antennas. You still need an additional modem and telephone line to upload information.

Gathering the Software You Need

Before you can access the Internet, you need to build a small collection of software. Fortunately, most of the software you need is inexpensive or free. You can get most of the software you need by installing one of the two leading Web browser suites: Microsoft's Internet Explorer or Netscape's Communicator. Both suites include tools for browsing the World Wide Web, accessing e-mail and Internet newsgroups, creating Web pages, and much more.

Internet Explorer

If you have a computer with Windows 95 (or later), you already have Microsoft's Internet Explorer. However, you may not have the latest version. If not, you can download a free copy from www.microsoft.com/ie, or you can order Internet Explorer on CD for a mere $6.95 by calling 1-800-485-2048. (See Book III, Chapter 4 for lots more on Web browsing with Internet Explorer.)

The complete Internet Explorer suite includes the following programs:

✦ **Internet Explorer Web Browser:** For viewing Web pages

✦ **Outlook Express:** For e-mail and Internet newsgroups

✦ **MSN Messenger Service:** For sending instant messages to other Internet users

✦ **NetMeeting:** For online conferencing

✦ **Chat:** For chatting online with other Internet users

✦ **FrontPage Express:** For creating simple Web pages

Netscape Communicator

Netscape Communicator is a complete package of Internet access tools from Netscape. You can download Netscape Communicator from home.netscape.com/computing/download/index.html, or you can order it on CD for $5.95 from cd.netscape.com.

Netscape Communicator includes the following components:

✦ **Navigator:** For viewing Web pages

✦ **Messenger:** For e-mail and Internet newsgroups

✦ **Netscape AOL Instant Messenger:** For sending instant messages to other Internet users

✦ **Netscape Calendar:** For scheduling meetings

✦ **Composer:** For creating simple Web pages

Other software you may need

Both Microsoft Internet Explorer and Netscape Communicator contain most of the software you need to access the Internet. The following list describes some other software you may find useful:

✦ **Instant messenger software:** Messenger software lets you chat one-on-one with other Internet users. You get Microsoft Messenger Service as a part of Internet Explorer, or you can download it from `messenger.msn.com`. Likewise, you get AOL Instant Messenger with Netscape Navigator, or you can download it from `www.aol.com/aim`. Besides these two, another popular instant messaging program is ICQ, which you can download from `www.icq.com`.

✦ **Filtering software:** This type of software protects your family from offensive Web sites. Some good ones are CyberPatrol (`www.cyberpatrol.com`), Net Nanny (`www.netnanny.com`), Pearl Software's Cyber Snoop (`www.pearlsw.com`), and Norton Internet Security 2000 (`www.symantec.com`).

✦ **Adobe Acrobat Reader:** Many Web sites let you download documents that require you to have the Adobe Acrobat Reader to read them. Sooner or later, you'll need to download and install this free software from `www.adobe.com`.

✦ **Macromedia Shockwave:** Many Web pages display complicated multimedia graphics by using a program called Shockwave. You can download it free of charge from `www.macromedia.com`.

✦ **RealPlayer:** RealPlayer (formerly known as RealAudio) is a must if you want to listen to real-time audio or watch real-time video over the Internet. You can get RealPlayer from `www.real.com`.

✦ **Windows Media Player:** Microsoft's media player is the standard program for playing sound and video files under Windows.

✦ **Compression software:** Many files that you can download from the Internet are stored in a compressed format. To access these files, you need compression software. You can get WinZip from `www.winzip.com`.

Book III
Chapter 1

Getting Started with the Internet

Getting Connected

Perhaps the most important — and confusing — decision you have to make to get on the Internet is figuring out how you want to connect. As this section shows, you can choose to connect to the Internet through an online service, which offers you some additional features besides just Internet access, or you can choose from a couple of other options, including contracting with a standard *Internet Service Provider (ISP)*. Read on to discover your available options.

Online services

An *online service* is a company that provides information online, separate from what is available on the Internet. The term *value-added* is often attached to these online services because they offer their members additional information above and beyond the basic Internet access provided by standard ISPs.

America Online (AOL) is by far the largest of these value-added online services, and many consider it to be the best service for beginners. AOL recently acquired CompuServe and promotes that service for business and professional users. Microsoft Network is still trying to become a player. Prodigy has faded somewhat. All these online services also provide access to the Internet itself, including sending and receiving Internet e-mail and viewing Web pages.

All of the major online services send you a free starter kit with the software you need and usually some promotional offer. Just give them a call.

Online Service	*Phone Number (s)*
America Online (AOL)	800-827-6364; 703-448-8700
CompuServe	800-848-8990; 614-718-2800
Microsoft Network (MSN)	800-386-5550

Internet Service Providers (ISPs)

Standard ISPs just connect you to the Internet. They can be big corporations, such as AT&T or Sprint, or they can be run from someone's garage. Bigger is not necessarily better. The most important feature to check about an ISP is that it has a local access number. Otherwise, your phone bill will go through the roof. Here are some other reasons to go with an ISP over an online service:

+ Lower cost

+ Higher speeds

+ A choice of access tools (Netscape Navigator, Internet Explorer, or Eudora, for example)

+ The capability to use the latest Internet services as soon as they hit the Net

+ Less censorship

+ Inclusion in your cable or DSL service package

To find an ISP, ask around, check the business pages in your local newspaper or peruse the Yellow Pages. If someone you know has access to the

World Wide Web, see if she'll let you get online long enough to check out `thelist.internet.com`, which provides a huge list of providers sorted by state or area code. Consider the following issues when you're picking an ISP:

✦ Flat fee versus hourly charge

✦ System availability during peak periods

✦ Good support, particularly when you're first getting connected and after normal business hours

✦ Space provided for building your own Web pages

✦ Modem speeds and support for 56 Kbps technology

✦ Arrangements to let you dial in from other locations

It's not unreasonable to try several ISPs before picking the one that you like best. Remember, however, that after you start giving out your e-mail address, it's harder to switch ISPs.

PPP accounts

Most dial-up ISPs offer *PPP accounts* — accounts that let your computer connect directly to the Internet. You can use all kinds of cool Windows software, such as Netscape Navigator, Internet Explorer, and Eudora. In case you're curious, PPP stands for *Point-to-Point Protocol.*

Shell accounts

If you have a very old computer or have special access needs, you may prefer a *shell account,* an account that connects your computer to the ISP's computer, usually a Unix machine. From there, you can hop on the Internet. With a shell account, you generally can see only text, not graphics, on Web pages, so you miss out on some of the glitz and excitement that the Internet has to offer.

See *UNIX For Dummies,* 4th Edition, by John Levine and Margaret Levine Young (published by IDG Books Worldwide, Inc.) for more information about how to use Unix shell accounts.

Free e-mail and Internet access services

Several companies offer free Internet access in return for showing you ads. Although these free services are perfect for nonprofit organizations or anyone with a tight budget, don't expect much support:

✦ **Juno:** Juno provides a free e-mail account for Windows users. You see advertisements when you check your mail. You can download the Juno software from `www.juno.com` or get a copy from a friend who has Juno.

+ **NetZero:** NetZero offers free, advertising-supported Internet and e-mail access for Windows 95/98/Me/NT users. Go to www.netzero.com for information or phone 1-888-279-8132 to request a CD-ROM containing the necessary software. You pay a small charge for shipping and handling.

+ **AltaVista:** AltaVista also offers free Internet access to Windows users. You have to download a small program that can fit on a floppy disk, so you first need to get access through a friend or a library. Visit microav.com for more information.

Many free services analyze what you do online so that they can target the ads they display to your interests.

Libraries and cybercafés

You don't have to spend any money to use the Internet. Many local libraries now have public Internet-access machines. With free e-mail services, you can have your own, private Internet address.

You can also visit a *cybercafé* — a coffee bar that rents time on online computers. You may meet some people at the cybercafé who can help you with whatever problems you encounter.

Internet Safety and Security Issues

Surfing the Web from your home may feel totally safe and anonymous. It isn't. Computer vandals and criminals can intercept the messages that you send (such as completed forms) as the information passes through the network. This section gives you the basics on privacy on the Net, tells you how to encrypt your messages for added security, and provides suggestions for controlling your kids' access to the Internet.

Privacy, security, and cookies

The messages your browser sends to get information from the Web are often recorded. Web sites can also ask your browser to save (or set up) a small lump of information, called a *cookie,* that the site can request the next time you visit. Cookies are commonly used to

+ Track how often you visit a site.

+ Save your logon name and site password so that you don't have to go through a logon procedure every time you visit.

+ Store your billing address and credit card number.

+ Save a user profile so that the site can present information customized to your needs.

Your browser enforces these rules to prevent cookie abuse:

✦ Cookies are limited in size (4K).

✦ Only the site that set the cookies can access them.

✦ Cookies must have an expiration date.

You can ask your browser to tell you when a Web site wants to set a cookie:

✦ **Netscape Communicator:** Choose Edit⇨Preferences, click Advanced on the Category list, and then click the Warn Me Before Accepting a Cookie option in the Cookies box.

✦ **Internet Explorer:** Choose Tools⇨Internet Options, click the Security tab, click the Custom Level button, scroll down to the Cookies heading, and click the Prompt option button under both of the subheadings.

Web sites can track visitors in ways other than the use of cookies. If the lack of Web privacy makes you nervous, visit www.anonymizer.com before you go surfing. This Web site blocks the common ways that sites use to track you and also provides details on what information is collected about your computer and connection when you visit a Web site.

Encryption and Internet security

As your e-mail message or filled-out credit card form travels through the Internet, it passes through many different computers. Someone with the proper skills and equipment can intercept and read your message anywhere along the way without much trouble. You can prevent anyone from reading your messages by *encrypting* them in a secret code. Many sites offer encrypted transactions for form submittals and credit card purchases. Unfortunately, the United States and other governments have attempted to hobble the use of this technology so that they can read messages that they believe pose a threat to their interests. This section describes methods people have developed for improving Internet and e-mail security.

If you obtained your browser via a free download without answering questions about your citizenship, the browser probably uses one of the weaker international security levels. Your browser's About box tells you which level you have. Try to get the U.S. or 128-bit version, if you can. International users can upgrade Netscape to U.S. security standards by using tools available from www.fortify.net.

Internet Explorer and Netscape Navigator

Internet Explorer and Netscape Navigator use encryption technology to let you send and receive encrypted information from special sites called *secure servers*. They use a version of encryption called *SSL*. This feature is particularly useful when you want to send your credit card number over the Net. These programs also enable you to encrypt e-mail.

Netscape Navigator and Internet Explorer show a closed lock icon in the status bar if the connection is secure. If the lock is missing or appears open, the connection is not secure.

Malicious individuals can hijack your connection and send you to their own, nonsecure site, just when a legitimate site is about to ask for your credit card number. Always look for the closed-lock icon in your browser window before giving out sensitive information!

Outlook Express and Netscape Messenger

✦ Both Outlook Express and Netscape Messenger enable you to send encrypted e-mail using public-key cryptography.

✦ To encrypt a message with Outlook Express, click the envelope-with-a-lock icon in the New Message window.

✦ To encrypt a message with Netscape Messenger, click the Security button on the toolbar of the Message Composition window.

Pretty Good Privacy

PGP, which stands for *Pretty Good Privacy,* is a freeware encryption program with a strong following on the Internet. Although other software manufacturers talk about e-mail security, PGP has been providing it for years. The latest version of PGP is available as a plug-in that adds encryption and electronic signatures to the menus of popular e-mail programs, including Eudora, Microsoft Exchange, Microsoft Outlook, and Claris Emailer.

The free version of PGP is distributed in the United States and Canada via the Massachusetts Institute of Technology PGP site at `web.mit.edu/ network/pgp.html`. You can purchase PGP from the PGP Division of Network Associates, at `www.pgp.com`.

An alternative to PGP is HushMail, at `www.hushmail.com`. HushMail is similar to other Web-based, advertising-supported, free e-mail sites, such as HotMail or Yahoo!, but HushMail offers strong encryption.

Kids, adult sites, and the Web

The World Wide Web abounds in great resources for kids. Many kids have their own home pages, and cyberspace is filled with scanned artwork of the kind that once adorned refrigerator doors. Though pornography and other dangerous material on the Internet has been overhyped, more than enough of it is available to fill anyone's hard drive. If you have underage children, you need to control their access to the Internet. You can exercise this control in three primary ways: Watch over your kid's shoulder, use filtering (censoring) software, and sign up with an Internet provider that filters out unwanted stuff.

Supervising kids' access

Using this method, you simply don't let your kid on the Net unless you or an adult that you trust is present. You may choose to have your kids save pages that they find and look at them later — offline. Although this method takes a great deal of your time and limits your kids' spontaneity online, it can be very effective and also encourages quality family time.

Buying filtering software

Several companies sell software that filters out Web pages that are inappropriate for kids. After you load the software on your computer, your kids are blocked from seeing inappropriate stuff without restricting your access. Here are some popular vendors:

- **CyberPatrol:** www.cyberpatrol.com
- **Net Nanny:** www.netnanny.com
- **SafeSurf:** www.safesurf.com
- **SurfWatch:** www.surfwatch.com
- **Cybersitter:** www.solidoak.com

Using an online service with built-in filtering

Both America Online and CompuServe help parents limit their kids' access. Although the filtering programs described in the preceding section work fine if you install and use them properly, your kids probably know more about them than you do. Software that runs at the service-provider level may be more foolproof.

- **On AOL:** Click in the keyword box (in the middle of the row of buttons just below the toolbar), type **parental controls**, and press Enter.
- **On CompuServe:** Click the Go button, type **controls**, and press Enter.

Book III
Chapter 1

Getting Started with the Internet

You must set some rules for your kids. Here are a few, based on the America Online guidelines:

+ Never agree to meet someone in person or call someone on the phone without asking a parent first.

+ Never give out your last name, address, phone number, Social Security number, or the name of your school without asking a parent first.

+ Never share your logon password, even with your best friend.

+ If someone tells you not to tell your parents about him or her, tell your parents right away!

+ If you see anything that makes you feel scared or uncomfortable, or if you just aren't sure, ask a parent or teacher.

Ask your kids to give *you* a tour of the Internet. You can find out a great deal by seeing it through their eyes.

Chapter 2: E-Mail Basics

In This Chapter

✓ Getting up to speed on e-mail basics

✓ Understanding e-mail addresses

✓ Managing e-mail with Outlook Express

✓ Managing e-mail with Netscape Messenger

✓ Attaching files to e-mail messages

*E*lectronic mail, or *e-mail,* is without a doubt the most widely used Internet service. Internet mail is connected to most other e-mail systems, such as those within corporations. That means that you can send messages to folks with accounts at most big organizations and educational institutions as well as to folks with accounts at Internet providers and online services. This chapter covers the e-mail basics you need to know, such as how to interpret acronyms and emoticons, how to figure out what your e-mail address is, and how to practice proper e-mail etiquette. In addition, the chapter covers what you need to know to get up and running with the Outlook Express and Netscape Messenger e-mail applications.

For more information about using e-mail, get a copy of *E-Mail For Dummies,* 2nd Edition, by John R. Levine, Carol Baroudi, Margaret Levine Young, and Arnold Reinhold (published by IDG Books Worldwide, Inc.).

ABCs of E-Mail

This section covers a few things that you need to know to survive in the world of e-mail, such as abbreviations, emoticons, and electronic etiquette.

Abbreviations and acronyms

EUOA! (E-mail users often abbreviate.) Abbreviations are frequently used in e-mail messages and chat rooms to help users communicate. Table 2-1 lists some abbreviations and acronyms.

Table 2-1	Abbreviations and Acronyms
Abbreviation	*What It Means*
AFAIK	As far as I know
AFK	Away from keyboard
BAK	Back at keyboard
BFN	Bye for now
BRB	Be right back
BTW	By the way
CYA	See ya!
FWIW	For what it's worth
GMTA	Great minds think alike
IMHO	In my humble opinion
IMNSHO	In my not-so-humble opinion
L8R	Later
LOL	Laughing out loud
NRN	No response necessary
OIC	Oh, I see
OTOH	On the other hand
ROFL	Rolling on floor, laughing
RSN	Real soon now (not!)
SO	Significant other
TIA	Thanks in advance
TTFN	Ta-ta for now
WB	Welcome back
WTG	Way to go!

Emoticons

Emoticons (sometimes called *smileys*) substitute for the inflection of voice that is missing in e-mail messages. Most emoticons are supposed to look like faces when you turn your head sideways. Other emoticons (such as <g> or <grin>) are not pictorial; they're hints about the writer's feelings or actions. Because emoticons are still the e-mail equivalent of slang, you probably shouldn't use them in a formal message at work. Table 2-2 lists some common ones.

Table 2-2	Everyday Emoticons
Emoticon	*What It Means*
:) *or* :-)	Smile
:(*or* :-(	Frown
;) *or* ;-)	Wink
:D *or* :-D	Big smile (or laugh)
:'(	Crying
8-) *or* B-)	Sunglasses
:-@	Screaming
:-o	Uh-oh!
:-#	Lips are sealed
>:-(	Mad
:-P	Sticking tongue out
o:-)	Angel
:-\	Undecided
\o/	Praise the Lord!
{}	Hug
{{{}}}	Hugs
:-*	Kiss
{*}	Hug and a kiss
@-} -- -- -	Rose
<g> *or* <grin>	Same as :-)
<sigh>	Sigh!
::	Action markers, as in ::picks up hammer and smashes monitor::

Electronic etiquette

Electronic mail uses an etiquette all its own, and it differs from the etiquette of normal spoken or written language. Because e-mail messages are entirely text and usually are short, paying attention to e-mail manners helps to avoid misunderstandings. Follow these suggestions:

✦ **Proofread, proofread, proofread.** The recipient sees only words on a page; if those words are horribly misspelled, they create an impression of you that may not be the one you want to convey.

✦ **Don't type everything in ALL CAPS.** Using caps makes your text LOOK LIKE YOU'RE SHOUTING. You can use all capitals occasionally for emphasis.

✦ **Your subject line should tell the recipient as much as possible about your message, without getting too long.** *Tonight's softball game canceled* is much better than *Important announcement.* Don't try to put your entire message on the subject line, though.

✦ **Double-check your humor — irony and sarcasm are easy to miss.** Sometimes, adding a smiley to a joke aids your reader's understanding (see "Emoticons," earlier in this chapter).

✦ **Let the other person have the last word.** If you get involved in a vitriolic exchange of messages, known on the Net as a *flame war,* let the discussion die down by letting the other party have the final word.

✦ **When in doubt, save your message overnight.** Read and edit it again in the morning before you send it. *Never send e-mail when you're upset!*

E-mail caveats

Here are additional caveats to keep in mind as you read and send e-mail:

✦ Forging e-mail return addresses is not very hard, so if you get a totally off-the-wall message that seems out of character coming from that person, somebody else may have forged it as a prank.

✦ Many people on the Internet adopt fictional personas. The lonely flight attendant you're chatting up may be a 15-year-old boy. "On the Internet, no one knows you're a dog," says a cartoon in the *New Yorker.*

✦ E-mail is not very private. As your mail passes from site to site, it can be read not only by hackers but also by your system administrator. Your employer may even have a legal right to read your e-mail at work.

✦ Do use the Bcc (blind carbon copy) field when you're sending mail to a long list of addresses. That way, each recipient doesn't have to wade through the entire list to read the message.

✦ Mass distribution of unsolicited e-mail, known as *spam,* is becoming more of a problem. Because most spammers use phony return addresses, replying with a complaint is usually a waste of time. In fact, your reply proves that your address is good and may result in your receiving even more spam.

✦ Not every mail address has an actual person behind it. Some are mailing lists, and some are *robots,* or *mailbots.* Mail robots have become popular as a way to query databases and retrieve files.

✦ Don't *ever* open *any* file attached to messages from strangers or people you don't trust — or even from people you do know if you're not expecting a file from them. Some viruses distribute themselves by sending messages to everyone in the unsuspecting victim's e-mail address book, so the messages appear to be from a friend.

Headers

Headers are the lines of text that appear at the beginning of every Internet mail message. Use Table 2-3 as a guide to understanding what these lines mean.

Table 2-3	Common E-Mail Headers
Header	**Description**
Subject	Describes message (recommended; sometimes required)
To	Lists recipients of the message (at least one required)
Cc	Lists carbon copy recipients (optional)
Bcc	Lists blind carbon copy recipients; recipients' names not listed with the message (optional)
From	Address of message author (required; provided automatically)
Organization	Where the sender works, or whatever
X-Sender	Used with mailing lists to show who sent the message originally
Reply-To	Address to send replies to if it's different than the From line (optional)
Date	Time and date message was sent (provided automatically)
Expires	Date after which message expires (optional)
Message-ID	Unique, machine-generated identifier for message (provided automatically)
Lines	Number of text lines in message (optional; provided automatically)

Rejected mail (bounces)

Every Internet host that can send or receive mail has a special mail address called `postmaster` that is supposed to be guaranteed to get a message to the person responsible for that host. If you send mail to someone and get back strange failure messages, you may try sending a polite message to the postmaster.

For example, if mail sent to `king@bluesuede.org` returns with an error, send e-mail to `postmaster@bluesuede.org` asking, "Does Elvis the King have a mailbox on this system? TIA, Ed Sullivan."

E-Mail Addresses

To send e-mail to someone, you need his address. Roughly speaking, mail addresses consist of these elements:

+ **Mailbox name:** Usually, the username of your account.

+ **@:** The *at* sign.

+ **Host name:** The name of the recipient's computer. (See "Host names and domain names," later in this chapter.)

For example, elvis@gurus.com is a typical address, where elvis is the mailbox name and gurus.com is the host name.

Internet mailbox names should *not* contain commas, spaces, or parentheses. Mailbox names can contain letters, numerals, and, some punctuation characters, such as periods, hyphens, and underscores. Capitalization normally doesn't matter in e-mail addresses.

The most common situation in which these restrictions cause problems is in numeric CompuServe addresses, which consist of two numbers separated by a comma. When you're converting a CompuServe address to an Internet address, change the comma to a period. For example, the address 71053,2615 becomes 71053.2615@compuserve.com as an e-mail address. Similarly, some AOL users put spaces in their screen names. You just drop the spaces when you're sending the e-mail. If, for some reason, you must send mail to an address that does include commas, spaces, or parentheses, you can enclose the address in double quotes.

"What's my address?"

If you're accessing the Internet through a service provider, your address is most likely

your_logon_name@your_provider's_host_name

If you're connecting through work or school, your e-mail address is typically

your_logon_name@your_computer's_host_name

A host name, however, is sometimes just a department or company name rather than your computer's name. If your logon name is elvis and your computer is shamu.strat.gurus.com, your mail address may look like one of these examples:

elvis@shamu.strat.gurus.com
elvis@strat.gurus.com
elvis@gurus.com

Or even this one:

elvis.presley@gurus.com

Host names and domain names

Hosts are computers that are directly attached to the Internet. Host names have several parts strung together with periods, like this:

```
ivan.iecc.com
```

You decode a host name from right to left:

+ The rightmost part of a name is its *top-level domain,* or *TLD* (in the preceding example, com). See "Top-level domains," later in this chapter.

+ To the TLD's left (iecc) is the name of the company, school, or organization.

+ The part to the left of the organization name (ivan) identifies the particular computer within the organization.

In large organizations, host names can be further subdivided by site or department. The last two parts of a host name are known as a *domain.* For example, ivan is in the iecc.com domain, and iecc.com is a *domain name.*

Most domain names in the United States are assigned by Network Solutions (www.networksolutions.com) and cost $70 to register and $35 per year after the first two years. Other registrars, such as Internet Domain Registrars (www.registrars.com) and Joker (www.joker.com), are cheaper and do at least as good a job. For a list of organizations that can register a domain name for you, go to the following URL:

```
www.icann.org/registrars/accredited-list.html
```

Internet Service Providers often charge substantial additional fees for setting up and supporting a new domain. Shop around!

IP addresses and the DNS

Network software uses the IP address, which is sort of like a phone number, to identify the host. IP addresses are written in four chunks separated by periods, such as

```
208.31.42.77
```

A system called the *domain name system (DNS)* keeps track of which IP address (or addresses, for popular Internet hosts) goes with which Internet host name. Usually, one computer has one IP address and one Internet host name, although this pattern isn't always true. For example, the Web site at www.yahoo.com is so heavily used that a group of computers, each with its own IP address, accepts requests for Web pages from that name.

The most important IP addresses to know are the IP addresses of the computers at the Internet provider you use. You may need them to set up the software on your computer; if things get fouled up, the IP addresses help the guru to fix the problem.

Top-level domains

The *top-level domain (TLD),* sometimes called a *zone,* is the last piece of the host name on the Internet (for example, the zone of gurus.com is com). TLDs come in two main flavors:

◆ Organizational

◆ Geographical

If the TLD is three or more letters long, it's an *organizational name.* Table 2-4 describes the organizational names that have been in use for years.

Table 2-4	Top-Level Domain Names
TLD	*Description*
com	Commercial organization
edu	Educational institution, usually a college or university
gov	U.S. government body or department
int	International organization (mostly NATO, at the moment)
mil	U.S. military site (can be located anywhere)
net	Networking organization
org	Anything that doesn't fit elsewhere, usually a not-for-profit group

In the past, most systems using organizational names were in the United States. Now, however, the com domain has become a hot property; large corporations and organizations worldwide consider it a prestige Internet address. Address *haves* and *have-nots* are contesting a plan to add additional top-level domain names to those already in use.

If the TLD is two letters long, it's a *geographical name.* The two-letter code specifies a country, such as us for the United States, uk for the United Kingdom, au for Australia, and jp for Japan. The stuff in front of the TLD is specific to that country. Often, the letter group just before the country code mimics the style for U.S. organizational names: com or co for commercial, edu or ac for academic institutions, and gov or go for government, for example.

The us domain — used by schools, cities, and small organizations in the United States — is set up strictly geographically. The two letters just before us specify the state. Other common codes are ci for city, co for county, cc for community colleges, and k12 for schools. The Internet site for the city of Cambridge, Massachusetts, for example, is www.ci.cambridge.ma.us.

URLs versus e-mail addresses

URLs *(Uniform Resource Locators)* contain the information that your browser software uses to find Web pages on the World Wide Web. URLs look somewhat like e-mail addresses in that both contain a domain name. E-mail addresses almost always contain an @, however, and URLs never do. (See Chapter 3 in Book III for more details on URLs.)

E-mail addresses usually are not case-sensitive — capitalization doesn't matter — but parts of URLs *are* case-sensitive. Always type URLs *exactly* as written, including capitalization.

Managing E-Mail with Outlook Express

If you're using Internet Explorer, you have Outlook Express — Microsoft's friendly e-mail program. This section tells you what you need to know to get up and running quickly and efficiently with Outlook Express.

Checking for new mail

After you start sending messages and giving out your e-mail address, your Inbox will fill up with new mail in no time at all. Normally, when you launch Outlook Express, the program does not automatically tell you when you have new e-mail except when you click the Send/Recv button on the toolbar. If you want, you can have Outlook Express inform you of new e-mail anytime you open the program.

To set this up, follow these steps:

1. **Click the Launch Outlook Express button on the Windows taskbar.**

You can also click the Mail button on the Internet Explorer toolbar and choose Read Mail from the pop-up menu.

2. **Choose Tools⊏>Options.**

The Options dialog box displays, with the General tab selected.

3. **Select the Check for New Messages Every 30 Minute(s) check box.**

4. **In the associated text box, replace 30 with the new number of minutes you desire.**

   When you enable the Check For New Messages Every "So Many" Minutes check box, Outlook Express automatically checks your mail server for new messages whenever you launch the program and then continues to check at the specified interval as you work in the program.

5. **Select the Play Sound When New Messages Arrive check box.**

   Selecting this option enables a chime to play when new e-mail messages are downloaded while you're running the program.

6. **Click OK.**

Outlook Express informs you of the delivery of new e-mail by placing an envelope icon on the Outlook Express status bar (and *dinging* if you enabled the Play Sound When New Messages Arrive check box).

Reading e-mail

To open the Inbox in Outlook Express and read your e-mail messages from Internet Explorer, follow these steps:

1. **In Internet Explorer, click the Mail button in the toolbar and then choose Read Mail on the pop-up menu that appears.**

   Outlook Express opens the Inbox — that is, as long as Outlook Express is configured as your e-mail program.

2. **Click the Send/Recv button on the Outlook Express toolbar to download any new messages.**

   As soon as you click the Send/Recv button, Outlook Express opens a connection to your mail server where it checks for any new messages to download for all e-mail accounts on the computer. New messages are then downloaded to your computer and placed in the Outlook Express Inbox, as shown in Figure 2-1.

   Descriptions of any new messages appear in bold in the top half of the Inbox, which is divided into six columns: Priority (indicated by the red exclamation point), Attachments (indicated by the paper clip), Flag Status (indicated by the flag), From, Subject, and Received (showing both the date and time that the e-mail message was downloaded to your computer).

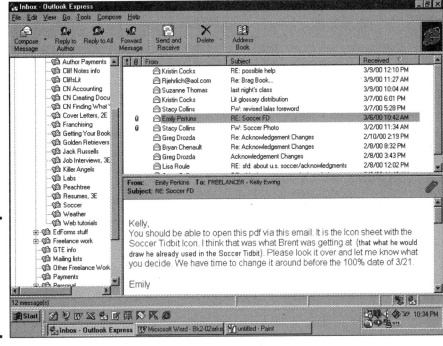

Figure 2-1:
Your new messages appear in the Outlook Express Inbox.

3. **To read one of your new messages, click the message in the top half of the Inbox.**

It doesn't matter if your mouse pointer is in the From, Subject, or Received column when you click the message. The message displays in the lower pane of the Inbox. The From and Subject information appears in a gray bar at the top of the lower pane.

If you want the message to open in its own window, rather than in the lower pane of the Inbox, double-click the message.

4. **After you finish reading your e-mail, click the Close box in the upper-right corner of the Outlook Express Inbox window.**

Sending a message

Outlook Express makes it easy to compose and send e-mail messages to anyone in the world who has an e-mail address. Follow these steps:

1. **From the Internet Explorer toolbar, click the Mail button and then choose New Message on the pop-up menu that appears.**

The Outlook Express New Message window opens. (Note that you can also start a new message from within Outlook Express by clicking the New Mail button on its toolbar.)

2. **Type the recipient's e-mail address in the text box of the To: field.**

   If the recipient is already listed in your Address Book, click the word To: to open the Select Recipients dialog box. Then in the Name list box, click the name of the recipient and click the To: button. If you don't want to send the message to anyone else, click OK.

3. **Click in the Cc: field, type the e-mail addresses separated by semi-colons, and press Enter.**

   Use this option to send carbon copies of the message to other recipients. If you want to send blind carbon copies, click the To: or Cc: button and indicate Bcc: in the Select Recipients dialog box.

4. **Click in the Subject: field and type a brief description of the contents or purpose of the e-mail message.**

   When your message is delivered, the descriptive text that you entered in the Subject: field appears in the Subject column of each recipient's Inbox.

5. **Click the Priority button on the New Message toolbar and select High Priority or Low Priority from the pop-up menu.**

   This option lets you (and others) prioritize your e-mail. Normal Priority is the default option, so you don't feel compelled to change it if your message isn't important.

6. **Click the cursor in the body of the message and type the text of the message.**

   Type the message just as you do in any text editor or word processor, ending paragraphs by pressing Enter. You can insert text directly into the body of the message from other documents via the Clipboard or, in the case of text or HTML documents, by choosing Insert⇨Text from File and selecting the name of the file in the Insert Text File dialog box.

7. **To spell check the message, click at the beginning of the message text and choose Tools⇨Spelling (or press F7).**

   If you choose to spell check a message, Outlook Express flags each word that's not in its dictionary and suggests an alternative word.

   • To replace the unknown word in the text with the word suggested in the Change To text box of the Spelling dialog box, click Change; or, if it's a word that occurs frequently, click Change All.

   • To ignore the unknown word and have the spell checker continue to scan the rest of the text for possible misspellings, click Ignore; or, if it's a word that occurs frequently in the text, click Ignore All.

8. **To send the e-mail message to the recipient(s), click the Send button on the Outlook Express toolbar.**

Replying to a message

Often, you want to reply to a message right away — especially if the e-mail message uses the High Priority (!) icon. Open the message you want to reply to and follow these steps:

1. **Click Reply to reply to the message's author.**

The e-mail address of the person to whom you're replying automatically appears in the To header of the new e-mail message window that appears. The text of the original e-mail also appears.

To reply to the author and send copies of the reply to everyone who received the original message, click the Reply All button instead. The e-mail addresses of the other recipients appear automatically.

2. **In the message window, type the text of your reply above the text of the original message.**

3. **Click the Send button.**

Forwarding a message

Sometimes, you need to send a copy of a message to someone who was not listed in the original message. To do so, forward a copy of the original message to new recipients of your choosing. When you forward a message, Outlook Express copies the Subject: field and contents of the original message to a new e-mail message, which you then address and send.

To forward an e-mail message to another e-mail address, open the message you want to forward and follow these steps:

1. **Click the Forward button on the Outlook Express toolbar.**

A new e-mail message window appears, with the text of the original e-mail, all ready to go.

2. **Fill in the recipient information in the To: field and, if applicable, Cc: and Bcc: fields.**

3. **Add any additional text of your own above that of the original message.**

4. **Click the Send button to send the forwarded message on its way.**

Attaching a file to a message

You can attach files to your e-mail messages to transmit information that you don't want to appear in the body of the message. For example, you may need to send an Excel 2000 worksheet to a client in another office.

**Book III
Chapter 2**

E-Mail Basics

To attach a file to an e-mail message in Outlook Express, follow these steps:

1. **From the Internet Explorer toolbar, click the Mail button and then choose New Message on the pop-up menu that appears.**

   Internet Explorer responds by opening a new message in Outlook Express.

2. **Add the recipient(s) of the e-mail message in the To: or Cc: field(s), the subject of the message in the Subject: field, and any message text explaining the attached files in the body of the message.**

3. **Choose Insert⇨File Attachment on the New Message menu bar or click the Attach button on the toolbar.**

   The Insert Attachment dialog box displays.

4. **In the Look In drop-down list box, choose the folder that contains the file you want to attach. Then click the filename in the main list box and click the Attach button.**

   Outlook Express adds an Attach field under the Subject: field displaying the icon(s), filename(s), and size of the file(s) attached to the message.

5. **Click the Send button to send the message to the recipient(s).**

Don't send files that are too large — your recipient's mail system may choke on large files. To send a file larger than 100K, use a file compression program, such as WinZip (www.winzip.com) or ZipMagic (www.zipmagic.com) to make the file smaller. Before you send someone an attached file, make sure that he wants it. Ask for permission to send the file, and ask whether the recipient has the necessary program to open the file that you're sending.

Managing E-Mail with Netscape Messenger

Netscape Messenger is the e-mail component in Communicator. This section covers the basics of using Netscape Messenger to manage your e-mail.

Checking for new mail

Messenger automatically alerts you when new messages arrive. The Inbox icon in the Component bar changes to include a downward-pointing green arrow. If you see that green arrow next to the Messenger icon in the Component bar, you have messages to download and read. (A yellow arrow indicates that Messenger has not checked for messages yet.) To check for e-mail, click the Get Msg button on the Messenger toolbar.

Reading e-mail

To read your e-mail, follow these steps:

1. **Launch Messenger by clicking the Inbox icon on the Component bar or by choosing Communicator➪Messenger.**

   The Inbox opens.

2. **Click the Get Msg button on the toolbar to begin downloading your new mail from the mail server to your Inbox.**

   A status window shows the progress of the download and tells you when the download is complete.

3. **Make the Inbox folder the active folder by clicking it in the folder list.**

   You see all the messages within the Inbox folder. New messages appear in bold type, with the New Message icon next to the folder names.

4. **Select the message that you want to read by clicking it.**

   To open a particular message in a separate window, double-click it.

5. **To read the next unread message in the Inbox, click the Next button on the Messenger toolbar.**

6. **To close a message that has been opened in its own window, click the Close (X) button in the upper-right corner of the window.**

Sending a message

Follow these steps to write and send your e-mail message:

1. **Click the New Msg button on the Messenger toolbar or choose Message➪New Message.**

   The Composition window appears, as shown in Figure 2-2.

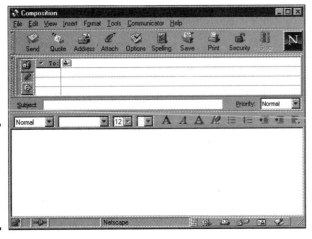

Figure 2-2:
The
Composition
window in
Netscape
Messenger.

2. **Type the e-mail address of the person you're sending the message to in the To: line.**

   You can save time by using the addresses and mailing list groupings in your Address Book or by typing the nickname.

3. **Type a brief description of the message in the Subject line to give your reader some indication of what your message is about.**

4. **Type the text of the message in the message composition area.**

5. **Click the Send button.**

At times, you may sit down to compose a message, get halfway through it, and get interrupted to attend to something else. Instead of sending an incomplete message or closing the message and starting all over again later, you can save the message as a draft. You can then edit the draft at any time. Follow these steps to create a draft:

1. **Click the New Msg button in the Messenger toolbar.**

2. **Begin writing your message.**

3. **Click the Save button.**

   The message is saved in the Drafts folder, but the Composition window stays open.

4. **Close the Composition window by clicking the Close (X) button in the upper-right corner of the title bar or by choosing File⇨Close.**

Okay, so you got halfway through a message, saved it as a draft, and now want to continue where you left off. Here's how you do that:

1. **Click the Drafts folder in the Messenger window.**

   All the messages within the Drafts folder appear.

2. **Double-click the message on which you want to work.**

   The message opens within the Composition window. You can now continue where you left off.

Replying to a message

To reply to an e-mail message that you receive, follow these steps:

1. **Highlight the message to which you want to reply by clicking it once.**

2. **Click Reply to send your reply to the sender of the message only or click Reply All to send your reply to all recipients of that message.**

Everyone on the To and Cc lines of the original message automatically gets copies of your reply if you click Reply All. The text of the original e-mail also appears.

3. **Type the text of your message in the message composition area.**

4. **Click Send.**

Forwarding a message

If you want to share a message that you received with others, you can forward it to them. To forward a message, follow these steps:

1. **Highlight the message that you want to forward by clicking it once.**

2. **Click Forward to send the message to the person of your choice.**

   A new e-mail message window appears, with the text of the original e-mail, all ready to go.

3. **In the To field, type the e-mail address(es) of the person(s) to whom you want to forward the message.**

4. **Type any text that you want to include above the forwarded message.**

5. **Click Send.**

Attaching a file to a message

Messenger enables you to send pictures, word processing files, Web pages, and other files attached to your messages. You can even attach more than one file to a message. To attach a file to a message, follow these steps:

1. **Click the New Msg button on the Messenger toolbar to begin composing a message.**

2. **Fill in the relevant information, such as the address of the person you're sending the message to and the text of the message.**

   Also, notice that the color of the paper clip to the left of the address window is blue.

3. **Click the Attach button on the Messenger toolbar.**

   A drop-down list opens and displays the attachment options.

   • **Click File if you want to attach a word processing document, spreadsheet, or picture to your e-mail message. Then select the file you want to attach and click Open.**

- **Click Web Page if you want to attach a Web page; then specify the URL of the Web page.** When you attach a Web page to a message, the recipient sees the actual Web page in the body of the message, complete with any images and links. The Web page appears as if you copied it in its entirety into the message.

The name of the attached file or URL appears on the Attach Files and Documents tab in the Composition window. Notice that the color of the paper clip on the attachment tab changes from blue to red, an indication that a document is attached to the message.

Some e-mail services and e-mail software have limitations on the size of the attachments you can send. Check with the recipient about such limitations before sending a file. If possible, use compression software (such as PKZip or WinZip) to compress files and package several files into a single file prior to sending them. Compressing files makes them smaller and, thereby, faster to send.

Chapter 3: Web Basics

The *World Wide Web* (or WWW or just *the Web*) is a system that uses the Internet to link vast quantities of information all over the world. You can use the Web to look for answers to almost any question under the sun. At times, the Web resembles a library, newspaper, bulletin board, and telephone directory — all on a global scale. Still very much a work in progress, the Web is destined to become the primary repository of human culture. This chapter explains all you need to know about the basics of the Web.

If Internet Explorer is your browser of choice, refer to Book III, Chapter 4 after you review this chapter. Otherwise, if you use Netscape Navigator as your Web browser, see Book III, Chapter 5 after you read this chapter.

ABCs of the Web

To start using the World Wide Web, all you need is an Internet connection and a program called a Web browser (such as Internet Explorer or Netscape Navigator). A *Web browser* displays, as individual pages on your computer screen, the various types of information found on the Web and lets you follow the connections — called *hypertext links* — built into Web pages.

Here are some basic Web concepts:

✦ **Hypertext:** A type of electronic document that contains pointers to other documents. These links (often called *hyperlinks*) appear in a distinct color or are highlighted when your browser displays the document. When you click a hypertext link, your Web browser displays the document to which the link points, if the document is available.

✦ **Uniform Resource Locator (URL):** The standard format used for hypertext links on the Internet, such as `http://www.microsoft.com`. (See "Uniform Resource Locators (URLs)," later in this chapter.)

✦ **Web site:** A collection of Web pages devoted to a single subject or organization.

✦ **Webmaster:** The person in charge of a Web site.

✦ **Surfing:** The art and vice of bouncing from Web page to Web page in search of whatever.

Uniform Resource Locators (URLs)

One of the key advances that Web technology brought to the Internet is the *Uniform Resource Locator,* or *URL.* URLs provide a single, standardized way of describing almost any type of information available in cyberspace. The URL tells you what kind of information you're accessing (such as a Web page or an FTP file), what computer it's stored on, and how to find that computer.

URLs are typically long text strings that consist of three parts:

✦ The document access type followed by a colon and two slashes (://)

✦ The host name of the computer on which the information is stored

✦ The path to the file that contains the information

Here's a typical URL:

```
http://www.microsoft.com/windows/ie/newuser/default.asp
```

The following list breaks down the different parts of the URL:

`http`   Indicates a hypertext document (a Web page)

`www.microsoft.com`   Indicates the host computer on which the Web page is stored (`www` indicates that the site is located on the World Wide Web)

`/windows/ie/newuser/default.asp`   Indicates the path and filename of the file

Common document access types include the following:

✦ **http:** For hypertext (the Web)

✦ **https:** For hypertext with a secure link

✦ **ftp:** For File Transfer Protocol files

✦ **gopher:** For Gopher files

✦ **mailto:** For e-mail addresses

The following list includes other mysterious things that you see in URLs:

✦ **.html** or **.htm:** The filename extension for a hypertext document; html stands for HyperText Markup Language, the set of codes used to build Web pages.

✦ **index.html** or **default.html:** The master page of a Web site (the actual file name depends on the server).

✦ **.txt:** A plain-text document without links or formatting.

✦ **.gif**, **.jpg**, **.jpeg**, **.mpg**, **.png**, and **.avi:** Pictures, graphics, or video.

✦ **.mp3**, **.mid** (MIDI), **.wav**, **.snd**, and **.au:** Music files. You can even purchase a Walkman-size unit that accepts and plays these files.

✦ **.zip**, **.sit**, **.hqx**, **.gz**, **.tar**, and **.z:** Filename extensions for files that have been compressed to save downloading time.

✦ **.Class:** A Java applet.

✦ **~george:** As suggested by the tilde (~) character, probably a Unix account belonging to someone with the account name of george.

Some browsers can fill in missing information, such as the `http://` prefix, if you leave it out. Some browsers go even further by letting you type **hungryminds** rather than the complete **http://www.hungryminds.com** to go to the Hungry Minds, Inc. Web site. Typing the complete address may load the page a little more quickly, however. Because many companies use their corporate name as their host name, you can often type **sony**, for example, in the URL text box, press Enter, and expect to end up at the Sony Corporation Web site.

Finding Your Way around the Web

The Web displays pages of information with hypertext links that take you to other pages. Browsers usually **highlight the links** to make them easy to spot by using a different color for the item and underlining it. You can customize the colors that a Web browser uses to indicate links to pages that you've already visited and links to pages that you have yet to view.

Some links are just areas you click inside an image or photograph. Currently, three different graphics file formats are used to display images on a Web page: GIF (Graphics Image Format), JPEG (Joint Photographic Experts Group), or PNG (Portable Network Graphics). You can always tell when one of these types of graphics contains a hyperlink and when it doesn't. Only graphics with hyperlinks cause your mouse pointer to assume the shape of a hand, as shown in Figure 3-1.

Hand pointer

Graphic with hyperlink

Text with hyperlinks

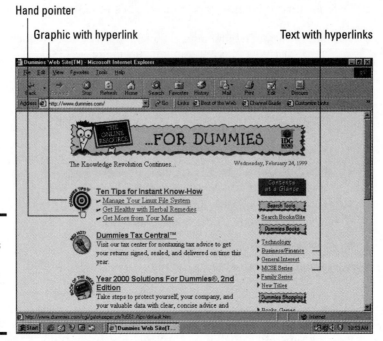

Figure 3-1:
Web pages
use both
text hyper-
links and
graphics
hyperlinks.

Here are some tips for using hyperlinks:

✦ On a system that uses windows and a mouse, and browsers such as Internet Explorer or Netscape Navigator, use the mouse to click the link. If the page doesn't fit on-screen, click the scroll bar (or drag the scroll box) to scroll up and down.

✦ On a text system, such as Lynx, press the up-arrow key or the down-arrow key to move the cursor to the link that you want and then press Enter.

✦ Many mail programs, such as Eudora, automatically detect and high-light URLs in e-mail messages. You can activate these links by clicking them in the mail program.

You can bring up a page on your browser in ways other than following a link:

✦ Select a page from your browser's list of bookmarks or favorites.

✦ Type a URL in the address field on your browser's screen and press Enter.

✦ If you have the page stored as a file on a disk or CD-ROM on your com-puter, most browsers let you open it by choosing the File⇨Open (or similar) command.

Web page components that appear in your browser can take on other functions, such as the following:

✦ **File items containing text, pictures, movies, or sound:** If your Web browser can handle the file, the browser displays or plays the file. If not, the browser just tells you about the file. If an image or element is missing, the browser displays a broken link icon.

✦ **Search query items that let you type one or more key words:** A Web page displays the results of your search.

✦ **Forms you fill out:** The answers are sent as a long URL when you click Done, Submit, or a similar button on the form.

✦ **Small computer programs called *Java applets:*** You download and run them on your computer.

Another way of accessing information on the Web is by using *channels.* Channels enable a Web site to deliver content to your computer whenever the site has new information for you. You can read the information at another time.

Working with Frames

At first glance, a Web page looks like any other nicely formatted document containing graphics and text. What differentiates a Web page from a regular document? In a Web page, text and graphics can be used as hyperlinks. When you click a *hyperlink,* you're transported to another Web page.

Many Web sites now include *frames,* which display multiple Web pages on-screen at one time. Figure 3-2 provides an example of a Web site with frames.

**Book III
Chapter 3**

Web Basics

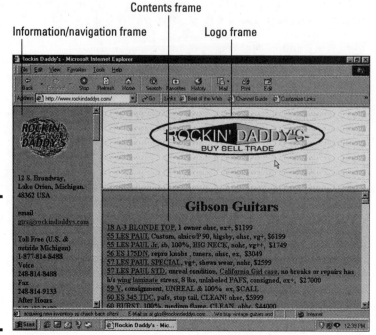

Contents frame

Information/navigation frame   Logo frame

Figure 3-2:
This Web
site uses
frames to
show three
different
Web pages
at once.

The three frames on this page are used for the following purposes:

✦ A *logo frame* displays the company's name and logo.

✦ An *information/navigation frame* displays the company's contact and ordering information. The hyperlinks in this frame take you to different sections of the company's inventory.

✦ A *contents frame* lists all the items in the company's current inventory.

Chapter 4: Web Browsing with Internet Explorer

In This Chapter

✓ Accessing Web sites with Internet Explorer

✓ Searching for information on the Web

✓ Changing your default Home page

✓ Keeping track of your favorite Web sites

✓ Printing a Web page

✓ Viewing the HTML source of a Web page

This chapter takes you on a tour of Microsoft's Web browser — Internet Explorer 5. You find out how to launch Internet Explorer, get to know the elements of the screen, and use the browser to begin your travels on the Web. In addition, this chapter shows you how to add links to the sites that you can't possibly live without and how to access the sites that you add to your Favorites list. Now boarding Internet Explorer. The next stop in cyberspace is totally up to you!

This chapter covers Internet Explorer 5. You can download the newest version of Internet Explorer from the Microsoft Web site.

Refer to Book III, Chapter 3 if you need a refresher on Web basics. If you use Netscape Navigator as your Web browser, see Book III, Chapter 5.

Getting Started with Internet Explorer

The Windows desktop includes several doorways to the Internet Explorer browser. To start the Internet Explorer, you can

✦ Double-click the Internet Explorer shortcut on your desktop.

✦ Click the Start button on the Windows taskbar and then choose Programs⇨Internet Explorer.

✦ Click the Launch Internet Explorer Browser button on the Quick Launch toolbar, located near the Start button in the taskbar. (If the Quick Launch toolbar doesn't display, right-click the taskbar and choose Toolbars⇨Quick Launch.)

Accessing a Web site

After you start Internet Explorer, you can tell the program which Web site you want to go to. If you haven't saved the Web site in your Favorites list (see the section "Keeping Track of Your Favorite Web Sites," later in this chapter), you must type the Web site's URL or choose it from a list of Web sites you recently viewed.

To access a Web site, follow these steps:

1. **In Internet Explorer, choose File⇨Open.**

The Open dialog box displays.

2. **In the Open text box, type the URL of the site you want to visit or click the drop-down arrow and select a site from the list.**

3. **Click OK.**

You also can access a Web site by positioning the cursor in the Address box of the Internet Explorer window, typing the URL of the Web site you want to go to, and pressing Enter.

Elements of the Internet Explorer window

Each of the launch methods covered in the preceding section opens Internet Explorer. Figure 4-1 describes the elements in the Internet Explorer window.

The following list provides a rundown of the parts of the Internet Explorer screen:

✦ **Menu bar:** As with all standard Windows menu bars, the Internet Explorer menu bar consists of pull-down menus that you can click to reveal a list of options and submenus.

Menu bar

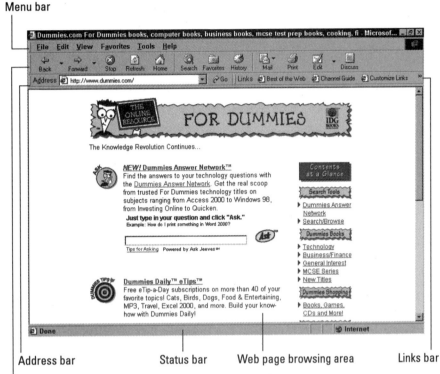

Figure 4-1:
The
elements of
the Internet
Explorer
window.

Address bar   Status bar   Web page browsing area   Links bar

Standard Buttons toolbar

✦ **Standard Buttons toolbar:** This toolbar contains the tools that you use most often for navigating and performing tasks, such as the following:

- **Back:** Enables you to return to any Web sites you may have previously visited during your Web session.

- **Forward:** Takes you to any available pages in the History listing.

- **Stop:** Lets you stop a page from loading.

- **Refresh:** Reloads or updates the current Web page. (Sometimes, the information on a page may not download to your computer properly the first time. *Refreshing* the page downloads the entire page again.)

- **Home:** Displays the Web page that you designate as the home (or *start*) page.

- **Search:** Displays or hides the Search Explorer bar.

- **Favorites:** Displays or hides the Favorites Explorer bar.

- **History:** Displays or hides the History Explorer bar.

- **Mail:** Opens a menu with options for sending e-mail or for reading e-mail or news.

- **Print:** Prints the current Web page.

- **Edit:** Opens the current Web page in a text editor.

- **Discuss:** Displays the Discussions toolbar so that you can review and add comments about the Web page.

◆ **Address bar:** A text box that displays the URL (Web address) of the current Web page. You can go to a new Web page by typing in a new URL in the Address bar's text box and pressing Enter (or clicking Go). (If the Address bar is hidden by the Links bar, double-click the word Address to reveal the full Address bar.) When you enter a URL, the AutoComplete feature helps you correctly complete the address.

As you visit different pages during a Web browsing session, Internet Explorer adds the URL of each site that you visit to the drop-down list attached to the Address bar. To revisit one of the Web pages that you've seen during the session, you can click the drop-down button at the end of the Address box and click its URL or its page icon in the drop-down list.

The Address bar also includes an Autosearch feature that lets you search for Web sites that meet your search criteria. Click the Address box and type **find**, **go**, or **?** (question mark) followed by a descriptive term or terms that you think describes the site (such as **find computer books**). Then press Enter. Internet Explorer opens the Search Explorer bar with a list of possible links to sites that meet your search criteria.

◆ **Links bar:** This toolbar contains buttons (called Quick Links) with shortcuts to various Microsoft Web pages — Best of the Web, Channel Guide, Customize Links, and various other pages. (If the Links bar is hidden by the Address bar, double-click the word Links to reveal the full Links bar.) You can, however, change the shortcuts listed on the Links bar to reflect the Web pages that you visit most often.

To add a Quick Link button for the Web page that you're currently viewing, drag its Web page icon (the icon that precedes the URL in the Address bar) to the place on the Links bar where you want the Quick Link button to appear. To remove a button from the Links bar, right-click the button and choose Delete from the shortcut menu.

✦ **Windows taskbar:** The standard Windows 95/98 taskbar contains the Start button and the Quick Launch toolbar, along with icons for all open programs.

✦ **Quick Launch toolbar:** This toolbar appears next to the Start button in the Windows taskbar and provides one-click access to Internet Explorer applications or features. This toolbar includes four buttons by default — Launch Internet Explorer Browser, Show Desktop, Launch Outlook Express, and View Channels.

✦ **Web page browsing area:** The space where the current Web page actually appears.

✦ **Status bar:** This toolbar provides information on your whereabouts as you travel the Web and also the status of Internet Explorer as it performs its functions.

✦ **Radio bar:** This toolbar appears immediately above the top of the browsing area when you choose View⇨Toolbars⇨Radio. The Radio bar is available only if you install Windows Media Player as part of the Internet Explorer installation. The Radio bar contains buttons for listening to online radio programs that support the ASF (ActiveMovie Streaming File) format.

You can display or hide most toolbars by right-clicking the menu bar and selecting the toolbar that you want to display or hide from the shortcut menu. In the shortcut menu, a check mark appears next to toolbars that are currently displayed.

Using the Explorer bar

The Explorer bar is a frame that appears on the left side of the Internet Explorer screen when you want to perform a search, work with your Favorites list, or display a history of recently viewed Web pages. Click the Search, Favorites, or History button on the Standard Buttons toolbar to display the Explorer bar and additional options for each of these functions. The contents of the current Web page appear in the area (frame) on the right.

If the need arises, you can change the width of both frames by positioning the mouse pointer on the border that the two frames share. When you do this, the mouse pointer changes to a double-headed arrow (the horizontal resize pointer), as shown in Figure 4-2. You can then modify the widths of the two frames by clicking and dragging the border to the right (to make the Explorer bar wider) or to the left (to make the Explorer bar narrower).

**Book III
Chapter 4**

Web Browsing with
Internet Explorer

Horizontal resize pointer

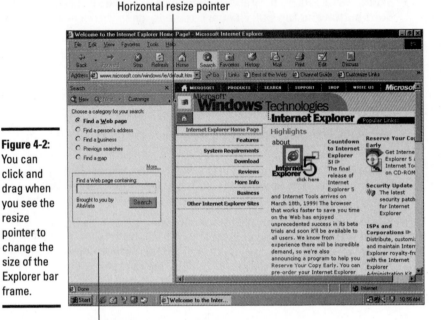

Figure 4-2:
You can
click and
drag when
you see the
resize
pointer to
change the
size of the
Explorer bar
frame.

Search bar is open

The Explorer bar comes in four different flavors:

✦ **Search bar:** The Search bar (refer to Figure 4-2) gives you access to the various search engines that you can use to search the Web. To open the Search bar, click the Search button, choose View⇨Explorer Bar⇨Search, or press Ctrl+E. (See "Searching the Web," later in this chapter.)

✦ **Favorites bar:** The Favorites bar contains links to the Web pages that you have marked as your favorites. Click the Favorites button, choose View⇨Explorer Bar⇨Favorites, or press Ctrl+I to open the Favorites bar. (See "Viewing pages from the Favorites folder," later in this chapter.)

✦ **History bar:** The History bar gives you access to links of all the Web pages that you visited recently. Click the History button, choose View⇨Explorer Bar⇨History, or press Ctrl+H to open the History bar. (See "Viewing Pages from the History Folder," later in this chapter.)

✦ **Folders bar:** The Folders bar (choose View⇨Explorer Bar⇨Folders) displays a map (in outline form) of the elements of your computer. Click the icon for a drive or folder in the Folders bar, and the contents of that drive or folder appear in the right pane. To get back to surfing the Internet, click the Internet Explorer icon in the Folders bar.

To remove the Explorer bar from the browsing area, click the Close button (the X) in the upper-right corner of the Explorer bar.

Getting Help

The Help feature in Internet Explorer is written in HTML so that it looks and acts like a Web page. To open Internet Explorer Help, click Help on the menu bar and then choose from the following options:

+ **Contents and Index:** Opens the Help window for Internet Explorer, which is divided into two panes. The left pane shows the categories available on the Contents tab or, in the case of the Index tab, an alphabetical list of subjects; the window on the right serves as a viewing area. You also can use the Search tab to search for specific keywords.

+ **Tip of the Day:** Provides a useful tip about Internet Explorer at the bottom of the program window. Click the Close button to remove the tip.

+ **For Netscape Users:** Opens the Help window and displays information on making the transition from Netscape Navigator to Internet Explorer.

+ **Tour:** Takes you to an online Web tutorial on the Microsoft Web site.

+ **Online Support:** Takes you to a Microsoft Web site page that includes these support options: a searchable knowledge base, downloads, phone numbers, FAQs, and custom support.

+ **Send Feedback:** Takes you to Microsoft's Contact Web page, where you can choose various types of feedback to send to Microsoft.

+ **About Internet Explorer:** Displays an About Internet Explorer dialog box with copyright and licensing information and the version number of the Internet Explorer software.

Searching the Web

The World Wide Web holds an enormous wealth of information on almost every subject known to humanity, but you need to know how to get to that information. To help Web surfers like you locate sites containing the information that interests them, a number of so-called *search engines* have been designed. Each search engine maintains a slightly different directory of the sites on the Web (which are mostly maintained and updated by automated programs called *Web crawlers, spiders,* and *robots!*).

Starting the search

Internet Explorer gives you access to all the most popular search engines through the Search bar, a special Explorer bar for searching the Web. (For details on the Explorer bars in Internet Explorer, see "Using the Explorer bar," earlier in this chapter.)

To open the Search bar, click the Search button on the Standard Buttons toolbar, choose View➪Explorer Bar➪Search, or press Ctrl+E.

In the Search bar, Internet Explorer automatically selects the Find a Web Page option button. Beneath the search category option buttons, you find a text box where you can type the kind of Web page to look for. After you enter the keyword or words (known affectionately as a *search string* in programmers' parlance) to search for in this text box, you begin the search by clicking the Search button.

Internet Explorer then conducts a search for Web sites containing the keywords by using the first search engine (the one listed in the Search bar). If that search engine finds no matches, Internet Explorer then conducts the same search by using the next search engine in its list.

When the search engine finishes processing your search string, it returns a list of hyperlinks in the Search bar that represents the top ten matches. You can then click any of the hyperlinks in the list to display that Web page in the area of the browser window to the right of the Search bar. If you aren't interested in the page that appears, try another of the hyperlinks to see whether it leads to a Web page that's of more interest.

Using additional search options

In addition to searching for Web pages, you can use the Search bar to search for people (Find a Person's Address), companies (Find a Business), redo a search that you conducted earlier (Previous Searches), or even to display a map for a particular address (Find a Map). If you click the More . . . hyperlink at the bottom of the category option buttons, the Search bar adds three additional option buttons: Look Up a Word, Find a Picture, and Find in Newsgroups.

If you're viewing a lengthy Web page, you can search for a specific word or phrase without having to page through multiple screens of text. To do so, choose Edit⇨Find (on This Page) or press Ctrl+F. In the Find dialog box, type the word or phrase that you want to find and click Find Next.

Limiting your searches

To avoid getting back thousands of irrelevant (or at the very minimum, uninteresting) search results, you need to consider telling the search engines to return links only to sites that contain all the terms you type in the search string. For example, say that you want to find sites that deal with koi (the ornamental carp that are very popular in Japan) ponds. If you type the search string **koi ponds** in the Find a Web Page Containing text box, the search engines will return links to Web sites with both *koi* and *ponds* (without any reference to the fish) in their descriptions as well as sites that contain both *koi* and *ponds* in their descriptions. The problem with this approach is that it can give you far too many extraneous results because many search engines search for each term in the search string independently as well as together. It's as though you asked for Web sites with descriptions containing koi *and/or* ponds.

The easiest way to tell the search engines that you only want links to a Web site returned if *all* the terms in your search string are matched in their descriptions is to enclose all the terms in double quotation marks. In the case of the *koi ponds* search string, you can find more Web sites that deal only with koi ponds (as opposed to frog ponds or other ponds containing just garden plants), by typing **koi ponds** in the Find a Web Page Containing text box. Taking this little extra step often brings you fewer, but more useful, results.

Browsing in full screen mode

One of the biggest drawbacks of Web surfing is the amount of scrolling that you have to do to see all the information on a particular Web page. To help minimize the amount of scrolling, Internet Explorer offers a full screen mode that automatically minimizes the space normally occupied by the menu bar, Standard Buttons toolbar, Address bar, and Links bar (see Figure 4-3). To switch to full screen mode, press F11 or choose View⇨Full Screen. To get out of full screen mode and return to the normal view, press F11 again.

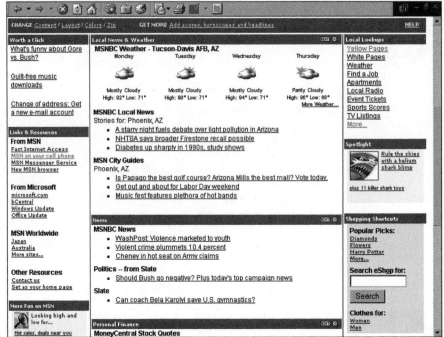

Figure 4-3:
Press F11 to
enter full
screen
mode and to
see more of
the Web
page.

Refreshing a Web page

Refreshing a page simply means asking Internet Explorer to download the
most current information available on the Web site. This feature is helpful
when you're viewing a page that provides rapidly changing information —
for example, a page providing running stock quotes. Because the page is
constantly updated at its source, you want to make sure that the version of
the page you're viewing is the most recent one. To refresh the page, click
the Refresh button on the toolbar.

Displaying previously viewed Web pages

As you browse different Web sites, Internet Explorer keeps track of your
progression through their pages. You can then use the Back and Forward
buttons on the toolbar or the equivalent commands on the View⇔Go To
menu to move back and forth between the pages that you visited in the current session.

If you use the Back and Forward buttons on the toolbar, you get the added
benefit of being able to tell in advance which page will be redisplayed when
you click the button. Simply position the mouse pointer on the Back or
Forward button and hold it there until the title of the Web page appears in a
ScreenTip box.

Both the Back and Forward buttons have drop-down lists attached to them. When you display these drop-down menus (by clicking the drop-down arrow to the immediate right of the Back or Forward button), they show a list, in most-recent to least-recent order, of the nine most recent Web pages visited in the work session before (Back) or after (Forward) the current Web page. (See "Viewing Pages from the History Folder," later in this chapter, for information on revisiting pages opened in the last few weeks.)

When the Back or Forward buttons are grayed out on the toolbar, this means that you're already viewing the first or the last of the Web pages that you visited in the current Internet Explorer session. You cannot go further back or forward.

Changing Your Default Home Page

Each time you start the Internet Explorer browser, it opens a designated page, called the *home page*. The home page is also where Internet Explorer goes when you click the Home button on the toolbar. If your computer isn't connected to the Internet when you click Home, Internet Explorer loads the home page locally from the cache. The *cache* is an area of a computer's hard disk used to store data recently downloaded from the Internet so that the data can be redisplayed quickly.

To change the default home page on your computer, follow these steps:

1. **Launch the Internet Explorer browser and display the Web page that you want to make the new home page.**

2. **Choose Tools➪Internet Options.**

The Internet Options dialog box appears. Click the General tab if it isn't already selected.

3. **In the Home Page section of the dialog box, click the Use Current button to make the current page your new home page.**

You can also type the URL of the page that you want to designate as your home page in the Address text box.

4. **Click OK.**

If, for the sake of speed, you want to use a blank Web page as the home page, click the Use Blank button. Internet Explorer then enters `about:blank` (the name of its standard blank page) in the Address text box. You also can click the Stop button on the navigation bar as soon as Internet Explorer starts loading the page.

**Book III
Chapter 4**

Web Browsing with
Internet Explorer

Keeping Track of Your Favorite Web Sites

As you browse the Web with Internet Explorer, you may come across Web sites that you want to revisit later. To make finding a site again easy, you can recall its home page (or any of its other pages) by placing a reference to the page in the Internet Explorer Favorites folder. You can then revisit the page by selecting its title from the Favorites pull-down menu or from the Favorites bar.

Adding Web pages to your Favorites folder

To add a Web page to the Favorites folder, follow these steps:

1. **Go to the Web page that you want to add to your Favorites.**

2. **Choose Favorites⇨Add to Favorites.**

   The Add Favorite dialog box opens.

3. **(Optional) Edit the Web page title in the Name text box, if you want to.**

   Keep in mind that this text is listed on the Favorites menu, so you want to make it descriptive but brief.

4. **(Optional) To make the Web page that you're adding to your Favorites available for offline browsing, click to select the Make Available Offline check box.**

5. **(Optional) To add the favorite to a subfolder of Favorites, click the Create In button to expand the Add Favorite dialog box (if the files and folders aren't already displayed in the list box); then click the icon of the appropriate subfolder (see Figure 4-4) or click the New Folder button to create a new folder for your new favorite.**

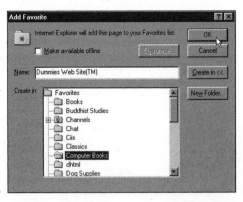

Figure 4-4: You can specify the folder where you want to add your favorite pages.

6. **Click OK to add the Web page to your Favorites.**

Viewing pages from the Favorites folder

The Favorites folder contains hyperlinks to all the Web pages that you've marked during your cyberspace travels on the Web as well as all the local folders and files on which you rely. From the Favorites list, you can open Web pages that you want to revisit, go to a channel home page, or open a favorite file with its native application (such as Word 2000 if it's a Word document or Excel 2000 if it's an Excel workbook).

To display the links in your Favorites folder, you can select the links directly from the Favorites pull-down menu, click the Favorites button on the Standard Buttons toolbar, or press Ctrl+I. When you click the Favorites button or press Ctrl+I, Internet Explorer presents the subfolders and links of your Favorites folder in the Favorites bar (a frame on the left side of the screen). The current Web page appears in a frame on the right. To display the links in one of the Favorites subfolders, click the folder icon containing the link in the Favorites bar. Then click the desired hyperlink to display a Web page, a list of folders and files, or to open a document in its own program.

Viewing Pages from the History Folder

The History folder contains a list of links to the Web pages that you visited within the last 20 days (unless you've changed this default setting). These hyperlinks are arranged chronologically from least recent to most recent, grouped by days for the current week, and then by weeks for all days further back.

To display the links in your History folder, click the History button on the Standard Buttons toolbar or press Ctrl+H. Internet Explorer shows the folders for each Web site that you visited on a particular day or during a particular week in the History bar (a pane on the left side of the screen).

To revisit a Web page in the History folder, click the Web site's folder icon in the History bar to display the links to its pages; then click the hyperlink for the particular page that you want to go to (see Figure 4-5).

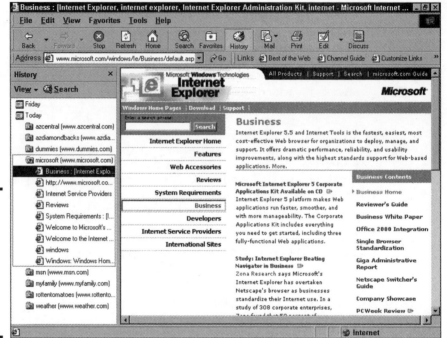

Figure 4-5:
Use the
History
folder to
quickly
locate sites
that you
recently
visited.

Printing a Web Page

Although you can save a Web page to your hard drive (using the File⇨Save As command), you may prefer to just print its contents. Internet Explorer makes it easy to print the contents of the Web page you're currently browsing. Just remember that a Web page (in spite of its name) can produce multiple printed pages due to the amount of information contained on that "page."

Before you print from Internet Explorer, you should check the page settings. You can change page settings from the Page Setup dialog box, which you open by choosing File⇨Page Setup. To change the page size, select a new size setting from the Size drop-down list. To change the orientation of the printing from Portrait (vertical) to Landscape (horizontal), click the Landscape option button. To change any or all of the page margins, enter a new value (in inches) in the Left, Right, Top, and Bottom text boxes. Click OK to save your settings.

When you're ready to print the contents of the current Web page, click the Print button on the Standard Buttons toolbar; alternatively, choose File⇨Print or press Ctrl+P to open the Print dialog box and then click OK.

When you print a Web page that uses frames, the Print dialog box gives you the option to print all the frames on the page as they appear in the browser, to print each one individually, or to print just a particular frame of your choice. Select the option you want and then click OK to begin printing.

Viewing the HTML Source of a Web Page

A Web page is no more than a special type of text document that makes extensive use of HTML (HyperText Markup Language) tags to format its contents. If you're a Web page designer (or have any inclination to become one), you can figure out a lot about Web design by viewing the HTML contents of the pages that you visit.

To see the HTML codes behind any Web page displayed in the Internet Explorer browsing window, choose View⇨Source. When you select this command, Internet Explorer launches the Windows Notepad utility, which displays a copy of the *HTML source page* (the page containing all of the HTML tags and text) for the current Web page, as shown in Figure 4-6. You can then print the HTML source page by choosing File⇨Print within Notepad.

Figure 4-6:
The HTML
source code
appears in
the Notepad
window.

```
asianart[1].htm - Notepad
File  Edit  Search  Help
<html>

<head>
<meta http-equiv="Content-Type" content="text/html;
charset=iso-8859-1">
<meta name="GENERATOR" content="Microsoft FrontPage 3.0">
<title>Asian Home Page</title>
</head>

<body background="images/backgrnd.gif" bgcolor="#FFFFFF">

<p><a href="index.html"><img src="art/aamh.gif" border="0" width="469"
height="72" </a><br>
<img src="art/homea.gif" border="0" width="61" height="25" </a></a><a
href="news.htm"><img
src="art/newsi.gif" border="0" width="62" height="25" </a></a><a
href="exhibits.htm"><img
src="art/exhibi.gif" border="0" width="81" height="25" </a></a><a
href="programs.htm"><img
src="art/progi.gif" border="0" width="92" height="25" </a></a><a
href="membership.htm"><img
src="art/membi.gif" border="0" width="100" height="25" </a
alt="Membership Information"></a><a
```

Chapter 5: Web Browsing with Netscape Navigator

In This Chapter

✔ Viewing Web sites with Navigator

✔ Performing a Web search

✔ Changing your default Home page

✔ Keeping track of your favorite Web sites

✔ Printing a Web page

✔ Viewing the HTML source of a Web page

*N*avigator is the world famous browser from Netscape that many Web surfers use to go globetrotting. You can also use Navigator for browsing your company's intranet, assuming, of course, that the intranet is not designed for use with Internet Explorer alone. In this chapter, we tell you what you need to know to successfully use Netscape Navigator. You get to know the elements of Navigator's screen and discover how to search the Web, keep track of your favorite sites, print Web pages, and view HTML source code.

This chapter covers Navigator 4.7, which is currently the most popular version of Netscape Navigator. You can download the newest version of Netscape Navigator 6 from the Netscape Web site.

If you need a refresher on Web basics, see Book III, Chapter 3. If your browser of choice is Internet Explorer, go to Book III, Chapter 4.

Getting Started with Netscape Navigator

The first thing you need to do to get started is launch Netscape Navigator. Use any of the following methods to start Netscape Navigator:

✦ Double-click the Netscape Navigator shortcut on your desktop.

✦ Click the Start button on the Windows taskbar and then choose Programs➪Netscape Communicator➪Netscape Navigator.

✦ Click the Netscape Navigator icon on the Quick Launch toolbar, located to the right of the Start button on the taskbar.

Accessing a Web site

When you fire up Navigator, you have to tell it which Web site you want to go to. If you don't have the Web site bookmarked (see the section "Keeping Track of Your Favorite Web Sites," later in this chapter), you must type the Web site's URL. To type the URL of a Web site that you want to visit, follow these steps.

1. **Choose File⇨Open Page.**

The Open Page dialog box appears.

2. **In the text box, type the URL of the site you want to visit.**

3. **Select the Open Location or File in Navigator option button.**

4. **Click Open.**

You also can position the cursor in the Location text box and type the URL of the Web site that you want to go to. Press Enter and voilà! Your Web page appears.

Elements of the Navigator window

If you're a first time Navigator user, you may wonder what's what in the Navigator window. Figure 5-1 shows you the elements of the Navigator window.

The following list describes the elements in the Navigator window:

✦ **Menu bar:** As with all standard Windows menu bars, the Netscape Navigator menu bar consists of pull-down menus that you can click to reveal a list of options and submenus.

✦ **Navigation toolbar:** This toolbar contains the tools that you use most often for navigating and performing tasks, such as the following:

 • **Back:** Enables you to return to any Web sites that you may have previously visited during your Web session.

 • **Forward:** Takes you to any available pages in the History listing.

 • **Reload:** Refreshes or updates the current page. (Sometimes, the information on a page may not download to your computer properly the first time. *Reloading* the page downloads the entire page again.)

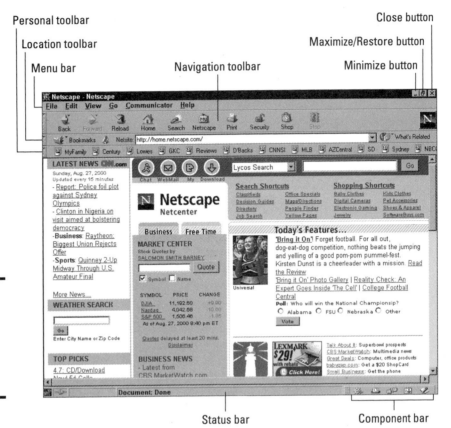

Personal toolbar

Location toolbar

Menu bar

Navigation toolbar

Close button

Maximize/Restore button

Minimize button

Figure 5-1:
The elements of the Netscape Navigator window.

Status bar

Component bar

- **Home:** Displays the Web page that you designate as the home (or *start*) page.

- **Search:** Displays a page containing a collection of search engines.

- **My Netscape:** Takes you to your personalized startup page.

- **Print:** Prints the current Web page.

- **Security:** Displays a page dedicated to security-related information.

- **Shop:** Takes you to the Shop At Netscape page.

- **Stop:** Lets you stop a page from loading.

✦ **Location toolbar:** This toolbar displays the URL (Web address) of the current Web page and also lets you access the Bookmark QuickFile. (See "Keeping Track of Your Favorite Web Sites," later in this chapter, for more information on bookmarks.) You can go to a new Web page by typing in a new URL in the Location text box and pressing Enter. The What's Related button displays a list of sites related to the page currently being displayed.

As you visit different pages during a Web browsing session, Netscape Navigator adds the URL of each site that you visit to the drop-down list attached to the Location text box. To revisit one of the Web pages that you've seen during the session, click the drop-down arrow at the end of the Location text box and click its URL in the drop-down list.

✦ **Personal toolbar:** Use this toolbar to create buttons for the URLs that you want to visit often. (If you don't see the Personal toolbar, choose View⇨Show⇨Personal Toolbar.) To add a button for the page that you're currently viewing, drag the Bookmark icon (the yellow-and-green icon that precedes the URL in the Location text box) to the place on the Personal toolbar where you want the button to appear.

All links on your Personal toolbar are saved in the Personal Toolbar Folder in your bookmark list. To remove a link from your Personal toolbar, you must remove it from the Personal Toolbar Folder. To do so, click the Bookmark QuickFile icon on the Location toolbar, choose Edit Bookmarks, right-click the link you want to remove from the Personal Toolbar Folder, and choose Delete Bookmark. Choose File⇨Close to close the Bookmarks window.

✦ **Minimize button:** Click this button to reduce Navigator to a button on the taskbar. (The program remains open.)

✦ **Maximize/Restore button:** When this button resembles a square (Maximize), click it to enlarge the page to fill the entire screen. When this button resembles two overlapping documents (Restore), click it to reduce the page to a less-than-full-size view.

✦ **Close button:** Click this button after you finish using Navigator.

✦ **Scroll bar:** Use the vertical scroll bar on the right side of your page to view the various areas of your screen. Occasionally, you may also see a horizontal scroll bar at the bottom of the Web page.

✦ **Status bar:** Provides information on your whereabouts as you travel the Web and also the status of Netscape Navigator as it performs its functions.

✦ **Component bar:** The Navigator Component bar provides one-click access to the Navigator browser, the Inbox, newsgroup messages, the Address Book, and the Composer window, via a set of icons.

Getting Help

Navigator features an extensive set of online help files, called NetHelp; each of the components described in this section has a link to NetHelp. To access it, just choose Help⇨Help Contents from the menu bar or press F1 at any point to bring up the NetHelp - Netscape window, shown in Figure 5-2.

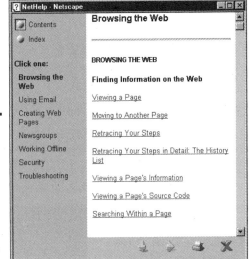

Figure 5-2:
The
NetHelp -
Netscape
window
provides
access
to Help
information.

To locate information on a particular component, follow these steps:

1. **Click any of the topics in the left pane of the NetHelp - Netscape window.**

On the right side of the Help window, a list displays the subtopics within the topic you select in the left pane.

2. **In the list of subtopics, click the subtopic on which you need help.**

To view an alphabetical listing of all help topics, follow these steps:

1. **Click Index.**

An alphabetical list of all topics appears.

2. **Scroll down the list or type the first few letters of the topic name in the textbox.**

3. **When the topic you want help with appears in the list, click it.**

4. **To exit from NetHelp, click the Close button in the upper-right corner of the NetHelp - Netscape window.**

TIP

The Help menu also provides several commands that enable you to access online help information on Netscape. These commands include a Reference Library, Release Notes, Product Information and Support, Software Updates, and Member Services.

Searching the Web

You find more information on the Web than in any library or museum in the world. Some of the information is useful — other information, utterly useless. Some information is so useless that you may wonder why the author wasted precious time putting it up. But the information is there if you want it, and Navigator provides an easy way to find what you want. Follow these steps:

1. **On the Navigation toolbar, click the Search button.**

The Netscape Net Search site appears, as shown in Figure 5-3. At this site, you can access a variety of search engines — software that finds the information you want — to look up people, businesses, and products.

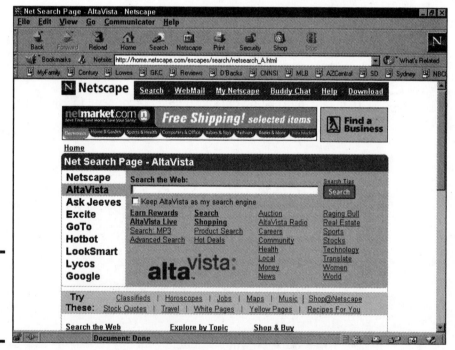

Figure 5-3:
The
Netscape
Net Search
site.

2. **To begin a search, type your query in the text box under Search the Web and then click a button that says something like Go or Search or Go Get It!, depending on the search engine that you're using.**

If results from a search engine don't satisfy you, try another, and another, and another, and . . . you get the picture.

Using (and clearing) the Location text box

Using the Location text box, you can quickly return to any site that you recently visited. To do so, follow these steps:

1. **Click the arrow at the end of the Location text box.**

   The URLs of the sites that you visited recently display.

2. **Click the URL of the site to which you want to return.**

   Whoosh! You're on your way.

Clearing this list of URLs from the Location text box takes just a few clicks of the mouse. Follow these steps:

1. **Choose Edit⇨Preferences.**

   The Preferences window displays, as shown in Figure 5-4. Select Navigator in the Category pane on the left side of the window.

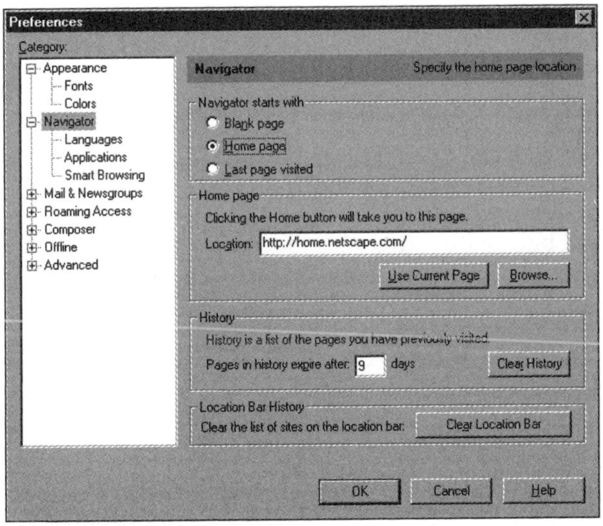

Figure 5-4:
The Navigator section of the Preferences window.

2. **Click the Clear Location Bar button in the Location Bar History section near the bottom of the window. Click OK to continue.**

3. **Click OK again to close the Preferences dialog box.**

    The URLs in the Location text box are deleted, and you're back to the Navigator window.

Reloading a Web page

Reloading a page simply means asking Navigator to download the most current information available on the Web site. This feature is helpful when you're viewing a page that provides rapidly changing information — for example, a page providing running stock quotes. Because the page is constantly updated at its source, you want to make sure that the version of the page you're viewing is the most recent one. To ask Navigator to go out and get the current version of the page, click the Reload button on the Navigation toolbar.

Displaying a previously visited Web page

To return to a Web site that you visited earlier in your Web session, you can do one of the following things:

✦ **Click the Back button on the Navigation toolbar.** Positioning the mouse pointer on the Back button for a second or two shows you the URL of the Web page to which you will return by clicking on that button.

✦ **Click the Back button and hold down the mouse button for a second.** A drop-down list displays the most recently visited pages. Scroll down to the page that you want to visit and then release the button.

✦ **Click the right mouse button and choose Back.**

✦ **Choose Go in the menu bar.** From the list that appears, select the Web site to which you want to go.

The Forward button becomes available only after you use the Back button in the current session. You can go forward to a site in any of the following ways:

✦ **Click the Forward button on the Navigation toolbar.** Positioning the mouse pointer on the Forward button for a second or two shows you the URL of the Web page to which you will return by clicking on that button.

✦ **Click the Forward button and hold down the mouse button for a second.** A drop-down list displays the most recently visited pages to which you can fast forward. Scroll down to the page that you want to visit again and then release the button.

+ **Click the right mouse button and choose Forward.**

+ **Choose Go in the menu bar.** From the list that appears, select the Web site to which you want to go.

Changing Your Default Home Page

One of the first things you can do to make Navigator your very own is to change your home page. You no longer have to see the standard Navigator page when you launch your browser; now you can load a specific page automatically each time you start it. To change your home Web page, follow these steps:

1. **Choose Edit⇨Preferences.**

   The Preferences dialog box opens.

2. **In the Category pane on the left side of the dialog box, click Navigator.**

   The Navigator screen appears in the Preferences dialog box (refer to Figure 5-4).

3. **In the Navigator Starts With section, click the Home Page option button.**

   If you don't want to see any page when you start Navigator, click the Blank Page option button and then click OK.

4. **In the Location text box of the Home Page section, type the URL for the page that you want to start with.**

5. **Click OK to apply your changes and close the Preferences dialog box.**

Sometimes you may be in such a rush that you don't want this page to appear when you start Navigator. Just click the Stop button on the Navigation toolbar as soon as the page starts to load and then type the URL of the page you want.

Keeping Track of Your Favorite Web Sites

You know what a bookmark is. It's a little mark you make in a book to help you find a particular page when you need it, fast. A *bookmark* within Navigator serves the same purpose. When you see a Web site that you think you may want to visit again, you bookmark it. The Bookmark feature is very helpful; if you cruise the Web as much as we do, you probably come across at least a handful of sites every day that you want to visit again.

Adding Web pages to the bookmark list

When you're viewing a Web site, adding a URL to the bookmark list is simple. To mark a site with a bookmark, follow these steps:

1. **Position the mouse pointer over the Bookmark QuickFile icon — the green and yellow icon just to the right of the word *Bookmarks* on the Location bar.**

   Notice that the mouse pointer changes to a hand.

2. **Click and drag this QuickFile icon over the Bookmark icon — the blue and green icon at the left end of the Location toolbar.**

   Notice that as you drag the icon, it changes to a chain-like link.

3. **Release the mouse button.**

   The URL for the current page is added to the bottom of the bookmark list. (You can click the Bookmark QuickFile icon to see it.)

Here are other ways to add the URL for the currently displayed page to the bookmark list:

✦ Right-click anywhere on the current page and choose Add Bookmark.

✦ Press Ctrl+D.

✦ Click the Bookmark QuickFile icon and choose Add Bookmark.

✦ Choose Communicator⇨Bookmarks⇨Add Bookmark.

You can add a URL to a specific folder within your bookmark list. Before you drop the link onto the Bookmark icon, hold the link on that icon for a second. Then drag the link over to your folder of choice and release the button.

Creating a new bookmark folder

After a few sessions of cruising the Web, you may notice that your bookmark file is longer than the tail of Haley's comet. To organize your bookmarks, you can store them in folders. Follow these steps:

1. **Open the bookmark file by clicking the Bookmark QuickFile icon and choosing Edit Bookmarks.**

   The Bookmarks window appears.

2. **In the Bookmarks window, choose File⇨New Folder.**

   The Bookmark Properties dialog box appears.

3. **Replace the generic name *New Folder* with something more descriptive.**

4. **Type a description in the Description box if you want.**

5. **Click OK.**

   The new folder should now appear in the bookmark list.

Be sure that no two folders have the same name. Navigator doesn't alert you if a folder with the same name already exists within your bookmark list.

Using a bookmark to view a Web page

To go to a URL listed within your bookmark file, click the Bookmark QuickFile icon on the Location toolbar and then choose the URL to which you want to go from those listed. To pick a URL bookmarked within a bookmark folder, hold the mouse pointer over a folder for a second; then choose your URL from the contents of that folder. To close the Bookmark QuickFile menu, click anywhere outside the menu or press Esc.

Viewing Pages from the History File

Navigator maintains a log of the Web sites that you visit during a Web session. This log is maintained in the History file and is like a set of footprints you leave behind as you surf the Web. You can ask Navigator to erase this log automatically after a fixed number of days. When Navigator erases the contents of the file, the log stays empty until you start a new Web session. At any time during a Web session, you can review the History file and directly jump to a Web site listed there — that is, a Web site you already visited.

To use the History file to get to a Web site, follow these steps:

1. **Choose Communicator⇨Tools⇨History or press Ctrl+H.**

   The History window appears. The most recent Web site you visited appears at the top.

2. **Double-click the Web site that you want to revisit.**

To close the History window, click the Close button in the upper-right corner.

Printing a Web Page

Navigator can help you find the information you want on the Web; but unless you plan to carry your computer around with you, you may need to print the information you find in order to show it to someone else. To see a preview of the page that you want to print, choose File⇨Print Preview.

To print a Web page, follow these steps:

1. **Choose File⇨Print, press Ctrl+P, or click the Print button on the Navigation toolbar.**

The Print dialog box appears.

2. **If you want to print only specific pages, specify those pages in the Print Range section.**

3. **Click Properties to specify the paper size and the print quality of the text and graphics.**

4. **Click OK to begin printing.**

Frames divide your browser window into separate panes, each displaying content from different HTML documents. If you view a page containing frames, the Print Frame option appears instead of the Print option in the File menu. Position the cursor anywhere within the frame that you want to print and then choose File⇨Print Frame.

When you print a Web page from Netscape Navigator, the program applies default page settings to the printout, such as: Letter for Page Size; Portrait for Orientation; and .50 for all margins. If you decide that you want to break out of the mold, you can adjust the page options as follows:

✦ To change the paper size, tray, or orientation, choose File⇨Print and then click the Properties button. Adjust your settings in the Properties dialog box (which differs depending on your printer). Click OK.

✦ To change formatting features, such as margins, choose File⇨Page Setup. Adjust your settings in the Page Setup dialog box, shown in Figure 5-5, and then click OK.

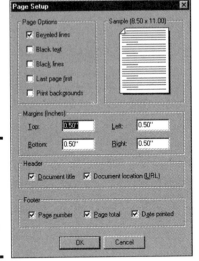

Figure 5-5:
Adjust the
page
settings
in the
Page Setup
dialog box.

Viewing the HTML Source of a Web Page

Behind every great Web page is a document of great HTML tags that present
and format the page's contents. To see the HTML code behind any displayed
Web page, choose View➪Page Source. The HTML source code appears in a
separate window, like the code shown in Figure 5-6. To close the window
after you finish, just click the Close button (X) in the upper-right corner of
the window.

Figure 5-6:
The HTML
source code
for a Web
page.

Chapter 6: Newsgroups, Chat, and Other Internet Communication

In This Chapter

- ✔ Participating in newsgroups
- ✔ Chatting online
- ✔ Using Web-based chatting
- ✔ Understanding Internet telephony
- ✔ Transferring files using FTP

The Internet is chock-full of information — you just have to know how to access it. One way that you can delve into some of the most current issues is through newsgroups. A *newsgroup* is a place on the Internet where people gather to discuss a topic of common interest. A newsgroup resembles an electronic bulletin board on which people post questions or comments, and others respond to these questions and comments.

The Internet also lets you communicate with people in more immediate ways, such as *chatting*, voice, and even video communication. In this chapter, you find out about the most popular forms of online communication and how to get the most from them. In addition, you discover how to copy files between your computer and other computers using File Transfer Protocol (FTP).

Newsgroup Basics

Reading Usenet is like trying to drink from a fire hose. Usenet now has more than 25,000 different newsgroups. Here are some tips for maintaining your sanity:

- ✦ Pick a few groups that really interest you or use an indexing service, such as Deja.com.
- ✦ Develop a tolerance for the numerous junk-mail messages that infest many groups.
- ✦ If you feel that you absolutely have to reply to a comment, save the message and sleep on it before sending the reply.

✦ Don't get into a flame war; however, if ever you do, let the other guy have the last word.

✦ Don't believe everything you read on Usenet.

You use a *newsreader* program to read newsgroup postings. Or you can use your browser to read newsgroup postings on the `Deja.com` Web site. To configure your newsreader program, ask your Internet Service Provider (ISP) for the name of its *news server,* the program that stores newsgroup postings for you to download.

Newsgroup "netiquette"

The e-mail etiquette rules listed in Chapter 2 also apply to newsgroup articles. Here are some additional Do's and Don'ts:

✦ **Don't** post to the whole group a follow-up intended solely for the author of the original article. Instead, reply via e-mail.

✦ **Do** be sure that each article is appropriate for the group to which you post it.

✦ **Don't** post a message saying that another message — a spam ad, for example — is inappropriate. The poster probably knows and doesn't care. The first message wasted enough of everyone's time; your response would waste more. Silence is the best answer.

✦ **Don't** criticize someone else's spelling or grammar — ever.

✦ **Do** make your subject line as meaningful as possible. If your reply is tangential to an article, change the subject line to reflect the new topic.

✦ **Don't** post a two-line follow-up that quotes an entire 100-line article. Edit out most of the quoted material.

✦ **Don't** *cross-post;* that is, don't post the same article to multiple newsgroups, unless you have a really good reason. Be especially careful when you're replying to multiple cross-posted messages; your response may be cross-posted, too.

✦ **Do** watch out for *trolls,* messages calculated to provoke a storm of replies. Not every stupid comment needs a response.

✦ **Do** read the FAQ before posting a question. Most groups periodically post a list of Frequently Asked Questions (or *FAQs*). See "Frequently Asked Questions (FAQs)" later in this chapter.

Newsgroup names

Usenet newsgroups have multipart names separated by dots, such as `comp.dcom.fax`, a data communication discussion group about fax machines. Related groups have related names. Groups about data communication, for example, all start with `comp.dcom`. The first part of a newsgroup name is called its *hierarchy.* In e-mail addresses and Internet host names, the top-level component (`edu`, for example) is on the *right.* In newsgroup names, the top-level component is on the *left.*

Table 6-1 lists the most popular Usenet newsgroup hierarchies.

Table 6-1	Newsgroup Names
Newsgroup	*Description*
comp	Computer-related topics
humanities	Discussions relating to humanities
misc	Miscellaneous topics that don't fit anywhere else
news	Topics having to do with the Usenet newsgroup system
rec	Recreational groups about sports, hobbies, the arts, and so on
sci	Science-related topics
soc	Social groups, both social interests and plain socializing
talk	Long arguments, frequently political
alt	Semiofficial "alternative" to the preceding newsgroup hierarchies (which are often called "the big eight")

Regional, organizational, and national hierarchies also exist:

Newsgroup	*Description*
ne	New England
ny	New York
uk	United Kingdom
ibm	IBM

Many hierarchies serve languages other than English:

Newsgroup	*Description*
de	German
es	Spanish
fj	Japanese
fr	French

New hierarchies are being started all the time. Lewis S. Eisen maintains a master list of Usenet hierarchies (567, at last count), at:

`www.magma.ca/~leisen/mlnh`

Frequently Asked Questions (FAQs)

Many newsgroups periodically post a list of frequently asked questions and their answers, or *FAQs*. They hope that you read the FAQ before posting a message they have answered a dozen times before, and you should.

MIT collects FAQs from all over Usenet, creating, in effect, an online encyclopedia with the latest information on a vast array of topics that is accessible with your Web browser or via FTP, at this URL:

```
ftp://rtfm.mit.edu/pub/usenet-by-hierarchy
```

FAQs are often quite authoritative, but sometimes they're just a contributor's opinion. Reader beware!

Posting articles to newsgroups

Standard Usenet dogma is to read a group for a few weeks before posting anything. It's still good advice, although Internet newbies generally aren't big on delayed gratification. Here are some tips on your first posting:

✦ Pick a newsgroup whose subject is one you know something about.

✦ Read the FAQ before you post.

✦ Reply to an article with specific information that you know firsthand or can cite in a reference and that is relevant to the topic being discussed.

✦ Read the entire preceding *thread* (a series of replies to the original article and replies to those replies) to make sure that your point hasn't been raised already.

✦ Edit included text from the original article to the bare minimum.

✦ Keep your reply short, clear, and to the point.

✦ Check your spelling and grammar.

✦ Don't be inflammatory, use foul language, or call people names.

✦ Avoid Netisms, such as ROFL ("rolling on floor laughing"). If necessary, use — at most — one smiley :-).

✦ Use a local hierarchy for stuff of regional interest. The whole planet does not need to hear about your school's bake sale.

✦ Save your message overnight and reread it before posting.

Some newsgroups are *moderated,* which means that

✦ Articles are not posted directly as news. Instead, they're e-mailed to a person or program that posts the article only if he, she, or it feels that it's appropriate to the group.

✦ Moderators, because they're unpaid volunteers, do not process items instantaneously, so it can take a day or two for items to be processed.

✦ If you post an article for a moderated group, the news-posting software mails your item to the moderator automatically.

✦ If your article doesn't appear and you really don't know why, post a polite inquiry to the same group.

Remember that Usenet is a public forum. Everything you say there can be read by anyone, anywhere in the world. Worse, every word you post is carefully indexed and archived.

Reading Newsgroups with Deja.com

Deja.com is a great place to find answers to problems that you may be having with your computer and its software. You can find a newsgroup for almost every system out there, including ones that are obsolete.

Deja.com updates its site from time to time, so the details described in this section may change.

Deja.com and Usenet indexes

Usenet has been around almost since the beginning of the Internet and is a bit old and creaky. Deja.com, at www.deja.com, has done much to bring Usenet into the modern Web era. The Web site has indexed Usenet articles since 1995. You can use Deja.com to

✦ Search for articles by keywords

✦ Look for newsgroups of interest

✦ Read newsgroup articles

✦ Send e-mail to an article's author

✦ Post a reply article to something you read

✦ Post a newsgroup article on a new topic

Watch out what you post on Usenet newsgroups because anyone can find your posts later by using Deja.com! A simple search for your name displays your e-mail address and a list of every message that you've posted — at least since 1995. If you include your home address, phone number, kids' names, political opinions, dating preferences, personal fantasies, or whatever in any message, that information also is easily retrieved. You have been warned.

Searching Deja.com

The traditional way to read Usenet is to go to a newsgroup and read the recent messages posted there. With tens of thousands of newsgroups, however, this method is very inefficient. Deja.com lets you search *all* newsgroups by content. To use Deja.com to search all newsgroups by content, follow these steps:

1. **Open your browser and go to** www.deja.com/usenet.

2. **At the top of the Web page, type some keywords in the Search Discussions text box and click Search.**

   You see a list of newsgroups that includes many articles (or contributor's names) with those keywords, followed by a list of specific articles. You can sort this list by date, subject, forum, or author; click the link at the top of each column. If you don't find what you want, change your keywords.

3. **Click an article to read it. To see other articles on the same topic, click the <u>Thread</u> link in the article window. To read other postings in the same newsgroup, click the <u>Forum</u> link. To return to the last search list, click Back to Search Results (or your browser's Back button).**

4. **To save an article, choose File⇨Save As in your browser.**

When you first perform a search, Deja.com looks at only the articles posted in the past month or so. If you want older articles, look for the search box at the bottom of the list of articles, change Recent to Past or All messages, and click Search. For additional search options, click the Power Search link, which is also located below the list of articles.

You also can use Deja.com as a newsreader, if you want to subscribe to specific newsgroups and create a personalized list of forums. Click the My Deja link on the Deja.com Web page and follow the steps provided to create your account.

Replying to an article by e-mail

To reply to a newsgroup article via e-mail, find the person's e-mail address in the article and copy it in the To field of your favorite e-mail program. (See Chapter 2 for more information on e-mail.)

To post an article following up on a message, click the <u>Post Reply</u> link. On the Post Message page, edit the quoted article to a reasonable size and add your response. You can also edit the list of newsgroups to which your article is posted. Click the Submit My Message button when it's ready for public viewing. Deja.com sends you e-mail asking for confirmation before posting your message.

Posting a new article

To post a new message to a newsgroup, display an article in the newsgroup and then click the <u>Post Reply</u> link. On the Post Message page, replace the text in the Subject box with your new title. Type the message in the list box. You can also edit the list of newsgroups to which your article is posted. When the message is ready to send, click the Submit My Message button.

Reading Newsgroups with Outlook Express

Outlook Express, the e-mail program that comes with Internet Explorer and Windows 98 (see Chapter 2), also works as a newsreader. You can receive (by subscribing) copies of all the messages being sent by the participants of the newsgroup, or you can peruse the chitchat (by not subscribing to the newsgroup). You must first set up a newsgroup account.

You can add and remove news server accounts or make an account your default account by choosing Tools➪Accounts and clicking on the News tab of the Internet Accounts dialog box.

Viewing newsgroup messages before you subscribe

To get a feel for a newsgroup by reading some of its messages before actually subscribing to it, follow these steps:

1. **From the Internet Explorer toolbar, click the Mail button and then choose Read News.**

   Internet Explorer opens the Outlook Express window for the news server that you selected when you set up your news account. An alert dialog box appears, indicating that you are not currently subscribed to any newsgroups.

2. **Click Yes to display a list of all available newsgroups in the Newsgroup Subscriptions dialog box.**

   This process takes a few minutes if your connection speed is slow.

3. **Select a newsgroup in the list box of the Newsgroup Subscriptions dialog box by clicking it.**

   If you want to limit the list of newsgroups, you can enter a term or series of terms used in the newsgroup's title (if you know that kind of thing) in the Display Newsgroups Which Contain text box.

4. **Click the Go To button to download all the messages from the newsgroup into the Outlook Express window.**

   You can read through the newsgroup messages just as you do your own e-mail messages. The Go To button is shown in Figure 6-1.

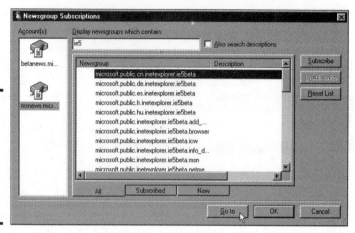

Figure 6-1:
Use the Go
To button
to view
newsgroup
messages
before you
subscribe.

5. **If you want to reply to a particular message, click it in the upper pane; then click the Reply button to reply to the author of the message or click the Reply Group button to reply to the entire group.**

   You don't have to reply to every message you receive; in fact, you should only send a reply if you have something specific you want to add to the discussion.

6. **Click the Newsgroups button on the Outlook Express toolbar.**

   You return to the list of newsgroups on your News server.

7. **After you finish perusing the newsgroups of interest, click OK to close the Newsgroup Subscriptions dialog box and then click the Close button in the Outlook Express window.**

Subscribing to a newsgroup

When you find a newsgroup in which you want to regularly participate, you can subscribe to it as follows:

1. **From the Internet Explorer toolbar, click the Mail button and then choose Read News.**

2. **If you see an alert dialog box telling you that you haven't subscribed to any newsgroups, click Yes.**

   The Newsgroup Subscriptions dialog box opens.

3. **In the list box, click the name of the newsgroup to which you want to subscribe.**

4. **Click the Subscribe button.**

   Outlook Express then adds a newspaper icon in front of the name of the newsgroup to indicate that you are subscribed to it. The program also adds the name of the newsgroup to the Subscribed tab of the Newsgroup Subscriptions dialog box.

5. **Repeat Steps 3 and 4 to subscribe to any other newsgroups of interest.**

6. **After you finish subscribing, click OK.**

   The Outlook Express window appears. You now see a list of all the newsgroups to which you are subscribed.

7. **To see the messages in a particular newsgroup, select the newsgroup by clicking its name in the Folders pane.**

8. **To have Internet Explorer go online and download any new messages for the selected newsgroup, choose Tools⇨Synchronize Newsgroup.**

   The Synchronize Newsgroup dialog box appears.

9. **Select the Get the Following Items check box and then choose the desired option button: All Messages, New Messages Only (the default), or Headers Only; then click OK.**

   After the messages are downloaded, you can get offline and peruse the messages at your leisure. If you want to send any replies to the messages, however, you must go back online.

10. **Read and reply to as many of the newsgroup messages as you want. Click the Reply button to reply to the author of the message or click the Reply Group button to reply to the entire group.**

    You don't have to reply to every message you receive; in fact, you should only send a reply if you have something specific you want to add to the discussion.

11. **After you finish with the newsgroup messages, click the Close button in the upper-right corner of the Outlook Express window.**

After subscribing to a newsgroup, click the Mail button on the Internet Explorer toolbar and choose Read News to return to the list of newsgroups in Outlook Express. Click the title of a newsgroup to download its current messages.

Unsubscribing from a newsgroup

If you decide that you no longer want to participate in a newsgroup to which you're subscribed, you can easily unsubscribe by following these steps:

1. **Click the Newsgroups button on the Outlook Express toolbar.**

   The Newsgroup Subscriptions dialog box displays.

2. **Click the Subscribed tab and then click the name of the newsgroup to which you want to unsubscribe.**

3. **Click the Unsubscribe button and then click OK.**

   You're immediately unsubscribed from the list and won't receive any mailings.

Reading News with Netscape Messenger

If you are using Netscape Communicator, Netscape Messenger is your gateway to newsgroups. If you haven't read newsgroups before, Messenger may not be set up for receiving news from a news server.

To ensure that Messenger is set up to view newsgroups, follow these steps:

1. **Choose Edit⇨Preferences.**

   The Preferences dialog box appears.

2. **Double-click the Mail & Newsgroups category to expand it, if necessary.**

3. **Click the Newsgroup Servers component in the Mail & Newsgroups category (see Figure 6-2).**

   The Newsgroup Servers dialog box appears. If the box under Newsgroup Servers is empty, you're not connected to a news server. In that case, contact the local computer guru in your office or the systems administrator to get the name of the news server that you type in that box. If your Internet connection is through an ISP, contact the ISP and get the name of the news server from them.

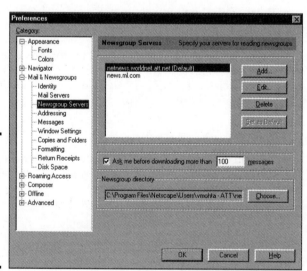

Figure 6-2:
Active news servers appear in the Newsgroup Servers list box.

4. **(Optional) To add a news server to the Newsgroup Servers list, click the Add button, type the name of the server, and click OK.**

5. **Click OK.**

Just like canceling a magazine subscription, you may at some point want to delete a news server from your list of subscribed servers. To do so, choose Edit⇨Preferences and double-click the Mail & Newsgroups category to expand it (if necessary). Next, Click the Newsgroup Servers component in the Mail & Newsgroups category, click the server that you want to delete, and then click Delete. Click OK to confirm the deletion.

Subscribing to a newsgroup

When you connect to a news server, you're presented with a list of all the newsgroups available on it. In some cases, the list can contain thousands of newsgroups. Each time you connect to the news server, you may need to scroll through this long list of newsgroups to get to the newsgroup you want to read. This process can get pretty annoying after awhile.

Instead of rooting out your newsgroup each time you want to read it, you can permanently list your newsgroup of choice in your Message Center listing, under the news server. This is what *subscribing to a newsgroup* means. Then, each time you connect to the news server, Messenger automatically connects to all subscribed newsgroups and displays the number of messages currently posted on each newsgroup.

To subscribe to a newsgroup, follow these steps:

1. **Choose Communicator⇨Tools⇨Message Center and right-click on the news server within the Message Center window.**

2. **From the shortcut menu, choose Subscribe To Newsgroups.**

   The Communicator: Subscribe To Newsgroups window appears, displaying a list of newsgroups on the server. As Messenger lists the newsgroups, the status bar at the bottom of the window reads Receiving Newsgroups. After Messenger lists all the newsgroups, the status bar reads Document: Done.

3. **In the Newsgroup box, type the name of the newsgroup to which you want to subscribe or scroll down the list until you find the one you want and select it.**

   If you type the name of the newsgroup and the newsgroup exists on the server, Messenger automatically scrolls down the list and highlights it. If a + sign is next to the newsgroup, that means the newsgroup contains subgroups within it. You can click the + sign to display all subgroups within the newsgroup.

4. **Click the newsgroup to which you want to subscribe.**

**Book III
Chapter 6**

Newsgroups, Chat, and Other Internet Communication

5. **Click again on the group you want to subscribe to, but this time click on the little dot that you see to the right of the group name, in the Subscribe column.**

   A check mark now appears in place of the dot.

6. **Repeat Steps 3 through 5 for all the newsgroups to which you want to subscribe.**

7. **Click OK.**

   Messenger now lists the newsgroups in the Message Center.

Your Internet Service Provider (ISP), or your employer, may maintain only a partial list of newsgroups on its news server. Your choice of newsgroups is limited to the newsgroups within that list.

To view all the newsgroups that you've subscribed to on a particular news server, double-click the news server's name or click the + sign to the left of the news server's name. All the newsgroups listed within the news server should appear. To hide the newsgroup list again, double-click the news server name or click the – sign to the left of the news server's name.

Unsubscribing from a newsgroup

Even though you may have subscribed to a newsgroup, you may rarely read what's in it. To unsubscribe from a newsgroup, follow these steps:

1. **Right-click the newsgroup within the Message Center window.**

2. **From the shortcut menu that appears, choose Remove Newsgroup.**

   A dialog box appears, asking you whether you're sure that you want to unsubscribe from the newsgroup.

3. **Click Yes to zap the newsgroup.**

Reading a newsgroup

Following a discussion is a lot easier if all the posts pertaining to a particular topic are *threaded,* or linked together. Messenger arranges posts in a thread hierarchically in the Netscape Newsgroup window. For example, if you post a message on a newsgroup asking for opinions about taxation, all suggestions posted in response to your query form a message thread. You can then follow this thread to see what people have suggested, thereby keeping this discussion separate from all others going on the newsgroup at the same time.

To read threaded message newsgroups, follow these steps:

1. **In the Netscape Newsgroup window, list the newsgroups within a news server by clicking the + sign next to the news server name.**

   A list of all the newsgroups you subscribe to appears.

2. **Click a newsgroup that you want to read.**

   The number of messages within a newsgroup may be greater than the download limit set in the Mail & Newsgroup Preferences settings. If this happens, Messenger displays a dialog box titled Download Headers. This dialog box offers you the option of downloading only a specific number of messages, thereby saving you time on a slow modem connection.

3. **If the Download Headers dialog box appears when you download messages, select the number of headers (messages) you want to download and then click Download.**

   If the number of messages within the newsgroup is less than the limit specified in the Mail & Newsgroup Preferences settings, Messenger automatically downloads all the messages within the newsgroup.

   In a three-pane window within Messenger, the top-right window lists the messages in the newsgroup; the bottom-right window lists the contents of the message selected in the top-right window. Each time you select a new message in the top-right window, the contents of the bottom window change accordingly.

4. **To read a post, click on the post.**

   The post's contents appear in the bottom-right window of the screen.

To download another batch of messages from the newsgroup, choose File➪ Get Next 100 Messages. The number next to Next is the maximum number of messages set by you within the Mail & Newsgroups Preferences options.

Searching for a post within a newsgroup

You may want to look up some information that you have read in a post, but you just can't remember which of the gazillion posts within the newsgroup you read that information in. If you forget to mark that post, you can still pull it up as long as you remember something specific about the post, such as the date, subject, name of sender, or a word or phrase in the text of the post.

To find the post that you've been looking for, follow these steps:

1. **Choose Edit➪Search Messages.**

   A search window pops up on your screen. This window is where you specify what you're looking for.

2. **Click Search.**

   Messenger begins a search through the current newsgroup and displays the search results.

To view a post that Messenger pulls up as a result of your search, just double-click the post. To begin a new search, click Clear Search.

You can tag specific posts with a flag, making them easier to find. Think of marking posts as dropping breadcrumbs as you read your way through a newsgroup. To mark your posts, click the post you want to mark or tag. On the message header, click the dot that is in the orange flag column. You should now see an orange flag in the header. To remove the flag, click it again.

Posting messages to a newsgroup

Online and offline discussions are similar in one important respect: You need to listen to the conversation before you jump in and start talking yourself. After you read a newsgroup for a while and get a feel for the type of conversation that takes place there, you may want to post a message or two to the newsgroup. You can either create a new post of your own or you can reply to someone else's post on the newsgroup.

While you're reading a newsgroup, you can create a new message to post by following these steps:

1. **Click the New Msg button on the toolbar.**

   The Composition window appears, as shown in Figure 6-3. Notice that the name of the current newsgroup automatically appears in the Group box.

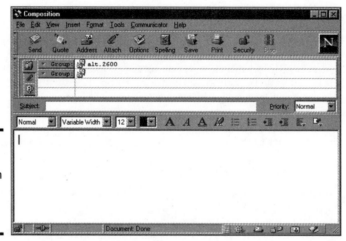

Figure 6-3:
Use the
Composition
window to
type your
message.

2. **Type a Subject for your post.**

3. **Type your post and click Send.**

Sometimes, you may want to contribute your two cents to an existing post on a newsgroup. Follow these steps to make your voice heard:

1. **Click the post you want to reply to.**

   The content of the post is displayed. You have the following options for your reply:

   • Reply to the sender of the message only.

   • Reply to the sender of the message and to all recipients of the message.

   • Post your response on the newsgroup only.

   • Send a reply to the person who posted the message *and* post your response on the newsgroup, too.

2. **Right-click the header of the post.**

3. **In the shortcut menu, choose who you want to send your reply to.**

   The Message Composition window appears.

4. **Type your reply and click Send.**

   Your post is on its way.

Don't be surprised if the post you send to a newsgroup doesn't show up immediately. It usually takes a couple of hours, sometimes longer, for your message to be posted.

Saving a post

When you come across (or write) a post that you want to save for posterity, you can save a post to a hard drive or floppy disk. If you save it to a hard drive, you can view the post later and edit it by using your favorite word processor, just like any other file.

To save a post, follow these steps:

1. **In the Netscape Newsgroup window, right-click the post that you want to save.**

2. **In the shortcut menu that appears, choose Save Message.**

   The Save Message As dialog box appears. You can save the post in HTML format or in Plain Text format. If the page has any HTML-formatted material in it, such as URLs, images, bulleted lists, or tables, you may want to retain those features by saving the post in HTML format. If it doesn't have any of this HTML formatted material in it, you can save it in Plain Text format.

3. **In the Save As Type box, select HTML Files or Plain Text (*.txt).**

Book III
Chapter 6

Newsgroups, Chat,
and Other Internet
Communication

4. **Give the file a name that is a little more descriptive than untitled.html.**

   You can thank me for this later after you have saved tons of posts.

5. **In the Save In drop-down list, select the destination for the post that you want to save.**

   You can choose your floppy drive, any folder on your hard drive, or any other storage device.

6. **Click Save.**

 Sometimes you want to take a Usenet post with you to a meeting or maybe even hang it up on your refrigerator door. To print a post, click the post and then click the Print button on the toolbar. Specify any appropriate printing options, such as the number of copies you want, and click OK.

Chatting Online

Online chat lets you communicate with people live, just as you do on the telephone — except that you type what you want to say and read the other person's reply on your computer screen. Here are some things that you need to know about chat:

✦ In chat, a window shows the ongoing conversation. You type in a separate box what you want to send to the individual or group. When you press Enter or click the Send button, your message appears in the conversation window, along with any responses.

✦ Chat differs from e-mail in that you don't have to address each message and wait for a reply. Though sometimes a small lag occurs in chatting, communication is nearly instantaneous — even across the globe.

✦ You're usually limited to a sentence or two in each exchange.

✦ You can select a group or an individual to chat with, or someone can ask to initiate a private chat with you. Many chat venues exist on the Net, including IRC (Internet Relay Chat), AOL chat rooms (for AOL users only), Web-based chat, and instant messaging systems such as ICQ and AIM (AOL Instant Messenger).

✦ Because tens of thousands of people are chatting at any instant of the day or night, the discussions are divided into groups. Different terms exist for chat groups. AOL and ICQ call them *rooms*. IRC (Internet Relay Chat) calls them *channels*.

✦ The chat facilities of the value-added service providers (such as AOL, CompuServe, and Microsoft Network) are accessible to only that service's members. Only AOL members can use the AOL chat rooms, for example. You cannot get to the AOL chat rooms from ICQ or IRC.

✦ People in chat groups can be unruly and even vicious. The online service providers' chat groups usually are tamer because the service provides some supervision.

✦ You may select a special name — called a *screen name, handle,* or *nickname* — to use when you're chatting. This name can and often does differ from your logon name or e-mail address.

Although your special chat name gives you some privacy online, someone could possibly find out your real identity, particularly if your online service or ISP cooperates. Don't go wild out there.

Following group conversations

Get used to following a group conversation if you want to make any sense of chats. Here's a sample of what you may see (screen names and identifying content have been changed):

```
BrtG221: hey Zeb!
Zebra795: Hello
ABE904: Where is everyone from...I am from Virginia
Zebra795: Hi Brt!
HAPY F: how should I know
Zebra795: Hi ABE
HAPY F: < -- Virginia
ABE904: Hi Zebra!!!
BrtG221: so StC... what
Zebra795: < -- was from Virginia!
ABE904: Hi HAPY ! Didn't see ya
BrtG221: is going on in FL?
HAPY F: HI ABE
Zebra795: Hap's been on all night!
Storm17: Brt...what?...i miss our heart to hearts
HAPY F: on and off
ABE904: Zeb, and wish you were back here!
DDouble6190: im 26 but i like older women
Zebra795: I was over July Fourth!!
Janet5301: Sorry...DD...call me in 10 yrs...
BrtG221: really DD?... where do you live?
BrtG221: lol.. so talk to me Storm..
ABE904: Gee, you didn't call, didn't write...
```

Here are a few tips for getting started:

✦ When you enter a chat group, a conversation is usually already in progress. You cannot see what went on before you entered.

✦ Wait a minute or two for a page full of exchanges to appear on-screen so that you can understand some of their context before you start reading and then determine with whom you want to converse.

✦ Start by following the comments from a single screen name. Then follow the people whom that person mentions or who replies to that person. Ignore everything else because the other messages are probably replies to messages that went by before you came in.

✦ After you can follow one thread, try picking up another. It takes practice to get the hang of it.

✦ Some services, such as AOL, let you highlight the messages from one or more screen names. This capability can make things easier to follow.

✦ Many services let you indicate screen names to ignore. Messages from these chatters no longer appear onscreen, though other members' replies to them do appear.

✦ Scroll up to see older messages if you have to, but remember that after you have scrolled up, new messages don't appear until you scroll back down.

✦ Many of the messages are greetings to familiar names as they join or leave the chat group.

✦ The real action often takes place in private, one-on-one side discussions, which you cannot see.

Chatting etiquette

Chatting etiquette isn't much different from e-mail etiquette (see Book III, Chapter 2), and common sense is your best online guide. Here are some additional chat behavior tips:

✦ The first rule of chat is that a real person with real feelings is at the other end of the computer chat connection. Hurting him or her is not okay.

✦ The second rule is that because you really have no idea who that other person is, being cautious is okay. (See "Safe chatting guidelines" in the following section.)

✦ Keep your comments short and to the point.

✦ Avoid insults and foul language.

✦ Many systems let you create a profile about yourself that other members can access. Having a profile is polite. You don't have to tell everything about yourself in your profile, although what you do say should be truthful.

✦ If you want to talk to someone in private, send a message saying hello, who you are, and what you want.

✦ If the rudeness and banality of the chat turn you off, try another group.

Safe chatting guidelines

Here are some guidelines for conducting safe and healthy chats:

✦ Many people in chat groups are totally dishonest about who they are. They lie about their occupation, age, locality, and, yes, even gender. Some think that they're being cute, and others are exploring their own fantasies; a few are really sick.

✦ Be careful about giving out information that enables someone to find you personally, including phone numbers, mailing address, and the schools that your kids attend.

✦ Pick a screen name or handle that's different from your logon name; otherwise, you'll receive a great deal of unwanted junk e-mail. If you're worried about people knowing your sex, pick a gender-neutral screen name.

✦ Never give out your password to anyone, even if she says that she works for your service provider, the phone company, the FBI, or the CIA. Never!

✦ If your chat service offers profiles and a person without a profile wants to chat with you, be extra cautious. Of course, those who do offer profile details may be giving out false information.

✦ If your children use chat, realize that others may try to meet them. Before your kids log on, spend some quality time talking to them about the guidelines in "Kids, adult sites, and the Web," in Book III, Chapter 1.

✦ Don't hesitate to report anyone who you believe is behaving inappropriately on a value-added service's chat group. On AOL, go to the keyword **Notify AOL**. On CompuServe, go to the keyword **feedback**.

AT&T has a service (currently available only through Excite! Chat) that lets you talk to someone you meet in a chat room without exchanging phone numbers. Visit chatntalk.att.com for details.

If you choose to meet an online friend in person, use at least the same caution you would use in meeting someone through a newspaper ad:

✦ Don't arrange a meeting until you talk to that person a number of times over the course of days or weeks.

✦ Have a few phone conversations first.

✦ Meet in a public place.

✦ Bring a friend along, if possible. If not, at least let someone else know what you're doing and agree to call that person at a specified time (a half-hour, for example) after the meeting time.

✦ If you travel a long distance to meet someone, stay in a hotel, not at that person's home.

Smileys, abbreviations, and emoticons

Chat abbreviations are similar to those used in news and e-mail, although some are unique to the real-time nature of chat. Table 6-2 provides abbreviations and emoticons common on AOL and other chat services.

Table 6-2	Common Chat Abbreviations
Abbreviation/Emoticon	*What It Means*
AFK	Away From Keyboard
A/S/L	Age/Sex/Location (response may be 35/f/LA)
BAK	Back At Keyboard
BRB	Be Right Back
BTW	By The Way
FTF	Face To Face
GMTA	Great Minds Think Alike
IC	In Character (playing a role)
ICQ	"I Seek You" (a chat service described later in this chapter)
IM	Instant Message
IMHO	In My Humble Opinion
IRC	Internet Relay Chat (a chat service described later in this chapter)
LTNS	Long Time No See
LOL	Laughing Out Loud
M4M	Men seeking other men
OOC	Out of Character (stepping out of a role)
RL	Real Life (opposite of RP)

Abbreviation/Emoticon	What It Means
ROFL	Rolling on Floor, Laughing
RP	Role Play (acting a character in a fantasy)
TOS	Terms of Service (the AOL member contract)
TTFN	Ta-Ta for Now!
WB	Welcome Back
WTG	Way To Go!
:) or :-)	Smile
:D	Smile/laughing/big grin
**	Kisses
;)	Wink
{}	Hug
:(or :-(	Frown
:'(	Crying
0:)	Angel
}:>	Devil
:X	My lips are sealed
:P	Sticking out tongue
(_|_)	Moon

Internet Relay Chat (IRC)

Internet Relay Chat (IRC) is the Internet's own chat service. IRC is available from most Internet Service Providers. You can even participate in IRC through most online services, although IRC is completely separate from the service's own chat services. You need an *IRC client program* (or just *IRC program*), which is simply another Internet program, like your Web browser or e-mail software. Freeware and shareware IRC programs are available for you to download from the Net. Most Unix systems come with an IRC program. One of the best shareware IRC programs for Windows is mIRC.

You can download updated versions of these programs and get detailed information about installing them from www.irchelp.org. These programs are also available from TUCOWS (www.tucows.com). Windows 98 comes with Microsoft Chat. You may have to install it from your Windows 98 CD-ROM, or you can download it from www.microsoft.com/downloads.

Check with your Internet Service Provider for any additional information you may need in order to use IRC. If you have a direct link to the Internet, ask your system administrator whether the link supports IRC.

You use IRC in two main ways:

✦ **Channel:** This is like an ongoing conference call with a bunch of people. After you join a channel, you can read what people are saying on-screen and then add your own comments just by typing them and pressing Enter.

✦ **Direct connection:** This is like a private conversation.

To learn more about IRC, check out these sources:

✦ **The official IRC home page in Finland:** www.funet.fi/~irc (where IRC was invented)

✦ **The New IRC user's page:** www.newircusers.com

✦ **The Usenet newsgroup:** alt.irc

✦ **The IRC FAQ:** www.irchelp.org

Getting ICQ

ICQ, pronounced "I seek you," is a popular program that lets you chat and exchange messages and files with other ICQ users. Developed by an Israeli company, Mirabilis, and sold to AOL, ICQ has more than 20,000,000 users. Even though ICQ is now owned by AOL, ICQ doesn't let you communicate with AOL chat or Instant Messages. You can download ICQ from www.icq.com or www.tucows.com.

For more information on ICQ, check out *ICQ For Dummies,* by Peter Weverka and published by IDG Books Worldwide, Inc.

ICQ asks a number of personal questions for marketing purposes when you first register. You don't have to answer the questions to use ICQ. Parents should review the questions with their kids before letting their kids sign up.

Web-Based Chatting

A number of sites on the World Wide Web let you chat by using just your Web browser. Sometimes, a Java applet is loaded automatically. Fewer people use Web-based chat than either America Online or IRC, although Web-based chat is becoming more popular. New chat sites appear all the time.

Chat rooms

Web-based chatting is similar to arriving in a crowded room at a party where clusters of people, all in the same room, are following different conversations. When you first join a chat room, like a party, the conversation is already under way (see Figure 6-4). You just need to figure out which *thread* of conversation you want to follow, get up to speed on what everyone is saying, and then join in. People respond who are interested in commenting or have advice to offer.

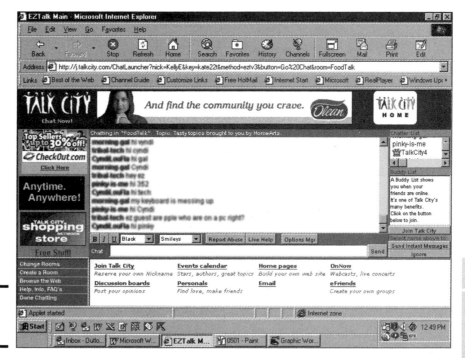

Figure 6-4: A Talk City chat room.

Book III Chapter 6

Newsgroups, Chat, and Other Internet Communication

No matter what topic you're interested in, you'll probably have no problem locating a chat room. Common topics include autos, computers, family, health, and sports, among many others.

Discussion boards

Discussion boards are slower paced than chat rooms (see preceding section). Like chat rooms, discussion boards revolve around one specific topic, such as relationships, family, or music. Discussion boards differ from chat rooms, however, in that they don't take place in real time. You click a category that piques your interest, and a list of subcategories appears (see Figure 6-5). When you choose a subcategory under the main category, you see that the discussion becomes even more focused. When you reach a discussion that interests you, post a message and return to the board later to see how others have responded.

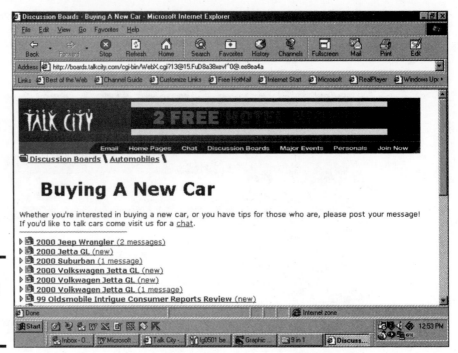

Figure 6-5:
The Buying
a New Car
discussion
board.

Accessing via a Web browser

If you've never participated in Web-based chatting and don't know where to begin, this section is for you. You may want to start with one (or all) of these three free communities. Just fire up your Web browser and head to these sites:

✦ **Excite Talk:** Located at `www.excite.com/channel/chat`, Excite Chat offers chat rooms and message boards on the following topics: Autos, Computers, Education, Entertainment, Family, Games, Health, Home, Lifestyle, Money, People, Politics, Relationships, Shopping, Sports, and Travel. Before you participate in anything, you need to register. To do so, you simply click the Sign Me Up button and follow the on-screen instructions. If you're already a member, you're prompted to sign in.

✦ **Talk City:** Located at `www.talkcity.com`, Talk City offers chat rooms and message boards on about 20 common topics, including Cities & Travel, Ethnic & Lifestyles, and Women. Like Excite Chat, you need to register or sign in before you can participate.

✦ **Yahoo!:** Yahoo! may be better known as a search engine, but it, too, boasts chatting — even voice chatting! — and discussion boards. Go to `www.yahoo.com` and click Chat. After you sign in, you can chat away.

Of course, free chatting comes at a price. Occasionally, on any of these three sites, advertising floating across your screen may interrupt your chat. In addition, advertising usually appears at the top and/or bottom of your screen.

Internet Telephony

The Internet doesn't limit you to communication by typing. Today's powerful personal computers and fast modems let you send voice and even pictures over the Net. Best of all, no long-distance charges apply — even for calls overseas. You do need a microphone or headset, a fast PC with a sound card, and a 28.8 Kbps or faster modem. You need the proper phone software, of course, although those packages cost less than a couple of months' worth of phone bills.

So why isn't everyone calling on the Internet yet? Here's the bad news:

✦ Internet phone software is complicated to set up and use.

✦ At best, the sound quality is not that great, and it can be downright poor.

✦ Both parties must have the equipment and have their computers turned on, which can be tricky to arrange.

✦ Internet phone software may not work well if you're behind a firewall (if your computer is connected to a corporate LAN, for example).

✦ Some packages require you to know the other person's IP address to make connections.

✦ Different software packages often don't work with one another.

✦ If Internet telephony is widely adopted, it will place a big strain on the Net and may raise the ire of phone regulators, especially in countries with state telephone monopolies.

Internet telephony will get better, though. The technology is improving all the time, with new features such as these:

✦ **Whiteboards:** Special screens that both parties can see and draw on

✦ **Text windows:** Enable you to write notes that others can see, similar to online chat

✦ **Conference calls:** Enable more than two people to talk together

✦ **Voice mail and voice e-mail:** Enables callers to leave a message at the beep

✦ **Video phone:** Displays the other person's image on-screen in a small picture that changes at rates as fast as several times per second

You can see up-to-date information about the fast-changing field of Internet telephony at the following Web sites:

+ **Voice on the Net:** www.von.com

+ **Iphone:** www.pulver.com/iphone

+ **Telirati:** www.phonezone.com/telirati

Using FTP to Transfer Files

The Internet copies files between your computer and other computers on the Internet by using a facility known as *FTP (file transfer protocol).* You connect your computer to an *FTP server,* an Internet host computer that stores files for transfer. Many publicly accessible FTP servers enable you to log in and retrieve a wide variety of files, including software, text files, and graphics files. On these systems, rather than log on with your own name and password, you log on as *anonymous* and use your e-mail address or the word *guest* as the password. A common use of FTP is to obtain updated drivers for your printer, video card, and other system components.

Your browser can usually log on as *anonymous* for you, download the file you want, log off, and unpack the file — all automatically. URLs that start with ftp:// take you to an FTP site.

Using FTP programs

Sometimes, you may want more control over the file transfer process — for example, when you're uploading files to a remote Web server. If your ISP uses a PPP (Point-to-Point Protocol) account, which enables your computer to connect directly to the Internet (most dial-up ISPs use PPP), you can use Winsock TCP/IP software to move files on the Internet. Check out WS_FTP Pro 6.5, from Ipswitch, Inc., at http://www.ipswitch.com.

On America Online and CompuServe, go to keyword ftp. On Unix systems, type **ftp** followed by the host name of the server; type your logon name and password for that server when prompted.

Navigating files and directories

Most Winsock TCP/IP programs use a full-screen interface that displays in one window the files in the current directory on the FTP server (the "Remote system") and in another window the files on your own computer (the "Local system"). Before you can transfer files, you want to display in one window the files to transfer and in the other window the directory you want to transfer them to.

To change directories, click the name of the directory you want to move files to in the FTP window. If you want to move to the parent directory of the current directory, click the ᴛ᠇ entry on the directory list. Depending on your browser, you may also see a hyperlink (such as Up to higher level directory) that you can click to move to the parent directory.

In Unix, you type FTP commands that are similar to standard Unix file-management commands. (If you're familiar with DOS, you may recognize some of them as the DOS commands for these same tasks.) To change to a directory, for example, you type **cd** followed by the name of the directory. To see a list of the files in a directory, type **dir**. To move to the parent directory of the current directory, you can type the **cd ..** command.

Uploading and downloading files

If you use an FTP program with a full-screen interface (such as WS_FTP), click all the names of the files that you want to transmit. Click the ASCII button if the files contain only text; otherwise, click the Binary button. Then click the transfer button that shows the arrow pointing from the system where the files are located to the system where you want to move them.

On Unix, type **ascii** if the files to be transferred contain only text; type **image** or **binary** if the files contain something other than text. To download a file from the other computer to your computer, type **get** followed by the name of the file. To upload a file from your computer to the other computer, type **put** followed by the name of the file.

After you finish copying files, disconnect from the FTP server.

+ If you're using a graphics FTP program, click the Disconnect button or choose Disconnect from the menu.

+ If you're using the Unix FTP program, type **quit**.

Chapter 7: Getting Started with Web Publishing

In This Chapter

✔ **Understanding the different kinds of Web sites**

✔ **Creating a Web site step by step**

✔ **Determining what to include on a Web site**

✔ **Finding space for your Web site**

*T*his chapter presents some basic information to help you get started with setting up your own Web site. You discover the basic steps for creating a Web site, what every Web site should include (and on every page in the site), how to effectively organize the pages in your site, and where to find space for your Web site. In addition, this chapter presents some recommendations and guidelines for creating a successful Web site.

For more detailed information about the process of designing and creating Web pages, see *Creating Web Pages For Dummies,* 5th Edition by Bud Smith and Arthur Bebak (published by IDG Books Worldwide, Inc.).

Understanding the Different Kinds of Web Sites

This section describes three very broad categories of Web sites. The site that you intend to publish probably falls into one of these three categories: personal home pages, company Web sites, and special-interest Web sites.

Personal home pages

Just about anyone with access to the Internet can create a personal home page. The simplest personal home pages contain basic information, such as your name, information about your family, your occupation, your hobbies, and any special interests you may have. You can also throw in one or more pictures. Links to your favorite pages on the Web are also commonly included. If you're looking for a job, include your resume on your site.

Company Web sites

More and more companies are joining the Web bandwagon. Even mom-and-pop pizza parlors are putting up Web pages. The simplest corporate Web pages provide basic information about a company, such as a description of the company's products or services, phone numbers, and so on. A more elaborate corporate Web site can include any or all of the following:

✦ An online catalog that enables users to see detailed information about products and services. The catalog may also include pictures and prices.

✦ Online ordering, which enables Internet users to actually place orders over the Internet.

✦ Lists of frequently asked questions (FAQs) about the company's products or services.

✦ Online support, where a customer can leave a question about a problem he or she is having with a product and receive a reply within a day or so.

✦ Articles and reviews of the company's products and press releases.

✦ Employment opportunities with the company.

✦ Biographies of company employees.

Special interest Web sites

Many of the most interesting Web sites are devoted to special interests. For example, if you are involved with a youth soccer league, you may want to create a Web page that includes team rosters, schedules, and standings. Or you can create a Web page that focuses on Christmas decorating. The list of possible topics for a special-interest Web site is limitless.

Creating a Web Site

Although you don't have to be obsessively methodical about creating a Web site, it's a good idea to follow at least the three basic steps described in this section. First, go over these helpful suggestions for creating a Web site.

Guidelines for creating a successful Web site

When you are planning the content, design, and layout of your Web site, keep the following guidelines in mind so that you create a Web site that people want to visit over and over again:

✦ **Offer something useful on every page.** Too many Web sites are filled with fluff — pages that don't have any useful content. Avoid creating pages that are just steps along the way to truly useful information. Instead, strive to include something useful on every Web site page.

✦ **Check out the competition.** Find out what other Web sites similar to yours have to offer. Don't create a "me too" Web site that offers nothing but information that already is available elsewhere. Instead, strive for unique information that can be found only on your Web site.

✦ **Make it look good.** No matter how good the information at your Web site is, people will stay away if your site looks as if you spent no more than five minutes on design and layout. Yes, substance is more important than style. But an ugly Web site turns people away, whereas an attractive Web site draws people in.

✦ **Proof it carefully.** If every third word in your Web site is misspelled, people will assume that the information on your Web site is as unreliable as your spelling. If your HTML editor has a spell-check feature, use it and proof your work carefully before you post it to the Web. In fact, you may want to consider having someone else proofread it for you; a fresh pair of eyes can catch mistakes that you may overlook.

✦ **Provide links to other sites.** Some of the best pages on the Internet are links to other Web sites that have information about a particular topic. The time you spend creating a directory of links to other sites with information similar or complementary to your own is worth it.

✦ **Keep it current.** Internet users don't frequent sites that contain old, out-of-date information. Make sure that you frequently update your Web pages with current information. Obviously, some Web pages need to be changed more than others. For example, if you maintain a Web page that lists the team standings for a soccer league, you have to update the page after every game. On the other hand, a page that features medieval verse romances doesn't need to be updated very often.

If your Web site contains links to other Web sites, frequently check all those links to make sure that they're still valid.

✦ **Don't tie it to a certain browser.** Exploiting the cool new features of the latest and greatest Web browser is a good idea. But don't do so at the expense of users who may be using the *other* browser, or at the expense of users who are still working with an earlier version. Some people still use browsers that don't support frames. Make sure that any pages in which you incorporate the advanced features of newer browsers work well with older browsers as well. In addition, it's always a good idea to include a statement on your home page stating which browser provides the optimum viewing for the pages.

✦ **Don't make hardware assumptions.** Remember that not everyone has a 21-inch monitor and a high-speed cable-modem connection to the Internet. Design your Web site so that it can be used by the poor sap who is stuck with a 14-inch monitor and a 28.8 Kbps modem.

✦ **Publicize it.** Few people stumble across your Web sites by accident. If you want people to visit your Web site, you have to publicize it. Make sure that your site is listed in the major search engines, such as Yahoo! and Lycos. You can also promote your site by putting its address on all your advertisements, correspondence, business cards, e-mail, and so on.

Step 1: Planning your Web site

Start by making a plan for your Web site. If all you want to do is create a simple, one-page "Here I Am" personal Web site, you don't really need to make a plan. But for a more elaborate Web site, you should plan the content of the site before you start creating actual pages.

One good way to plan a Web site is to sketch a simple diagram on paper showing the various pages you want to create, with arrows showing the links between the pages. Alternatively, you can create an outline that represents your entire site. You can be as detailed or as vague as you want.

Step 2: Creating your Web pages

You can take several different approaches to creating the pages that comprise your Web site. If the mere thought of "programming" gives you hives, you can use a simple Web page editor to create your Web pages. Both Microsoft Internet Explorer and Netscape Navigator come with basic Web page editors that enable you to create simple Web pages without any programming. You can also purchase inexpensive programs for creating complete Web sites. One of the best known Web site development programs is Microsoft FrontPage 2000.

On the other hand, if you dream in Boolean, feel free to fire up NotePad and start banging away HTML code from scratch. You have to learn the intricacies of using HTML codes to format your Web pages, but you'll gain satisfaction from knowing that you did it the hard way.

If you need help writing HTML code, check out *HTML 4 For Dummies,* 3rd Edition, by Ed Tittel, Natanya Pitts, and Chelsea Valentine (published by IDG Books Worldwide, Inc.).

Step 3: Publishing your Web pages

After your Web pages are complete, it's time to publish them on the Internet. First, you have to find a Web server that can host your Web pages. The section "Finding Space for Your Web Site," later in this chapter, gives you ideas for finding a Web server. Next, you copy your Web pages to the Web server. Finally, you can publicize your Web site by cataloging it in the major search services.

What to Include on Every Web Site

Although every Web site is different, you can find certain common elements on most Web sites. The following sections describe the items you should consider including on your Web site.

Home page

Every Web site should include a home page that serves as an entry point into the site. The home page is the first page that most users see when they visit your site. As a result, devote considerable time and energy to making sure that your home page makes a good first impression. Place an attractive title at the top of the page. Remember that most users have to scroll down to see your entire home page. They see just the top of the page first, so make sure that the title is visible.

After the title, include a site menu that enables users to access the content available on your Web site. You can create a simple text menu or a fancy graphics-based menu in which the user can click on different parts of the image to go to different pages. However, if you use this type of menu, called an *image map,* be sure to provide a text menu as an alternative for users who don't want to wait for the image map to download or who have turned off graphic downloads.

Here are a few other goodies that you may want to include on your home page.

**Book III
Chapter 7**

**Getting Started with
Web Publishing**

✦ **An indication of new content that is available on your Web site.** Users who return to your site often want to know when new data is available.

✦ **The date your site was last updated.**

✦ **A copyright notice.** You can include a link to a separate copyright page where you spell out whether others can copy the information you place on your site.

✦ **A reminder to bookmark the page so that users can return easily.**

✦ **A hit counter.** If users see that 4 million people have visited your site since last Tuesday, they automatically assume that yours must be a hot site. On the other hand, if users see that only three people have visited since Truman was president, they'll yawn and leave quickly. If your site isn't very popular, you may want to skip the hit counter.

Avoid placing a huge amount of graphics on your home page. Your home page is the first page on your Web site most users see. If it takes more than 15 seconds for your page to load, users may lose patience and skip your site altogether.

Cover page

A cover page displays temporarily before your home page displays. Cover pages usually feature a flashy logo or animation. On most cover pages, the user must click the logo or some other element on the page to enter the site's home page. You can also program the page so that it automatically jumps to the home page after a certain amount of time elapses — say 10 or 15 seconds.

Many users become annoyed with cover pages, especially those cover pages that take more than a few seconds to download and display. Think carefully about whether the splashy cover page actually enhances your site or is more of an annoyance.

Site map

If your site has a lot of pages, you may want to include a site map. A site map is a detailed menu that provides links to every page on the site. By using the site map, a user can bypass intermediate menus and go directly to the pages that interest him or her.

Contact information

Be sure that your site includes information about how to contact you or your company. You can easily include your e-mail address as a link on the home page. When the user clicks this link, most Web browsers fire up the user's e-mail program with your e-mail address already filled in.

Help page

If your Web site contains more than a few pages, consider providing a help page that provides information about how to use the site. The help page can include information about how to navigate the site as well as information on how you obtained the information for the site, how often the site is updated, how someone can contribute to the site, and so on.

FAQ

Frequently Asked Questions (FAQ) pages are among the most popular sources of information on the Internet. You can organize your own FAQ page on any topic you want. Just come up with a list of questions and provide the answers. Or solicit questions and/or answers from readers of your page.

Related links

At some sites, the most popular page is the links page, which provides a list of links to related sites. As the compiler of your own links page, you can do something that search engines, such as Yahoo! cannot. You can pick and choose the links that you want to include, and you can provide your own commentary about the information on each site.

Discussion group

A discussion group adds interactivity to your Web site by enabling visitors to post articles that can be read and responded to by other users. Other similar Web page elements that encourage interactivity include a feedback page or a guest book. Those who visit your Web site can use these elements to comment on your site.

What to Include on Every Page

Although every Web page should contain unique and useful information, all Web pages must contain the following three elements:

Title

Place a title at the top of every page. The title should identify not just the specific contents of the page but also the Web site itself. A specific title is important because some users may not enter your site through your home page. Instead, they may go directly to one of the content pages in your site.

Navigation links

All the pages of your Web site should have a consistent set of navigation links. At the minimum, provide a link to your home page on every page in your site. In addition, you may want to include links to the next and previous pages if your pages have a logical sequential organization.

Author and copyright information

Every page should also include author credits and a copyright notice. Because users can enter your site by going directly to any page, placing the authorship and copyright notices on only the home page is not sufficient.

Organizing the Content

The following sections describe several popular ways to organize the information on your Web site.

Sequential organization

In sequential organization, you simply organize your pages so that they follow one after another, like the pages in a book, as shown in Figure 7-1. On each page, provide navigation links that enable the user to go to the next page, go to the previous page, or return directly to the first page.

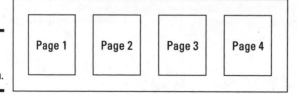

Figure 7-1:
Sequential
organization.

Hierarchical organization

With a hierarchical organization, you organize your Web pages into a hierarchy, categorizing the pages according to subject matter. The top-most page serves as a menu that enables users to access other pages directly (see Figure 7-2). On each page you should provide a navigation link that returns the user to the menu.

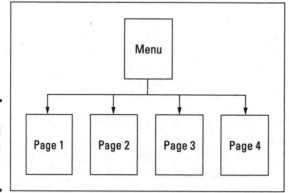

Figure 7-2:
Hierarchical
organization
with one
menu level.

You can include more than one level of menu pages, as shown in Figure 7-3. However, don't overdo the menus. Most users become frustrated with Web sites that have unnecessary menus, in which each menu has only two or three choices. When a menu has more than a dozen choices, however, consider splitting the menu into two or more separate menus.

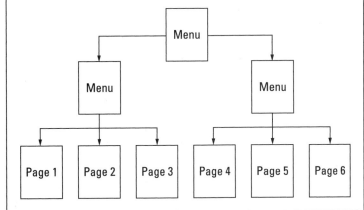

Figure 7-3:
Hierarchical
organization
with
multiple
menu levels.

Combination sequential and hierarchical organization

Many Web sites use a combination of sequential and hierarchical organization, in which a menu enables users to access content pages that contain sequential links to one another, as in Figure 7-4. In a combination organization style, each content page includes a link to the next page in sequence, in addition to a link back to the menu. The menu page contains links to the pages that mark the start of each section of pages.

Book III
Chapter 7

Getting Started with
Web Publishing

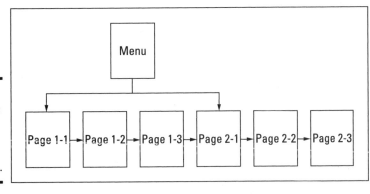

Figure 7-4:
Combination
sequential
and
hierarchical
organization.

Web organization

Some Web sites have pages that are connected with links that defy a sequential or hierarchical pattern. In extreme cases, every page in the site is linked to every other page, creating a structure that resembles a web, as shown in Figure 7-5.

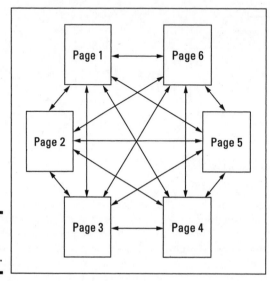

Figure 7-5:
Web
organization.

Finding Space for Your Web Site

If you don't have a home for your Web site, the following sections give you some ideas for where to find space for your Web pages.

Internet Service Providers

If you access the Internet through an Internet Service Provider (ISP), you probably already have space set aside to set up a home page. Most ISPs give each user a small amount of disk space for Web pages included in their monthly service. The space may be limited to a few megabytes, but that should be enough to set up several pages. You can probably get additional disk space if you need it for a modest charge. You may also have to pay additional fees for any type of commercial use on your site. Your ISP can give you step-by-step instructions for copying your Web pages to the ISP's Web server.

Online services

Two of the major online services — CompuServe and America Online — let you publish your own Web pages.

CompuServe (CSi) lets you publish your Web page in an area called *Our World,* which already has more than 100,000 home pages. Our World includes authoring tools that make creating Web pages easy. CSi limits each user to 5MB of disk space. CompuServe also has a service called CSi BusinessWeb that provides 30MB of disk space and your own domain name (such as www.mycompany.com) for $79/month, plus a $50 setup fee.

America Online (AOL) also lets you publish your own Web page. Each AOL member can have up to 7 screen names, and each screen name is limited to 2MB of disk space. (For more information on building a home page in AOL, see Book VI, Chapter 4.)

Free Web servers

If you can't find a home for your Web page at your Internet Service Provider or your online service, consider using a free Web server to host your site.

The best-known free home page service is GeoCities, which hosts more than 1 million home pages. Each free Web site can use up to 11MB of disk space. The only limitation is that you must include a banner advertisement at the top of your Web page and a link to the GeoCities home page at the bottom of your page. (For $4.95 per month, you can eliminate the advertising and increase your space allotment to 25MB.) For more information, go to www.geocities.com.

Many other free home page services are available, although most cater to specific types of home pages, such as those for artists, churches, chambers of commerce, and so on. To find a good directory of free home page services, go to Yahoo! (www.yahoo.com) and search for *Free Web Pages.*

Index

continued

Book IV

Microsoft Works 6

The 5th Wave   By Rich Tennant

"Can't I just give you riches or something?"

Contents at a Glance

Chapter 1: Getting Familiar with Microsoft Works

In This Chapter

▶ **Discovering what's inside Works**

▶ **Getting your programs started**

▶ **Mastering the Task Launcher**

▶ **Using menus and toolbars**

▶ **Switching and exiting programs**

▶ **Asking for help**

*M*icrosoft Works is a nice program. It lets you do what you want, simply and quickly, without much to-do. Sure, you may not have a lot of fancy options like some of the other, more advanced programs, but if you're a basic user, you'll probably find your needs more than fulfilled with this useful program. In fact, you may even find several options that you have no desire to use! (Who needs fancier options?) Whether you want to write, crunch numbers, make lists, or plan, Works is the program for you.

What's Included with Microsoft Works 6?

If you like to do a lot of different tasks by using one neat program, you're in luck! Microsoft Works 6 offers a virtual cornucopia of goodies to its users, from a word processor and spreadsheet, all the way to e-mail and browser software. And drop that planner — you won't need it anymore now that you have access to Works' handy-dandy calendar!

The following sections give you a basic rundown of the tools and *utilities* — tech-speak for programs with a very specialized function — you'll encounter while working in Works. For more details about the workings of each program, see its respective chapter.

Word processor

The Works word processor works just like any other word processor. If you want to write, this tool is your destination. You can create documents, letters, invitations, newsletters, you name it — if you can type it, you can create it.

If you're the literary type, make sure to check out Chapters 2 and 3 in Book IV so that you can find out how to use the word processor to do all that cool writing stuff.

Spreadsheet

If you're a list or numbers person, then you'll be visiting the Works spreadsheet a lot. This friendly tool lets you crunch numbers to your heart's content and plan, plan, plan all you want. And if you hate math, then you'll be happy to discover a tool that can do all the dirty work for you.

Chapter 4 in Book III gives you the inside scoop on the spreadsheet and how it works.

Database

If a big wave of satisfaction rushes over you every time you're able to look around a room and see everything in the correct place, then you'll probably be a big fan of the database. This little tool lets you organize whatever you want — and then organize it some more. You can store almost anything you want in this database as well as create forms and reports to impress your boss.

For more information on the database, see Book IV, Chapter 5.

Calendar

Are you always running 5 minutes . . . errr, 15 minutes . . . late? Constantly scheduling yourself to be in two places at once? And forgetting important business meetings? Then the Works Calendar utility is for you.

Using the Calendar, you'll be able to keep track of your life — both personal and professional — in a streamlined way. You can even arrange for a little reminder to pop up on your screen to warn you of an upcoming appointment. (Okay, so you have to be at your computer to actually see it!) And when you finally show up on time and on schedule, your coworkers and friends will be in awe . . . all because of Works Calendar utility.

For more on mastering your calendar, see Book IV, Chapter 6.

Address Book

I know it's around here somewhere. I mean, I remember writing down that darn address on my bright yellow sticky note, which I piled on all those other darn bright yellow sticky notes with addresses scrawled on them. Now where did it go?

This now-just-where-did-that-address-go problem will be a thing of the past once you start taking advantage of Works' Address Book utility. Type it in once and then forget-about-it!

For more on the workings of the Address Book, see Book IV, Chapter 6.

Outlook Express

Can you imagine going a day without e-mail? And the think-of-everything creators of Works 6 made sure that you didn't have to, either. That's why you'll find Outlook Express ready and waiting for your fast-flying typing fingers (or maybe you use the hunt-and-peck method).

For more on composing e-mail with Outlook Express, see Book III, Chapter 2.

Internet Explorer browser software

With a click, click here, and a click, click there . . . oh, sorry. You know how it is when you get carried away searching the Internet. You don't? Then you definitely want to check out Book III, Chapter 4 so that you find out all about the Internet Explorer browser software included in Works 6. Enjoy!

Portfolio

Are you one of those people who has all your photo albums up to date? (Okay, if you just laughed here, we're with you!) If you're a picture maniac and you actually do something with those pictures, then check out Works' new Portfolio. By using this utility, you can organize all your photo and art clippings so that you can arrange them in any document you'd like. Now how's that for photo archiving at its finest?

Due to space limitations, this book doesn't cover the Portfolio application.

Starting Programs

If you've used another Microsoft application, then it won't be too hard for you to figure out how to start Works; it operates just like Microsoft's other programs. But if you're new to Microsoft products or just need a refresher course, then check out the following sections.

Starting from an icon

When you installed Works, the Microsoft Works icon should have appeared on your desktop. To start Works:

1. **Double-click the Microsoft Works icon.**

The Microsoft Works Task Launcher, shown in Figure 1-1, appears.

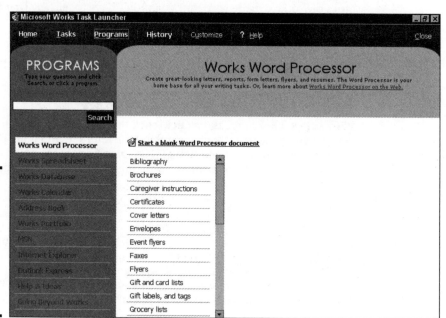

Figure 1-1:
The Task Launcher makes it easy for you to launch different Works programs.

2. **On the Task Launcher screen, simply click the program, utility, or task of choice, and you're off and running.**

If you've never used the Task Launcher, see the section "Using the Task Launcher," later in this chapter.

Starting from the Start menu

If you're more of a menu person or somewhere along the way your Microsoft Works icon disappeared, don't despair. Like every other Microsoft program, you have the option of starting Works by using the Start menu. Here's how:

1. **Click Start.**

2. **Click Programs from the menu that appears.**

A menu containing all the programs on your computer appears.

3. **Slide down to the Microsoft Works menu choice.**

If you don't immediately see Microsoft Works in your list, then simply click the down arrow on the bottom of the menu. (My, you have a lot of programs on your computer!)

Another menu appears, listing your Works program and utility options.

4. **Click the program of your choice.**

Works takes you to the program you chose.

Using the Task Launcher

The Works Task Launcher is a nice little tool that coordinates all the programs and utilities in Works. Instead of having to start each program individually, you can now start Works and choose from your Works programs in one centralized location.

Not sure what program you want to use? No sweat. The Task Launcher even gives you descriptions of common tasks in each program. You can't go wrong!

The Task Launcher appears when you start Microsoft Works. (If you've already started Works and want to use the Task Launcher, choose File⇨New from the menu bar.) To use the Task Launcher:

1. **Choose the program of your choice from the Task Launcher list on the left side of the screen.**

A list of common tasks accomplished by the program appears, as shown in Figure 1-2.

2. **Click the link to create a new document or click the task you want to accomplish.**

A description appears.

3. **If that blurb sounds like what you want to do, then click Start This Task.**

Now's your chance to be creative!

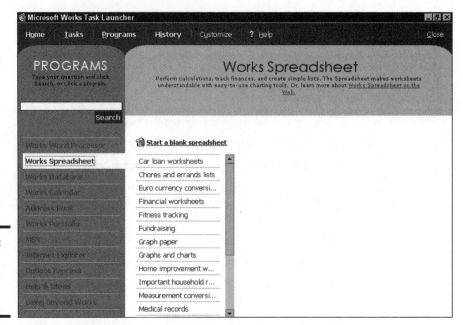

Figure 1-2:
What do
you want
do? Take
your pick!

Getting to Know the Menus and Toolbars

Whether you're a word person or a picture person, you're in luck. Works gives you two main ways to navigate around its programs: menus and toolbars. Menus are the words that appear across the top of your screen. Toolbars are the buttons underneath the menus. Figure 1-3 shows you both menus and toolbars.

Navigating menus or toolbars is fairly simple to do. Simply click the menu you want to use, and another menu appears. From this secondary menu, click a command. If another menu appears, click a command again.

Using a toolbar button is even easier. (It's knowing which button you want to use that's harder!) This time, you just click once — on the button that performs the task you want to accomplish — and you're done.

In Book IV, we walk you through the word processor toolbar in Chapter 2, the spreadsheet toolbar in Chapter 4, and the database toolbar in Chapter 5. We also give you specific menu commands throughout the book. If you don't know which menu item or toolbar button to click, look up the task you want to accomplish in the index and then flip to the page where we tell you how.

Menu bar   Toolbars

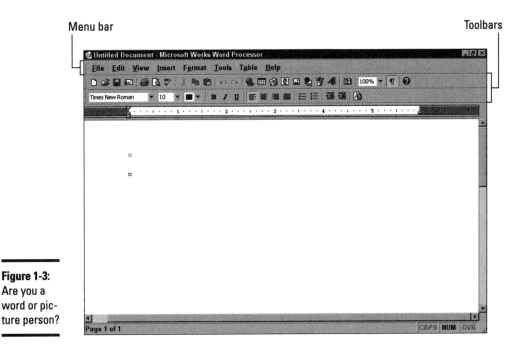

Figure 1-3:
Are you a
word or pic-
ture person?

Switching Among Programs

Say that you're working in the word processor and you get the sudden urge
to make a spreadsheet. No problem! Works makes opening and switching
between multiple programs easy. Simply choose File⇨New to return to the
Task Launcher and then click the program of your choice in the left column.
Have fun!

You can press Alt+Tab to toggle between Works and other open programs in
Microsoft Windows.

Exiting Programs

Exiting programs is a simple task; in fact, if you really think about it, you'll
probably be able to figure it out on your own. Simply choose File⇨Exit. (Get
it? Your document is a file, and you want to exit it.)

A lot of tasks in Works (and other Microsoft programs) are intuitive after
you get used to the system. If you want to do something that involves the
entire document (file, in Microsoft speak), such as printing, closing, or
saving, then click the File menu. Chances are, the task you want will appear
in the list. If you want to do something related to formatting, then pick the
Format menu.

Getting Help

Okay, while you may be able to figure out some things in Works by great guesswork, there's going to come a time when you have to ask for help. Fortunately, Microsoft made it easy for you to ask for help. In fact, whenever you open a Works program, the Works Help window greets you on the right side of the screen.

The Help screen even displays possible questions you may have relevant to the task that you are currently working on. For example, you can open a new word-processor document, and Help anticipates that your questions will center around that topic. If Help is wrong, you even have the opportunity to type your question in the blank Answer Wizard section at the top of the screen and click Search.

Can't find the Help window? Then someone must have closed it. For Help to make its appearance, simply click the Help button in the word processor or Calendar, choose Help⇨Works Help from the menu bar, or press F1.

Find that handy-dandy Help window annoying? Then close it. Simply click the X in the top-right corner of the Help window. Now you have space! If you decide you need it, follow the directions in the preceding paragraph.

Or, if you've finally found the inside scoop on what you were looking for, but you find the width of the Help screen annoying, then enlarge it. Simply click the Resize Help button next to the Close button in the right corner of your screen, and your Help screen almost doubles in width. When you're done, click the button again, and it shrinks back to its original size.

Listing the Help contents

If you're not sure what you want to ask, try browsing the Help Contents by clicking the Contents buttons. The screen appears, containing an alphabetical list of all topics covered in Help. Simply click the folder of the category that sounds interesting, as shown in Figure 1-4, and a list of any subtopics appears. Keep going until you find what you want. As soon as the Contents area is as specific as it can be, you'll see a series of links. Simply click the link and find out everything that you want to know about that particular topic.

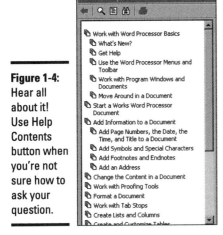

Figure 1-4:
Hear all
about it!
Use Help
Contents
button when
you're not
sure how to
ask your
question.

Using the Help index

 Another Help option is to click the Index button. Using the Help index, you can type a word, such as Table, that you want to find out about. Or, if you're not feeling too creative, you can simply choose from the alphabetical list of all Help topics available. (Don't forget to double-click.) No matter which method you use, a list of topics appears in the Topics found.

Chapter 2: Using the Word Processor

In This Chapter

- Mastering the word processor toolbar
- Starting a document from scratch
- Maximizing the use of TaskWizards
- Working with existing documents
- Saving and closing your documents
- Printing your masterpieces
- Getting fancy with mail merge

The Works word processor provides some magical, timesaving shortcuts. You can use TaskWizards to create documents without all the work, take advantage of the Undo feature, and even do mail merges at the drop of a hat. In this chapter, we let you in on all the secrets. After you try these shortcuts, you'll never use the long way again!

Getting to Know the Word Processor Toolbar

In this day and age, every timesaving shortcut is welcome. And that's why you'll be especially fond of the word processor toolbars. Instead of scrolling and clicking through several menu commands, the toolbars enable you to click just once to perform common actions.

The word processor has two toolbars — the Standard toolbar and the Formatting toolbar. The Standard toolbar focuses more on daily tasks, such as creating documents, saving, and sending e-mail, while the Formatting toolbar is only for formatting needs.

Tables 2-1 and 2-2 show you which buttons on each toolbar match up with each task.

If you're using the Formatting toolbar, you need to highlight the text you want to format before you click the appropriate button.

Table 2-1	Word Processor Standard Toolbar Buttons
Button	**Function**
	Creates a new document.
	Opens a document.
	Saves a document.
	Lets you e-mail the document.
	Prints the document.
	Gives you a preview of the document.
	Spell-checks and grammar-checks the document.
	Cuts highlighted text.
	Copies highlighted text.
	Pastes the text you've cut or copied to the Clipboard.
	Undoes the action.
	Redoes the action.
	Inserts a hyperlink.
	Inserts a table.
	Inserts a spreadsheet.
	Inserts clip art.
	Inserts a picture.

Button	Function
	Launches Microsoft Draw so that you can create a new drawing.
	Launches Microsoft Paint so that you can paint your drawing.
	Lets you create WordArt.
	Accesses your Address Book.
100%	Zooms the size of your page in or out.
¶	Enables you to view or hide formatting codes, such as paragraph marks.
?	Accesses Help.

Table 2-2	Word Processor Formatting Toolbar Buttons
Button	*Function*
Times New Roman	Changes the font.
10	Changes the font size.
	Changes the font color.
B	Bolds text.
I	Italicizes text.
U	Underlines text.
	Left aligns text.
	Centers text.

Book IV
Chapter 2

Using the Word
Processor

(continued)

Table 2-2 *(continued)*

Button	Function
	Right aligns text.
	Justifies text.
	Creates a bulleted list.
	Creates numbered list.
	Increases text indent.
	Decreases text indent.
	Accesses the Format Gallery.

Creating a Document

Sometimes you just want to start anew. If you find yourself feeling that way, you're in luck. You can create a brand-new document in the Works word processor in one of two ways: by creating a blank document by using the Task Launcher or by using a TaskWizard.

Creating a blank document

Probably the easiest way to create a new document is to use the Task Launcher. (See Book IV, Chapter 1 for more on the Task Launcher.) After you start Works and you're in the Task Launcher, simply click Works Word Processor. Then click Start a Blank Word Processor Document, and a new document appears.

Using a TaskWizard

If you use the Task Launcher very much at all, you may have wondered about the list that appears below the Start a Blank Word Processor Document. These TaskWizards are new documents that already contain for-matting — so you don't have to waste the time! For example, you can create customized gift labels and tags simply by clicking one of the TaskWizards, as shown in Figure 2-1. The TaskWizard walks you through each step of the process.

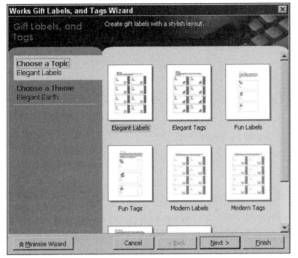

Figure 2-1:
Customized
gift labels
and tags
don't have
to take a lot
of time to
create,
thanks to
TaskWizards.

To start a TaskWizard:

1. **Go to the Task Launcher.**

2. **Click the program or utility you want to use.**

3. **Click the TaskWizard you want to use.**

4. **Follow each step of the TaskWizard, making sure to click Next after you complete each step.**

5. **After you're done, click Finish.**

Now that saved a lot of time and effort, didn't it?

You can also access the TaskWizards by clicking the Tasks button at the top of the page. A list of task categories appears on the left side of the screen. Click the category you're interested in and then click the task you want to try. Then click the Start button, and you're good to go.

Works also has simpler versions of TaskWizards. Instead of creating a finished, formatted document, these simpler wizards walk you through a process. However, the wizards work the same way as TaskWizards.

Opening a Document

After you've been working in the word processor a while, you'll have several documents that you've created or that others have sent to you. While you may end up forgetting about some of your creations, more than likely you will need to open most of them again. You're not limited to just one way with Works!

**Book IV
Chapter 2**

Using the Word
Processor

In the word processor

When you're working in your word processor, you have three easy ways to open files:

+ Choose File⇨Open from the menu.

+ Click the Open button on the toolbar.

+ Choose File and then choose the recently used file you want to open from the bottom of the menu.

All methods get the job done effectively!

From outside Works

If you're not working in Works, don't despair. Instead, you can simply open a word-processing file, and your program launches. You can do this in one of three ways:

+ **From the desktop:** Double-click the icon for your document on the desktop.

+ **From Windows Explorer:** Right-click on the Start button and choose Explore to open Windows Explorer. Or, if you prefer to do things the long way, click Start⇨Programs. Then click through the drives and folders until you find the document you want to open. (**Hint:** This is not the fastest way to open a file!)

+ **From the Documents menu:** If you've opened the document recently — like in the last 15 files — click Start and then choose Documents from the list that appears. Then click the document you want to open.

Editing a Document

Think you're done with that file? Not yet! You need to give it the once-over to make sure that it's indeed ready for the world. And the word processor is ready to step up and help with this editing process. If you did poorly in English, the word processor has you covered — it offers a spelling and grammar checker as well as a thesaurus to find words to impress your peers. And when you find something that you're not so proud of — say, an incoherent sentence that doesn't make sense — you have the tools on hand to remove it from the file.

Checking spelling and grammar

The word processor's spelling and grammar feature is a popular editing tool. If you want your document to be perfect, you won't want to miss this step.

Keep in mind that if a word is spelled correctly and you just used the wrong spelling for that usage — for example, *it's* for *its* or *your* for *you're* — your word processor won't always catch it. That's why it's crucial for you to proofread the document instead of relying solely on the computer.

Follow these steps to check spelling and grammar:

1. **Click the Spelling and Grammar Check button on the toolbar or choose Tools⇨Spelling and Grammar from the menu.**

   If you're document is spotless, you get an A! Spell-check tells you everything looks A-Okay. If spell-check sees anything suspicious, the Spelling and Grammar dialog box appears, as shown in Figure 2-2.

Figure 2-2: You didn't pass the spelling and grammar check with flying colors. Uh-oh!

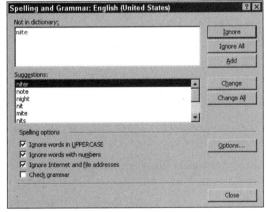

2. **Click one of the buttons on the right side of the screen, depending on what you want to do.**

   • **Ignore:** If you disagree with the suggestion, click Ignore. Spell-check ignores the word or phrase.

   • **Ignore All:** If you want spell-check to ignore the word or phrase *every* time it appears, click this button.

   • **Add:** If you want spell-check to add the word to the dictionary so that it can recognize it later, click this button.

   • **Change:** Uh-oh. If spell-check caught you and you need to make a change, select the word you really want and then click this button.

- **Change All:** Bad habits are hard to break. If you repeatedly made the same mistake, click this button to make the change throughout the document.

- **Options:** You probably won't need to use this button. Stick with the options that appear in the Spelling and Grammar dialog box. If you want spell-check to follow any of them, just make sure that you have a check in the box next to the option.

- **Close:** If you've had enough of spell-check's criticism, click the Close button to return to your document.

  When the Works word processor has had enough of you, a box appears to tell you that spell-check is done.

3. **Click OK.**

Using the thesaurus

If you truly love words or you find yourself using the same ones over and over again, check out the Works thesaurus. This nice little tool suggests better words to replace some of the ones you've chosen. It's like having a real thesaurus at your fingertips — but you don't have to turn the pages.

To use the thesaurus:

1. **Highlight the word or phrase you want to find a substitute for.**

2. **Choose Tools⇨Thesaurus from the menu.**

   The Thesaurus dialog box appears with a list of possible replacements for your word or phrase.

   If your word or phrase has multiple meanings, make sure that you choose the correct one for your purpose in the Meanings section.

3. **If you like the word or phrase in the Replace With Synonym text box, click Replace; otherwise, scroll through the list of words and click the one that you prefer.**

   Works replaces your original word or phrase.

The Thesaurus places what it considers to be the best replacement in the Replace With Synonym text box.

Selecting text

With many of Works' editing functions, one of the first steps you need to take is to *select,* or highlight, the text you want to change. And selecting text is as easy as click, click, click:

+ Click once to position the cursor.

+ Double-click to highlight a word.

+ Triple-click to select the whole paragraph.

+ Click at the beginning of the text you want to highlight and drag the cursor to the end of a section of text to select it.

+ Choose Edit⇨Select All (or press Ctrl+A) to highlight all text within a document.

And deselecting — well, that's as easy as clicking anywhere in your document.

Deleting text

Have you ever typed something and gone back later and tried to get back inside your mind? What in the world were you thinking when you typed that paragraph? What were you trying to say? And what word is *ljwkt* supposed to be?

No matter what kind of mess-up you have on hand, Microsoft Works word processor can rescue the day. Just select the text you'd like to delete and press the Delete key. The text vanishes.

Undoing mistakes

If you find yourself typing away and catching yourself repeating that same pesky mistake time and time again, then you'll like this tip: Undo it!

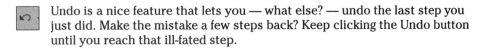 Undo is a nice feature that lets you — what else? — undo the last step you just did. Make the mistake a few steps back? Keep clicking the Undo button until you reach that ill-fated step.

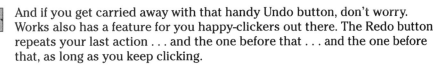 And if you get carried away with that handy Undo button, don't worry. Works also has a feature for you happy-clickers out there. The Redo button repeats your last action . . . and the one before that . . . and the one before that, as long as you keep clicking.

If you're a menu fan, choose Edit⇨Undo or Edit⇨Redo, depending on what you're trying to do.

Inserting special characters

Sometimes the keyboard just can't fulfill your needs. No problem! You can insert all types of special characters and symbols by using the word processor. To do so:

1. **Position your cursor where you want the symbol or special character to appear.**

2. **Choose Insert⇨Special Character.**

   The Insert Special Character dialog box appears, as shown in Figure 2-3.

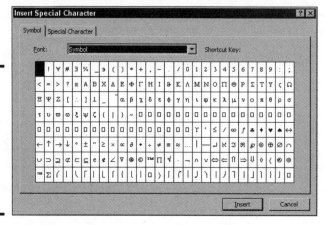

Figure 2-3: Use this dialog box to insert all kinds of funny little marks in your document.

3. **Choose the symbol or special character you want to insert.**

   If you want to insert a symbol, make sure that you're on the Symbol tab. Likewise, if you want to insert a character, make sure that you select the Special Character tab.

4. **Click Insert.**

   Your symbol or character appears in the document.

Using Find and Replace

Maybe you just realized that you made a mistake. It's somewhere in the document, but you just can't remember where. That's when the word processor's Find and Replace features are useful. The two features work basically the same, but with a few minor differences.

✦ The *Find* command only finds the word or phrase you indicate.

✦ The *Replace* command not only finds but replaces the specified word or phrase, as well. If you know you want to replace the text when you find it, this one is the most effective methods.

Here's how the Find command works:

1. **Choose Edit⇨Find.**

   The Find and Replace dialog box appears.

2. **In the Find What text box, type the word or phrase you're looking for.**

   You aren't limited to finding just words. Works also lets you replace special characters. Simply click the Special button, and a list of special characters appears.

3. **Indicate whether you'd like Works to look for the exact case you've specified and whether to look for whole words only.**

4. **Click the Find Next button.**

   If Works can't find the word or phrase specified, it lets you know. If Works finds the word or phrase, it highlights it in your document.

If you know you ultimately want to replace the word or phrase when you find it, you should use the Replace command instead of the Find command. Here's how it works:

1. **Choose Edit⇨Replace.**

   You get a dialog box similar to the one shown when you use the Find feature, but this time the Replace tab is displayed.

2. **In the Find What text box, type the word or phrase you're looking for.**

   You aren't limited to replacing just words. Works also lets you replace special characters. Simply click the Special button, and a list of special characters appears.

3. **In the Replace With text box, type the word or phrase you want to replace it with.**

4. **Indicate whether you want Works to look for the exact case you've specified and whether to look for whole words only.**

5. **Click one of the buttons at the bottom of the dialog box.**

   If you click Replace, Works replaces the first instance of the word or phrase. If you click Replace All, Works replaces all instances. And if you click Find Next, Works merely locates the word or phrase.

   Like Find, if Works can't find the word or phrase specified, it lets you know.

The Find and Replace commands work basically the same in all of the Works programs. However, in the database, you're only able to use the Find command in the Form or List views. (For more on the Works database, see Chapter 5 in Book IV.)

Using Go To

Another derivative of the Find and Replace commands, described in the preceding section, is the Go To feature. This feature enables you to look for footnotes, headers, fields, and tables. You can also go directly to a particular page in your document.

To use the Go To command:

1. **Choose Edit⇨Go To.**

   The Go To tab of the Find and Replace dialog box appears.

2. **From the Go To What list, click the item you want to go to.**

3. **Type the number of the item you want to go to.**

   For example, if you want to go to page 12, type **12**. If you want to go to footnote 22, type **22**.

4. **Click Go To, and Works locates what you're looking for.**

Viewing a Document

Works keeps a lot of things hidden from you, but it has your best interest in mind. It doesn't want to clutter up your page with more than you need. But if you're one of those types who wants to see everything, then check out the View menu. You can view toolbars and formatting, among other things, by simply clicking what you want to see. If a check appears next to the menu item, you're looking at it currently in your document. If you don't see a check, then you don't see that particular item.

To check and uncheck menu items, just drag down to the menu command and release the mouse button. If the menu item was unchecked, it's now checked; if it was checked, it's now unchecked.

Saving a Document

Save, save, save. What more important advice can we give you when it comes to working with computers that have minds of their own (or so we think!)? This little step takes just seconds but can cost you hours if you forget to do it and a power outage occurs.

To save your document:

1. Click the Save button or choose File⇨Save.

The Save As dialog box appears.

If you already saved the file, Works doesn't show you a dialog box. It simply saves the new version of the file over the old one. If you don't want that to happen, then you need to choose File⇨Save As and give your file a new name, such as *Report2,* to indicate that's its the second version of the document.

2. Using the drop-down arrow, browse the Save In box to find the folder you'd like to save your document to.

If the folder has any subfolders, they appear in the big white area in the middle of the dialog box.

3. Type your name in the File Name text box.

You want to choose a name that's descriptive of the file, so you know what it contains in the future.

4. Click Save.

Now you're ready for a thunderstorm!

Printing a Document

There's something about seeing your document on paper. It makes it so offi-cial. After you reach that point, Works makes the job easy for you. But first, save some trees — preview your document to make sure that it looks the way you want it to before you print. And, of course, don't forget to recycle your paper by using the back of it for copies that won't go to other people and then hauling it off to a recycling bin instead of a dumpster.

Previewing pages

If you think you have your document just right, but you're not sure, then you can preview it. And even if you think that it's perfect, this feature comes in handy as a quick and easy double-check.

To use Print Preview, click the Print Preview button or choose File⇨Print Preview. Either way, you're taken to the Print Preview mode, where you can check your document out to your heart's content.

To leave Print Preview, click Print if you like what you see or click Close if you decide to make some changes. Either way, you return to your document.

Printing pages

 After your document is just like you want it, you're ready to print. If you want to print your entire document, just click the Print button.

If you want to print only part of your document or you're adverse to buttons, then you can print via another route:

1. **Choose File⇨Print.**

The Print dialog box appears.

2. **In the Print Range section, indicate whether you want to print all or part of the document.**

To print part of a document, type the beginning and ending page numbers in the boxes next to the Pages option button.

3. **Indicate the number of copies you want to print.**

If it's your first time printing the document, you'll probably want to print just one, even if you used the Print Preview feature. (See the preceding section.) You never know what can go wrong!

4. **If you're printing multiple copies and you want each set to be in order, make sure that the Collate box is checked.**

Otherwise, if you're printing five copies of a 15-page document, you'll have five copies of page 1, then five copies of page 2, and so on. Why collate when you can have Works do it automatically?

5. **Click OK to print your document.**

Creating a Template

 If you've put a lot of work into your file and ended up with a masterpiece, consider making a template. That way, you can use the file as a basis for future documents.

To create a template:

1. **Open the document you want to use as the basis of your template.**

2. **Choose File⇨Save As.**

The Save As dialog box appears.

3. **Click the Template button.**

The Save As Template dialog box appears.

4. **Type a name for your template in the text box.**

   Be creative! You want the name to tell you instantly what the template creates. For example, if you created a birthday invitation, save it as Birthday, not Doc1.

5. **Click OK.**

   The next time you start the word processor, your template will appear in the TaskWizards list.

Creating a Mail Merge Document

If you want to send the same letter to a number of people or companies, you'll be happy to hear about the word processor's *mail merge* feature. When you use mail merge, you create a *source document* — the one that contains your mailing list — and combine it with a *destination document* (usually a letter).

If you're not using the Works Address Book as your source document, you need to create a source document elsewhere. More than likely, you'll do that in the Works database. To find out more about the Works database and the Address Book, see Book IV, Chapters 5 and 6 respectively.

Developing form letters

After you have your source document ready, creating form letters is easy. You just need to create the letter you want to use as the destination document and then follow these steps:

1. **With your destination document open, choose Tools⇨Mail Merge⇨Open Data Source.**

   The Open Data Source dialog box appears.

2. **Choose your source document.**

   If you're using the Works Address Book, click Merge From the Address Book. If your source document comes from somewhere else, click the Merge Information From Another Type of File button.

   If you choose a source document other than the Address Book, you need to browse the folders until you find that document and then click Open.

   No matter where your source document originates — the Address Book or another source — you next see the Insert Fields dialog box.

3. **In your destination document, move your cursor to the place where you want to insert a field.**

4. **From the list of fields in the Insert Fields dialog box, select the field you want to insert and then click Insert.**

   The field appears in your document.

5. **Repeat Steps 3 and 4 to continue inserting fields until you finish.**

6. **After you insert the last field, click the View Results button.**

   The View Results dialog box appears, enabling you to see each document with the merge completed.

7. **When you finish viewing your merged documents, click the X in the top-right corner of the dialog box to close it.**

   Now wasn't that easier than typing each letter individually? We thought you'd like this!

Creating envelopes

The gurus at Microsoft thought of everything when they developed this mail merge feature. After all, what good is a bunch of personalized form letters without envelopes?

To use mail merge to create envelopes:

1. **Choose Tools⇨Envelopes.**

   The Envelopes dialog box appears.

2. **Select the Mail Merge Envelopes option button and then click OK.**

   The Envelope Settings dialog box appears.

   If you want to create just one envelope, you can select the first option button.

3. **Choose the size of your envelope from the Envelope Size list box.**

   If you don't see your envelope size, click the Custom Size button and enter the width and height of your envelopes and then click OK to return to the Envelope Settings dialog box.

4. **After you choose your envelope size, click New Document.**

   A word-processing document with the dimensions you specified appears, with space mapped out for your mailing and return addresses.

   Because you chose the mail merge option in Step 2, you also see the Open Data Source dialog box.

5. **Choose your source document.**

   If you're using the Works Address Book, click Merge From the Address Book. If your source document comes from somewhere else, click the Merge Information From Another Type of File button.

   If you choose a source document other than the Address Book, you need to browse the folders until your find that document and then click Open.

   No matter where your source document originates — the Address Book or another source — you next see the Insert Fields dialog box.

6. **Move your cursor to the place on your envelope where you want to insert a field.**

7. **From the list of fields in the Insert Fields dialog box, select the field you want to insert and then click Insert.**

   The field appears on your envelope.

8. **Repeat Steps 6 and 7 to continue inserting fields until you finish.**

   If you want commas or other punctuation to appear in your addresses, type them between the fields.

9. **After you insert the last field, click the View Results button.**

   The View Results dialog box appears, enabling you to see each envelope with the merge completed.

10. **When you finish viewing your envelopes, click the X in the top-right corner of the dialog box to close it.**

Printing envelopes

There's more to creating envelopes than just finalizing the text and clicking Print. You need to tell Works how you're going to insert your envelope in the printer. To do so:

1. **Choose File⇨Page Setup.**

   You see the Page Setup dialog box.

2. **Click the Envelope Feed tab, if it's not already selected.**

3. **Indicate how you will be inserting the envelope into the printer by selecting the appropriate option button.**

4. **Click OK, and you're ready to print!**

Creating labels

If you find yourself sending letters to the same people or companies over and over again, why go through the hassle of repeatedly printing envelopes each time (see the preceding section)? Instead, create labels!

Like other mail merge features, you need a source document, which can be your Address Book or a database you created. You can then use the Labels Wizard to create your labels.

To create labels, follow these steps:

1. Choose Tools⇨Labels.

The Labels dialog box appears.

2. Select the option button that best describes the labels you want to create and then click OK.

No matter which option you select, you see the Label Settings dialog box.

3. In the Printer Information section, select the type of printer you're using.

4. From the Label Products list box, select the manufacturer of the labels you're using.

5. From the Product Number list box, select the product number of the labels you're using.

If you can't find the manufacturer or product number, click the Custom button and enter your labels' configurations. Then click OK to return to the Label Settings dialog box.

6. Click New Document.

If you chose the Mail Labels option in Step 2, you see the Open Data Source dialog box.

If you chose the Multiple-Entry Labels option in Step 2, you are taken through a series of dialog boxes representing each label. Type away! If you chose the Return Address Label option in Step 2, type your information in the only active text box. For both these options, skip to the last step.

7. Choose your source document.

If you're using the Works Address Book, click Merge From the Address Book. If your source document comes from somewhere else, click the Merge Information From Another Type of File button.

If you choose a source document other than the Address Book, you need to browse the folders until you find that document and then click Open.

No matter where your source document originates — the Address Book or another source — you next see the Insert Fields dialog box.

8. **Move your cursor to the place on your label where you want to insert a field.**

9. **From the list of fields in the Insert Fields dialog box, select the field you want to insert and then click Insert.**

 The field appears on your label.

10. **Repeat Steps 8 and 9 to continue inserting fields until you finish.**

11. **After you insert the last field, click the View Results button.**

 The View Results dialog box appears, enabling you to see each label with the merge completed.

12. **When you finish viewing your labels, click the X in the top-right corner of the dialog box to close it.**

13. **Print your labels.**

 Unlike the envelopes feature in the preceding section, you don't need to adjust any page settings.

**Book IV
Chapter 2**

**Using the Word
Processor**

Chapter 3: Changing Your Document's Look

In This Chapter

✔ Making your text look nice

✔ Adding creative touches, such as column, bullets, and tables

✔ Getting fancy with borders and shading

There's more to creating a document than just putting words in a file. After all, if you want to make your point, you need to make sure that your text is not only readable but also attractive. You want to draw people into your document. And that's where the extra touches — such as headers and footers, bullets and numbered lists, and spreadsheets — enter into the picture. In this chapter, you find out how to add these finishing touches to your word-processor document.

Formatting Your Text

If you want people to want to read your document, you need to make it as legible as possible. That includes using readable, friendly fonts, adjusting the line spacing and alignment, and adding paragraph indents. If you truly want to pull out all the stops, then don't forget to add headers and footers — you never know when someone will drop a printed copy of your document and need to collate it again!

Changing fonts

A first step to making your document presentable is choosing a font you like. You can also change your font color and size at the same time. To change fonts:

1. **Highlight the text you want to change.**

   If you want to change all text, press Ctrl+A to select all.

2. **Choose Format⇨Font.**

   The Font dialog box appears, as shown in Figure 3-1.

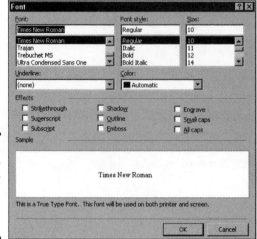

Figure 3-1:
You can
change your
font, color,
and size in
one swoop.

3. **From the Font drop-down list, click the font you want to use.**

   A preview appears in the Sample area at the bottom of the dialog box. If you don't like that font, simply choose another one.

4. **Choose a font style from the Font Style drop-down list.**

   Italics can be hard to read, so you probably want to use that style only for a limited selection of text.

5. **Choose the size of text you want to use from the Size drop-down list.**

6. **Indicate the color of text you'd like in the Color drop-down list.**

7. **If you want to use any special effects, such as strikethrough, sub-script, or all caps, click in the checkbox next to that effect.**

   Again, most special effects are difficult to read, so if you use one limit it to a small selection of text.

8. **If you like what you see in the Sample area, click OK; if not, adjust the settings and then click OK.**

   Your changes appear in the document.

If you're a toolbar person, you can also change many of these selections by using the Formatting toolbar. See Book IV, Chapter 2 to find out what does what on the Formatting toolbar.

Setting the line spacing

If your lines look a little crowded to you on-screen, you can adjust the line spacing. You can also use this feature to tighten the spaces vertically in between lines of text.

To adjust line spacing:

1. **Select the paragraphs you want to format.**

   To change the entire document, press Ctrl+A.

2. **Choose Format⇨Paragraph.**

   The Format Paragraph dialog box appears.

3. **Click the Spacing tab if it's not already selected.**

4. **Indicate the amount of spacing you want between lines by using the up and down arrows in the Spacing section.**

   You also see a preview of your selections on the right-hand side of the screen.

5. **When you're satisfied with what you see, click OK.**

   Your line spacing changes on-screen.

Aligning text

If you want to change how your text lines up on the page, use the aligning text option. To change your text alignment:

1. **Select the text you want to change.**

2. **Choose Format⇨Paragraph.**

3. **In the Format Paragraph dialog box, click the Indents and Alignment tab.**

4. **Select the option button that describes how you want your text aligned.**

5. **Click OK.**

You can also use the Formatting toolbar to change alignment. Just select your text and click the appropriate alignment button. (See Chapter 2 in this book if you're not sure which button does what.)

Indenting paragraphs

To indent the first line of each paragraph or to indent a particular paragraph within your document, follow Steps 1 through 3 in the preceding section, "Aligning text." Then, in the Indentation section, use the arrows to set the indentation you want. (Don't forget to check out the Preview area.) To indent the first line of each paragraph you've highlighted, change the setting in the First Line text box. When you see how you want your paragraph to appear in the Preview area, click OK.

For toolbar people, select your text and then just click the Decrease Indent button or Increase Indent button on the Formatting toolbar.

Controlling page breaks

For the most part, you don't need to worry about adding page breaks to your document. Works does that for you. However, if you really want a page to break in a particular spot, you can exercise control. Here's how:

1. **Place your cursor where you want the page to end.**

2. **Choose Insert⇨Break⇨Page Break (or press Ctrl+Enter).**

A new page appears.

Adding footnotes

If you need to add footnotes, don't worry. You can do that in the word processor, too. To do so, follow these steps:

1. **Place your cursor where you want the footnote to appear.**

2. **Choose Insert⇨Footnote.**

The Footnote and Endnote dialog box appears.

3. **Indicate whether you want to insert a footnote (appears at the end of your current page) or an endnote (all footnotes appear at the end of your document) by selecting the appropriate option button.**

4. **In the Numbering section, select the AutoNumber option button.**

No matter where you insert a new footnote, Works takes care of the numbering for you.

5. **Click OK.**

The appropriate footnote number appears in your text, and your cursor moves to the bottom of the page.

6. **Type your footnote.**

You're all done! Just return to your document to resume work.

Adding headers and footers

If you want the same words to appear at the top *(headers)* or bottom *(footers)* on every page of your document, then you're in luck. To add headers or footers, follow these steps:

1. **Choose View⇨Header and Footer.**

   A Header text box appears at the top of your document, while a Footer text box appears at the end.

2. **Place your cursor on either the Header or Footer text box and type your header and/or your footer in the Footer text box.**

   For example, your header may include your name, document title, or date.

3. **After you finish, double-click outside the box.**

4. **If you typed a header in Step 2 and want to add a footer as well, repeat these steps.**

   Your header and/or footer appears.

Being Creative with Text Presentation

If you're tired of seeing paragraph after paragraph of boring documents, then try something different. In the Works word processor, you can add columns, bullets, numbered lists, and tables. And although the results look impressive, the effort required on your part is minimal.

Creating columns

To create columns in a document:

1. **Choose Format⇨Columns.**

   The Format Columns dialog box appears.

2. **In the Number of Columns text box, use the arrows to indicate the number of columns you want to use.**

3. **In the Space Between text box, indicate the amount of space you want between each column.**

4. **If you want a line to appear between columns, click that checkbox.**

5. **If you like what you see in the Preview section, click OK.**

Creating bullets and numbered lists

If you want to make your document as easy to read as possible and spice it up visually, then try adding a bulleted list.

To create a bulleted list as you're typing, simply click the Bullets button on the Formatting toolbar and begin typing. When you finish typing your last bullet, click the Bullets button again to turn the feature off or press Enter twice in a row.

If you've already typed your list and now you want to turn it into a bulleted list, don't fret. It's not too late:

1. **Select the paragraphs you want to make into a bulleted list.**

2. **Choose Format⇨Bullets and Numbering.**

   The Bullets and Numbering dialog box appears, as shown in Figure 3-2.

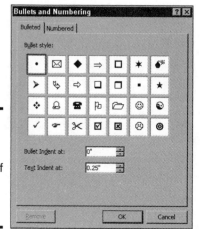

Figure 3-2: Choices, choices! What kind of bullet best suits your document?

3. **If you want to create a bulleted list, click the Bulleted tab and then click the bullet you want to use.**

4. **In the Bullet Indent At text box, use the arrows to select how far you want your bullet to be indented from the margin.**

5. **In the Text Indent At text box, use the arrows to select how far you want the text to be indented from your bullet.**

6. **Click OK.**

Creating numbered lists

Numbered lists work just like bulleted lists. You can use the Numbering button on the toolbar and then type your text, or you can create a numbered list from existing text by following these steps:

1. **Select the paragraphs you want to make into a numbered list.**

2. **Choose Format⇨Bullets and Numbering.**

   The Bullets and Numbering dialog box appears.

3. **Click the Numbered tab and then click the number style you want to use.**

4. **In the Starting Number text box, use the arrows to select the number you want your list to begin with.**

5. **In the Number Indent At text box, use the arrows to select how far you want your number to be indented from the margin.**

6. **In the Text Indent At text box, use the arrows to select how far you want the text to be indented from your number.**

7. **Click OK.**

Working with tables

If you decide that a table is just what you need to spice up your document, then follow these steps:

1. **Place your cursor where you want your table to appear and click the Insert Table button or choose Table⇨Insert Table.**

   The Insert Table dialog box appears, as shown in Figure 3-3.

Figure 3-3:
Custom-
design your
very own
table.

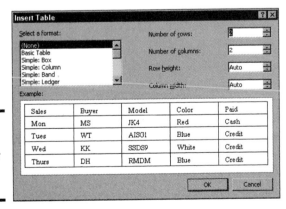

2. **From the Select a Format drop-down list, choose the type of table you want to insert.**

   The Example section gives you a preview of each table.

3. **Type the number of rows and columns you want to appear in your table in the Number of Rows and Number of Columns text boxes.**

4. **Choose the Auto feature for both the Row Height and Column Width text boxes.**

5. **Click OK.**

 After you enter your text in your table, you can use the commands on the Table menu to format it. For example, you can insert and delete rows and columns, delete text, or change the cell height and width. You can also format your table by choosing Table⇨Table Format. To move from one table cell to another, simply press the Tab key or use your arrow keys.

Adding Borders and Shading

Borders and shading can help draw attention to important information in your document and improve your document's overall appearance. To add borders or shading:

1. **Select the text that you want to place the border around or shade.**

2. **Choose Format⇨Borders and Shading.**

   The Borders and Shading dialog box appears. If you're only adding shading, skip to Step 6. If you're adding a border, continue to Step 3.

3. **In the Apply To drop-down list, select whether to place the border around a paragraph or the entire page.**

4. **In the Line Style and Line Color drop-down lists, choose the style and color of your line.**

5. **In the Border section of the dialog box, indicate how you want the border to appear.**

   For example, the Outline option surrounds the selected text, while the other options only place a border on the side indicated. If you don't want to add shading, skip to Step 8.

6. **In the Shading section of the dialog box, select the type of shading that you want to use from the Fill Style drop-down list.**

7. **In the Colors section, choose the color that you want to use for the shading.**

8. **Click OK.**

   Your border and shading changes take effect.

Chapter 4: Using the Spreadsheet

In This Chapter
- Creating a spreadsheet
- Working with formulas and functions
- Inserting and deleting rows and columns
- Advancing to charts

*I*f you're an organization guru — or you want to be — then you'll like working with the Works spreadsheet program. You can create rows and columns of information to hold all the data you want as well as use your new spreadsheet to create snazzy-looking charts. In this chapter, you find out all you need to know about the workings of the Works spreadsheet.

Creating a Spreadsheet

Chances are, if you're reading this chapter, one thing you probably want to know most is how to create a spreadsheet. Although a spreadsheet looks hard to create, it's really not. In the Task Launcher, you simply click Start a Blank Spreadsheet, and you're on your way. You just need to add your text and numbers and format.

But you know what's even easier than that? Using a Spreadsheet Wizard. In the Task Launcher, simply click the Spreadsheet program, and a list of wizards appears. Click the one that sounds the most like what you want to do, read the description that appears, and then click Start This Task. Then follow the steps in the Wizards, clicking Next or Finish as prompted. A spreadsheet appears, and you just have to update the figures, as shown in Figure 4-1.

Figure 4-1:
Replace the numbers in the spreadsheet created by the Financial Worksheets Wizard to create your very own budget.

[Screenshot of Microsoft Works Spreadsheet titled "Unsaved Spreadsheet - Microsoft Works Spreadsheet" showing cell E13 with value 2450.5]

Home Budget, Monthly

September 2000

Summary

	Actual	Budgeted	Over/Under	Notes
Total income	5,653.00	5,525.00	128.00 over	
Total expenses	4,977.25	4,896.25	81.00 over	
Income less expenses	675.75	628.75	47.00 over	

Income

			Over/Under	Notes
Salary 1	2,874.50	2,874.50	at budget	
Salary 2	2,450.50	2,450.50	at budget	
Investment	200.00	200.00	at budget	
Stocks and bonds				
Other	128.00		128.00 over	Garage sale
Total income	5,653.00	5,525.00	128.00 over	

Expenses

Withholdings	Actual	Budgeted	Over/Under	Notes
Federal income tax	448.00	450.00	2.00 under	
State income tax			at budget	

Opening a Spreadsheet

If you've worked in the word processor, then don't let the spreadsheet intimidate you. It works just like Microsoft's other programs!

To open a spreadsheet you've already created, you have several options:

✦ Click the Open button. In the Open dialog box, look through the folders to find your spreadsheet and then click Open.

✦ Choose File⇨Open from the menu.

✦ Choose File and then choose the recently used file you want to open from the bottom of the menu.

Mastering Spreadsheet Basics

Whether you want to create a spreadsheet from scratch or use a Wizard, you need to know certain processes to finalize it. In the following sections, you find out the basics, such as selecting cells and ranges, entering text, naming ranges, and formatting.

Selecting cells and ranges

First, a little terminology: When you type in a spreadsheet, you're typing in a *cell,* which is the meeting of a particular row and column, identified by a *cell address* — say, A4, for column A, row 4. A *range,* on the other hand, consists of several cells.

Before you can change the formatting or add formulas to a cell or range, you need to select it. Here's how:

✦ Click the row or column heading to select that particular row or column.

✦ Click the first cell and drag to the last cell to select a particular range.

✦ Press Ctrl+A to select the entire spreadsheet.

You know you've successfully selected cells when they appear highlighted.

Entering data

One of the first steps you need to do when creating a spreadsheet is to insert data. To type information into a cell:

1. **Select the cell that you want the information to appear in.**

2. **Type your data.**

3. **Press Enter.**

Your data appears in the cell and in the formula bar.

If you want the same information to appear in multiple cells, here's a shortcut for you:

1. **Click the cell containing the text you want to repeat.**

2. **Click the lower-right corner of that cell so that the Fill button appears.**

3. **Holding your mouse down, drag to the end of the cells where you want the information to repeat.**

4. **Release the mouse.**

You can also use this feature to copy formulas. (See the section "Creating Formulas," later in this chapter.)

Naming ranges

If you've used Excel, then you'll have no problem using range addresses in the Works spreadsheet. Just as in Excel, range addresses appear as letters and numbers with colons inserted between each address, such as A4:A12.

However, you may prefer to name your ranges. Here's how:

1. **Select the cells that make up the named range.**

2. **Choose Insert⇨Range Name.**

The Range Name dialog box appears.

3. **Type the range name in the Name text box.**

4. **Click OK.**

Formatting cells

Just like in the Works word processor, you can format your spreadsheet to maximize its readability. The AutoFormat feature makes formatting a snap. No more hard work for you!

To use AutoFormat:

1. **Select the cell(s) you want to format.**

2. **Choose Format⇨AutoFormat.**

The AutoFormat dialog box appears.

3. **In the Select a Format list, click once on a format that you think you may like.**

The format appears in the Preview area, as shown in Figure 4-2.

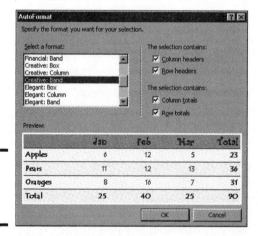

Figure 4-2: Try this formatting shortcut.

If you double-click by mistake, the dialog box disappears, and the format you double-clicked is automatically applied. If you didn't mean to apply that format, choose Edit⇨Undo Format.

4. Click OK.

The format is applied to your cells.

If you like to do things the hard way, you can format your cells without using the AutoFormat feature. Simply select the cells you want to format and choose Format⇨Number. The Format dialog box, complete with tabs for Number, Alignment, Font, Border, and Shading, appears. Go through each tab, choose the formatting features you want, and then click OK after you finish.

Working with Rows and Columns

You may decide that you need more or less rows and columns as you fiddle with your spreadsheet. No problem. Not only can you insert and delete rows as needed, but you can even size them to your heart's content. Have fun!

Inserting rows and columns

To insert a row:

1. Click any cell in the row below the spot where you want to insert the new row.

2. Choose Edit⇨Select Row to highlight the entire row.

3. Choose Insert⇨Insert Row.

A new row appears above the selected row.

To insert a column:

1. Click any cell in the column to the right of the spot where you want to insert the new column.

2. Choose Edit⇨Select Column to highlight the entire column.

3. Choose Insert⇨Insert Column.

A new column appears to the left of the selected column.

Deleting rows and columns

If you got a little carried away inserting rows or columns, don't despair. To delete them, select the row or column (by clicking the row number or column letter) and choose Insert⇨Delete Row or Insert⇨Delete Column. All gone!

Sizing rows and columns

You may discover that a column is constantly too narrow to accommodate the data you're entering or it's so wide that it leaves a bunch of wasted white space. To not only maximize your space but also enhance the attractiveness of your spreadsheet, you may want to resize your rows or columns.

Follow these steps to resize your rows or columns:

1. **Click the row or column heading that you want to resize.**

2. **Choose Format⇨Row Height or Format⇨Column Width.**

   If you're resizing the row, the Row Height dialog box appears. If you're resizing the column, the Column Width dialog box appears.

3. **Indicate how you want to set the row height or column width and then click OK.**

The first option button is usually your best option, unless you want to set the height or width manually.

You can also position your cursor on the dividing border of the row or column and drag to resize. Be sure that you are on the border to the right of a column or the bottom of a row.

Freezing row and column titles

If you have a big spreadsheet and you always want the same titles to appear on-screen as you scroll the spreadsheet, then try *freezing* a row or column. By doing so, that row or column remains on-screen no matter where you are in the spreadsheet. That way, you're not stuck on page 7 with data that's meaningless to you!

To freeze a row or column:

1. **Click the row below or the column to the right of the row or column you want to freeze.**

2. **Choose Format⇨Freeze Titles.**

   A checkmark appears next to the menu to tell you that the Freeze Titles option is turned on.

To unfreeze titles, choose Format⇨Freeze Titles again.

Creating Formulas

Whether you're a numbers person or not, you'll like the formula feature in the Works spreadsheet. In fact, if you're not a numbers person, you'll love it! By typing a simple formula, you order the spreadsheet to do all the hard number-crunching for you — your very own mathematician. By creating a formula, you force Works to do the math as you change and update data so that you don't have to redo it. (Don't you just love this!)

Using simple math operators

To create a formula, you need to type the information in a certain way. Say, for example, that you want to add two cells together:

1. **Click in an empty cell where you want the sum to appear and then type the equal (=) sign.**

2. **Click the first cell you want to add.**

3. **Type the plus (+) sign.**

   If you prefer to do another operation, such as division, type the slash (/) instead. You also can use the asterisk (*) for multiplication and the minus sign (–) for subtraction.

4. **Click the second cell you want to add.**

5. **Press Enter.**

   Tada!

If you feel comfortable with those steps, then try this shortcut: Go to the cell that you want the result to appear that and type the following: *=celladdress/operation/cell address*. So, for example, if you're trying to add cells A3 and A9, you'd type =A3+A9. It's that easy!

You probably know all the basic math operators from elementary school, but here's one you may not remember: ^. This exponent sign multiplies the first number by itself the amount of times indicated by the second number. For example, if your first number is two and the second one is three (as in 2^3), two is multiplied by itself three times, as in 2 x 2 x 2 for a total of 8.

Calculating with Easy Calc

If you don't want to create your own formulas, you're in luck. You can use the Easy Calc tool to walk you through the formula process.

To use Easy Calc:

1. **Choose Tools⇨Easy Calc.**

The Easy Calc dialog box appears, as shown in Figure 4-3.

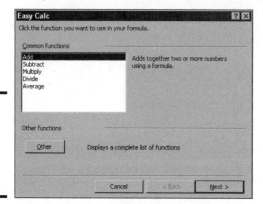

Figure 4-3:
Easy Calc
walks you
through
creating a
formula.

2. **From the Common Functions area, choose the type of calculation you want to do; click Next.**

You can also click the Other button if you don't see the calculation you want; find your function and then click Insert.

3. **In the next dialog box, enter the Range and then click Next.**

If you want to at this point, you can go back to your spreadsheet and select the cells in the range. The Easy Calc dialog box returns after you select the cells.

4. **In the next and final dialog box, indicate which cell you want the result to appear in; click Finish.**

Using functions

Here's another shortcut to creating formulas: Instead of developing them yourself, you can also use the spreadsheet's functions. Here's how:

1. **Select the cell where the function should go.**

2. **Choose Insert⇨Function.**

The Insert Function dialog box appears, as shown in Figure 4-4.

Figure 4-4:
Let the
spreadsheet
do the work
for you
when
inserting
functions.

3. **In the Select a Category area, click the category of the function you want to create.**

   The list of available functions for that category appears in the Choose a Function area.

4. **Click the function that you think you want to use.**

   A description appears at the bottom of the screen.

5. **After you find the function you want, click Insert.**

   The formula appears in your spreadsheet, with the first word in the formula highlighted.

6. **Click the cell that contains the information needed for the first word; continue clicking cells to replace each word in the formula.**

7. **When you finish, press Enter.**

Displaying formulas

If your numbers just don't seem to be coming out right, you may want to check your formulas. To do so, choose View⇨Formulas. Your formulas, instead of the results, appear in the cells. To return to your spreadsheet, choose View⇨Formulas to remove the checkmark from the command.

Sorting Data

Thanks to the sorting feature, you can reorder your spreadsheet entries. Alphabetical, numeric, ascending, and descending orders are just a click away, so you can check them all to your heart's content.

To sort your data:

1. **Highlight the entries you want to sort.**

2. **Choose Tools⇨Sort.**

The Sort dialog box appears.

3. **In the Sort Using section, click The Selected Cells option button.**

If you don't want your header to be rearranged during the sort, select the Selection Has a Header Row option button.

4. **In the Select the Column You Want To Sort By selection, select the Ascending or Descending option button.**

5. **Click Sort.**

Working with Charts

If you really want to spice up a presentation, try creating a chart. Talk about visual! Charts show your audience or readers at a glance what you're trying to say. After all, a picture is worth a thousand words!

Creating a chart

No matter how much you like charts, you can't get around creating a spreadsheet first. So if you haven't already created a spreadsheet, then peruse the first half of this chapter.

After you have your spreadsheet created, you're ready to create a chart:

1. **Open the spreadsheet that you want to base your chart on.**

2. **Select the information that you want to include in your chart.**

3. **Choose Tools⇨Create New Chart.**

The New Chart dialog box appears.

4. **Click the chart type you like best.**

Don't forget to check out the Preview area on the right side of the screen to see how your data looks in that chart type.

5. **Type the name of your chart in the Chart Title text box.**

6. **If you want to add a border or gridlines, check the appropriate boxes.**

7. **Click OK.**

If you decide that you don't like the way an existing chart works, then change it to another chart type. To do so, choose View⇨Chart, choose the chart you want, and then choose Format⇨Chart Type. Then choose a new chart in the Chart Type dialog box that appears.

Viewing a chart or spreadsheet

After you create a chart based on a spreadsheet, you can easily toggle between viewing the spreadsheet and viewing the chart. If you're in your spreadsheet and want to see your chart, choose View⇨Chart. Your chart appears. (If you have multiple charts associated with the spreadsheet, you just need to choose the chart from the View Chart dialog box that appears.) To return to your spreadsheet, choose View⇨Spreadsheet.

Changing the chart values

After you create a chart, you can still change the numbers it's based on. You just need to update the numbers in your original spreadsheet, and your chart will update itself automatically.

Deleting, copying, and renaming charts

Change your mind about a chart? No problem. You can always delete or rename it, and if you really like it, even create a copy of it:

✦ To delete a chart, open the chart's spreadsheet and choose Tools⇨ Delete Chart. In the Delete Chart dialog box, select the chart you want to delete and click Delete.

✦ To copy a chart, open the chart's spreadsheet and choose Tools⇨ Duplicate Chart. Again, select the chart you want to copy. Type a name and then click Duplicate. The duplicate chart name is added to the listing.

✦ To rename a chart, open the chart's spreadsheet and choose Tools⇨ Rename Chart. Select the chart you want to rename, type the new name, and click Rename.

Changing chart colors

What's a chart without color? Boring! If you decide, though, that you're not fond of the colors and patterns that Works assigns automatically, get creative and change them.

To change colors and patterns in your chart:

1. **Open the spreadsheet and select the chart you want to change.**

2. **Choose Format⇨Shading and Color.**

The Shading and Color dialog box appears.

3. From the Select Series list, choose the series you want to change.

4. Choose a color in the Color list.

5. Choose a pattern in the Pattern list.

6. Click Format to apply the color change or click the Format All button to apply the changes across the entire chart.

7. Repeat Steps 3 through 6 for each series.

8. Click the Close button when you finish.

Printing a Chart or Spreadsheet

After your chart or spreadsheet looks just right, you're ready to print it. First, to save trees, check out your creation in print preview mode by choosing View⇨Print Preview. If you feel satisfied, click the Print button. Or, if you want to skip the preview, simply choose File⇨Print.

Saving a Chart or Spreadsheet

You can save a chart or spreadsheet the same way you save a word processing document. Here's how:

1. Click the Save button or choose File⇨Save.

   The Save As dialog box appears.

   If you already saved the file, Works doesn't show you a dialog box. It simply saves the new version of the file over the old one. If you don't want that to happen, then you need to choose File⇨Save As and give your file a new name to indicate that it's the second version of the chart or spreadsheet.

2. Using the drop-down arrow, browse the Save In box to find the folder you want to save your spreadsheet to.

   If the folder has any subfolders, they appear in the big white area in the middle of the dialog box.

3. Type your name in the File Name text box.

   You want to choose a name that's descriptive of the file, so you know what it contains in the future.

4. Click Save.

Chapter 5: Getting Organized with the Database

In This Chapter

- ✔ Starting a new database
- ✔ Mastering fields and records
- ✔ Understanding forms
- ✔ Generating reports

*D*on't let the Works database intimidate you. You can do a lot of useful things with this program, such as keeping lists and using forms. We even give you a brief section on database basics, just in case you're still nervous. So if you're ready to delve in, read on!

Mastering Database Basics

No doubt about it, databases can be scary. I'm not talking about Halloween scary but more along the lines of "Wow, that looks so cool, I bet it's really hard to do" scary. But here's a little secret. Working with databases isn't difficult at all — especially if you know the language:

- ✦ **Cell:** The basic building block of a table. You must have more than one cell to create a table.

- ✦ **Field:** A column in a table. Fields contain categories — for example, last names only.

- ✦ **Record:** A row in a table. Records contain all entries for one listing — for example, one person's entire address.

- ✦ **Form:** A database view in which you see one record at a time on-screen.

- ✦ **Filter:** A tool that gives you only certain information that you request — for example, only the names of individuals living in Indiana.

- ✦ **Report:** Summaries of your data.

Creating a Database

Obviously, the Works database program lets you create a database file, which is similar in structure to a table. After you have the basic database created, you can change the format of your information, as well.

If you want to create a basic inventory list or recipe book, then Works offers you TaskWizards. In the Task Launcher, simply click the TaskWizard you like and follow the steps. If none of these wizards fit your needs — and they probably won't for the majority of people — then you need to create your own database.

To create a new database:

1. **In the Task Launcher, click the Works Database button and then click Start a Blank Database.**

The Create Database dialog box appears, as shown in Figure 5-1.

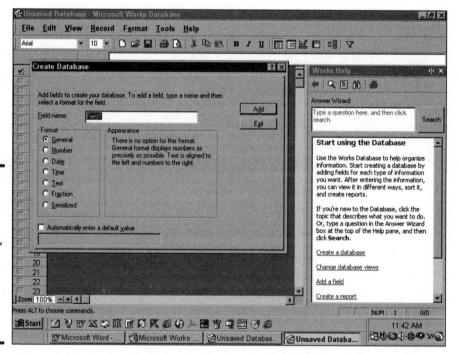

Figure 5-1: If you don't want to use a database TaskWizard, you can create your own database from scratch.

2. Type the name of your first field in the Field Name text box.

Each of your fields represents a category of the information you're entering. For example, if you're organizing addresses, one field would be the person's first name, another the person's last name, another the street address, another the city, and so on.

3. In the Format area of the dialog box, select the format you want to use for this particular field.

You can see examples of each format in the Appearance section of the dialog box.

4. Click Add.

Your field is added, and the Create Database dialog box reappears, this time with a Done button below the Add button.

5. Repeat Steps 2 through 4 for each field in your database.

6. Click Done after you finish adding all your fields.

Reserve Number fields for anything that needs to be calculated — in other words, *not* your zip codes or phone numbers!

Saving a Database

After you create a database and periodically while you're working in it, you want to save your database to ensure that you don't lose any work.

To save your database:

1. Click the Save button or choose File⇨Save.

The Save As dialog box appears.

If you've already saved the file, Works doesn't show you a dialog box. It simply saves the new version of the file over the old one. If you don't want that to happen, you need to choose File⇨Save As and give your database a new name.

2. Using the drop-down arrow, browse the Save In box to find the folder you want to save your document to.

3. Type your file name in the File Name text box.

4. Click Save.

Opening a Database

To open an existing database, you have several options:

 ✦ Click the Open button. In the Open dialog box, look through the folders to find your database and then click Open.

✦ Choose File⇨Open from the menu.

✦ Choose File and then choose the recently used file you'd like to open from the bottom of the menu.

Working with Fields

After you create a database, you may decide that you didn't do your fields justice. Perhaps you omitted a few fields that you need to add. Perhaps you chose an inappropriate format. Or maybe you don't really need that field for birthdays after all. The following sections provide you with information on what you can do with your database fields.

Adding new fields

It's never too late to add fields to your database. You just need to know *how* to do it. To insert a new field:

1. **Make sure that your document is in List view by choosing View⇨List from the menu.**

2. **Place your cursor in one of the columns next to the column where you want to insert the new field.**

3. **Choose Record⇨Insert Field.**

A submenu appears.

4. **Click whether you want the new field to appear before or after the column where your cursor is.**

No matter which one you choose, the Insert Field dialog box appears.

5. **Type the name of the new field in the Field Name text box.**

6. **Select the type of format you want to use for the new field.**

7. **Click Add.**

Your field is added, and the Insert Field dialog box reappears — just in case you want to add another field.

8. **Repeat Steps 5 through 7 if you want to add another field.**

9. **Click the Done button after you finish.**

Formatting fields

If you want to change a field's formatting, no problem:

1. **In List view, click the title bar of the field you want to format.**

   If you're not sure that you're in List view, choose View⇨List from the menu bar.

2. **Choose Format⇨Field.**

   The Format dialog box appears. The Field tab should be selected, and the field you selected in Step 1 should also appear in the Field Name text box.

   If you want to change the field name, simply type the new name in the Field Name text box.

3. **Select your new formatting from the Format area.**

4. **For most of the formatting options, you need to select the specific type of formatting you want from the Appearance options; do so now.**

5. **Click OK.**

Deleting fields

Oops! Didn't mean to add that field after all? Don't worry. You can delete it.

In List view, simply select the field you want to delete and choose Record⇨ Delete Field. Then click OK to confirm the deletion.

Changed your mind again? To recover the deleted field, immediately choose Edit⇨Undo Delete Field. But note that word *immediately* — if you don't do it the very next step after your original deletion, you're out of luck!

Working with Records

Records are groupings of related fields that make up entries in a database. For example, if you're creating an address book, one person's information — although made up of many fields — is collectively called a record.

Showing and hiding records

If you're working in your database and you'd rather not see a particular record, then hide it:

1. **In List view, click within the record that you want to have disappear.**

2. **Choose Record⇨Hide Record.**

   The record disappears.

If you want to see a hidden record, simply choose Record⇨Show⇨4 Hidden Records. If you want to see all records, simply click the checkbox at the top-left of the screen.

Deleting records

Don't like that person anymore? Then delete his entire record. In List view, click the row heading for the record you want to delete and then choose Record⇨Delete Record. It's outta there!

If you want to delete several records at once, click the check box for all the rows you want to delete and then choose Record⇨Show⇨2 Marked Records. Then press the Delete key. Gone!

Filtering records

Filters are pretty cool. After you enter your information into a database, you can use filters to find certain information in your database. Using the criteria you supply, the filters search your database and then give you a list of the matching records.

To create a filter for your database:

1. **Choose Tools⇨Filters.**

If you haven't created a filter for this database, you see the Filter Name dialog box. If you've already created a filter in this database, you see the Filter dialog box instead.

2. **If you see the Filter Name dialog box, type a name for your filter and click OK. If you see the Filter dialog box, click the New Filter button to see the Filter Name dialog box, type a filter name, and click OK.**

Either way, you return to the Filter dialog box.

3. **Select the Easy Filter option button.**

4. **In the Field Name column, choose the field you want the filter to find.**

5. **In the Comparison column, choose what kind of comparison you want, as shown in Figure 5-2.**

You can choose up to five criteria per filter, one for each box.

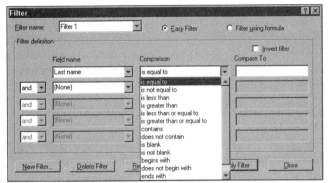

Figure 5-2:
What kind of
comparison
do you want
to make?

6. In the Compare To column, type what you want Works to look for.

Again, you can choose up to five criteria.

7. Click Apply Filter

The dialog box closes, and the entries that match your criteria appear.

If you have more than one criterion in a filter, you need to use either the AND or OR operator. Use AND when you want to conduct a narrower search, such as locating a person who is named Ann and who lives in Indiana. Use OR when you want to find either one of the criteria: a person named Ann or a person who lives in Indiana.

Creating Forms

If you want to see your database in a form, choose View➪Form. Your database is converted to a form, and you can start entering your data. Using a form helps you focus on the record that you need to enter or change.

Modifying Forms

If you don't like the way your form looks — and you probably won't — then use the Form Design view of your database to improve it.

Inserting a label

You can use labels to add explanation to a form. Here's how:

1. Choose View➪Form Design to work in Form Design view.

2. Select the current label of the field you want to change.

3. Choose Insert⇨Label.

4. In the Insert Label dialog box, type the name of the label and click Insert.

Sizing a field

To change the size of a field:

1. In Form Design view, select the field you want to resize.

2. Choose Format⇨Field Size.

3. In the Format Field Size dialog box, enter the width or height that you want to change.

4. Click OK.

Positioning items

If you don't like where your fields and labels appear, then move them. To reposition fields and labels:

1. Click the field or label you want to reposition and move your cursor to the center of the field.

   If you've done this step correctly, you see the word *Drag*.

2. Click your mouse button, drag the field to its new location, and then release the mouse button.

   You're all done!

Generating Reports

If you want to know how everything in your database relates or if you want to present the database information to others, then generate a report.

You may think that if you want to see your report, you should go to Report view. Wrong. Despite its confusing name, Report view is actually a template for designing the layout of your report — you won't find any information there.

To create a report:

1. In List or Form view, choose Tools⇨ReportCreator.

2. In the Report Name dialog box, enter the report name and click OK.

   The ReportCreator dialog box appears. The Title tab automatically appears.

3. **Type the title of your report in the Report Title text box.**

4. **In the Report Orientation area, select how you want your report to appear — either Portrait (vertical) or Landscape (horizontal).**

5. **From the drop-down lists in the Report Font area, choose the font and size you want to use in your report.**

   You can see a preview of your font in the Sample area.

6. **Click Next to advance to the Fields tab, shown in Figure 5-3.**

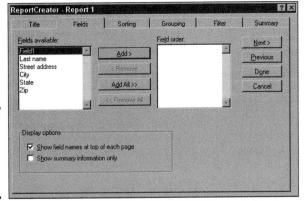

Figure 5-3:
Now you need to specify your fields.

7. **From the Fields Available list, select the field you want to appear in your report and click Add.**

   The field appears in the Field Order box.

8. **Repeat Step 7 until you've added all the fields you want to appear in your report.**

9. **In the Display options area, select whether you want the field names to appear as column heads on each page of the report (the top option) or whether you want to show only the totals.**

10. **Click Next to advance to the Sorting tab.**

11. **From the Sort By drop-down list, select the field you want to sort by first; then choose Ascending or Descending order.**

12. **(Optional) From the first Then By drop-down list, select the field you want to sort by second; then choose Ascending or Descending order.**

13. **(Optional) From the last Then By drop-down list, select the field you want to sort by last; then choose Ascending or Descending order.**

14. **Click Next to advance to the Grouping tab; click Next again to advance to the Filter tab.**

Grouping is a bit advanced, so you don't need to worry about that for now.

15. **Click Next again to move on to the Summary tab.**

If you decide that you want to add a filter later, see the section "Filtering records," earlier in this chapter.

16. **To create a summary, click the first field you want summarized in the Select a Field list box.**

17. **In the Summaries area, select the boxes you want to see in your report.**

18. **In the Display Summary Information area, indicate where you want the information to appear.**

19. **Click Done.**

Your report is finally created!

Printing Reports

After your form or report is to your liking, you're ready to print. If you want to preview your document (always a good idea), choose View⇨Print Preview. If you like what you see, click the Print button. Or, if you want to skip the preview, simply choose File⇨Print. Your document awaits you at your printer!

Chapter 6: Managing Your Calendar and Address Book

In This Chapter

✔ Managing your schedule with the Calendar

✔ Keeping up-to-date with your Address Book

*I*f you like to plan and be up-to-date in your professional life and your personal life, then you've come to the right chapter. In this chapter, you find out how to maximize the Works Calendar and Address Book utilities.

Using the Calendar

The Works Calendar utility helps you manage your schedule and remember birthdays and other special events — icing on the cake! You'll never forget your spouse's birthday or your boss's anniversary again when you use this nifty utility.

Adding appointments

To remember an appointment, you first need to add it into your Works Calendar. You can schedule appointments to occur one time only or on a regular basis, such as a weekly team meeting. You can also use the Calendar to send e-mail and give you on-screen reminders. Works Calendar is like your very own personal assistant!

Follow these steps to schedule an appointment:

1. **In the Task Launcher, click Works Calendar and then Start The Calendar.**

2. **In the Works Calendar, click the New Appointment button or choose File⇨New Appointment.**

The New Appointment dialog box appears.

3. **In the Title text box, type the name of the appointment.**

4. **In the Location text box, type where the meeting or appointment is to be held.**

5. **Click the Change button to open the Choose Categories dialog box.**

6. **(Optional) Choose the category, such as Anniversary, that the appointment falls under and then click OK.**

   You return to the New Appointment dialog box.

7. **From the Appointment Starts drop-down lists, click the arrow and choose the day that the meeting is scheduled; then, from the next drop-down list, choose the starting time.**

   The times listed are in half-hour increments. If you want to use another time increment, you can manually type in the time you prefer in the text box.

8. **From the Appointment Ends drop-down lists, choose the ending day and time.**

9. **If the appointment lasts the entire day, such as a vacation day or an off-site seminar, click the All-Day Event check box.**

10. **If the meeting is to occur on a regular basis, click the Make This Appointment Repeat check box and then click the Recurrence button if you want the appointment to repeat on a different schedule other than weekly; if weekly works for you, skip to Step 11.**

    The Recurrence Options dialog box appears, as shown in Figure 6-1.

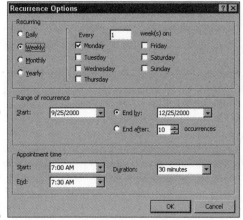

Figure 6-1:
You can even schedule a recurring appointment.

11. **Complete the Recurrence Options dialog box and click OK after you finish.**

    You return to the New Appointment dialog box.

12. **If you want a reminder of the meeting, click the arrow next to the Reminder text box and choose the time that you want the reminder to occur.**

If you want a different time than the ones listed, simply type it in the text box. Either way, a reminder appears on-screen at the designated time. As long as you're at your computer, you have no excuse for missing your appointment!

13. **After you fill in the New Appointment dialog box to your satisfaction, click OK.**

Your appointment is scheduled!

Title, Appointment Starts, and Appointment Ends are the only text boxes you really have to complete to schedule an appointment.

Editing or deleting appointments

Maybe you've attended a few weekly meetings of a committee and have realized that someone else is better suited to attend. No sweat. You can just delete the appointment from your Calendar. Open your Calendar, go to the day the appointment is scheduled, highlight it, and click Delete Item button. Click OK when Works pops up a confirmation dialog box, and it's gone. It's that simple.

Likewise, if you decide that you want to change the time of an appointment, you can edit it. Again, open your Calendar, go to the day the appointment is scheduled, and double-click it. The Edit Appointment dialog box appears. Click the appropriate option button and click OK, and the Edit Appointment dialog box appears. Change what you want to change and click OK. You're all done!

Adding birthdays and holidays

If you're using your Address Book to its fullest capabilities, then you're typing all the information you can about your friends, family, and coworkers into your Address Book — including birthdays and anniversaries! (See the section "Using the Address Book," later in this chapter.) If that's the case, then you don't need to manually add birthdays and anniversaries to your Calendar because the Calendar can work with your Address Book to get the information. What a relief!

To import the Birthdays from your Address Book into your Calendar:

1. **In your Address Book, choose Edit⇨Birthdays.**

2. **In the Works Calendar dialog box that appears, place a check mark in the only box in the dialog box and click OK.**

The Calendar copies the birthday and anniversary information from your Address Book into the Calendar.

If you want to include birthday or anniversary information for someone who isn't in your Address Book, add the event to your Calendar just as you do for any appointment. (See the section "Adding appointments," earlier in this chapter.)

If you want a reminder of the event, you need to open each event and ask for a reminder, as described in the section "Adding appointments," earlier in this chapter.

Viewing your events

Just like you can purchase planners that show you your schedule on each page in daily, weekly, or monthly format, you can view your Works Calendar in any of these formats. Either click the View Day button, View Week button, or View Month button, according to your preference, as shown in Figure 6-2.

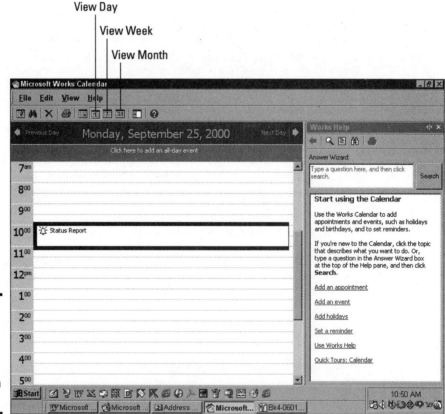

Figure 6-2: Choosing your Calendar format is just a button click away.

Finding events

If you know that you scheduled a meeting or appointment and you just can't remember when, don't despair. You can use the Calendar's Find feature to help you. Follow these steps:

1. **Click the Find button or choose Edit➪Find.**

The Find dialog box appears.

2. **Click the tab that best indicates how you want to conduct the search.**

The Keyword tab searches by any word you type in the appointment. So if you know that you entered *Dentist,* then you can search by keyword.

The Time tab searches by timeframe. So if you know that you scheduled the appointment in October, you can search that month.

You also have the option of selecting the Search Title Only or the Search Title and Notes buttons.

The Category tab searches by category.

3. **After you complete the appropriate tab, click Find Now.**

Your search results appear. Hopefully, you've found what you were looking for!

Using the Address Book

The Works Address Book lets you maintain everything you need to know about your friends, family, and coworkers in one place — on your computer. Better yet, you can use this utility with your Calendar to make sure that you never forget an appointment, birthday, or anniversary again. (See the section "Adding birthdays and holidays," earlier in this chapter, for more information.)

Adding individual contacts

Meet a new person? Then add them to your Works Address Book:

1. **In the Task Launcher, click Address Book and then Start The Address Book.**

2. **In the Address Book, choose File➪New Contact.**

The Properties dialog box appears. Each of the seven tabs collects information about your new contact.

3. **In each tab, type all the information you know about the individual.**

4. **After you complete all the tabs, click OK.**

It's official. Your new contact now appears in your Address Book.

Adding group information

The Works Address Book lets you create a mailing group in your Address Book — say for a group of managers to whom you send a weekly report. In addition, you can continue to add and delete names down the road.

To create a mailing group:

1. **In the Address Book, choose File⇨New Group.**

The Properties dialog box appears.

2. **In the Group tab, type your group name in the first text box.**

3. **Click Select Members to choose the members of your mailing group.**

The Select Group Members dialog box appears.

4. **As you select each member, click Select.**

The new member appears in the Members list box.

5. **After you finish creating your group, click OK to exit the Select Group Members dialog box.**

6. **Click OK one last time to exit the Properties dialog box.**

Modifying Address Book contacts

To modify information about an individual contact or a group, double-click the name in your Address Book. The Properties dialog box appears. For an individual contact, you then need to click the tab that contains the information you want to change. Make your change and then click OK. For a group, you then need to add or remove members as necessary and then click OK when you finish.

Index

Book V

Microsoft Office 2000

The 5th Wave By Rich Tennant

"It's a ten-step word processing program. It comes with a spell-checker, grammar-checker, cliche-checker, whine-checker, passive/aggressive-checker, politically correct-checker, hissy-fit-checker, pretentious pontificating-checker, boring anecdote-checker, and a Freudian reference-checker."

Contents at a Glance

Chapter 1: Getting to Know Microsoft Office 2000

In This Chapter

✔ **What applications does Microsoft Office 2000 include?**

✔ **Other Microsoft Office applications**

*O*ne thing's for sure: You get your money's worth with Microsoft Office 2000. In one convenient bundle, you get a world-class word processor, spreadsheet, presentation program, and time-management program. Plus, you get a grab bag full of other useful features and programs. What a bargain! All these Office 2000 applications and features work together seamlessly to help you simplify all your day-to-day computing tasks.

This chapter provides a general overview of the various programs that make up Office 2000 so that you can get an idea of how the pieces fit together.

What's Included with Microsoft Office 2000?

The Standard Edition of Microsoft Office 2000 includes four main applications: Word 2000, Excel 2000, PowerPoint 2000, and Outlook 2000. Each application is covered in a separate chapter of Book V. (In addition, Book V, Chapter 2 covers common tasks that all Microsoft Office applications share.)

The more expensive Professional Edition of Microsoft Office 2000 includes the same four applications, plus the Access 2000 database program and the Publisher 2000 desktop publishing program. These two programs are briefly described at the end of this chapter but are not covered elsewhere in this book.

The Premium Edition of Microsoft Office 2000 is the most comprehensive (and most expensive) package. In addition to the six applications mentioned previously, the Premium Edition also includes the FrontPage 2000 Web site creation and management program and the new PhotoDraw 2000 business graphics program.

Small business owners may prefer to purchase the Small Business Edition of Microsoft Office 2000, which includes these applications: Word 2000, Excel 2000, Outlook 2000, Publisher 2000, and some additional small business tools.

Word 2000

Microsoft Word 2000 (also called Word 9) is one of the best word-processing programs available (see Figure 1-1). You can use Word to create business and personal documents of all shapes and sizes — including letters, mailing labels, envelopes, newsletters, reports, proposals, brochures, and much more. If you want to get fancy, you can use Word to format the text, check the spelling and grammar, and change the page layout. You also can easily add tables, bulleted and numbered lists, drawings, charts, graphics (such as clip art), and hyperlinks to your Word documents.

For lengthier documents, you can use Word to add headers and footers, indexes, tables of contents, and footnotes and endnotes. You also can track document revisions, compare documents, and view documents using outline levels.

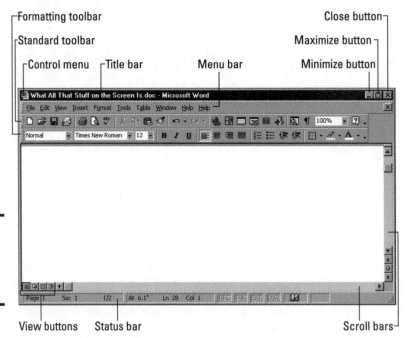

Formatting toolbar
Standard toolbar
Control menu
Title bar
Menu bar
Close button
Maximize button
Minimize button

Figure 1-1:
Elements in the Word 2000 window.

View buttons   Status bar   Scroll bars

See also Book V, Chapter 3 for more information about Word 2000.

Excel 2000

Excel 2000, also known as Excel 9, is a spreadsheet program (see Figure 1-2). It's the bean counter of the Office 2000 operation. Excel 2000 excels at adding up budget totals, calculating sales commissions, figuring loan payments, and performing other math-oriented chores. Just like other spreadsheet programs, Excel 2000 presents its data as a large table that consists of rows and columns. The intersection of a row and column is called a *cell*. You can use cells to store text, numbers, or formulas that calculate results based on the contents of other cells.

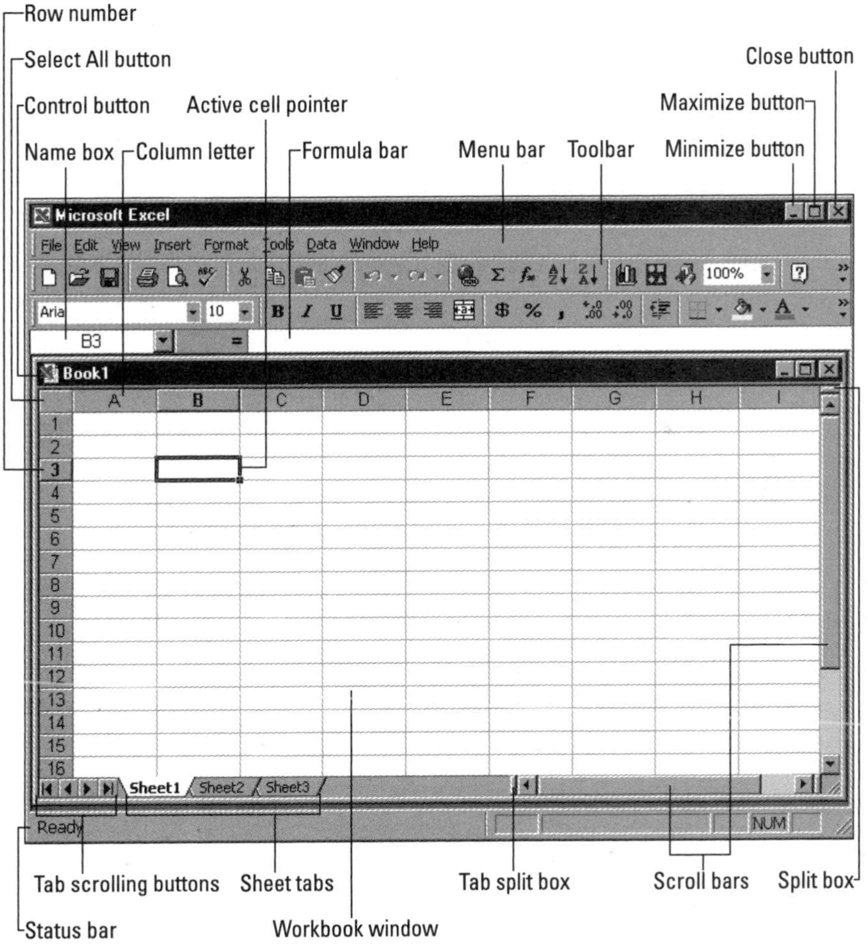

Figure 1-2:
The important parts of the Excel 2000 window.

You can easily spruce up your spreadsheets to create a more polished look by formatting the data. For example, you can change fonts and number formats, add borders, apply different colors to text or cell backgrounds, and use attributes such as bold, italics, and underlining.

See also Book V, Chapter 4 for more details on Excel 2000.

PowerPoint 2000

PowerPoint 2000 (also sometimes known as PowerPoint 9) is a desktop presentation program, which means that the program is designed to help you make presentations (see Figure 1-3). You can use PowerPoint 2000 whether you're speaking in front of hundreds of people at a shareholders' meeting, to a group of sales reps at a sales conference, or with a client one-on-one at a restaurant.

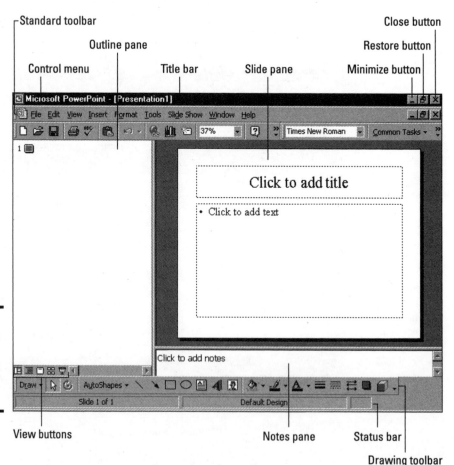

Figure 1-3: The Normal view of the PowerPoint 2000 window.

If you work with overhead transparencies or 35mm slides, PowerPoint 2000 is just the program you need. PowerPoint 2000 can create slides in any of several formats and can also create handouts for your audience as well as notes for you so that you don't get lost in the middle of your speech. You can also use PowerPoint 2000 to create files that you can publish on the Web.

See Book V, Chapter 5 for additional information about PowerPoint 2000.

Outlook 2000

Outlook 2000 is the computer equivalent of one of those fancy combination appointment book/address books — a time-management program that enables you to schedule appointments, create a To Do list, and keep track of your important contacts (see Figure 1-4). But more than that, Outlook 2000 is also an all-in-one e-mail program from which you can send and receive electronic mail over the Internet, your office network, or any of several popular online services.

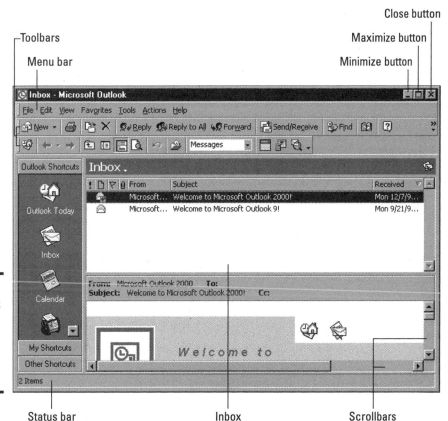

Close button

Maximize button

Minimize button

Toolbars

Menu bar

Figure 1-4:
The Outlook 2000 window with the Inbox displayed.

Status bar

Inbox

Scrollbars

See Book V, Chapter 6 for more information on Outlook 2000.

Other Applications

As mentioned previously in this chapter, Access 2000 and Publisher 2000 come with the more expensive Professional and Premium Editions of Microsoft Office 2000. Although we don't have enough room to cover these applications in this book, we thought that you might want to find out a little bit about them.

Access 2000

Access 2000, a database program, is the computer equivalent of the shoebox in which you store your tax records. Access 2000 helps you keep your records in order and enables you to print reports that list and summarize your data in any form imaginable. On the negative side, Access 2000 is a lot harder to use than your average shoebox.

Database programs, such as Access 2000, are well-suited for keeping mailing lists, but if a mailing list is the only reason you think that you need Access 2000, don't bother. Word 2000 does a pretty good job of storing mailing lists all by itself. In addition, Microsoft Works includes a database program that is simple to use. (For more information, see Book IV, Chapter 5.)

If, however, you want to keep an inventory of your CDs or books or if you want to keep a record of sales orders or employee performance, Access is unbeatable. You can also use Access 2000 to set up databases that you can access from the Web.

For details on using Access 2000, pick up a copy of *Access 2000 For Dummies* by John Kaufeld, published by IDG Books Worldwide, Inc.

Publisher 2000

Publisher 2000 is the Microsoft desktop publishing program, and it's available in the Office 2000 Professional Edition. You can use Publisher to create professional-looking documents that are suitable for publication. Publisher can create everything from single-page leaflets to posters to newsletters with full-color photographs.

Publisher provides you with document templates to cover nearly every imaginable type of document you want to create, and then it enables you to customize your document so that you can create your own personal look and feel.

For more information on how to use Publisher 2000, refer to *Microsoft Publisher 2000 For Dummies* by Jim McCarter, published by IDG Books Worldwide, Inc.

Chapter 2: Performing Common Tasks

In This Chapter

- ✓ Starting and exiting programs
- ✓ Creating, opening, and closing files
- ✓ Finding the help you need
- ✓ Saving and printing files
- ✓ Checking spelling in a document
- ✓ Using time-saving shortcuts

The applications that comprise Microsoft Office 2000 work together to help make your life easier. Not only do the programs resemble each other, but they also include several common tools and commands to help you quickly get up to speed and become more efficient. In this chapter, you find out how to work with tools and commands that are fairly common among the different programs of the Microsoft Office 2000 suite. You'll discover that some of these tools and commands are fairly basic, while others are more advanced.

Starting Programs

To start a Microsoft Office 2000 program, follow these steps:

1. **Turn on your computer.**

2. **Click the Start button.**

   Normally, the Start button is located at the bottom-left corner of the screen in the taskbar. After you click the Start button, the Start menu pops up.

3. **Point to Programs in the Start menu.**

4. **Locate and click the program that you want to start from the menu that appears.**

You can place a shortcut for the programs you use most frequently on the top level of the Start menu or on your desktop. To do this quickly and easily, open the Start menu and locate the program that you want to make a shortcut for, click and hold the left mouse button on it, and drag it to where you want it. (If you want the shortcut on the top of the Start menu, drag it to the area of the Start menu over Programs. If you want the shortcut on the desktop, drag it there.)

Creating a Document

You have several ways to create a new document in Word, Excel, or PowerPoint:

✦ **Choose File⇨New.** Choosing this command displays the New dialog box, which enables you to select one of several available templates you want to use as the basis of your new document. All of the major applications in Office 2000 provide templates for the most common types of documents created in these programs.

 ✦ **Click the New button in the Standard toolbar.** Clicking the New button bypasses the New dialog box and creates a blank, new document.

✦ **Press Ctrl+N.** This keyboard shortcut also creates a blank, new document.

Opening a File

After you save your file to disk, you may want to retrieve the file later to make changes to it or to print it. Unless you've worked with the file recently, you must display the Open dialog box to open a file. Use any of these methods:

 ✦ Click the Open button on the Standard toolbar.

✦ Choose File⇨Open.

✦ Press Ctrl+O.

✦ Press Ctrl+F12.

If you have used the file recently, chances are that you can find it without using the Open dialog box (or even having the application running). To find the file quickly, click the Start button and select Documents. You get a list of the last 15 documents that you have opened. If what you need is there, simply click the document name. The document and its application open for you.

If the Open dialog box (shown in Figure 2-1) shows the document folder where the file you want is located, simply double-click the file you want to open. If your file isn't listed, use the Look In drop-down list to select the folder containing the file and then double-click the file.

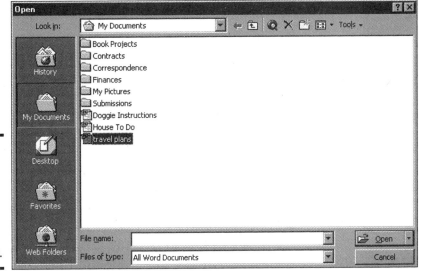

Figure 2-1:
The Open
dialog box
works the
same way
in Word,
Excel, and
PowerPoint.

Other controls on the Open dialog box are listed in Table 2-1:

Table 2-1	Open Dialog Box Controls
Control	*What It Does*
←	Moves you back to the last location that the Open dialog box showed. If you hold your pointer over this button, a ScreenTip (yellow box) appears to tell you what that last location is.
⬆	Moves you up one level in your computer's directory.
🔍	Opens the Internet Explorer to enable you to search the World Wide Web, which is useful if you're looking for a Web page.
✕	Deletes the highlighted document or folder. This means that you don't have to open the Windows Explorer to get rid of files.
📁	Creates a new folder in the current location of the Open dialog box.

(continued)

Table 2-1 *(continued)*

Control	What It Does
	The Views button changes what information displays in the Open dialog box. If only the icons and filenames are showing (called the List view), one click provides you with information about the size of all the files, the type of file, and the date they were modified (this is called the Details view). If you select one particular file and click this button again, the dialog box shows you a split screen. A window appears on the right with information about that file (this is called the Properties view). Click the button a third time to see a small picture of the document. This Preview is handy if you want to know what the document says without opening it. Click the button again, and you're back to seeing just the icons and file-names.
	If you click the arrow to the right of the Views button, you get a drop-down list of the different possible ways of displaying the documents and files of your system. In fact, these are the same views that you saw by clicking the main button (rather than the arrow) repeatedly (see the pre-vious entry in this table). However, one other feature, Arrange Icons, enables you to organize how your files appear in the dialog box.
Tools ▾	This button is actually a menu button. Clicking it gives you a drop-down list of commands, including Find, Delete, Rename, Print, Add to Favorites, Map Network Drive, and Properties.
	Shows you a list of the documents that you've recently had open, regardless of their location.
	Shows the contents of the My Documents folder.
	Shows the contents of your desktop, including any shortcuts you've placed there.
	Displays your Favorites folder.
	Displays any Web folders that you've saved to your system.

All the Office 2000 programs keep track of the last few files you opened and display the names of those files at the bottom of the File menu. To reopen a recently opened file, click the File menu and inspect the list of files at the bottom of the menu. If the filename you want appears in this list, click it to open that file.

If you look through a folder and don't see a file that you *know* has to be there, click the Files of Type list box. The Open dialog box displays only the types of files indicated in this box, so if Files of Type is set to show only Word files, you could have a dozen Excel files in the folder and not see them. If this problem happens, scroll to the type of file you want (or select All Files) and click it. The correct file formats appear.

Switching among Programs

Microsoft Windows enables you to run several programs at the same time and switch back and forth among those programs. By using this feature, for example, you can start up Word, PowerPoint, and Excel at the same time and quickly switch to any of the programs to access or exchange information among them.

After you have more than one program running, you can switch among them by using any of the following techniques:

+ **Press Alt+Esc:** You can switch to the next program in line by pressing Alt+Esc. If more than two programs are running, you may need to press this key combination several times to get to the program you want.

+ **Press Alt+Tab:** Alt+Tab displays a menu of icons, representing all the programs currently running, in a window that appears in the middle of the screen. To switch to a program, hold down the Alt key and press the Tab key repeatedly until you select the program you want to use. Then release both keys to switch to that program.

+ **Use the taskbar:** You can switch programs easily by using the taskbar. Just click the button in the taskbar that represents the program to which you want to switch — and you're there!

The taskbar usually sits at the bottom of the screen, but you can also configure the taskbar to rest on any edge of the screen. You can even configure the taskbar so that the feature vanishes entirely if not in use. In that case, you must move the mouse pointer to the extreme bottom edge of the screen (or the left, right, or top edge, if you moved the taskbar) to access the feature again. If all else fails, you can locate the taskbar by pressing Ctrl+Esc, which reveals the taskbar no matter where it is. (Pressing Ctrl+Esc also opens the Start menu as if you had clicked the Start button.) After you locate the taskbar, you can then switch to any other running program by clicking that program's button on the taskbar.

Getting Help

Lost within the dark woods of Microsoft Office 2000 and don't know how to get out? Fret not, for all the Office programs boast an excellent Help system that can answer all your questions — provided, of course, that you know what your questions are.

The following list summarizes the more notable methods of getting help:

+ The universal Help key is F1. Press F1 at any time, and the Office Assistant rushes to your aid (see "Using the Office Assistant"). If you have turned the Office Assistant off, then a Help window opens instead.

✦ If you have not turned off the Office Assistant and you press F1 while you're in the middle of something, the Office Assistant tries to figure out what you're doing so that it can give you help tailored for that task. This slick little bit of wizardry is called *context-sensitive Help*.

✦ After you click Help in the menu bar, you get an entire menu of Help stuff. Choosing Help⇨Help displays the Office Assistant or opens the Help window.

✦ You can also call up Help in just about any dialog box by clicking the question mark button that appears in the top-right corner of the dialog box. The mouse pointer changes to an arrow with a question mark. You can then click anything in the dialog box to get specific information about that feature.

✦ You can also click the Office Assistant button on the Standard toolbar to display the Office Assistant.

✦ For a really cool kind of help, try choosing Help⇨What's This? This Help feature changes the mouse pointer into a pointy question mark, with which you can click just about anything on-screen in order to get an explanation of the object that you click.

Using the Office Assistant

The Office Assistant is a friendly little helper that lives on your screen. The Assistant watches you work and periodically chimes in with a tip about how you can perform a task more efficiently.

To ask a question, click the Office Assistant. If the Office Assistant is nowhere to be found, you can display it quickly by clicking the Office Assistant button on the Standard toolbar. A balloon dialog box appears, as shown in Figure 2-2.

Figure 2-2:
The Office
Assistant
awaits your
question.

Tell the Assistant what you want to do by typing a few keywords in the balloon's text box (for example, you can type **create a bullet list** or even just **bullet list**) and then click the Search button. The Assistant thinks for a moment and then shows you a list of Help topics related to your keywords (see Figure 2-3). Click the topic you're interested in to display the Help.

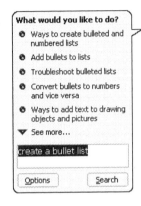

Figure 2-3:
Select the appropriate Help topic from the list.

If you don't like Clippit, the animated paper clip object that is your default Office Assistant, you can change it to another Assistant: Rocky the Dog, Links the Cat, the Genius, Mother Nature, a robot, or several other choices. To change the Assistant's character, right-click the Office Assistant and select Choose Assistant from the Office Assistant dialog box. Use the Back and Next buttons to look at the available choices. When you see the one you like best, click OK. The Assistant appears on your screen. (If you didn't install all of the Assistants when you installed Office, you'll be prompted to insert the Office CD when you attempt to switch to a different Assistant.)

You can customize your Office Assistant to behave in ways that are most appealing or useful to you. To do this, click the Options button in the Office Assistant's balloon (or right-click the Office Assistant and select Options from that dialog box). The Options tab of the Office Assistant dialog box appears (see Figure 2-4). You can use the check boxes on this dialog box to specify exactly how you want your Office Assistant to work for you, up to and including turning the Office Assistant off. Choose the settings you want and then click OK.

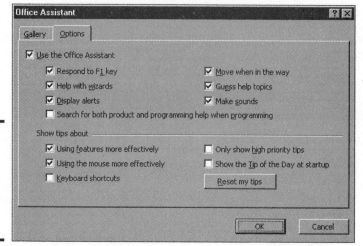

Figure 2-4:
You can customize the settings for the Office Assistant.

Getting help the old-fashioned way

If you yearn for the good old days, back when you actually had to *search* for Help topics, you can always revert to Windows-style Help. Here's how to search for Help on a specific topic the old-fashioned way:

1. **Before you can open the Help window, you first must turn off the Office Assistant. Do this by right-clicking the Office Assistant, clicking Options from the shortcut menu, and deselecting the Use the Office Assistant check box. Then click OK.**

2. **Choose Help⇨Help or press F1.**

    The actual name of the item on the Help drop-down menu depends on the application you're using. If you are asking for help in Word, for example, the menu says Microsoft Word Help. If you're using PowerPoint, the menu says Microsoft PowerPoint Help.

    The Help window appears, as shown in Figure 2-5 for Word 2000.

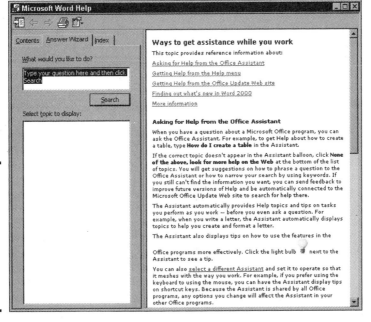

Figure 2-5: The Help window provides different ways of accessing help information.

The left side of the Help window has three tabs: Contents, Answer Wizard, and Index. Each one of the tabs enables you to find the same information through a different route.

- **The Answer Wizard tab** (shown in Figure 2-5) works like the Office Assistant. The *What would you like to do?* text box enables you to ask a question about a topic. Type in the task you want more information about and click the Search button. The information appears in the right window.

- **The Contents tab** (see Figure 2-6) organizes help information by topic, like the chapters of a book. Click the plus sign to the left of the topic, and the topic expands to show you a list of tasks associated with that topic. Click the task you want to find out about, and the right window shows you the information you requested or gives you a list of specific tasks. If you see the list of specific tasks, click the one you need information about, and you (finally!) get to the directions to complete the task. Generally, the more complex the task, the more levels of the Contents directory you have to go through to get to the information.

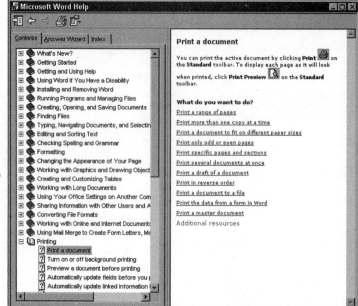

Figure 2-6:
The
Contents
tab displays
help infor-
mation
organized
by category.

- **The Index tab** (see Figure 2-7) is like the index in the back of a book. There are two ways to use this tab. You can enter a keyword into the Type Keywords text box, or you can scroll through the Or Choose Keywords list box until you find what you're looking for. After you type in the keyword or find it in the list, click the Search button. You get a list of topics in the Choose a Topic window, located at the bottom of the Index tab. Scroll through this list until you find the specific topic you want and double-click it. The information you want appears in the right window.

3. **After you finish looking up the information, click the Close button in the upper-right corner of the Help window.**

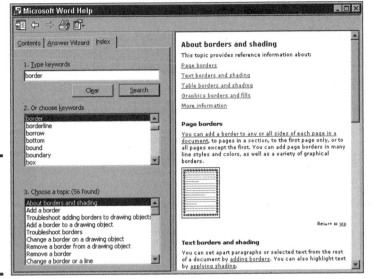

Figure 2-7:
Use the
Index tab to
search for
help infor-
mation by
keyword.

Locating help on the Internet

You can also get help directly from Microsoft via the World Wide Web, assuming that you have access to the Internet from your computer. The Help⇨Office
on the Web command launches your default Web browser and displays the
Microsoft online support page for the program you're using. From this page,
you can access useful articles about specific topics of interest.

But the most valuable link on the online support page is the Office
Newsgroups link. Click this link to enter the Microsoft product support
newsgroups, where you can leave a detailed question that should be
answered within a few days.

Using the Detect and Repair feature

Like everything else in our lives, computer programs can suffer wear-and-
tear from regular use. Eventually, applications can become tattered and
ragged, which can result in crashed programs and lost or garbled data.
When a crash happened in the bad old days, you had no choice but to erase
the program from your system and reinstall it, which is an annoying and
time-consuming task and one that would have lost any customized settings
that you had made on your system. But no more! We now have the Detect
and Repair feature as part of the Help menu.

Detect and Repair is actually a feature of Windows 98, so if you're running Office 2000 on Windows 95, you're out of luck. But for the rest of us, Detect and Repair can be a godsend. This wonderful little tool scans your application for damage and fixes it for you in a fraction of the time you need to delete and install the application again. And this tool enables you to retain your customized settings.

To use the Detect and Repair feature, follow these steps:

1. **Open the Office program that you need to repair.**

2. **Select Help⇨Detect and Repair.**

The Detect and Repair dialog box opens.

3. **Make sure that a check mark appears in the Restore My Shortcuts While Repairing check box.**

Selecting this option saves your customization.

4. **Click the Start button.**

After you set the process in motion, your system thinks about things for a few moments and then asks you to insert the Office installation disk.

5. **When prompted, insert the Office installation disk and then click OK.**

At this point, Windows starts analyzing the application. Depending on the speed of your system, this may take a few minutes, so go get a snack while you're waiting for Office to do its thing.

After Detect and Repair is finished, you see a dialog box that tells you that you must restart your computer for the changes to take effect.

6. **Either click Yes to restart immediately (which is what we recommend) or click No and do it yourself later.**

Using the Clipboard

The *Clipboard* is the program that enables you to copy and move data within a file, between files, or between programs, and it has been a standard part of all Windows programs since the first version of Windows. The following sections describe how to copy and move data by using the Clipboard.

Copying data

You can make a copy of a selection of a document and put that copy somewhere else. The procedure for copying data is the same whether the new location for the copied data is in the same document, a different document using the same program (such as copying data from one Word document to another Word document), or a different program (such as copying data from Word to Excel).

To copy data, follow these steps:

1. **Select the text (or object) that you want to copy.**

 2. **Choose Edit⇨Copy, press Ctrl+C, or click the Copy button on the Standard toolbar.**

3. **Position the insertion point where you want to insert the data.**

 4. **Choose Edit⇨Paste, press Ctrl+V, or click the Paste button on the Standard toolbar.**

Moving data

The procedure for moving data is basically the same within all the applications of Office 2000, whether you're moving data within the same document, between two documents in the same program, or between two documents in different programs (such as moving a range from an Excel worksheet to a Word document).

To move data, follow these steps:

1. **Select the text (or object) that you want to move.**

 2. **Choose Edit⇨Cut, press Ctrl+X, or click the Cut button on the Standard toolbar.**

3. **Position the insertion point where you want to insert the data.**

 4. **Choose Edit⇨Paste, press Ctrl+V, or click the Paste button on the Standard toolbar.**

Dragging and dropping text

You can move text from one location to another by using the drag-and-drop technique. Before using this feature, be sure to enable the drag-and-drop option. To do this, choose Tools⇨Options. When the Options dialog box appears, click the Edit tab and make sure that the drag-and-drop feature is checked. (The name of the drag-and-drop feature varies between programs; for example, in Word the feature is called Drag-and-Drop Text Editing, but in Excel it's called Allow Cell Drag and Drop.)

When drag-and-drop text editing is enabled, you can use it as follows:

1. **Select the text (or object) that you want to move.**

2. **Place the mouse pointer anywhere over the selected text and then press and hold the left mouse button.**

If you're using Excel, you must point to an edge of the selected cell or range before you can move it; the mouse pointer changes to an arrow.

3. **Drag the text to the location where you want to move the text.**

4. **Release the mouse button.**

To use drag-and-drop to copy rather than move text, press and hold the Ctrl key while dragging the text.

Spell Checking a Document

You can check your spelling in any of the main Office 2000 applications. If you're using Word or PowerPoint, the program can check your spelling as you type, highlighting misspelled words so that you can immediately correct them. (To correct a misspelled word, right-click the word and then choose the correct spelling from the shortcut menu that appears.) In addition, all main Office 2000 applications enable you to check your spelling after you finish typing your document. This feature enables you to forget about spelling as you type, with the knowledge that you can correct any mistakes later on.

To spell check a document, follow these steps:

1. **Position the insertion point where you want to begin the spell check.**

2. **Choose Tools⇨Spelling (in Word, the command is Tools⇨Spelling and Grammar), press F7, or click the Spelling button in the Standard toolbar.**

3. **Depending on whether the word is misspelled, take one of the following actions:**

    • If the word is misspelled, select the correct spelling from the list of suggested spellings in the dialog box and click Change.

    • If the correct spelling doesn't appear among the suggestions, type the correct spelling in the Not in Dictionary box (or the Change To box in Excel) and click Change.

    • If the word is correctly spelled, click Ignore. Or click Ignore All to ignore this and any subsequent occurrences of the word.

4. **Repeat Step 3 until the spell checker is finished.**

    After Office 2000 finishes checking your spelling, a message appears to tell you it's done.

If you're annoyed by the wavy red underlines that appear under misspelled words in Word or PowerPoint, you can disable this spell-as-you-type feature. Choose Tools⇨Options. In Word, click the Spelling & Grammar tab. In PowerPoint, click the Spelling and Style tab. Deselect the Check Spelling as You Type check box and click OK.

Saving a File

When you create a new file or modify an existing file, the changes you make aren't permanent until you save the file. What happens if you shut down your applications before saving your files? You lose all your work since the last time you saved the file (*if* you saved it at all!). Be sure to save your work frequently to avoid accidental data loss. You never know when you may experience a power outage or when your computer may lock up.

Use any of the following methods to save the current Office 2000 file to disk:

+ **Choose File⇨Save.**
+ **Click the Save button on the toolbar.**
+ **Press Ctrl+S.**

The first time you save an Office 2000 file, you can accept the default name (such as Doc1.doc in Word) or provide a new name for the file (see the following section). You also specify the drive and folder in which you want to store the file. If you save a file that's previously been saved, the file in memory automatically replaces the file with the same name on disk.

Saving a file under a new name

If you want to make a duplicate of the current file by saving the file under a different filename, follow these steps:

1. **Choose File⇨Save As.**

   The Save As dialog box (which closely resembles the Open dialog box) appears.

2. **In the Save In drop-down list, find the folder in which you want to save the file.**

   You can click the Create Folder button if you want to create a new folder instead of using an existing one.

3. **Type a new name for the file in the File Name text box.**

4. **Click the Save button.**

To save your file in a different file format, use the Save as Type drop-down list in the Save As dialog box. You may choose to do this, for example, if you need to exchange files with coworkers who use an earlier version of the program.

You may lose some formatting or other file information if you save to an older file format or to a different file format. Information loss normally happens if you use features or commands that aren't available in the older version of that application. When you save a file to an older file format, be sure to change the file name so that you can always revert to your original file.

Saving a file as a Web document

Web documents are saved in what is called *HTML* format. HTML is a computer language that you use to format material for the Internet's World Wide Web. All the Office 2000 applications can easily save documents in the HTML format so that you can display them on the Web.

To save a Word, Excel, or PowerPoint document as a Web page, all you need to do is choose File⇨Save as Web Page. This command opens the Save As dialog box, specifically set to save the file as a Web page. Simply find the folder where you want to store the file and click the Save button. You can then upload the file to your server.

Printing a File

You can print an entire document, specific pages, or any text or object that you select. Before you print, you can adjust settings such as the margins, page orientation (portrait or landscape), and paper size. To do so, choose File⇨Page Setup, select the settings you want in the Page Setup dialog box, and click OK.

Follow these steps when you're ready to print your document:

1. **Turn on you printer**

2. **Choose File⇨Print or press Ctrl+P.**

   The Print dialog box opens.

3. **Specify the print settings you want to use and then click OK.**

 To print a single copy of your document quickly, without fussing with the Print dialog box, click the Print button in the Standard toolbar. One copy of your document prints to your default printer.

Shortcuts That Work Everywhere in Office 2000

The following Tables 2-2 through 2-5 list keyboard shortcuts and toolbar buttons that work in all (or at least most of) the Office 2000 applications.

Table 2-2	**File Commands**	
Toolbar button	*Keyboard Shortcut*	*Equivalent Command*
	Ctrl+N	File⇨New
	Ctrl+O or Ctrl+F12	File⇨Open
	Ctrl+S	File⇨Save
	F12	File⇨Save As
	Ctrl+W	File⇨Close
	Ctrl+P	File⇨Print
	Alt+F4	File⇨Exit

Table 2-3	**Editing Commands**	
Toolbar button	*Keyboard Shortcut*	*Equivalent Command*
	Ctrl+X	Edit⇨Cut
	Ctrl+C	Edit⇨Copy
	Ctrl+V	Edit⇨Paste
	Ctrl+Z	Edit⇨Undo
	Ctrl+Y	Edit⇨Repeat
Ctrl+A	Edit⇨Select All	
Ctrl+F	Edit⇨Find	
Ctrl+H	Edit⇨Replace	

Table 2-4	**Quick Formatting**	
Toolbar button	*Keyboard Shortcut*	*Equivalent Command*
B	Ctrl+B	Bold
I	Ctrl+I	Italic
U	Ctrl+U	Underline

Table 2-5	Switching Programs
Keyboard Shortcut	*What It Does*
Alt+Esc	Switches to the next program in line.
Alt+Tab	While holding the Alt key, press Tab to display a list of icons for all the programs that are currently running. Keep pressing the Tab key until the icon for the program you want to switch to is highlighted and then release both keys to switch to that program.
Ctrl+Esc	Pops up the taskbar and the Start menu. Click the button on the taskbar for the program you want to switch to.

If you have a Microsoft IntelliMouse, you can use its wheel control to scroll through your document. Just roll the wheel to scroll forward and back or click the wheel to switch to "pan" mode, which enables you to scroll through your document by dragging the mouse up or down. Click the wheel again to quit pan mode. You can also zoom in and out by pressing and holding the Ctrl key as you roll the wheel on the IntelliMouse. Refer to Book I, Chapter 3 for more on using the IntelliMouse.

Using the Web Toolbar

The Web toolbar enables you to browse Office documents that are linked together with hyperlinks more easily and to browse the Web. Choose View⇨Toolbars⇨Web to display the toolbar. At the far right side of the Web toolbar is an Address list box in which you can type the filename of a file you want to open or the URL of an Internet address you want to visit. Table 2-6 describes the other buttons in the Web toolbar:

Table 2-6	Web Toolbar
Button	*What It Does*
	Displays the previous page.
	Displays the next page in sequence.
	Cancels a download in process.
	Obtains a new copy of the document or HTML page and refreshes your screen.
	Takes you to your start page, which is the first page to display when you access the Internet.
	Calls up a search page that enables you to search the Internet for specific information.

Button	What It Does
Favorites ▾	Displays a list of your favorite documents so that you can quickly access them. Also includes an Add to Favorites command so that you can add items to your Favorites menu.
→	Displays a menu that lists these commands: Open, Back, Forward, Start Page, Search the Web, Set Start Page, and Set Search Page.
▣	Shows only the Web toolbar so that more space is available on your screen to display the document.

Sending an Office 2000 File as an E-Mail Attachment

If your computer is connected to a network or to the Internet, you can send a copy of the file you're working on to a friend or co-worker via e-mail by following these steps:

1. **Choose File⇨Send To⇨Mail Recipient (as Attachment).**

   If the program asks you to specify a user profile, select the profile you normally use when sending and receiving e-mail. User profiles control such things as which e-mail services you have access to and where your address book is stored. If more than one person uses your computer, you can set up a separate profile for each user.

2. **Type someone's e-mail address in the To text box.**

   You also can click the To button to display your address book, which should contain the e-mail addresses of the people you routinely e-mail.

3. **Type a message in the message box, if desired.**

4. **Click the Send button to send the message.**

Closing a File

To close a file, choose File⇨Close, use the keyboard shortcut Ctrl+W, or click the Close button, which is located in the upper-right corner of the screen. When you look at the upper-right corner of the screen in Excel and PowerPoint, you see two Close buttons. The top button of the two closes the *program;* the Close button just below it closes the *file.* If you don't want to close the program you're working in, make sure that you click the Close button for the file.

You don't need to close files before exiting a program. If you exit the program without closing a file, the program closes the file for you. But closing files you're no longer working with is a good idea because doing so saves memory, which can help your programs run faster.

If you close a file and have made changes to the file since you last saved it, a dialog box appears, offering to save the changes for you. Click Yes to save the file before closing or click No to abandon any changes you made to the file.

If you have only one file open and you close that file, you may discover that you inadvertently rendered most of the program's commands inaccessible — the commands appear "grayed out" on the menus, and clicking them does nothing. Don't panic. Create or open another file, and the commands return to life.

Exiting Programs

Had enough excitement for one day? Use any one of the following techniques to shut down your program:

- ✦ **Choose File⇨Exit.**

- ✦ **Click the Close button that appears at the upper-right corner of the program window.**

- ✦ **Press Alt+F4.**

Save your work before you abandon ship. If you made changes to any files that you haven't saved, a dialog box asks whether you want to save your files. Click Yes to save your changes.

Never just turn off your computer while a program is running. Doing this can damage your computer and can leave file fragments cluttering up your hard drive. Always exit all programs that are running *before* you turn off your computer. Notify Windows before you turn off your computer by clicking the Start button and then choosing the Shut Down command. Click OK in the Shut Down dialog box that appears.

Chapter 3: Word 2000

In This Chapter

✔ Typing and formatting text

✔ Working with tabs

✔ Discovering the most useful Word 2000 keyboard shortcuts

✔ Using Mail Merge

✔ Applying themes and styles to simplify formatting chores

✔ Creating Web pages using the Web Page Wizard

*O*ffice 2000 comes with the latest and greatest version of the premier word processing program, Microsoft Word 2000. This chapter covers the basics of using Word 2000. You can find lots more information about Word 2000 in *Word 2000 For Windows For Dummies,* by Dan Gookin, published by IDG Books Worldwide, Inc.

Typing Text

When you begin typing in a document, the text appears at the location of the *insertion point* — the blinking cursor that you see in the document area on-screen. Don't confuse the insertion point with the mouse pointer. The mouse pointer normally appears as an I-beam shape in a Word document; use this pointer to click the location in the document where you want to insert text.

Follow these steps to type text in a Word document:

1. Position the insertion point where you want the text to appear.

If you've just created a new, blank document, the insertion point appears at the beginning of the first page.

2. Type your text.

Keep in mind that you don't need to press Enter at the end of a line. Word automatically wraps your text to the next line when it reaches the end of the current line, and it automatically begins a new page when your text reaches the end of the current page.

Selecting Text

In most cases, you need to select text in a document before you can do any-thing that affects the text (such as formatting, editing, copying, moving, or deleting). You can use either the mouse or the keyboard to select text in a document.

Always be careful when selecting a large amount of text — anything you type replaces the selection! If this happens, and you catch it right away, you can click the Undo button in the Standard toolbar to reverse the action.

Selecting text by using the mouse

Here are the common mouse actions for selecting text:

+ Drag the mouse over the text you want to select.

+ Click the mouse at the start of a block of text, press and hold the Shift key, and then click again at the end of the block. This procedure selects everything in between the clicks.

+ Double-click to select a single word.

+ Triple-click to select an entire paragraph.

+ Press and hold the Ctrl key and then click to select an entire sentence.

+ Press and hold the Alt key and then drag the mouse to select any rec-tangular area of text.

+ Click the selection bar (the invisible vertical area to the left of the text) to select a line.

+ Double-click the selection bar to select an entire paragraph.

Selecting text by using the keyboard

You can use the following keyboard techniques to select text:

+ Place the insertion point at the beginning of the text you want to select, press and hold the Shift key, and then move the insertion point to the end of the text you want to select by using the arrow keys. Release the Shift key after you select the text you want.

+ Press Ctrl+A to select the entire document.

+ Press F8 and then press any key to extend the selection to the next occurrence of that key's character. For example, to select text from the current location to the end of a sentence, press F8 and then press the period key.

You can keep extending the selection by pressing other keys. For example, if you press the period key again, the selection extends to the next period. To stop extending the selection, press the Escape key.

Creating a Bulleted List

To create a bulleted list, follow these steps:

1. **Type one or more paragraphs to which you want to add bullets.**

2. **Select the paragraphs to which you want to add bullets.**

3. **Click the Bullets button on the Formatting toolbar.**

To add additional items to the bulleted list, position the insertion point at the end of one of the bulleted paragraphs and press Enter. Because the bullet is part of the paragraph format, the bullet format carries over to the new paragraph.

The Bullets button works like a toggle. Click the button once to add bullets and click the button again to remove them. To remove bullets from an entire list, select all the paragraphs in the list and click the Bullets button.

If you want to create a bulleted list as you compose your text, start by formatting the first paragraph with a bullet. Word 2000 carries the bullet format over to subsequent paragraphs as you type them. After you finish typing your last bulleted paragraph, press Enter and then click the Bullets button again to turn off the bullet format.

To change the appearance of the bullet, choose Format⇨Bullets and Numbering and click the Bulleted tab (see Figure 3-1). Select the bullet style you want to use and then click OK.

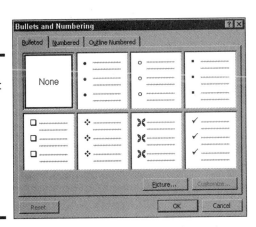

Figure 3-1: Many bullet styles are available; click the Picture or Customize button for even more options.

Creating a Numbered List

To create a numbered list, follow this procedure:

1. **Type one or more paragraphs that you want to number.**
2. **Select all the paragraphs that you want to number.**

3. **Click the Numbering button on the Formatting toolbar.**

If you add or delete a paragraph in the middle of the numbered list, Word 2000 renumbers the paragraphs to preserve the order. If you add a paragraph to the end of the list, Word 2000 assigns the next number in sequence to the new paragraph.

The Numbering button works like a toggle. Click the button once to add numbers to paragraphs; click the button again to remove them. To remove numbering from an entire list, select all the paragraphs in the list and click the Numbering button.

If you insert an unnumbered paragraph in the middle of a numbered list, Word 2000 breaks the list in two and begins numbering from one again for the second list. If you simply turn off numbering for one of the paragraphs in a list, however, Word 2000 suspends the numbering for that paragraph and picks up where the sequence left off for the next numbered paragraph.

For more advanced numbering options, choose Format⇨Bullets and Numbering and then choose the Numbered or Outline Numbered tabs.

Creating Tables

Tables are a nifty feature of Word 2000 that enable you to organize information into a grid. You can create tables by using any of several predefined formats.

Follow this procedure to create a table:

1. **Position the insertion point where you want to insert the table into your document.**
2. **Choose Table⇨Insert⇨Table.**

   The Insert Table dialog box appears.
3. **Select the size of the table by setting the Number of Columns and Number of Rows text boxes.**
4. **If you want to apply predefined formats to your table, such as borders and shading, click the AutoFormat button. Then choose the format and other settings you want to use in the Table AutoFormat dialog box (see Figure 3-2) and click OK.**

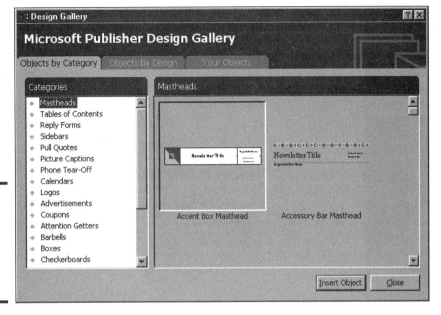

Figure 3-2:
You can
easily add
fancy for-
matting to
your Word
tables.

5. **Click OK to create the table.**

To quickly insert a simple table in your document, click the Insert Table
button on the Standard toolbar. This produces a drop-down box that shows
a grid of columns and rows. Drag your insertion point diagonally across the
drop-down box to highlight the number of rows and columns you want in
your table. When you release the mouse button, your table is inserted at the
insertion point position.

After you create a table, you can type data into its cells by clicking the cell
where you want to enter data and typing the data. You can use the arrow
keys to move from cell to cell in any direction you want, or you can press
the Tab key to move to the next cell in the table.

Browsing Through a Document

Word 2000 offers a Browse control located at the bottom of the vertical
scroll bar, as shown in the margin. After you click the Select Browse Object
button sandwiched between the two double-arrow controls, a menu appears
that enables you to access several navigation features from one convenient
location.

Two of the buttons on this menu invoke the familiar Edit⇨Go To and
Edit⇨Find commands. The ten remaining buttons change the unit by which

the document is browsed after you click the double up or double down arrow controls immediately above and below the Select Browse Object button. Table 3-1 describes the function of each of the buttons on the Browse menu.

Table 3-1	Browse Buttons
Button	*What It Does*
→	Invokes the Edit⇨Go to command
🔍	Invokes the Edit⇨Find command
✎	Browse by edits (works in conjunction with revision tracking)
≡	Browse by heading, as indicated by standard heading styles
🖼	Browse by graphic objects
▦	Browse by Word table objects
{a}	Browse by Word fields
📑	Browse by endnote
📄	Browse by footnote
💬	Browse by comment
🔖	Browse by section
📄	Browse by page

 The *Document Map* is a cool feature that enables you to view your document's outline side-by-side with the text. Click the Document Map button in the Standard toolbar. After the Document Map is open, you can quickly move to any spot in your document simply by clicking the appropriate heading in the Document Map. Click the button again to return to your previous document view.

Finding Text

You can use the Edit⇨Find command to find text anywhere in a document. Just follow these steps:

1. **Choose Edit⇨Find or press Ctrl+F.**

   The Find and Replace dialog box opens.

2. **In the Find What text box, type the text that you want to find.**

   You can type a single word or a phrase. You can use spaces, too.

3. **Click the Find Next button.**

   After Word finds the text, the program highlights the text on-screen. Repeat this step as needed to find the next occurrence of the text.

4. **After Word finds the last occurrence of the text, click OK.**

Click Cancel to exit the Find and Replace dialog box at any time.

You can change how Word 2000 searches for your text by clicking the More button in the Find and Replace dialog box to reveal a set of additional search options. The available search options are listed and described in Table 3-2:

Table 3-2	Search Options
Search Option	*What It Does*
Search	Enables you to specify the direction in which Word searches the document for text. The choices are Down, Up, and All.
Match Case	Indicates that whether the search text appears in uppercase or lowercase letters matters.
Find Whole Words Only	Finds your search text only if the text appears as a whole word.
Use Wildcards	Enables you to include wildcard characters in the Find What text box. Here are three of the most useful wildcards:
?	Finds a single occurrence of any character. For example, **f?t** finds *fat* or *fit*.
*	Finds any combination of characters. For example, **b*t** finds any combination of characters that begins with *b* and ends with *t*, such as *bat*, *bait*, or *ballast*.
[abc]	Finds any one of the characters enclosed in the brackets. For example, **b[ai]t** finds *bat* or *bit* but not *bet* or *but*.
Sounds Like	Finds text that is phonetically similar to the search text, even if the spelling varies.
Find All Word Forms	Searches for all forms of the search text word. For example, if you search for *sink*, Word 2000 also finds *sank* and *sunk*.
Format	Enables you to search for text that has specific formatting applied — for example, to search for text formatted in the Arial font.
Special	Enables you to search for special characters, such as paragraph or tab marks.

Replacing Text

You can choose Edit⇨Replace to replace all occurrences of one bit of text with other text. Follow these steps:

1. **Press Ctrl+Home to get to the top of the document.**

If you skip this step, the search-and-replace operation starts at the position of the insertion point.

2. **Choose Edit⇨Replace or press Ctrl+H.**

The Find and Replace dialog box displays with the Replace tab active.

3. **Type the text you want to find in the Find What box and then type the text you want to substitute for the Find What text in the Replace With box.**

4. **Click the Find Next button.**

After Word finds the text, the program highlights the text on-screen.

5. **Click the Replace button to replace the text.**

6. **Repeat Steps 4 and 5 until you finish searching the document.**

Word displays a message to tell you that it's finished.

If you're absolutely positive that you want to replace all occurrences of your Find What/Replace With text, click the Replace All button. This feature automatically replaces all occurrences of the text. The only problem is that you're bound to encounter at least one spot where you don't want the replacement to occur. Replacing the word *mit* with *glove,* for example, changes *Smith* to *Sgloveh.* (And no, Sgloveh is *not* the Czechoslovakian form of the name Smith.)

Formatting a Document

Word gives you more ways to format your document than any mere mortal would ever need. The following sections describe common formatting procedures.

If you already have some text formatted the way you like, the fastest way to format characters or paragraphs is to use the Format Painter. Highlight the already formatted text and click on the Format Painter button on the Standard toolbar. Then move your insertion point down to the text that you want to look just like the formatted text and highlight it. Word automatically formats the new text to look just like the previously formatted text. If you have text scattered through your document that you want formatted identically, highlight the text you want to use as your template and then double-click the Format Painter button. The Format Painter continuously formats text that you highlight until you click the Format Painter button again or press Escape.

Setting the character format

You can set character formats by using the formatting keyboard shortcuts or the buttons that appear in the Formatting toolbar, as described in the section "Using Keyboard Shortcuts," later in this chapter. Or you can use the following procedure to apply character formats via the Format⇨Font command:

1. **Highlight the text to which you want to apply the formatting.**

If you skip this step, Word applies formatting to all new text you type until you repeat the procedure to deactivate the formatting.

2. **Choose Format⇨Font.**

The Font dialog box appears, as shown in Figure 3-3.

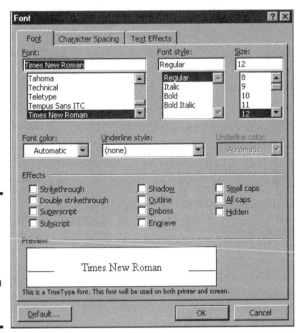

Figure 3-3:
You can apply multiple character formats at once with the Fonts dialog box.

3. **Select the settings you want to change, such as the Font, the Font style (bold, italic, and so on), and the Size; select any of the Effects area check boxes you want (Strikethrough, Superscript, and so on); and use the drop-down list boxes to set the Underline and Font color.**

   The Preview box at the bottom of the dialog box shows how text appears after Word applies the formatting options you select.

4. **Click OK after you finish.**

Setting the paragraph format

Follow these steps to apply formats to entire paragraphs in your document:

1. **Click anywhere in the paragraph you want to format.**

   You don't need to select the entire paragraph as long as the insertion point is somewhere in the paragraph you want to format.

2. **Choose Format⇨Paragraph.**

   The Paragraph dialog box appears (see Figure 3-4).

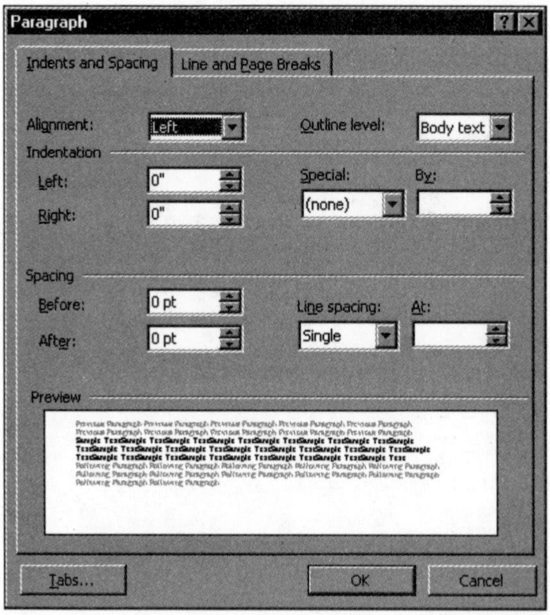

Figure 3-4:
Use the
Paragraph
dialog box
to set for-
mats for an
entire para-
graph.

3. **Specify the paragraph's Alignment, Indentation, and Spacing settings.**

   You can monitor the effect of each setting in the Preview box that appears at the bottom of the Paragraph dialog box.

4. **Click OK after you finish formatting your paragraph.**

You can quickly set paragraph formats by selecting the paragraphs you want to format and then using the buttons on the Formatting toolbar or keyboard shortcuts listed in the section "Using Keyboard Shortcuts," later in this chapter.

Setting Tabs

The most common method of setting tabs is by clicking the ruler, which sits atop the document window. (If the ruler isn't visible, choose View⇨Ruler.)

Word enables you to create four types of tab alignments: *left, center, right,* and *decimal.* To change the type of tab that you create as you click the ruler, click the Tab Alignment button at the far-left edge of the ruler. Each time you click this button, the picture on the button changes to indicate the alignment type:

Left tab   Text left-aligns at the tab stop.

Center tab   Text centers over the tab stop.

Right tab   Text right-aligns at the tab stop.

Decimal tab   Numbers align at the decimal point over the tab stop.

Follow these steps to set tabs using the ruler:

1. **Type some text that you want to line up with tab stops.**

2. **Select the paragraph(s) for which you want to set tabs.**

If you are adding tabs for a single paragraph, you only need to position the insertion point in the paragraph.

3. **Click the Tab Alignment button to the left of the ruler to switch to another tab type if necessary.**

4. **Click the ruler at each spot where you want a new tab stop.**

To adjust a tab setting, just use the mouse to grab the tab marker in the ruler and slide the tab to the new location. After you release the mouse button, text in the currently selected paragraph adjusts to the new tab position.

To remove a tab stop from the ruler, click the tab stop you want to remove and drag the tab off the ruler. After you release the mouse button, the tab stop disappears.

TIP

To remove all tab stops at once, choose Format⇨Tabs and then click the Clear All button in the Tabs dialog box. You also can use this dialog box to type the exact position of a tab stop or to create *leader tabs* that have rows of dots or dashes instead of spaces between tab stops.

Working with Styles

Styles are one of the best ways to improve your word processing efficiency. A *style* is a collection of paragraph and character formats that you can apply to text in one fell swoop. You can use styles to format your headings to ensure that they are all formatted in the same way. And you can quickly change the appearance of all headings by simply changing the style.

Applying a style

To apply a style to a paragraph, follow these steps:

1. **Put the insertion point in the paragraph you want to format.**

   To apply a style to two or more adjacent paragraphs, select a range of text that includes all the paragraphs you want to format.

2. **Select the style you want from the Style drop-down list on the Formatting toolbar (see Figure 3-5).**

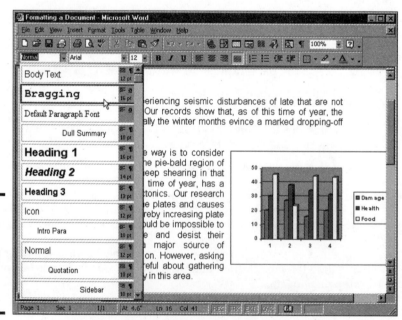

Figure 3-5:
Click the
Style drop-
down list to
see the
styles in a
document.

If the style you want doesn't appear in the drop-down list, press and hold the Shift key and then click the Style drop-down arrow. Word lists only the most commonly used styles if you don't hold down the Shift key.

Creating a new style

To create a new style, follow these steps:

1. **Tweak a paragraph until the text is formatted just the way you want.**

   Set the font and size, line spacing, before and after spacing, and indentation. Also set tabs and any other formatting you want, such as bullets or numbers. You can set these formatting options by using either the Formatting toolbar or the commands on the Format menu.

2. **Click anywhere in the paragraph on which you want to base the style and then press Ctrl+Shift+S or click the Style box on the Formatting toolbar.**

3. **Type a descriptive name for the style.**

4. **Press Enter to add the style to the list of styles for the document.**

Alternatively, you can choose Format⇨Style to display the Style dialog box and then click the New button. A New Style dialog box that enables you to set all the formatting options for a new style appears (see Figure 3-6).

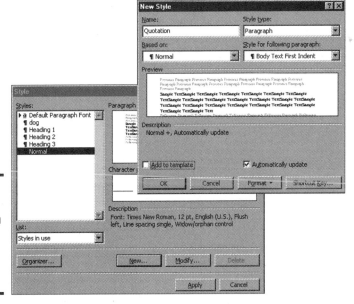

Figure 3-6:
Word enables you to create your own unique styles.

Applying Borders

To add a border around a text paragraph, follow these steps:

1. **Place the insertion point anywhere in the paragraph to which you want to add a border.**

2. **Choose Format⇨Borders and Shading.**

   The Borders and Shading dialog box displays, as shown in Figure 3-7.

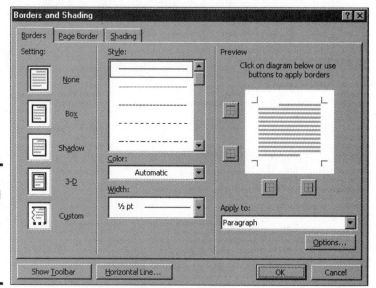

Figure 3-7:
You can add borders to one or more sides of a selected paragraph.

3. **Select the type of border you want from the Setting area of the Borders tab (Box, Shadow, 3-D, or Custom, for example). Or click None if you want to remove a border.**

4. **Select a line style from the Style list, a color from the Color list, and a line width from the Width list if you don't like the default settings.**

   Scroll through the entire list of styles; Word 2000 offers lots of interesting lines from which to choose. If you want each side of the border to have a different style, select the style and then click the appropriate button in the Preview area to apply the style to just that edge.

5. **Click OK.**

You can apply common border styles quickly by clicking the arrow to the right of the Border button on the Formatting toolbar and then selecting the desired border style from the drop-down palette.

Creating Columns

To create multiple columns in your Word document (like columns you see in a newsletter), follow these steps:

1. **Click the Columns button on the Standard toolbar.**

2. **Drag the mouse to pick the number of columns you want.**

For example, if you want three columns in your document, drag the mouse over the columns until three are highlighted.

3. **Release the mouse button.**

Voilà! The document appears formatted with the number of columns you select. In Normal view (choose View➪Normal), the text is formatted according to the width of the column, but the columns don't appear on-screen side by side. To see all columns side by side on-screen, choose View➪Print Layout.

If you want to change the width and spacing of the columns, choose Format➪ Columns and experiment with the settings in the Columns dialog box.

Using Keyboard Shortcuts

Tables 3-3, 3-4, and 3-5 list the most useful Word 2000 keyboard shortcuts for editing, character formatting, and paragraph formatting, respectively. See also "Shortcuts That Work Everywhere in Office 2000," in Book V, Chapter 2.

Table 3-3	Editing Shortcuts
Shortcut	*What It Does*
Ctrl+Del	Deletes from the insertion point to the end of the word.
Ctrl+Backspace	Deletes from the insertion point to the start of the word.
Ctrl+F	Finds text.
Ctrl+H	Replaces occurrences of one text string with another text string.
Ctrl+A	Selects the entire document.

Table 3-4	Character Formatting Shortcuts	
Shortcut	*Button*	*What It Does*
Ctrl+B	**B**	**Bolds** text.
Ctrl+I	*I*	*Italicizes* text.
Ctrl+U	U	<u>Underlines text (continuous)</u>.
Ctrl+Shift+W		<u>Underlines words</u>.
Ctrl+Shift+D		Double-underlines text.
Ctrl+Shift+A		Sets the font to ALL CAPS.
Ctrl+Shift+K		Sets the font to SMALL CAPS.
Ctrl+=		Uses subscript font.
Ctrl+Shift+=		Uses superscript font.
Ctrl+Shift+H		Makes the text hidden.
Shift+F3		Changes from uppercase to lowercase and vice versa.
Ctrl+Shift+*		Displays nonprinting characters.
Ctrl+K		Inserts a hyperlink.
Ctrl+Shift+F		Changes the font.
Ctrl+Shift+P		Changes the point size.
Ctrl+]		Increases size by one point.
Ctrl+[		Decreases size by one point.
Ctrl+Shift+>		Increases size to next available size.
Ctrl+Shift+<		Decreases size to preceding available size.
Ctrl+Shift+Q		Switches to Symbol font (Greek Tragedy).
Ctrl+spacebar		Removes character formatting.

Table 3-5	Paragraph Formatting Shortcuts	
Shortcut	*Button*	*What It Does*
Ctrl+L		Left-aligns a paragraph.
Ctrl+R		Right-aligns a paragraph.
Ctrl+J		Justifies a paragraph.

Shortcut	*Button*	*What It Does*
Ctrl+E		Centers a paragraph.
Ctrl+M		Increases left indent.
Ctrl+Shift+M		Decreases left indent.
Ctrl+T		Creates a hanging indent.
Ctrl+Shift+T		Reduces a hanging indent.
Ctrl+1		Single-spaces a paragraph.
Ctrl+2		Double-spaces a paragraph.
Ctrl+5		Sets line spacing to 1.5.
Ctrl+0 (zero)		Removes or sets space before a line to one line.
Ctrl+Shift+S		Applies a style.
Ctrl+Shift+N		Applies Normal style.
Ctrl+Alt+1		Applies Heading 1 style.
Ctrl+Alt+2		Applies Heading 2 style.
Ctrl+Alt+3		Applies Heading 3 style.
Ctrl+Shift+L		Applies List style.
Ctrl+Q		Removes paragraph formatting.

Assigning Your Own Keyboard Shortcuts

If Word doesn't supply enough keyboard shortcuts to fill your needs, you can easily create your own shortcuts. You can assign your own keyboard shortcuts to styles, macros, fonts, AutoText entries, commands, and symbols.

To assign a keyboard shortcut, follow these steps:

1. **Choose Tools⇨Customize.**

The Customize dialog box displays.

2. **Click the Commands tab and then click the Keyboard button.**

The Customize Keyboard dialog box appears, as shown in Figure 3-8.

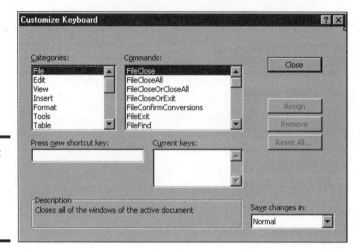

Figure 3-8:
Create
your own
keyboard
shortcuts
here.

3. **Select the command, style, macro, font, or other item for which you want to create a keyboard shortcut by using the Categories and Commands lists.**

4. **Click inside the Press New Shortcut Key text box and then type the new keyboard shortcut.**

   If the keyboard shortcut is already assigned, a message appears in the dialog box stating this; you may want to choose a different shortcut key.

5. **Click the Assign button to assign the shortcut and then click Close.**

To reset all keyboard shortcuts to their defaults, choose Tools⇨Customize, click the Keyboard button on the Commands tab, and then click Reset All.

Adding Headers and Footers

To add a header or footer to a document, follow these steps:

1. **Choose View⇨Header and Footer.**

   The Header and Footer toolbar appears, along with the header of the current page. (If you haven't yet created a header for the document, the header area is blank.)

2. **To switch between headers and footers, click the Switch Between Header and Footer button in the toolbar.**

3. **Type your header or footer text in the header or footer area, formatting the text any way you want.**

Book V
Chapter 3

Word 2000

You can click the Insert AutoText button in the toolbar to see a drop-down list of the information that is most commonly placed in a header or footer. Just scroll down the list and click the features you want. The information is automatically inserted for you.

4. **Click the other buttons in the Header and Footer toolbar to add the page numbers or the date or time.**

5. **Click the Close button after you finish adding a header or footer.**

Table 3-6 describes what each button does:

Table 3-6	Buttons on the Header and Footer Toolbar
Button	*What It Does*
🔲	Inserts the number of the current page.
🔲	Inserts the total number of pages in the document.
🔲	Enables you to specify a format for page numbers.
🔲	Inserts the date.
🔲	Inserts the time.
🔲	Enables you to control the layout of the headers and footers of the document.
🔲	Hides the document text from your screen while you are working with your headers and footers.
🔲	Sets up the same header or footer as you used previously in the document. This is useful if you need to have different headers or footers in the same document.
🔲	Shows the previous header or footer in the document.
🔲	Shows the next header or footer in the document.
Close	Closes the Header and Footer toolbar.

Mail Merging

Mail Merge is one of the most tedious of all Word tasks. Fortunately, the Mail Merge Helper is ready to help you at a moment's notice. Mail Merge is a three-step process: First, you create the form letter (the *main document*); then you create a mailing list of names and addresses (the *data source*); and finally, you merge the form letter and the mailing list to create a letter for each person on your mailing list. The following sections spell out the procedures for these steps.

Creating the main document

To create a main document to use in a mail merge, follow these steps:

1. **Choose Tools⇨Mail Merge.**

The Mail Merge Helper dialog box appears, as shown in Figure 3-9.

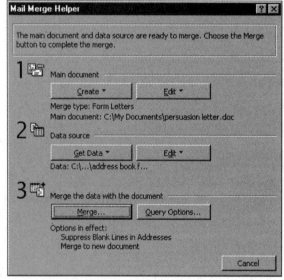

Figure 3-9:
Use the Mail Merge Helper to step through the mail merge process.

2. **Click the Create button and then choose Form Letters.**

3. **Click the New Main Document button.**

4. **Click the Edit button to reveal a menu of documents you can edit.**

The menu should have only one entry, Form Letter: Document #.

5. **Click this selection to create the letter.**

6. **Type the letter, leaving blanks where you want Word to insert custom data later, such as in the inside address or the salutation.**

When you edit a mail merge main document, a special Mail Merge toolbar appears. You'll use some of the buttons on this toolbar in later steps.

7. **Choose File⇨Save to save the file after you're done.**

Creating the data source

The next big step in Mail Merge is creating the data source, which may be
the hardest part of the procedure, because creating a data source requires
you to type in all the names and addresses of those to whom you want the
form letter sent.

To create the data source, follow these steps:

1. **Choose Tools⇨Mail Merge.**

The Mail Merge Helper dialog box returns to life.

2. **Click the Get Data button and then choose Create Data Source.**

The Create Data Source dialog box appears, as shown in Figure 3-10.

Figure 3-10:
Choose the
fields you
want to
include in
the merge
data source.

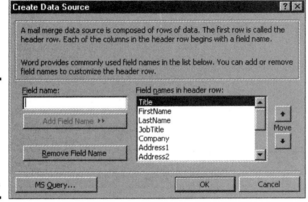

3. **To add a field, type a name in the Field Name text box and then click
the Add Field Name button.**

4. **To remove a field, click the field in the Field Names in Header Row
list to select the field and then click the Remove Field Name button.**

5. **To change the order in which the fields appear, select the field you
want to move in the Field Names in Header Row list and then click
the up-arrow or down-arrow Move button to move the field.**

6. **Click OK when you're done choosing the fields for the data source.**

The Save As dialog box appears.

7. **Type an appropriate name for your mailing list document in the File
Name text box and then click Save.**

A dialog box appears to inform you that the data source is empty.

8. **Click the Edit Data Source button in the dialog box to begin adding names and addresses to the data source.**

   A Data Form dialog box appears, similar to the one shown in Figure 3-11.

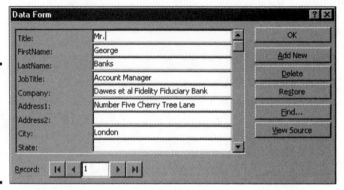

Figure 3-11:
Use the
Data Form
dialog box
to enter the
data source
information.

9. **Type the information for one person you want to add to the data source.**

   Use the Tab key to move from field to field or to skip over those fields in which you don't want to enter any data. (You don't need to enter a value for every field.)

10. **After you type all the data for the person, click the Add New button to add that person's data to the table in the data source.**

11. **Repeat Steps 9 and 10 for each person's data you want to add to the data source.**

12. **After you add all the names that you want to add, click OK.**

Notice that you can use the arrow buttons at the bottom of the Data Form dialog box to move forward or backward through the data source records. You can recall a previously entered record to correct a mistake if necessary.

To delete a record, use the arrow buttons at the bottom of the Data Form dialog box to move to the record you want to delete and then click the Delete button.

Inserting field names in the main document

After you finish adding names and addresses to the data source, return to the main document. (Because the main document is still open, you can select it from the Window menu.) Now you need to add field names to the main document so that Word knows where to insert data from the data source into the form letter.

Follow these steps to insert the field names into your document:

1. **Position the insertion point where you want to insert a field from the data source.**

2. **Click the Insert Merge Field button on the Mail Merge toolbar.**

A menu of field names from the data source appears.

3. **Click the name of the field that you want to insert into the document.**

4. **Repeat Steps 1 through 3 for each field that you want to insert.**

Figure 3-12 shows what a document looks like with all the fields inserted.

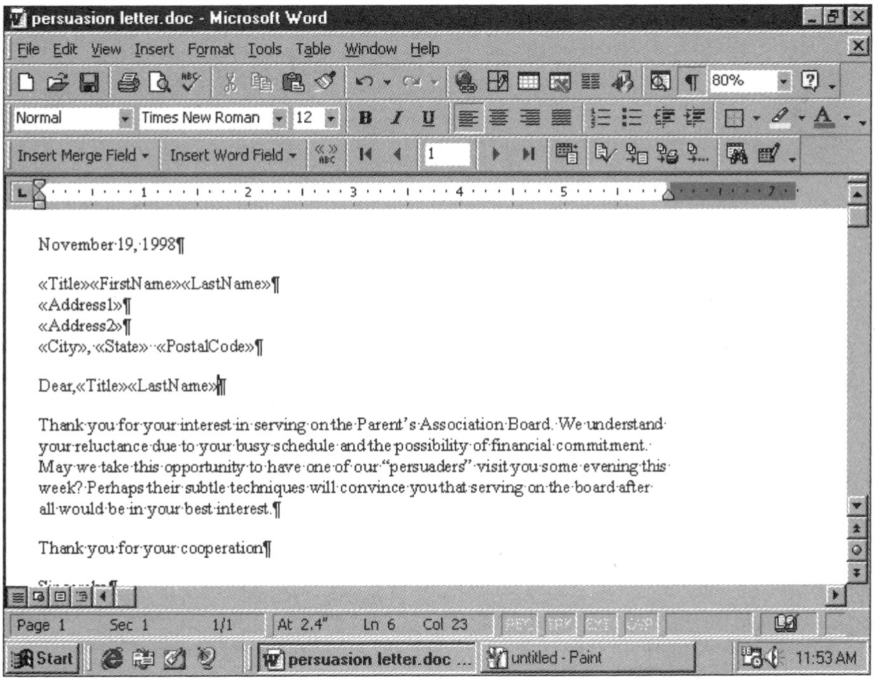

Figure 3-12: The merge document now includes the merge fields.

5. **After you finish inserting fields, choose File⇨Save to save the file.**

Merging the documents

After you set up the main document and the data source, follow these steps to merge the main document with the data source to produce form letters:

1. **Choose Tools➪Mail Merge and click the Merge button.**

   The Merge dialog box appears.

2. **Click the Merge button.**

   Word creates a new document that contains one complete copy of the main document for each record in the data source, with data from the data source substituted for each merge field. Section breaks separate the merged copies.

3. **Scroll through the merged document to make sure that the merge worked the way you expected.**

4. **To save the merged document, choose File➪Save.**

   Saving the file is a good idea, but that file may be quite large, depending on how many records you merged from the data source.

5. **To print the merged document, choose File➪Print.**

Creating Envelopes and Labels

Word makes it easy for you to print addresses on envelopes as well as labels. Follow these steps:

1. **If you're writing a letter to put in the envelope, create and print the letter first and leave the document open.**

   Doing so saves you the trouble of typing the mailing address twice.

2. **Choose Tools➪Envelopes and Labels.**

   The Envelopes and Labels dialog box appears, as shown in Figure 3-13.

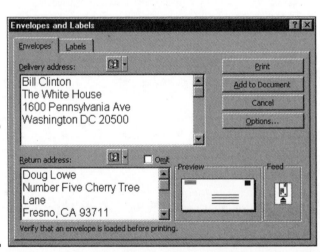

Figure 3-13: Enter the delivery and return address information here.

3. **Check the address in the Delivery Address field.**

   Word can usually find the mailing address from an ordinary letter. If not, you must type the address yourself.

   If you want a return address printed on the envelope, type the return address in the space provided. (Notice that you can set a default return address by choosing the Tools⇨Options command, clicking the User Information tab, and typing your return address in the space provided.)

4. **Insert an envelope into your printer.**

   The Feed option in the Envelopes and Labels dialog box suggests how to insert the envelope into the printer.

5. **Click the Print button when you're ready to print.**

Using Templates

Suppose that you toiled for hours on a document, and now you want to make its styles, macros, and other goodies available to other documents you may create someday. You can do that by creating a *template*. Then, if you create a new document based on your template, that document inherits the styles, AutoText entries, macros, and text from the template.

Here's how to create a template:

1. **Open the document that contains all the styles, AutoText, macros, and other goodies you want to save in a template.**

2. **Choose File⇨Save As.**

3. **In the Save as Type list box, select Document Template.**

4. **In the File Name text box, type a filename for the template.**

   Don't type the file extension; Word takes care of that element.

5. **Click the Save button to save the document as a template file.**

6. **Delete any unnecessary text from the file.**

   Any text that you do not delete appears automatically in any new documents that you create based on the template.

7. **Save the file again.**

You can also create a template by choosing File⇨New and then clicking the Template option button in the New dialog box. Doing so creates an empty template based on the template you select in the dialog box. You can then modify the template as you see fit and save that template under a new name.

Using Themes

Themes are a new feature in Word 2000. A *theme* is sort of like a template; it defines the fonts and style of your documents. However, there are significant differences. Themes do not automatically include macros, AutoText, or customized settings. What themes give you that templates do not is a unified design scheme that can include background images, fonts, bullets, horizontal lines, and other design elements. Using themes enables you to create consistently professional-looking documents, and they are especially good for Web page design.

If you don't like any of the themes that come with Word 2000 and don't want to go through the work of creating your own, you can choose Help⇨Office on the Web and follow the directions to download more themes onto your computer.

Applying a theme to a document

To start your document with a theme already applied, follow these steps:

1. **With the document open, choose Format⇨Theme.**

The Theme dialog box opens, as shown in Figure 3-14. Whether or not you've already worked on the document doesn't matter. Just make sure that you see an active insertion point within the document screen and that no text is highlighted.

Figure 3-14: Choose from dozens of available themes for your document.

2. **The Theme dialog box shows you a list of available themes in the Choose a Theme window on the left, and the window on the right displays a preview of the selected theme.**

    Scroll through the list and look at the samples until you find one you like.

3. **Choose among the three check boxes in the lower-left corner of the dialog box: Vivid Colors, Active Graphics, and Background Image.**

    These options enable you to refine your control of the theme. Experiment with these options to see how they affect the look of your document.

4. **Click OK.**

If you've just begun working with your document, Word 2000 applies the styles appropriate for the theme you've chosen as you write. If you're applying the theme to a document you've worked on, Word changes your formatting to match the theme.

You can mix and match themes with predetermined styles. If you click the Style Gallery button in the Theme dialog box, the Style Gallery dialog box opens. From this dialog box, you can choose different styles and see what your document will look like if you use that style with the theme you've chosen. Nifty, eh?

Changing the default theme

Word 2000 applies a default theme when you first open a Word document. You can change this default so that a new theme always appears whenever you open a new Word document.

To change the default theme, follow these steps:

1. **Choose Format➪Theme.**

2. **Determine what theme you want to use and click Set Default.**

    A dialog box appears, asking you if you want to set a new default theme for new documents.

3. **If you really want to use this theme, click Yes.**

4. **Click OK.**

    From now on, every new Word 2000 document you create will have that theme applied to it, until you decide to change it.

Using the Web Page Wizard

Do you want to make yourself known on the Web with your own Web page but are afraid that you're not enough of a geek for the complex HTML programming? Fear not! Word 2000 comes with a slick Web Page Wizard that can automatically create several different types of Web documents based on options you select. Anyone who can create a Word document can create a Web site using the Web Page Wizard.

To use the Web Page Wizard, follow these steps:

1. **Choose File⇨New.**

2. **In the New dialog box, click the Web Pages tab, click Web Page Wizard, and then click OK.**

   The Web Page Wizard dialog box appears.

3. **Click the Title and Location button on the left side of the window or click Next to move to the next screen on the list.**

   Doing this lets you give your site a title (which also functions as its file name) and the location where you want to save it on your system.

4. **After you enter that information, click the Next button.**

5. **Click the Navigation button.**

   A dialog box that lets you determine how your readers can navigate through the links in your Web page opens. You have three options:

   - **Vertical Frame.** Divides your screen with a vertical line. Click the links on the left to view the right side of the screen.

   - **Horizontal Frame.** Divides the screen into a top half and a bottom half. The links appear on the top, while the content appears in the bottom half.

   - **Separate Page.** Every time a link is activated, this option opens a new page to display the information.

   Choose the option that works best for you; however, be aware that not all browsers can support vertical or horizontal frames, so the Separate Page option is probably your best bet.

6. **After you make your choice, click the Next button.**

The next screen shows the Add Pages portion of the Web Page Wizard. With this feature, you can select what types of documents are associated with your Web page.

You can use Add New Blank Page for plain text, Add Template Page for specific Web templates (such as FAQ, Tables of Contents, or columns), and Add Existing File, which enables you to add any document from your computer system.

7. **Select those pages you want to include and then click Next.**

The Organize Pages feature lets you to determine the order in which the individual pages appear on your Web site. Simply highlight one of the pages and then click on either the Move Up or the Move Down button to position it where you want. Repeat with the different pages until everything is in the order you want.

8. **Click Next.**

This screen lets you apply a visual theme to your document or use a plain white background. See "Using Themes," earlier in this chapter.

9. **After you determine what theme you are using, click Next again.**

That's it! Your Web page is organized and ready for you to enter the information you want on it.

10. **Click the Finish button.**

The document appears on your screen.

For more information on designing and publishing Web pages, see Book III, Chapter 6.

Chapter 4: Excel 2000

In This Chapter

- ✓ **Understanding worksheet basics**
- ✓ **Formatting cells**
- ✓ **Working with formulas and functions**
- ✓ **Using styles with your worksheet**
- ✓ **Charting and printing worksheet data**

*Y*ou can think of Excel 2000 as the bean counter of Microsoft Office 2000. This program enables you to create worksheets — large grids of cells — that can perform meticulous calculations with uncanny accuracy. In this chapter, you find out about the basics of using Excel 2000. If you're interested in going beyond the basics, check out *Excel 2000 For Windows For Dummies,* by Greg Harvey (IDG Books Worldwide, Inc).

Understanding Worksheet Basics

Excel files are known as *workbooks.* A single workbook can store as many sheets as can fit into memory. These sheets are stacked like the pages in a notebook. Sheets can be either *worksheets* or *chart sheets.* Most of the time, you work with worksheets — each has exactly 65,536 rows and 256 columns. Rows are numbered beginning with 1. Columns are labeled with letters — from A to Z; then AA to AZ, BA to BZ, and so on through column IV.

The intersection of a row and column is called a *cell.* Each cell's *address* is a combination of its column letter and row number. Therefore, the cell at the intersection of column E and row 5 is cell E5. A *range* of cells is a rectangular area that is identified by two cells at opposite corners and is separated by a colon. For example, the range C7:E10 represents all the cells in a rectangle with its upper-left corner at cell C7 and lower-right corner at cell E10.

Before you get started with worksheet tasks, you'll want to know how to get around the worksheet. Table 4-1 summarizes the keyboard techniques you can use to navigate within Excel.

Table 4-1	Moving Around the Worksheet
Shortcut	*What It Does*
Home	Moves to the beginning of the current row.
←	Moves left one cell.
→	Moves right one cell.
↑	Moves up one cell.
↓	Moves down one cell.
PgUp	Scrolls the window up one screen.
PgDn	Scrolls the window down one screen.
Alt+PgDn	Scrolls the window right one screen.
Alt+PgUp	Scrolls the window left one screen.
Ctrl+Home	Moves to the beginning of the worksheet.
Ctrl+← or End,←	Moves to the left of a data range.
Ctrl+→ or End,→	Moves to the right of a data range.
Ctrl+↑ or End,↑	Moves to the top of a data range.
Ctrl+↓ or End,↓	Moves to the bottom of a data range.
Ctrl+PgUp	Displays the preceding sheet in the workbook.
Ctrl+PgDn	Displays the next sheet in the workbook.
Ctrl+End or End, Home	Moves to the last cell of the worksheet that contains data.
End, Enter	Moves to the last cell in the current row that contains data.
F5 or Ctrl+G	Goes to a specific location.

Selecting Cells and Ranges

In Excel, you normally select a cell or range before performing an operation that works with the cell or range. To select a single cell and (make it the active cell to the cell with the dark border), click the cell with the mouse. If you don't see the cell on-screen, move to that cell by using the arrow keys or the scroll bars or by pressing F5 and then typing the cell reference. (See Table 4-1 in the previous section "Understanding Worksheet Basics," for more information)

To select a range of cells, click a cell in any corner of the range and then drag to the opposite corner of the range. Alternatively, you can click a cell in any corner of the range and hold down the Shift key and then click the opposite cell. (The latter method is useful if you cannot see the entire range on-screen at one time.) To select a 3-D range across multiple worksheets, select the range in the first worksheet and hold down the Shift key and then click the sheet tab for the last sheet in the range.

To select an entire row in a worksheet, click the row number. To select multiple adjacent rows, drag up or down the row numbers. Similarly, to select an entire column in a worksheet, click the column letter. Drag across column letters to select multiple adjacent columns. To select an entire worksheet, click the gray rectangle that appears just above the row numbers. Click any cell to cancel the selection.

The selected range is usually a group of adjacent cells, but it doesn't have to be. Just select the first cell or range and then hold down the Ctrl key as you select additional cells or ranges. This method works for selecting nonadjacent rows and columns, too.

Entering and Editing Data

How do you build a worksheet? You enter data into it, of course! You can enter any of the following types of data in a cell:

+ Text (also called *labels*)
+ Numbers (also called *values*)
+ Dates and times
+ Formulas (see "Formulas," later in this chapter)

Entering text and numbers

To enter text in a cell, select the cell, type the text, and press Enter. If the text doesn't fit in the cell, it either spills into adjacent cells (if those cells are blank) or it appears to be truncated. You can edit the entry to make it shorter (see "Editing data," later in this chapter) or widen the column to display all of the data.

To change the width of a column, move the mouse pointer to the column border in the worksheet frame — to the right of the column letter you want to resize. When the pointer changes to a double-sided arrow, drag left or right to resize the column. To change the height of a row, move the mouse pointer to the bottom border of the row number (within the worksheet frame) that you want to resize and then drag up or down.

To force Excel to use multiple lines of text within a cell, press Alt+Enter to start a new line in the cell.

To enter a numeric value in a cell, select the cell, type the value, and then press Enter. You also can include a decimal point, dollar sign, plus sign, minus sign, and comma when you enter the value. If you precede a value with a minus sign or enclose it in parentheses, Excel considers the value to be a negative number. Excel may convert very large numbers to scientific notation. The formula bar always displays the value that you originally entered. If you make the column wider, the number displays as you entered it.

AutoFormatting your data

You can create an attractively formatted worksheet by using the AutoFormat feature to apply predefined formatting. Here's how:

1. **Create your worksheet as you normally do.**

   The AutoFormat feature works best when the first row and the first column of the worksheet contain headings and the last row contains totals because many of the AutoFormats apply special formatting (such as colors, shading, or borders) to the first row and column.

2. **Highlight the range that contains the data you want to format.**

3. **Choose Format⇨AutoFormat.**

   The AutoFormat dialog box appears.

4. **Select the table format you want to use.**

5. **Click OK.**

   Excel 2000 applies the selected AutoFormat to your worksheet. If you don't like the formatting applied by the AutoFormat, press Ctrl+Z, choose Edit⇨Undo, or click the Undo button to undo the AutoFormat operation.

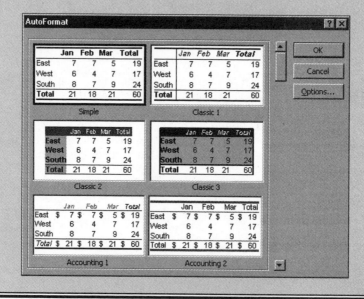

If you're entering data across a row (rather than down a column), press the right-arrow key to accept the current entry and to immediately move to the next cell.

Entering dates and times

To Excel, a date or time is simply a value that is formatted to appear as a date or a time. Excel automatically recognizes familiar date formats, such as MM/DD/YY and MM/DD or time formats, such as HH:MM:SS and HH:MM. To be safe, enter a date using a four-digit year value and then format the value to display the date how you want it to appear. (See "Formatting Data," later in this chapter.)

Editing data

After you enter data in the worksheet, you may want to change the data. You can either type a new entry in the cell to replace the previous entry, or you can edit the existing entry. To edit data within a cell, double-click the cell, use the normal editing keys (arrow keys, Backspace, and Delete) to edit the cell, and then press Enter.

Formatting Data

You can set formats for a cell or range by using formatting keyboard shortcuts or by using the buttons on the Formatting toolbar. You also can use the following procedure to apply character formats by using the Format➪Cells command:

1. **Highlight the cell or range to which you want to apply the formatting.**

2. **Choose Format➪Cells (or press Ctrl+1).**

    The Format Cells dialog box appears, as shown in Figure 4-1. You can use the settings in this dialog box to change number formats, alignment, and font styles. You also can add borders and patterns, and you can lock cells.

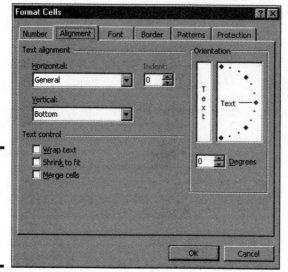

Figure 4-1:
The
Alignment
settings in
the Format
Cells dialog
box.

3. Experiment with the controls under the six tabs to set the formatting options you want.

4. After you select a formatting option, click OK.

To quickly apply common formats, highlight the cells you want to format and then click the button on the Formatting toolbar. For example, the button with a *B* applies boldface to selected cells.

Centering Text over Several Columns

Excel enables you to center text over several columns. Suppose, for example, that you put projected net sales for three consecutive years in columns B, C, and D, and actual net sales for those years in columns E, F, and G. You can then add a Projected Net Sales heading centered over the projected net sales columns and an Actual Net Sales heading centered over the actual net sales columns.

You can accomplish this effect by merging cells from the three columns to create a single cell that spans multiple columns. Follow these steps:

1. Move the cell pointer to the left-most cell in the range of columns over which you want to center the text.

For example, if you want text centered over the range B2:D2, move the cell pointer to cell B2.

2. **Enter the text that you want to center into the cell you've selected.**

3. **Highlight the range of cells that you want the text centered within.**

 4. **Click the Merge and Center button.**

If you change your mind and don't want to center the text across columns, highlight the merged cell, choose Format⇨Cells to display the Format Cells dialog box, and deselect the Merge Cells check box on the Alignment tab.

Naming a Range of Cells

To make your formulas easier to create and understand, Excel 2000 enables you to assign meaningful names to individual cells or ranges.

To assign a name to a cell or range, follow these steps:

1. **Select the cell or range to which you want to assign a name.**

2. **Choose Insert⇨Name⇨Define.**

   The Define Name dialog box displays.

3. **Type a name for the cell or range in the Names in Workbook text box.**

 You have some restrictions on what characters you can use in the name. The name cannot contain spaces — it must use only alphanumeric characters (no symbols) and must start with at least one letter, even if the rest of the "name" is numeric.

4. **Click OK.**

 To use a range name in a formula, type the name anytime you would type a range. Instead of typing **=Sum(D4:D15)**, for example, you can type the formula **=Sum(Sales)** if you've assigned the name *Sales* to the range D4:D15. (See "Functions," later in this chapter for more information.)

To delete a range name, choose Insert⇨Name⇨Define to open the Define Name dialog box, select the range name that you want to delete from the list, and then click the Delete button.

 To quickly select a named range, press F5 or choose Edit⇨Go To to open the Go To dialog box. Then double-click the range name in the list box.

Using Formulas

A *formula* is a special type of cell entry that returns a result. The formula itself appears in the formula bar (which is just below the toolbars near the top of the Excel window) when the cell is selected. In Excel, a formula begins with an equal sign (=) and can consist of any of the following elements:

✦ Operators such as + (for addition), - (for subtraction), * (for multiplication), and / (for division)

✦ Cell references, including addresses such as B4 or C12, as well as named cells and ranges

✦ Values and text

✦ Worksheet functions (such as SUM; see "Functions," later in this chapter)

You can enter a formula into a cell in three ways: manually (typing it in), by pointing to cell references, or with the assistance of the formula palette.

Entering formulas manually

To enter a formula manually, follow these steps:

1. **Select the cell that you want to contain the formula.**

2. **Type an equal sign (=) to signal the beginning of a formula.**

3. **Type the formula and press Enter.**

As you type, the characters appear in the cell as well as in the formula bar. You can use all the normal editing keys (Delete, Backspace, arrow keys, and so on) when entering and editing a formula.

Entering formulas by pointing

The pointing method of entering a formula still involves some manual typing. The advantage is that you don't have to type the cell or range references. Rather, you point to them in the worksheet, which is usually more accurate and less tedious.

The best way to explain this procedure is with an example. To enter the formula =**A1/A2** into cell A3 by using the pointing method, follow these steps:

1. **Type values (any number will do) into cells A1 and A2.**

(These are the cells that the example formula references. If you leave these cells blank, the formula results in an error.)

2. **Select cell A3.**

   This cell is where you want the formula (and the result) to appear.

3. **Type an equal sign (=) to begin the formula.**

4. **Press the up arrow twice.**

   As you press this key, notice that Excel displays a marquee around the cell and that the cell reference appears in cell A3 and in the formula bar.

5. **Type a division sign (/).**

6. **Press the up arrow once.**

   A2 is added to the formula.

7. **Press Enter to end the formula and see the formula result in cell A3.**

Entering formulas using the formula palette

The *formula palette* helps you create formulas and enter worksheet functions (see "Functions," later in this chapter). To use the formula palette to help you create a formula, click the = icon on the formula bar. Excel displays the formula palette directly below the formula bar. The formula's result displays in the formula palette as you create the formula (see Figure 4-2).

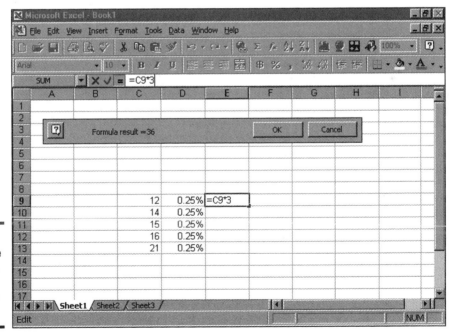

Figure 4-2:
You can use the formula palette to help create formulas.

You can move the formula palette anywhere you want. Just click and drag it to a new location.

Referencing worksheet cells

In Excel, you sometimes see cell addresses that use dollar signs ($), such as D$9, $E7, or H22. The dollar sign designates the row or column portion of an address as *absolute,* meaning that Excel shouldn't try to adjust the address if you move or copy a formula that includes the absolute address. For example, suppose that you type the formula **=D3+D4** into cell D5 and then copy cell D5 to cell E5; Excel adjusts the formula to =E3+E4. But if you make the formula in cell D5 **=$D3+$D4**, Excel does *not* adjust the formula if you copy it to another column.

One trick you can use with Excel 2000 is that the program can use labels that appear above a column of numbers as cell addresses. For example, suppose you set up a worksheet as shown in Figure 4-3.

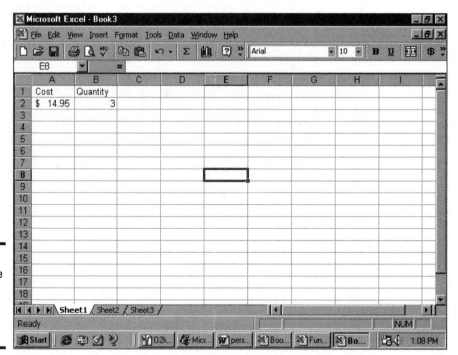

Figure 4-3: You can use labels to help enter formulas in Excel 2000.

To create a formula in cell C2 that multiplies cells A2 and B2, you could enter **=A2*B2**. With Excel 2000, however, you can enter the formula as **=Cost*Quantity**. Excel uses the column headings in row 1 to figure out that *Cost* is cell A2 and *Quantity* is cell B2.

Using Functions

Excel 2000 provides more than 300 built-in functions that can make your formulas perform powerful feats and save you a great deal of time. Take a look at the Help files in Excel 2000 for an explanation of all the functions. Table 4-2 provides examples of some of the most popular functions:

Table 4-2	Popular Functions
Function	*Action*
AVERAGE(*range*)	Calculates the average value of the cells in *range*.
COUNT(*range*)	Returns the number of cells in *range*.
IF(*logical_test, value_if_true, value_if_false*) value_if_false	Tests the condition specified in the logical test. If the condition is true, Excel returns *value_if_true*. Otherwise, the program returns.
MAX(*range*)	Returns the largest value in *range*.
MIN(*range*)	Returns the smallest value in *range*.
NOW()	Returns the current date and time. No arguments are required.
PMT(*rate, nper, pv*)	Calculates payments for a loan. *Rate* is the interest rate per period; *nper* is the number of periods; *pv* is the present value (that is, the amount of the loan).
PRODUCT(*range*)	Multiplies all the cells in the specified *range*.
SUM(*range*)	Adds the values of all cells in the specified *range*.
TODAY()	Returns the current date. No arguments are required.

Entering functions manually

If you're familiar with the function you want to use, you may choose to type the function and its arguments into your formula. Often this is the most efficient method. A function is composed of three elements:

+ The equal sign (=) to indicate that what follows is a formula.

+ The function name, such as SUM or AVERAGE, which indicates what operation is to be performed.

+ The argument, which indicates the cell addresses of the data that the function will act on. Some functions, such as IF and PMT, use multiple arguments. In addition, depending on the function, some arguments may be represented by text or values.

The formula =B1+B2+B3+B4+B5 can also be expressed as a function by typing:

=SUM(B1:B5)

Using the Function Wizard

Although you can type functions into worksheets manually, you also can use the Function Wizard to help you enter functions. The Function Wizard asks you to select a function from one of several function categories and to complete the function by providing all the information the function requires.

Here's the procedure, using a simple MAX function as an example:

1. **Select the cell in which you want to insert the function.**

2. **Choose Insert⇨Function or click the Paste Function button in the Standard toolbar.**

The Paste Function dialog box appears, as shown in Figure 4-4. The Paste Function dialog box initially lists the functions you used most recently.

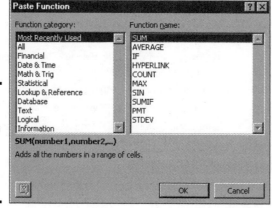

Figure 4-4: Choose the function you want from the Paste Function dialog box.

3. **Click one of the categories in the Function Category list and then select the desired function from the Function Name list.**

4. **Click OK.**

The formula palette for the specified function appears, similar to the one shown in Figure 4-5.

Figure 4-5:
Specify the
arguments
for the func-
tion in the
formula
palette.

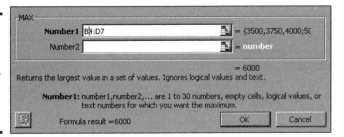

5. **Read the instructions for completing the function and then type whatever entries you need to complete the function.**

   If the function requires a single argument, Excel uses the cell or range
   that was selected at the time you accessed the Function Wizard. You
   don't need to do anything in this dialog box except click OK.

   If the function requires more than one argument, you can type a value,
   cell reference, or range into the text boxes for the additional arguments.
   If you want, you can select a cell or range in the worksheet by clicking
   the button that appears to the right of the text box for the argument you
   want to enter. This action returns you to the worksheet, where you can
   highlight the cell or range. Press Enter to return to the Function Wizard;
   the range you selected appears in the text box for the argument.

   If you need more detailed information on the function that you are
   entering, click the Help button in the lower-left corner of the formula
   palette.

6. **Click OK after you complete the function.**

Applying Conditional Formatting

Conditional formatting enables you to format a cell or range to have specific
formatting dependent upon the value or formula in that cell. To do this:

1. **Select the cell or range to which you want to apply conditional
   formatting.**

2. **Choose Format⇨Conditional Formatting.**

   The Conditional Formatting dialog box displays, as shown in Figure 4-6.

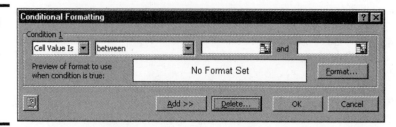

Figure 4-6:
Use this
dialog box
to specify
the condi-
tional
formats.

3. **In the Condition 1 drop-down box, select whether you want the formatting to be used when a cell value is determined or if a particular
   formula is active within a cell.**

   The appearance of the dialog box changes to match this condition.

4. **If you want to use a formula, type the formula in the text box
   provided.**

   Remember that every formula must begin with an equal sign (=).

   If you are using a cell value, you have to determine how the condition
   relates to the statement. The second drop-down box on the left enables
   you to determine if the condition to be met is *between, equal to, greater
   than, less than,* or any one of several other relationship statements.
   Select the one that you want. For example, if you want to see all cells
   that have a value of more than $19,000.00, select "greater than" from
   this drop-down box. Type the value you want to compare the number in
   the cell against in the text box provided.

5. **After you have the cell value or formula set, click the Format button.**

   The Format Cells dialog box opens.

6. **Apply the formatting you want and click OK.**

   Conditional formatting enables you to set up to three conditions for formatting on a cell or range. You can have one set of formatting if the
   numbers in the cell indicate that you met minimum expectations, but
   you can show an entirely different formatting if the numbers indicate
   that you met or exceeded your goals.

7. **If you want to set an additional condition, click the Add button.**

   (The dialog box expands to include Condition 2. Repeat Steps 3
   through 6 to specify the settings for Condition 2.)

8. **Click OK after you finish.**

Finding Data

You can find text anywhere in a worksheet. Just follow these steps:

1. **Press Ctrl+Home to move to the top of the worksheet.**

This step is optional; if you omit it, the search starts at the current cell.

2. **Choose Edit⇨Find or press Ctrl+F.**

The Find dialog box displays.

3. **In the Find What text box, type the text you want to find.**

4. **Click the Find Next button.**

When Excel 2000 finds the cell that contains the text you're looking for, it highlights the cell. The Find dialog box remains on-screen so that you can click Find Next to find yet another occurrence of the text.

5. **Press Esc after you finish.**

The Find dialog box offers several options for controlling the search, as I describe in Table 4-3.

Table 4-3	Search Options
Option	*What It Does*
Search	Indicates whether you want to search by rows or columns.
Look In	Indicates whether you want to search cell values, formulas, or notes attached to cells.
Match Case	Finds only text with the case that matches the search text you type.
Find Entire Cells Only	Finds text only if the entire cell entry matches the Find What text.

You can use the following wildcard characters in the Find What text box:

✦ **?** finds a single occurrence of any character. For example, **f?t** finds *fat* and *fit*.

✦ ***** finds any combination of characters. For example, **b*t** finds any combination of characters that begins with *b* and ends with *t*, such as *bat*, *bait*, and *ballast*.

If you find the text you're looking for and decide that you want to replace it with something else, click Replace. This action opens the Replace dialog box. You can then type replacement text in the Replace With text box and then click Replace to replace a single occurrence of the Find text or Replace All to replace the Find text wherever it appears in the document.

Charting Worksheet Data

Excel 2000 offers so many charting capabilities that we could write an entire *Quick Reference* just on charting. Follow these steps to quickly create a simple chart:

1. **Select the cells that contain the data on which you want to base a chart.**

2. **Click the Chart Wizard button on the Standard toolbar.**

The Chart Wizard displays, as shown in Figure 4-7.

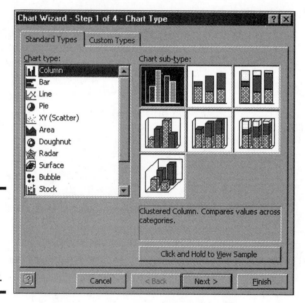

Figure 4-7:
Use the
Chart
Wizard to
create an
Excel chart.

3. **From the Chart Type list, select the type of chart you want to create.**

For each chart type, you can choose from several subtypes. To see a preview of how the selected data appears charted with a particular chart type and sub-type, click and hold the mouse button on the Click and Hold to View Sample button.

4. **Click the Next button.**

5. **Check the range shown in the Data Range box to verify that the range listed is the range you want to chart.**

The Chart Wizard initially assumes that the data you are trying to chart is grouped by row. In other words, the first row of the range contains the first series of values, the second row contains the second series, and so on. If this isn't the case, you can click the Columns option button so that the data is grouped by column, with the first data series in the first column of the range, the second series in the second column, and so on.

6. Click the Next button.

The dialog box shown in Figure 4-8 appears.

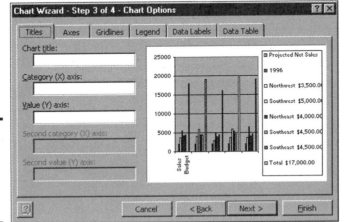

Figure 4-8:
You can set a variety of chart options here.

7. Add any optional features to your chart by filling in the text boxes and setting various option buttons that appear in the Chart Options dialog box.

Notice that the Chart Options dialog box has six tabs that display various charting options. Be sure to check the settings on all six tabs before proceeding.

8. Click the Next button.

The Chart Wizard displays its final dialog box.

9. Choose where you want Excel 2000 to place your chart — as a new sheet or as an object in any sheet in the current workbook.

10. Click Finish to create the chart.

If you added the chart to an existing sheet, you may need to drag and possibly resize the chart to its correct location and size.

After you add a chart to your worksheet as an object, you can display a toolbar that enables you to continue to manipulate the chart. You can use the buttons to change the grouping of the data, to angle your text, to add, format, or remove the legend, or even to change the chart type. This toolbar enables you to play with the chart to your heart's content without having to return to the Wizard to make a new chart. To open the Chart toolbar, choose View➪Toolbars➪Chart.

Inserting Comments

Excel 2000 enables you to add an electronic version of those yellow sticky notes to your worksheets. You can use this feature as a reminder to yourself and others who may use the worksheet, such as a reminder about why you created a formula the way you did or where you got a particular number you entered into the worksheet.

Follow these steps to insert a comment in the worksheet:

1. **Click the cell to which you want to add the comment.**

2. **Choose Insert⇨Comment or press Shift+F2.**

   A yellow text box appears.

3. **Type anything you want in the box.**

4. **Click anywhere outside the yellow comment box.**

   The comment box disappears, and Excel adds a red marker to the cell to indicate that a comment is attached to that cell.

To access the comment later, point to the cell; the comment box appears. The box disappears after you move the mouse pointer away from the cell.

To delete a comment, right-click the cell and choose Delete Comment from the shortcut menu that appears.

Printing a Worksheet

Printing in Excel 2000 is pretty much the same as printing in any other Office 2000 application: You can choose File⇨Print, press Ctrl+P, or click the Print button in the Standard toolbar to print the current worksheet. However, Excel offers a few printing tricks that can help you:

✦ By default, Excel prints the entire worksheet. However, you can set a print area to print just part of the worksheet. First, highlight the range you want to print. Then choose File⇨Print Area⇨Set Print Area.

✦ To clear the print area so that the entire worksheet prints, choose File⇨Print Area⇨Clear Print Area.

✦ If annoying grid lines appear on your printed output, choose File⇨Page Setup to display the Page Setup dialog box and click the Sheet tab. Then deselect the Gridlines check box and click OK.

Chapter 5: PowerPoint 2000

*I*f you like to stand in front of a group of people with a flip chart and a pointer, either trying to get them to buy something from you or trying to convince them to vote for you, then you'll love PowerPoint 2000. PowerPoint 2000 enables you to quickly create dazzling presentations that can be printed out on plain paper, made into transparencies or slides, and displayed on-screen or as a Web presentation.

In this chapter, you find out how to perform the most common PowerPoint 2000 tasks. For more information about using PowerPoint 2000, get a copy of *PowerPoint 2000 For Windows For Dummies,* by Grace Jasmine (IDG Books Worldwide, Inc.).

Creating a New Presentation

The easiest way to create a new PowerPoint 2000 presentation is to use the AutoContent Wizard. Follow these steps:

1. **Start PowerPoint 2000 (click the Start button in the taskbar and then choose Programs⇨Microsoft PowerPoint).**

PowerPoint 2000 opens and displays the PowerPoint dialog box, as shown in Figure 5-1.

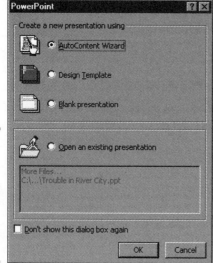

Figure 5-1:
You can
start the
AutoContent
Wizard
from the
PowerPoint
dialog box.

If you already have PowerPoint running, you can get to the AutoContent Wizard by choosing File⇨New and selecting the AutoContent Wizard from the General tab.

2. Click the AutoContent Wizard option button and then click OK.

The AutoContent Wizard displays.

3. Click Next.

The AutoContent Wizard asks what type of presentation you want to create (see Figure 5-2). To see a full list of the options, click All.

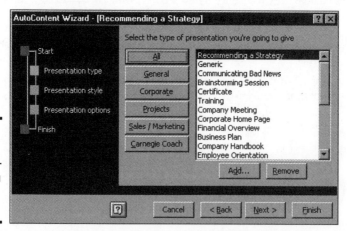

Figure 5-2:
Choose the
type of pres-
entation you
want to
give.

4. **Select the presentation type from the list box and then click Next.**

   The Wizard asks what kind of output you want to create.

5. **Select the type of output you want and then click Next.**

   The Wizard prompts you for a presentation title and enables you to specify what elements to include on each slide, including a footer and the date you last updated your presentation. You can also decide whether you want the slides numbered.

6. **Enter the requested information and then click Next.**

7. **Click Finish to create the presentation.**

Using Templates

A *template* is a PowerPoint 2000 presentation that is used as a model to create other presentations. When you create a new presentation using the AutoContent Wizard (as described in the preceding section), the Wizard automatically selects a template for your presentation. As an alternative, you can select a template yourself when creating a presentation by choosing File⇨New and selecting a template from the Design Templates tab.

If at any time you decide that you don't like the appearance of your presentation, you can change the presentation's look without changing its contents by assigning a new template to the presentation.

Understanding PowerPoint's views

PowerPoint 2000 provides five presentation views that enable you to see your work in different ways. To switch among the views, click the small buttons that appear near the lower-left corner of the PowerPoint window. The following list provides brief descriptions of these views:

✦ **Normal view** shows three panes simultaneously — the presentation outline on the left, the slide on the right, and speaker notes at the bottom.

✦ **Outline view** shows an ordered list of the text information on your slides.

✦ **Slide view** shows a single slide under construction.

✦ **Slide Sorter view** displays thumbnails of all slides in the presentation.

✦ **Slide Show view** displays an on-screen preview of a presentation.

You also can access the Normal, Slide Sorter, and Slide Show views from PowerPoint's View menu.

To assign a new template, follow these steps:

1. **Choose Format➪Apply Design Template.**

    The Apply Design Template dialog box appears (see Figure 5-3).

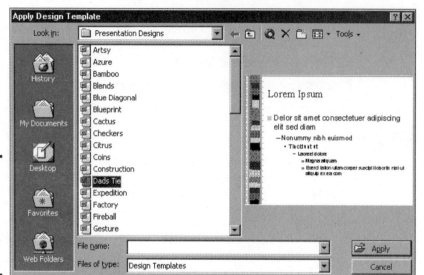

Figure 5-3:
You can
assign a
new design
template
to a presen-
tation.

2. **Select the template you want to use.**

    The Preview area shows a preview of each template as you select it.

3. **Click Apply to assign the selected template to the presentation.**

Applying Color Schemes

A presentation's *color scheme* is a set of coordinated colors that represents the various elements of your presentation's slides, such as the slide background, title text, body text, and so on.

You can change the color scheme for an entire presentation or for individual slides:

✦ To change the color scheme for an entire presentation, switch to Slide Master view (choose View➪Master➪Slide Master).

The *slide master* is a model slide layout that governs the appearance of all the slides in a presentation. You can find out more about the slide master in the section, "Hiding Background Objects."

♦ To change the color scheme for a specific slide, switch to Normal view and display the slide you want to change.

After you've made the choice to change the color scheme to an entire presentation or to just one slide, follow these steps:

1. **Choose Format⇨Slide Color Scheme.**

The Color Scheme dialog box appears.

2. **Click the color scheme you want to use.**

3. **Click Apply to All.**

To customize the color scheme of an individual slide or the whole presentation, click the Custom tab and then choose whatever colors you want to use for the various slide elements.

Inserting Recurring Text

To add recurring text (such as a company name) to each slide, follow these steps:

1. **Choose View⇨Master⇨Slide Master to display the slide master.**

2. **Click the Text Box button on the Drawing toolbar.**

3. **Click where you want to add text.**

4. **Type the text that you want to appear on each slide.**

5. **Format the text.**

6. **Return to Normal view.**

To add a graphic that recurs on each slide, click the Insert Clip Art button on the Drawing toolbar to insert any clip art picture supplied with PowerPoint 2000 or choose Insert⇨Picture to insert a picture file.

To delete an object from the slide master, click it and press Delete. To delete a text object, you must first click the object and then click the object frame again. Then press Delete.

If the object won't select when you click it, you're probably in Normal view. Choose View⇨Master⇨Slide Master again to display the slide master.

Inserting Clip Art

Follow these steps to add clip art to your presentation:

1. **Move to the slide that you want to decorate with clip art.**

   If you want the clip art to appear on every slide, move to the master slide by choosing View⇨Master⇨Slide Master.

2. **Choose Insert⇨Picture⇨Clip Art or click the Insert Clip Art button on the Drawing toolbar.**

   The Clip Gallery opens, as shown in Figure 5-4.

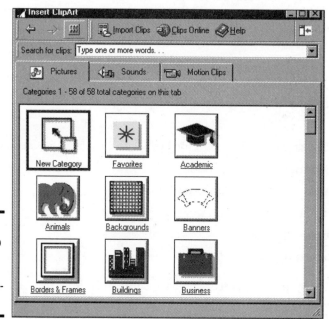

Figure 5-4: Use the Clip Gallery to add clip art to your presentation.

3. **Select a category on the Pictures tab or type a search string in the Search for Clips text box.**

4. **Scroll through the clips and select the specific picture you want.**

5. **Click the Insert Clip button (the top button) from the drop-down list of buttons.**

   PowerPoint 2000 inserts the picture on the slide. You can move and resize the picture by dragging it with the mouse.

The first time you use the Clip Gallery after installing PowerPoint 2000, the Clip Gallery realizes that it hasn't added the PowerPoint 2000 clip art to the gallery, so it automatically adds the clip art. This process may take a while, so be prepared.

Notice that the Clip Gallery has tabs for sounds and videos as well as pictures. You can use these tabs to add sounds and movies to your presentations, following the same procedure described previously.

If your computer has an Internet connection, you can click the Clips Online button in the Clip Gallery to connect to Microsoft's clip art page on the Web. There, you find additional clip art pictures, sounds, and videos for your presentations.

Hiding Background Objects

PowerPoint 2000 lets you add background objects to the slide master so that the objects appear on every slide in your presentation. For example, you can create a fancy logo or slick graphic effect to add spice to your slides.

Occasionally, though, you may want to create a slide or two that doesn't have these objects in the background. To hide the background objects, follow these steps:

1. **In Normal view, display the slide you want to show with a plain background.**

2. **Choose Format⇨Background.**

   The Background dialog box displays.

3. **Select the Omit Background Graphics from Master check box.**

4. **Click Apply.**

To hide the background objects for all the slides in a presentation, follow Steps 1 through 3 and then click Apply to All.

Creating a Summary Slide

You can include a summary slide in your presentation that acts as an outline for your audience by guiding them through the presentation. Follow these steps to quickly create a summary slide that contains the titles of some or all of the slides in your presentation:

1. **Switch to Slide Sorter view.**

2. **Select the slides you want to include in the summary.**

    To summarize the entire presentation, press Ctrl+A to select all the presentation's slides.

 3. **Click the Summary Slide button.**

    PowerPoint 2000 inserts the summary slide in front of the selected slides.

Adding Slide Transitions

A *slide transition* is a visual effect that appears when a PowerPoint 2000 slide show moves from one slide to the next. PowerPoint 2000 lets you choose from among many different transition effects, and you can specify a different effect for each slide. In addition, you can easily add sound effects to add even more pizzazz to your presentations.

To set the transitions between slides, follow this procedure:

1. **Switch to Normal view or Slide Sorter view.**

2. **Select the slide to which you want to add a transition.**

    Note that the transition always occurs *before* the slide you select. So to set the transition to occur between the first and second slides, select the second slide.

3. **Choose Slide Show⇨Slide Transition.**

    The Slide Transition dialog box appears, as shown in Figure 5-5.

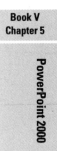
Figure 5-5:
PowerPoint
supplies
dozens of
slide transi-
tions for
your pres-
entations.

4. **Select the transition effect from the Effect drop-down list box.**

5. **Select the speed of the transition by clicking the Slow, Medium, or Fast option button. (Fast is almost always best.)**

6. **If you desire, choose a sound to accompany the transition from the Sound drop-down box.**

7. **If you want the slide show to run automatically, select the Automatically After check box and then enter the number of seconds you want the slide to be displayed.**

8. **If you want to control the pace of the slide show, check the On Mouse Click check box.**

9. **Click Apply.**

Animating a Slide

Animation enables you to add movement to your slides, which can help keep your audience awake. Every object on a slide can have its own anima- tion effect. You can control the order in which objects are animated and whether animations are manually controlled or happen automatically after a certain amount of time passes.

To add animation to your presentation, follow these steps:

1. **In Normal view, display the slide you want to animate.**

2. **Choose Slide Show⇨Custom Animation.**

   The Custom Animation dialog box displays, as shown in Figure 5-6.

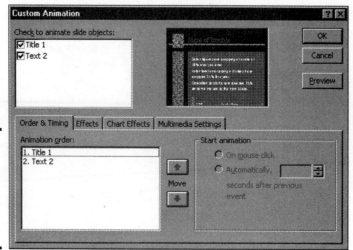

Figure 5-6:
Capture
your audi-
ence's
attention by
animating
your slides.

3. **At the top of the dialog box, select the check boxes representing the slide objects you want to animate.**

4. **On the Order & Timing tab, click the slide element you want to animate (such as Title or Text).**

   If you want the animation to occur automatically, select Automatically in the Start Animation area and then set the number of seconds you want to pass before the animation starts. If you want the animation to occur when the user clicks the mouse, select On Mouse Click.

5. **Click the Effects tab and choose the effects you want to use.**

   You can right-click any option in the dialog box and choose What's This? to see a brief pop-up description of that option.

6. **Click Preview to see a preview of your animation settings.**

7. **Repeat Steps 4 through 6 for any other objects you want to animate.**

8. **Click OK when you finish.**

Choose View⇨Toolbars⇨Animation Effects to display the Animation Effects toolbar, which contains buttons that apply several common animation effects with a single mouse click.

Manipulating Slides

You can quickly rearrange slides by switching to Slide Sorter view, which displays a thumbnail version of each slide in a presentation. Follow these steps:

1. **Switch to Slide Sorter view (see Figure 5-7).**

Use the scroll bars to display additional slides if necessary. To display more slides on-screen at once, click the drop-down arrow beside the Zoom button and select a smaller zoom percentage.

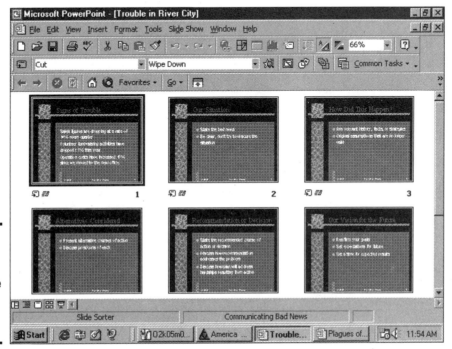

Figure 5-7:
Use Slide Sorter view to rearrange the slides in a presentation.

2. **To move a slide, click and drag it to a new location.**

A vertical line indicates where the slide will be dropped when you release the mouse button. PowerPoint 2000 adjusts the display to show the new arrangement of slides and automatically renumbers the slides.

3. **To delete a slide, click the slide and press Delete or choose Edit➪ Delete Slide.**

(The Delete key works on an entire slide only in Slide Sorter view.)

4. **To add a new slide, click the slide that you want the new slide to follow and then click the New Slide button. Then select the desired slide layout and click OK.**

To edit the contents of the slide, return to the Normal view.

Choose Insert⇨Slides from Files to display the Slide Finder, which enables you to import existing slides from other presentations.

Displaying a Slide Show

To display a slide show, follow these steps:

1. **Click the Slide Show View button.**

   The presentation displays on-screen, beginning with the current slide. If you want to run your presentation from the first slide, display that slide before you click the Slide Show View button.

2. **To advance to the next slide, press Enter, press the spacebar, or click the left mouse button.**

3. **Press Esc to end the slide show before it completes.**

Table 5-1 lists keyboard tricks you can use during your slide show.

Table 5-1	Keyboard Tricks for Displaying Slides
To Do This	*Press Any of These Keys*
Display next slide	Enter, spacebar, right arrow, down arrow, PgDn, N
Display previous slide	Backspace, left arrow, up arrow, PgUp, P
Display first slide	1+Enter
Display specific slide	Slide number+Enter
Toggle screen black	B, period
Toggle screen white	W, comma
Show or hide pointer	A, = (equals)
Erase screen doodles	E
Stop or restart automatic show	S, + (plus)
Display next slide even if hidden	H
Display specific hidden slide	Slide number of hidden slide+Enter
Change pen to arrow	Ctrl+A
Change arrow to pen	Ctrl+P
End slide show	Esc, Ctrl+Break, – (minus)

TIP

Setting up a professionally-timed slide show

You can set up a presentation so that it runs continuously on the computer without you having to stop talking and move on to the next slide. Here's what you do:

1. Choose Slide Show⇨Set Up Show.

2. Check the Loop Continuously until 'Esc' option and the Using Timings, if Present option and click OK.

3. Choose Slide Show⇨Rehearse Timings to open the slide show and display a timer dialog box that lets you manually set the timing for your slide show.

   As soon as the presentation opens, the timer starts counting.

4. Determine how long you want the slide to remain on-screen and click the Next arrow when you reach that time.

The screen moves to the next slide in the sequence, so you can set the timing for that slide. You may want to rehearse your presentation and figure out how much time you need to talk to customize the slide show's length.

When you get to the end of the slides, a dialog box appears asking whether you want to use these timings.

5. If you're happy with the timings, click Yes.

   The screen opens to Slide Sorter view, which enables you to see the times you've set for each slide.

Adding Notes to Your Presentation

PowerPoint 2000 enables you to create separate notes to accompany your slides to help you remember what you want to say. The beauty of the notes feature is that the audience doesn't see the notes, so they think you are winging it when in fact, you are relying on your notes. You can print notes pages that include a small image of the complete slide along with the notes for that slide.

Follow these steps to add notes to a slide:

1. **In Normal view, display the slide for which you want to add notes.**

2. **Click in the Click to Add Notes window near the bottom of your screen and type your notes.**

3. **To see your Notes page, select View⇨Notes Page.**

4. **Adjust the zoom factor with the Zoom drop-down list on the Standard toolbar if necessary, so you can read the notes text.**

   If necessary, scroll the display to bring the notes text into view. (The notes text appears beneath the slide image.)

After you switch to Notes Page view, you don't have to return to Normal view to add notes for other slides. Use the scroll bar or the PgUp and PgDn keys to add notes for other slides.

Keyboard Shortcuts

Tables 5-2, 5-3, and 5-4 list the most useful keyboard shortcuts in PowerPoint 2000. These are shortcuts that are specific to PowerPoint. Many of the shortcuts that can be used in all Office 2000 programs are covered in Book V, Chapter 2.

Table 5-2	Keyboard Shortcuts for Editing Slides
Shortcut	*What It Does*
Ctrl+Delete	Deletes from the insertion point to the end of the word.
Ctrl+Backspace	Deletes from the insertion point to the beginning of the word.
Ctrl+M	Inserts a new slide by using the AutoLayout dialog box.
Ctrl+Shift+M	Inserts a new slide without using the AutoLayout dialog box.
Alt+Shift+D	Inserts the date on the slide master.
Alt+Shift+T	Inserts the time on the slide master.
Alt+Shift+P	Inserts the page number on the slide master.
Ctrl+D	Duplicates the selected objects.
Ctrl+←	Moves the insertion point one word to the left.
Ctrl+→	Moves the insertion point one word to the right.
Ctrl+↑	Moves the insertion point to the preceding paragraph, except in Outline view, in which it moves to the preceding slide.
Ctrl+↓	Moves the insertion point to the next paragraph, except in Outline view, in which it moves to the next slide.
Ctrl+End	Moves the insertion point to the end of the page.
Ctrl+Home	Moves the insertion point to the top of the page.
Ctrl+Alt+PgUp	Moves to the preceding slide in Slide Sorter view.
Ctrl+Alt+PgDn	Moves to the next slide in Slide Sorter view.

Table 5-3	Keyboard Shortcuts for Formatting Text
Shortcut	*What It Does*
Ctrl+Shift+F	Activates the font control in the Formatting toolbar, so you can change the font.
Ctrl+Shift+P	Activates the font size control on the Formatting toolbar, so you can change the point size.
Ctrl+Shift+>	Increases the point size to the next available size.
Ctrl+Shift+<	Decreases the point size to the preceding size.
Ctrl+L	Left-aligns the paragraph.
Ctrl+R	Right-aligns the paragraph.
Ctrl+J	Justifies the paragraph.
Ctrl+E	Centers the paragraph.

Table 5-4	Keyboard Shortcuts for Working with Outlines
Shortcut	*What It Does*
Alt+Shift+←	Demotes the selected paragraphs.
Alt+Shift+→	Promotes the selected paragraphs.
Alt+Shift+↑	Moves the selected paragraphs up.
Alt+Shift+↓	Moves the selected paragraphs down.
Alt+Shift+A	Shows all text and headings.
Alt+Shift+−	Collapses all text under a heading.
Alt+Shift++	Expands all text under a heading.
/ (on numeric keypad)	Hides or shows character formatting.

Using Viewer to Transfer Presentations

You can transfer a PowerPoint 2000 presentation to a disk, from which you can run the presentation on any computer running Windows 95 or above, by using a special program called the PowerPoint 2000 Viewer. The following sections present the procedures for using the Viewer.

Using the Pack and Go Wizard

To prepare a presentation for use with the PowerPoint 2000 Viewer, use the Pack and Go Wizard:

1. **Open the presentation you want to copy to disk.**

2. **Choose File⇨Pack and Go.**

The Pack and Go Wizard appears.

3. **Click Next.**

The Wizard asks which presentation you want to include (see Figure 5-8). You can choose between the presentation you have open (Active Presentation), another presentation (Other Presentation), or both.

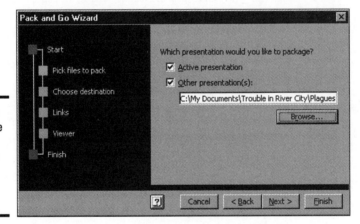

Figure 5-8:
Choose the presentation(s) you want to transfer to disk.

4. **Select the presentation(s) you want to include and then click Next.**

The Wizard asks whether you want to copy the presentation to drive A or to a different drive.

5. **Change the drive letter if necessary and then click Next.**

The Wizard now asks whether you want to Include Linked Files and Embed TrueType fonts. It's usually a good idea to check both options.

6. **Select the options you want and click Next.**

The Wizard asks whether you want to include the PowerPoint 2000 Viewer. It's best to include the Viewer, just in case the computer you want to run the presentation on doesn't have PowerPoint 2000 installed.

7. **Select the option you want and click Next.**

8. **Insert a disk in the disk drive and then click Finish.**

Copying a packed presentation onto another computer

You can't run a presentation directly from the disk created by the Pack and Go Wizard. Instead, you must first copy the presentation from the disk to another computer's hard drive. Follow these steps:

1. **Insert the disk that contains the packed presentation into the disk drive on the computer from which you want to run the presentation.**

2. **Open the My Computer window by double-clicking its icon and then select the disk drive into which you inserted the disk.**

3. **Double-click the Pngsetup icon to run the Pack and Go Setup program.**

4. **Follow the instructions that appear on-screen.**

Using the Viewer to run a slide show

After you copy the presentation to the other computer, you can run it with the Viewer by following these steps:

1. **Start the PowerPoint 2000 Viewer by double-clicking its icon in the folder into which you copied the presentation.**

   The system extracts the Viewer onto your hard drive, and the program asks whether you want to run the slide show at this time.

2. **Click Yes.**

   Your slide show starts automatically.

Chapter 6: Outlook 2000

In This Chapter

✔ **Creating and maintaining a contact list**

✔ **Tracking appointments and events**

✔ **Sending and receiving e-mail**

✔ **Managing daily tasks**

*T*his chapter covers Outlook, the all-in-one personal information manager that comes with Microsoft Office 2000. Outlook functions as an e-mail program, an address book, a calendar, and a task organizer. For more information about Outlook 2000, pick up a copy of *Microsoft Outlook 2000 For Dummies,* by Bill Dyszel (IDG Books Worldwide, Inc.).

Using the Address Book

 Outlook includes an address book, which enables you to maintain a list of your contacts with addresses, telephone numbers, and other information pertinent to each person. To work with the Outlook Address Book feature, click the Address Book button, choose Tools⇨Address Book, or press Ctrl+Shift+B. Figure 6-1 shows how Outlook appears when you call up your contacts.

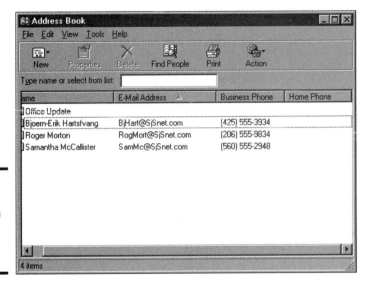

Figure 6-1:
A list of contacts in Outlook's Address Book.

Adding entries

To add a name to the Outlook address book, follow these steps:

1. Click the New button in the toolbar and select Contact (or New Contact) from the drop-down list.

The Properties dialog box displays, as shown in Figure 6-2.

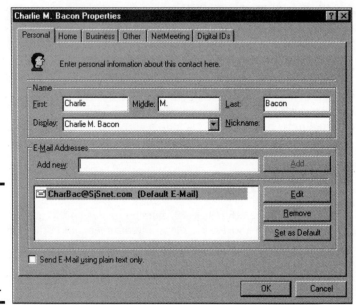

Figure 6-2:
Use the Properties dialog box to add contact information.

2. On the Personal (or Name) tab, type the person's contact information.

You can use the other tabs in this dialog box to add other information or make notes regarding the person for future reference.

3. Click OK after you finish.

Your Address Book displays your new contact.

You also can view your Address Book by clicking the Contacts button on the left side of the Outlook window.

Updating entries

To update an Address Book entry for an existing contact, follow these steps:

1. **Click the Address Book button.**

2. **Double-click the contact you want to change.**

The Properties dialog box for the selected person opens.

3. **Type your changes.**

4. **Click OK.**

Using the Calendar

One of the main functions of Outlook is keeping a calendar so that you can track appointments and upcoming events. To switch to the Outlook Calendar, click the Calendar icon in the Outlook bar. (The Outlook bar is the list of icons along the left edge of the Outlook window.)

Outlook gives you four calendar views: Day, Work Week, Week, and Month. To change views, click the applicable button in the toolbar. The Outlook Calendar also enables you to view active appointments, scheduled events, annual events, and recurring appointments. You can see these views via the drop-down list that appears when you choose View⇨Current View.

After you install Office 2000 on your system, you may notice icons for both Microsoft Outlook and for Outlook Express. *These icons are not the same thing!* This chapter covers Microsoft Outlook. Do not uninstall Outlook Express, because other Microsoft Office applications use components in this software.

Creating appointments

To create an appointment, follow these steps:

1. **Switch to the calendar view in which you prefer to work.**

Daily or weekly views are best for scheduling appointments.

2. **Click the day on which you want to schedule the appointment.**

3. **Click the time slot during which you want to schedule the appointment.**

If you want the appointment to stretch beyond a single time interval, drag the mouse across the desired time periods.

4. **Type a description for the appointment.**

Figure 6-3 shows two appointments scheduled, shown in Day view.

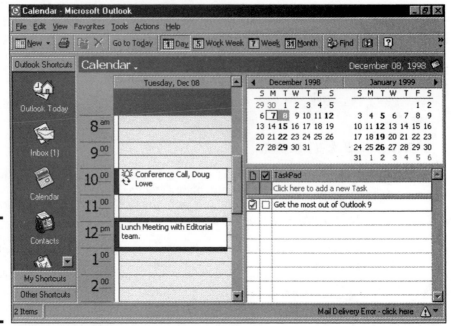

Figure 6-3:
The Outlook
Calendar
shows two
appoint-
ments.

Scheduling recurring appointments

You can use Outlook to schedule recurring appointments, such as staff meetings or other appointments that occur every day, week, or month. First, follow the procedure in the section "Creating appointments" to create an appointment for the next occurrence of the recurring date. Then follow these steps:

1. **After you create an appointment, double-click the appointment to open the Appointment window.**

2. **Click the Recurrence button to open the Appointment Recurrence dialog box (see Figure 6-4).**

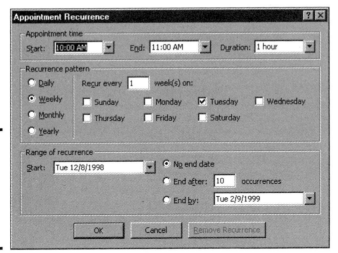

Figure 6-4:
Use this
dialog box
to schedule
recurring
appoint-
ments.

Outlook initially assumes that the appointment occurs every week on
the same day and time. If this is not the case, you can change this.

3. **If necessary, change the Recurrence Pattern options to indicate the
frequency of the appointment (Daily, Weekly, Monthly, or Yearly).**

   If you change the frequency option, a new set of controls appears in the
   Recurrence Pattern area of the dialog box, enabling you to specify the
   exact schedule for the recurring appointment.

4. **Click OK after you finish.**

5. **Click the Save and Close button in the Appointment window.**

   Outlook adds a special icon to the appointment in the calendar to indicate that the appointment is recurring.

Rescheduling appointments

Follow these steps to reschedule an existing appointment:

1. **Switch to a calendar view that shows both the appointment that you
want to reschedule and the date to which you want to reschedule it.**

2. **Click the appointment to select it.**

3. **Drag the appointment to the new time and/or day.**

   You can also reschedule an appointment by double-clicking the appointment
to open the Appointment window and then adjusting the Start Time and End
Time fields in the dialog box.

Canceling appointments

To cancel an appointment, follow these steps:

1. **Highlight the appointment you want to cancel to select that appointment.**

2. **Click the Delete button.**

   The appointment disappears from the calendar.

Adding events

An *event* is an item that occurs on a specific calendar date but does not have a particular time associated with it. Examples of events include birthdays, anniversaries, vacations, and so on.

To add an event to your calendar, follow these steps:

1. **Switch to the calendar view in which you want to work — Day, Week, or Month.**

2. **Click the date on which the event occurs.**

3. **Choose Actions⇨New All Day Event.**

   The Event window appears, as shown in Figure 6-5.

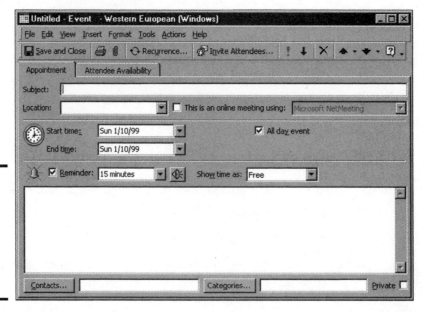

Figure 6-5:
Use the Event window to schedule birthdays and vacations.

4. Type a description for the event in the Subject box.

5. If the event continues for more than one day, change the ending date by selecting a date from the End Time drop-down list.

6. If it is a reminder of a birthday, anniversary, or some other similar event make sure to check the All Day Event check box; then click the Recurrence button, select the Yearly option button, and click OK.

7. Select Free in the Show Time As drop-down list.

The Free setting reminds you of the date but doesn't block your day from other appointments.

8. If this reminder is a personal matter, you want to make sure that you mark the Private check box.

Doing this prevents others on your network from receiving this message.

9. After you finish, click the Save and Close button.

The event appears on your calendar.

Scheduling meetings

If everyone in your office uses Outlook and your computers are connected via a network, you can use the Plan a Meeting feature to schedule meetings electronically. Outlook automatically picks a time slot that's available for each participant and notifies everyone of the time and place of the meeting.

Follow these steps to plan a meeting:

1. Choose Actions⇨Plan a Meeting.

The Plan a Meeting dialog box appears, as shown in Figure 6-6.

2. Type the names of the people with whom you want to schedule a meeting in the All Attendees column. Or click the Invite Others button to display the Select Attendees and Resources dialog box.

Use this dialog box to select names from your address book.

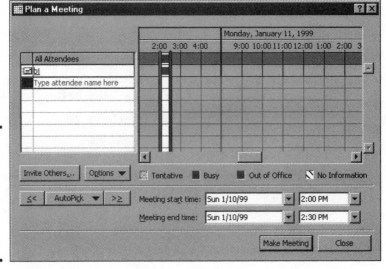

Figure 6-6:
The Plan a
Meeting
dialog box
enables you
to schedule
meetings
with others.

3. **After you select everyone you want to invite, click OK to close the Select Attendees and Resources dialog box.**

   Outlook reviews each person's schedule so that you can see who has free time (and when).

4. **Choose a time when everyone is free by clicking the time in the schedule area of the Appointment window. Or click AutoPick to have Outlook pick the time for you.**

5. **Click the Make Meeting button.**

   The Meeting window displays.

6. **Type a subject for the meeting in the Subject box and a location in the Location box.**

7. **Click the Send button in the toolbar to send the invitations.**

If someone invites you to a meeting, you receive an e-mail message that includes three buttons you can click to reply to the invitation: Accept, Decline, or Tentative. Click the appropriate button to reply to the invitation.

Working with E-Mail

Outlook includes an integrated e-mail feature that can send and receive electronic mail from your various e-mail services. If you receive e-mail from your local area network, from the Internet, and from the Microsoft Network, for example, Outlook can read e-mail from all three sources. That way, you don't need to fuss around with three separate e-mail programs.

 To access the Outlook e-mail feature, click the Inbox icon. Figure 6-7 shows the Inbox.

Figure 6-7:
The Outlook
Inbox can
display
e-mail from
multiple
e-mail
services.

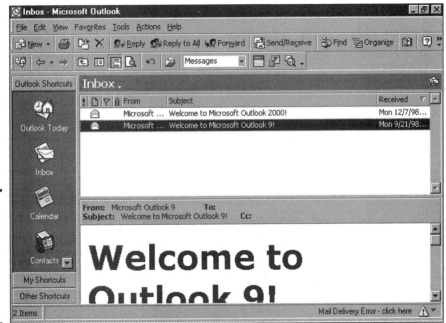

Sending e-mail

To send a new e-mail message, follow these steps:

1. **Click the New button.**

The Message window appears, as shown in Figure 6-8.

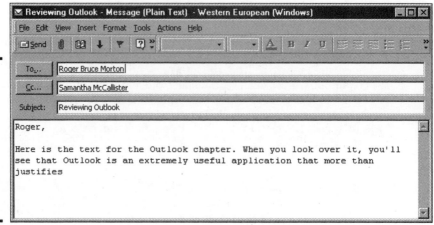

Figure 6-8:
Use the
Message
window to
type the
e-mail
recipient(s)
and the text
of your
message.

2. **In the To text box, type the e-mail address of the recipient(s).**

   If you want to pick names from your Address Book, click the To button.
   A dialog box listing all your contacts who have e-mail addresses
   appears; select the recipient you want and then click OK.

3. **In the Cc box, type the e-mail address of anyone you want to send a
   courtesy copy of your e-mail message to.**

   To pick names from your Address Book, click the Cc button.

4. **Type the subject of your message in the Subject text box.**

5. **Type the body of your message in the message area, the large text
   box at the bottom of the Message window.**

6. **After you finish typing, click the Send button in the toolbar.**

To attach a file to your message, click the Insert File button. In the Insert
File dialog box, select the file you want to attach and then click OK.

Reading e-mail

Reading e-mail is easy in Outlook. All you do is double-click the message
you want to read in the Inbox. The message appears in its own window.

After you finish reading the message, close the window by clicking the Close
button in the upper-right corner of the window. Or click any of the buttons
described below to respond to the message or to read other messages:

♦ Click this button to reply to the message's sender.

 ♦ Click this button to reply to everyone on the message's e-mail list.

 ♦ Click this button to forward the message to another recipient.

 ♦ Use this button to place a flag next to the message in the In Box. Using a flag helps you find the message later so that you remember to follow it up.

 ♦ Click the Move to Folder button to save your e-mail to a folder that you determine or to Outlook's Calendar feature.

 ♦ Click this button to delete the message.

 ♦ Click the Previous Item button to open a drop-down list that enables you to look at previous e-mail from any one of a number of categories. Outlook lets you sort your e-mail into different folders by topic, to flag the message as important, or to organize your e-mail by topic. Use this drop-down list to select which earlier piece of e-mail you want to read.

 ♦ Click the Next Item button to open a drop-down list that lets you select any item in your e-mail queue that fits the category you select.

Replying to e-mail

To reply to an e-mail message, follow these steps:

 1. **Click the Reply button.**

2. **Type your response in the message area.**

   Outlook automatically displays the contents of the original message below your response. You can delete as much of the original message as you want by selecting the text and pressing the Delete key.

 3. **After you finish typing, click the Send button.**

Using the Task List

 Outlook provides a Task List that enables you to keep track of all the tasks you need to do and when your tasks need to be completed. To access the Task List, click the Tasks icon in the Outlook bar. Figure 6-9 shows the Outlook Task List.

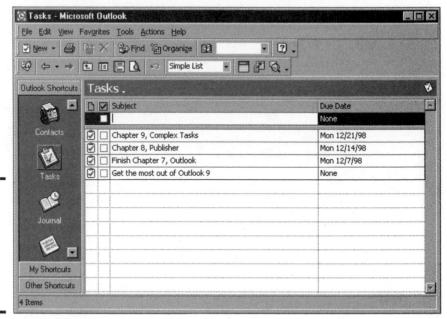

Figure 6-9:
Use the
Tasks
window to
track the
tasks you
need to
complete.

Creating a task

To add an item to your Task List, follow these steps:

1. Click the New button.

The Task window opens, as shown in Figure 6-10.

2. Fill in the Task window with the details of your task.

The Task window has two tabs. The Task tab enables you to fill in the general information about that task. This information appears on the Task List.

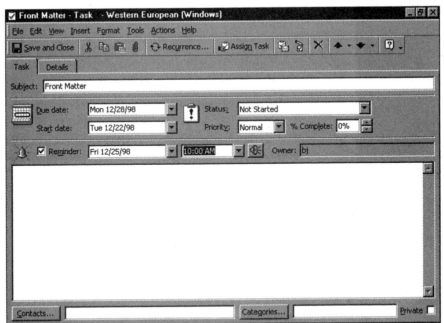

Figure 6-10:
Type a new
task in the
Task
window.

The Details tab enables you to keep a record of the work you do on the task. This tab is helpful for billing companies for your work.

3. **After you type a task, click the Save and Close button.**

The task is added to the top of the Task List.

Assigning tasks to others

Outlook enables you to create a task and then give that task to someone else on your network. This feature is useful for distributing jobs to subordinates or team members. As soon as you assign a task to another person, as far as Outlook is concerned, you give up ownership of the task. You can keep the task in your Task List and receive updates from the person performing the task, but you can't change any of the information regarding the task. Only the person doing the work can do that.

To use Outlook to assign a task to another person, follow these steps:

1. **Click the Tasks icon to open the Task List.**

2. **Click the arrow next to the New button on the toolbar and select Task Request from this list.**

   The Task Request window opens.

3. **Type the e-mail address of the person who you're assigning to the job in the To text box.**

4. **Type the assignment in the Subject text box and complete the Due Date and Start Date list boxes.**

5. **Specify the Priority and Status of the task.**

   To track the other person's progress, select the Keep an Updated Copy of This Task on My Task List check box. If you want to know when the task is finished, select the Send Me a Status Report When This Task Is Complete check box.

6. **Type your message in the message area at the bottom of the window.**

7. **Click the Send button.**

   Outlook gives the other person the option of accepting or rejecting the assignment. After the person accepts or rejects the task request, Outlook automatically notifies you via e-mail.

Index

Book VI

America Online 6.0

The 5th Wave   By Rich Tennant

It started as a wrap around porch, and then Stuart found information on medieval architecture on AOL.

Contents at a Glance

Chapter 1: Getting Started with America Online

In This Chapter

- ✓ Starting the AOL software
- ✓ Finding your way through the menus and toolbars
- ✓ Creating and changing your member profile
- ✓ Understanding screen names
- ✓ Setting the America Online preferences
- ✓ Getting help and using Parental Controls
- ✓ Getting offline and closing AOL

This chapter is your pre-online checklist of the basics you need to know to get into (and out of) America Online Version 6.0. Your new America Online account works pretty well right from the start, but with a few tweaks here and there, it becomes a high-performance technology machine. From account preferences to custom news wires, this chapter also explores the available tools and services that you can use to make America Online uniquely yours.

Starting AOL and Signing On

If you haven't installed the America Online software yet, insert the CD-ROM that came with your AOL information packet into the CD-ROM drive. Follow the installation instructions that appear on-screen and enter the registration number and password (also from your packet) when AOL prompts you to do so. During installation, AOL asks you to choose your own screen name and password; follow the guidelines provided. You use this screen name and password each time you log on to AOL. After you finish installing and registering the software, AOL displays help information to get you started with the program. When you're done using AOL, you sign off and exit the program. (See "Signing Off and Exiting AOL," later in this chapter, for more information.)

The next time you want to use AOL, follow these steps:

1. **If you have an external modem (or a PC Card modem in a laptop), turn it on and get the modem ready.**

2. **Find the America Online icon and double-click it to start the software.**

    You can usually find the icon on your desktop or inside an area called America Online 6.0. At this point, you can sign on to America Online. The Sign On dialog box appears, as shown in Figure 1-1.

Figure 1-1: Before you can begin using AOL, you must sign on.

3. **If you have more than one screen name, choose the screen name you want to use from the Select Screen Name drop-down list.**

4. **Press Tab to move the cursor into the Password box and then carefully type your password.**

    If you're accessing America Online from your home computer, continue to Step 5. If you want to connect to the service from some other location, choose that location from the Select Location drop-down list.

5. **Take a moment to make sure that your modem is turned on and nobody else in the family is using the phone line. When you're ready, press Enter or click Sign On.**

    A series of cool graphics displays your progress toward a finished connection. America Online may also have a few commercials for you; click No Thanks if you just want to get on with the show. When the Welcome screen appears (see Figure 1-2), you're ready to use America Online.

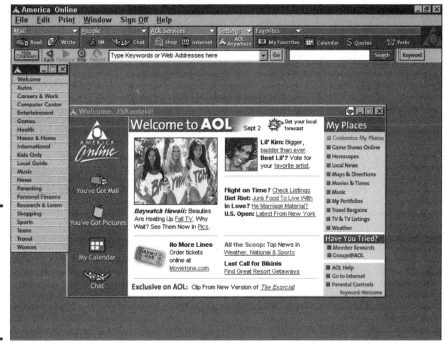

Figure 1-2:
The AOL
Welcome
screen
greets you
after a suc-
cessful
logon.

Every now and then, your connection attempt doesn't quite go through. When that happens, click Cancel and try again. If the connection still doesn't work, wait a few minutes and then give it one more attempt before you seek help from the America Online toll-free support line (800-827-3338).

Changing Your Password

Your password is the key to your account. To keep your account safe, change the password every month or so. Pick a password that's hard for other people to guess. For example, try making your password from two unrelated words and a number, such as `coincard3`, `cow8box`, or `clock4pad`.

To change your password, follow these steps:

1. **Press Ctrl+K, type the keyword** Password **in the text box, and then press Enter.** (See Book VI, Chapter 2, for more on using keywords.)

2. **Click Change Password.**

AOL Anywhere

As part of an ongoing effort to make life easier, the America Online programmers created AOL Anywhere. This feature ties several customizable areas together into a single dialog box. To get into AOL Anywhere, click the AOL Anywhere toolbar button. Of course, keyword **AOL Anywhere** works just fine, too. If you don't see the AOL Anywhere Web site open automatically, click the large Go button in the introductory screen that appears.

For new members, AOL Anywhere is a great starting point for learning about the system. More advanced members may discover some new features or get reacquainted with old favorites they haven't used in a while.

3. **Type your current password in the Current Password box and then press Tab.**

   The password appears as asterisks on-screen.

4. **Carefully type your new password in the two boxes at the bottom of the screen.**

   Capitalization doesn't matter, but spelling does.

5. **When you finish, click Change Password.**

   If the two new password entries match, AOL changes your password. If the passwords don't match, AOL asks you to try again.

Understanding the AOL Interface

Before you dive into your AOL session, familiarize yourself with the elements of the interface. In this section, you find out about AOL's menus, the toolbar, and the navigation bar.

Menus

The *menu bar* decorates the top of your America Online window. The menu bar is your main tool for controlling the software and communicating your desires to America Online itself. Table 1-1 describes the menu bar choices.

Table 1-1	Items Available on the AOL Menu Bar
Menu Item	*Description*
File	Deals with printing, saving, downloading, and using online features, such as You've Got Pictures. This menu also covers the Personal Filing Cabinet.
Edit	Includes the ever-popular text-editing commands, plus a Capture Picture command. Whether you need to check spelling or have a quick glance at a dictionary or thesaurus, you find those options here.
Window	Focuses on window management and offers an option that adds the top window to your Favorite Places list. This menu's most important (and arguably coolest) feature is the list of open windows that fills the bottom of the menu.
Sign Off	Switches between your account's screen names. This menu item also lets you exit the program when you finish playing online.
Help	Comes in handy when you have a general AOL question. Get comfy and click Help⇨Offline Help.

Book VI Chapter 1

Getting Started with America Online

Toolbar buttons

Although the toolbar buttons do add a dash of color to an otherwise utilitarian screen, their main goal is to make your online life easier. The toolbar buttons function in two ways. Buttons *without* a downward-pointing triangle provide a shortcut to either an America Online command (such as Write) or an online area (such as Quotes). Buttons that do sport such triangles reveal a pull-down menu when you click them; they function much like the menu bar items mentioned in the "Menus" section. Use the toolbar buttons to save time and frustration. Table 1-2 provides a description of the buttons on the AOL toolbar.

Table 1-2	AOL Toolbar Buttons	
Tool	*Name*	*Description*
	Mail	Use the Mail drop-down menu to look at e-mail you've sent, change e-mail preferences, create a signature file for your e-mail messages, run Automatic AOL, or open your online Address Book. (Some portions are available offline.)
	Read	Open a window full of your incoming mail.
	Write	Write a new e-mail message. (This option is available offline.)

(continued)

Table 1-2 *(continued)*

Tool	Name	Description
People ▼	People	Use the People drop-down menu to chat, talk, giggle, and laugh in a chat room, or locate other members online. Also, look here for the online White Pages and Yellow Pages.
IM	IM	Open the Instant Message window with a click of the IM button.
Chat	Chat	Find a chat room via the main People Connection window.
AOL Services ▼	AOL Services	Use this drop-down menu to check movie times, get directions for your next trip, find a recipe, and check the latest sports scores from the AOL Services toolbar list. AOL lists popular and useful services here.
Shop	Shop	Browse and buy from the main Shopping Channel window.
Internet	Internet	Open the AOL.com Web page and surf the Internet's worldwide information network.
Settings ▼	Settings	Make AOL your own with this drop-down menu. Change your preferences, create or delete screen names or passwords, set Parental Controls, or design news profiles. With News Profiles, AOL drops interesting news stories directly into your e-mail box. (Some selections are available offline.)
AOL Anywhere	AOL Anywhere	Pick your news, sports, stocks, and comics — and have it all delivered to you via the AOL Anywhere browser window.
Favorites ▼	Favorites	Use this drop-down menu to open the Favorite Places window, edit shortcut keys to your favorite AOL areas, open the Keyword window, or visit some of the general top areas online. (Some selections are available offline.)
My Favorites	My Favorites	Open your Favorite Places window.
Calendar	Calendar	Schedule outings and appointments with friends, keep your finger on the pulse of upcoming events, and remind yourself of the special days in your life with the AOL Calendar.
$ Quotes	Quotes	Track your favorite stocks.

Navigation bar

Nestled right under the toolbar resides a thin bar with a text field in it. This navigation bar (shown in Figure 1-3) helps you navigate the online service and the Internet in one fell swoop. After you figure out how to use it, you'll never want to see the Keyword dialog box again.

Figure 1-3:
The navigation bar appears just below the toolbar.

Table 1-3 describes the items on the navigation bar.

Table 1-3	Items Available on the AOL Navigation Bar	
Tool	*Name*	*Description*
Hide Channels	Hide Channels	Hide the channels list. Click it again to show the channels list.
Back	Back	Look at the last window you saw. Keep clicking the button to go backward one window at a time.
Forward	Forward	Go forward through the windows you've already opened online.
Stop	Stop	Stop your Web browser from loading the current page.
Reload	Reload	Reload the current Web page to update what you see.
http://www.aol.com	Text field	Type a keyword or URL to view that area or Internet site.
▼	Arrow	See the online areas or Web pages you already viewed during this online session.
Go	Go	Go to the area or Internet site highlighted in the text field.
	Search text field	Type a word or phrase that describes what you want AOL to find.
Search	Search	Fire up the system-wide Search service and go looking for stuff.
Keyword	Keyword	Type keywords directly into the Keyword dialog box rather than using the navigation bar text field.

Using Screen Names

Part of the fun on AOL is creating cool screen names that contribute to your online identity. Often, people choose to use one screen name for work and another for play. If you want to use Parental Controls to limit your kids' online activities, then the kids need individual screen names, too.

Each account has space for a primary screen name (the name you create when you sign up for America Online) and up to six secondary names. America Online now lets you create more than one master screen name for an account, in case you have more than one adult in a household. Your primary screen name automatically classifies as a master screen name. All master screen names have the capability to change America Online billing options and set Parental Controls for all the other screen names on the master screen names' account.

Creating a screen name

To create a screen name, follow these steps:

1. **Before signing on to America Online, think up a few possible screen names and write them down.**

   (That way, if someone else snarfed the name you wanted, you won't waste online time trying to think up another, equally cool name to replace it.)

2. **Sign on to the system with a master screen name.**

   Only a user bearing the master screen name can create new screen names.

3. **Press Ctrl+K, type the keyword** Screen Names, **and press Enter.**

   The Screen Names dialog box appears.

4. **Click Create a Screen Name.**

   A dialog box appears to ask if this screen name is for a child. If you click Yes, AOL presents you with a Note to Parents. Click Continue to proceed to the Create a Screen Name dialog box.

   If you click No, the Create a Screen Name dialog box appears immediately, explaining that the screen name you create will be public.

5. **Click the Create Screen Name button to continue.**

   The Choose a Screen Name dialog box appears.

6. **Carefully type the screen name you want in the box at the bottom of the screen.**

7. **Double-check the spelling; then click the Continue button.**

   The Choose a Password dialog box pops up to announce your success. If someone else already has that screen name, however, AOL informs you that the specific name is already in use. Whip out that list of backup names and keep trying until something works.

8. Type a password for the new screen name; press Tab, and type it again.

9. Click the Continue button.

If you type the same password in both boxes, AOL presents another dialog box. If you mistyped one of the passwords, AOL asks you to try doing the password thing one more time. A Parental Controls dialog box jumps to the screen.

10. Select the age range of the screen name's owner, and America Online automatically installs Parental Controls on that screen name. Click the Continue button.

If you select 18+ as the age range for the new screen name, AOL asks whether you want the new screen name to function as a Master Screen name, complete with the power to change billing options and set Parental Controls for all other screen names on the account. If you don't want the new screen name holder to exercise that much freedom, select No. (See also "Parental Controls," later in this chapter.)

11. A final Confirm Your Settings dialog box appears, listing your new screen name and the access features that go along with the age range you selected. If everything looks okay to you, press Enter to accept the settings and create your new screen name.

AOL then creates the screen name and adds it to your access software; the screen name appears in the AOL Screen Names window.

Deleting a screen name

When the time comes to bid a fond farewell to a screen name, don't get too sentimental — just delete the little fellow. You can delete any of the six secondary screen names on your account. However, you can't delete the primary screen name (you're stuck with that one). Follow these steps:

1. Sign on to AOL with the master screen name.

2. Press Ctrl+K, type the keyword Screen Names, and press Enter.

The Screen Names dialog box hops into action.

3. Click Delete a Screen Name; then click Continue in the Are You Really Sure You Want to Do This? dialog box.

The Delete dialog box takes the stage, displaying only your account's secondary screen names. (You can't delete the primary screen name.)

4. Click the screen name you want to delete; then click Delete.

A dialog box pops up and announces the screen name's demise.

Restoring a screen name

You deleted a favorite screen name by mistake, and five minutes later you decide you want it back. America Online provides a way to reactivate those hasty (or erroneous) screen name deletions. You can recover your screen name for up to six months after you delete it. Follow these steps:

1. **Sign on to AOL with the master screen name.**

2. **Press Ctrl+K, type the keyword** Screen Names, **and press Enter.**

3. **Click the Restore a Screen Name button.**

   If you recently deleted one or more screen names from your account, the Recover Previous Screen Name window hops onto the screen, help-fully listing the deleted screen names.

4. **Highlight the screen name you want to recover and click Recover.**

   The system reinstates your screen name and updates your screen name list.

Creating Your Member Profile

Your member profile tells the world who you are. If you want everyone on America Online to know something about you, put that information into your profile. You use the same steps to both create and change a member profile.

To create (or update) your member profile, follow these steps:

1. **Press Ctrl+K, type the keyword** Profile, **and press Enter.**

   The People Directory window opens.

2. **Click the My Profile button.**

   The Edit Your Online Profile window appears, but the window is unread-able due to the large warning dialog box that jumps to the screen directly on top of the Profile window. The warning dialog box begins by telling you that your AOL member profile is available to be seen by all America Online members. Then it suggests that no member include per-sonal information in any profile — all good stuff to know.

3. **Read the warning message. If you don't want to see this warning again, check Please Do Not Show Me This Again. Then click OK.**

4. **Type your information in the spaces in the profile window.**

   Include as little or as much information as you want; some members include only their screen names and general geographic location, while others complete each line and even include a personal quote.

5. **Click Update to store your changes or click Cancel to forget the changes.**

   Within a few minutes (sometimes longer), the new profile proudly takes its place in the People Directory.

If you want to include more information than the profile allows, try creating your own Web page. Clicking the Create a Home Page button in the Edit Your Online Profile window takes you to Hometown AOL, where you can upload your current Web page (if you have one) or design a new one. You can also get to Hometown AOL by typing keyword **Hometown**.

America Online gives you the capability to customize your profile. *America Online For Dummies,* 7th Edition, by John Kaufeld (published by IDG Books Worldwide, Inc.) contains a whole chapter on cool profile tricks.

Changing Your Preferences

The Preferences settings fine-tune your America Online experience. Almost every aspect of online life includes some Preferences settings. Whether you want to make file copies of e-mail messages automatically, turn off the system sound effects, or manage the Personal Filing Cabinet, the Preferences settings cover your needs.

The AOL Anywhere Preferences area offers all the preferences and also throws in short descriptions of each option at no extra charge. To get to this area, use keyword **Preferences**. To select a preferences item, click its link in the list.

You don't need to sign on to America Online to use the Preferences window — it's always available.

Association

Association selects America Online as your default application for Internet access. Selecting AOL as your Internet application can save you a lot of frustration if AOL is the only Internet service you use. Then, when you click a link in a document and you're not currently online, instead of watching Microsoft Internet Explorer open and then tell you it can't reach the Internet, you watch AOL open and load the Web site.

If you do use another Internet service, or you think you'd ever want to try a separate Internet Service Provider, do *not* select OK to establish America Online as your default Internet application.

Auto AOL

Auto AOL is short for Automatic AOL. Auto AOL enables you to download new e-mail messages onto your computer, send e-mail you've written offline, or get and send any new newsgroup postings that wait for your attention.

You probably want to set your Auto AOL preferences so that Auto AOL sends mail and gets unread mail. We generally leave the Download Files option unchecked, and download each attached file by hand as we need it. That way, we don't mistakenly download and open a hacker's contribution to our hard drive.

Chat

Chat options control the chat room window, and they change the way you see all chat rooms on the whole system. The most useful settings here are Alphabetize the Member List (turn this option on — it simplifies your life) and Enable Chat Room Sounds (turn this option off when someone won't stop playing sounds).

Download

Downloading cool stuff from the file libraries makes life worth living. To make downloading even easier, turn on Automatically Decompress Files at Sign-off. This choice automatically expands ZIP files after you sign off — it's pretty cool stuff.

Two options to turn off are Delete ZIP Files After Decompression and Confirm Additions to My Download List. If you want downloads to go to a specific place (other than the regular AOL Download folder), this window is where you change the download destination directory.

Filing Cabinet

Although the Personal Filing Cabinet is the neatest thing to hit the online world since high-speed modems, not too many preferences cover it. The only preferences really worth mentioning are the two deletion options — Confirm before deleting single and Confirm before deleting multiple items. If you're confident of your editing skills, turn these options off and save some time. On the other hand, if your life includes small children ("What does the DEL key do, Dad?"), leave these options turned on to protect your carefully filed information.

Font, Text, & Graphics

Font preferences give you the flexibility to change the fonts you see in chat rooms, e-mail, and Instant Messages. Be aware, however, that America Online has gone to great lengths to use fonts that are readable. If you choose some esoteric font for your chat rooms, reading the text may become more of a challenge — but hey, that's half the fun!

Also use this window to set the text size for e-mail, chat rooms, and Instant Messages. If you want to fit more words to a window without manually changing the text size each time you send an Instant Message or e-mail, select the Small text option. On the other hand, if larger letters would *really* be of help, select Large as your text preference.

**Book VI
Chapter 1**

One of the most useful items in the Font, Text, & Graphics window is Maximum Disk Space to Use for Online Art. If you're low on disk space, try reducing this setting to 10MB. (Getting a bigger hard drive is a *really* good idea, though.)

If you open and close several windows while you're online, you may come close to the maximum disk space amount you set. When that happens, every window you attempt to open brings a warning dialog box explaining that a graphic on the window can't be displayed due to low memory. Don't panic or run out to purchase a new hard drive — simply return to the Graphics window and increase the Maximum Disk Space to Use for Online Art. Poof! No more annoying dialog boxes.

Internet Properties (WWW)

The Web settings resemble a cross between a 747 cockpit and the control room of your local nuclear power plant. When you tweak the Windows 95/98 Web preferences, you're actually altering the Microsoft Internet Explorer settings.

Depending on your level of comfort with complexity, you may want to change several settings in the AOL Internet Properties window. Use the tabs at the top of the window to flip among the setting topics. Use the General tab to customize link colors and specify the Web page that you want to use as your home page. This tab also lets you clear the History folder — the list of Web page links you've visited. If you surf the Web often, you'll want to click Clear History every now and then to empty the folder. The Security Tab lets you set Internet safety preferences. The default setting for general Internet surfing is set at medium; with a medium setting, the software gives you a Warning dialog box when you attempt to download files from Web sites. The Security tab also lets you include specific Web sites as Trusted Sites or Restricted Sites by clicking the corresponding icon and then entering the site's Web address in the dialog box that appears. (We recommend that you take the easy way out and set Web preferences in the AOL Parental Controls if you want to shield the kids from harmful content.)

Web Graphics, the next tab in the lineup, gives you one lonely option. Web Graphics offers to compress Web graphics as they load. Leave that one marked to trim a little delay off the World Wide Wait.

Shopping Assistant takes its place as the final tab in the Windows 95/98 AOL Internet Properties window. Inside you find a check box that offers to show you the America Online Shopping Assistant each time you shop online. Unchecking the box doesn't seem to do a whole lot. Check or uncheck the box, as you prefer.

Mail

The e-mail preferences are quick and simple. The most useful ones are the *retain* options — Retain All Mail I Send in My Personal Filing Cabinet and Retain All Mail I Read in My Personal Filing Cabinet. If you do business through America Online e-mail, turn these options on — no doubt about it. A copy of every message you send or receive automatically lands in your Personal Filing Cabinet on your computer's hard drive, in the cleverly named Incoming/Saved Mail and Mail You've Sent folders.

Make sure that Use White Mail Headers is checked. This option lets you see exactly who sent you that mass-marketing message with the black background. Keeping white mail headers lets you track and report the spammers more easily.

On a related note, we recommend turning off Confirm Mail After It Has Been Sent. If you send more than two e-mail messages each month, this option gets very old very fast.

At the very bottom of the window, you see Keep My Old Mail Online X Days After I Read It. The default is set to three days; we recommend setting it to seven days, which is as high as the setting goes. The system zaps read e-mail messages by the send date rather than by the first-read date. So, if you read a message that arrived in your box four days ago and then want to reread it from your Read Mail list the next morning, that message will be history unless you increase the number of days the system keeps your old mail.

Marketing

Call us hermits-in-the-making, but we're burned out on junk mail and *have we got an offer for you* phone calls. If you're like us, run — don't walk — to the Marketing Preferences window. Here is your chance to strike a blow for empty mailboxes and quiet phone lines.

The Marketing Preferences dialog box is available through keyword **Marketing Prefs**. (It's also in AOL Anywhere Preferences, but why bother?) In the Marketing Preferences dialog box, click the button next to your pet peeve. Your choices are U.S. Mail from Other Organizations, U.S. Mail from AOL, Telephone, E-mail, Pop-up, and Additional Information. *Pop-up* is America Online's term for those advertising dialog boxes that appear occasionally when you sign on to the system. When you select a topic, a brief dialog box appears that explains why this particular type of junk mail is desirable. Click Continue and then choose either Yes I Do Want . . . or No I Don't. Then click OK to make it so.

Two other options deserve a quick mention as tools of a dedicated anti-annoyance crusader. Take a look at the Direct Marketing Association Mail Preference Service and Telephone Preference Service choices for details on how to truly remove yourself (at least temporarily) from the world of junk communications. You can find addresses for both these organizations under the Additional Information button.

Multimedia

The Multimedia Preferences window contains one lonely check box, called Attempt to Play All Multimedia Content with the Internal Player. Keep this one checked unless you've collected other players during your Internet excursions, and you prefer to use one or more of those.

Passwords

If you're tired of typing a password every time you sign on to America Online, use this preference setting to fix the problem once and for all. Type the password next to its associated screen name, and America Online won't ever ask you about it again. Unfortunately, anyone who wanders by your computer can then sign on to your account without knowing the password, so use this option only if your computer is in a secure area.

Privacy

Decide who you want to be able to contact you and make your preferences known in the Privacy Preferences window. By default, the preference is set to allow all AOL members and AOL Instant Message users to see you on their Buddy Lists and send you Instant Messages. If you want to exclude a few select people or you want to welcome only a designated group of screen names into your online world, you can do that, too. (You can also get to this window by clicking the Privacy Preferences button in your Buddy List window. Open the window with keyword **Buddy**.)

Spelling

The Spelling Preferences dialog box enables you to set your America Online software to capitalize the first word in a sentence, notify you if you type the same word twice, and choose a preferred dictionary (instead of the default AOL U.S. English dictionary) for spell-checking. Click the Advanced button to see additional settings. All Spelling preferences are turned on; if you really know your grammar and want a challenge, turn off any of them. Otherwise, leave them on — you now have one less thing to worry about.

Toolbar & Sound

With Toolbar preferences, you can change how the toolbar looks and where it appears (at the top or bottom of your screen). One of its most useful features is that you can set the preferences to clear your History Trail each time you sign off the system. Doing so deletes that long list of windows you opened while online — which America Online diligently keeps track of, in case you want to return to a window you saw yesterday (or even last week). Check Clear History After Each Sign Off or Switch Screen Name if you want the software to clean the slate each time you leave. To delete the list yourself, click the Clear History Now button and then click Yes when it asks whether you really want to erase your trail.

This window also enables you to turn off AOL sounds, such as "You've Got Mail" and the Buddy List sounds. Uncheck Enable AOL Sounds, such as the Welcome Greeting and Instant Message Chimes, if you want a quiet America Online experience. On the other hand, it may be easier to reach up and turn off your speakers.

Getting Help

Although the online world is a great deal of fun, it also provides more than a few confusing moments. That's why America Online offers many places to turn for help and consolation in your time of trouble. Most Help options listed here are free of connect charges if you subscribe to an hourly usage plan.

AOL Help area

America Online provides free help to members in the AOL Help area (keyword **Help**). If you have questions about online accounts, billing, or America Online itself, you can find answers in AOL Help (see Figure 1-4). Plus, you can find information on everything from downloads to chat areas and from online safety to the Internet.

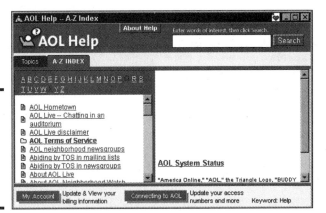

Figure 1-4:
AOL Help
provides
information
on a multi-
tude of
topics.

Free of connect time charges, this area offers members information about AOL by giving you the following options:

✦ Click any of the Topics links to open a window filled with articles about the corresponding topic or, depending on the subject, another window that provides more choices. Sooner or later, you reach a window with article listings.

✦ Type one or more words in the Search text box and then click the Search button to open a dialog box that starts a search of AOL Help information. Double-click an entry to read the article.

Billing problems

If you need to check your current bill and find the answers to billing questions, keyword **Billing** takes you to the window. Time spent in this area is free of online charges.

Use the Billing area to perform any of these tasks:

✦ Check your current bill summary.

✦ Change your name or address with America Online.

✦ Change your billing method and information.

✦ Read the answers to questions most often asked about America Online billing.

To request credit for a download that went awry or an evening when the America Online computers didn't feel like talking to you, type the keyword **Credit**. Only members who use America Online's measured service need to use the Credit window.

Free help from other members

Who knows America Online better than your fellow members? Nobody! Some of the best help on the whole system is available from other people, like yourself, in the AOL Help Community area. This area is only a keyword away — and it won't cost you a penny to access it.

Follow these steps to browse the AOL Help Community message board for answers to questions on billing, e-mail, uploading files, and more:

1. **Press Ctrl+K, type the keyword** Help Community, **and press Enter.**

The AOL Help Community window opens.

2. **Click the button next to Message Boards.**

A window opens that offers you two message board links: one for Windows and the other for Macintosh. Click Windows and the AOL Help Community message board opens.

You also can get help with your computer and America Online through the Computing channel's Get Help Now window. Here you can link to nightly Help Desk chats, where live volunteers answer your computer questions. Open any folder or document you find here to learn about everything from creating a new folder in Windows 95/98 to online safety and security. Use keyword **Get Help Now** to open the window.

Insider Tips window

Turn to the AOL Insider Tips window (keyword **AOL Tips**) for tips on viruses, ideas for fun and useful areas online, suggestions for making your AOL experience faster, and tips on using AOL like a pro. Whether you're a beginner or a veteran at AOL, you find some good information here (see Figure 1-5).

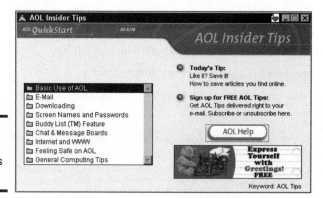

Figure 1-5:
The AOL Insider Tips window.

The AOL Help button opens the AOL Help window. Here you can find further information on the problem that perplexes you.

Use the folders in the item list to read tips organized by subject. Here you find the goodies on navigating the system and enhancing your time on AOL.

Calling America Online for help

Most of the time, you can find help about America Online while connected to the service. Once in a while, though, connecting to AOL is the problem. In that case, you need some human help. Talk to a technical support staff member live at 800-827-3338. If possible, be near the computer when you call (the technician may need to know some specific info about your computer).

Here are the toll-free numbers you need to contact America Online:

+ For technical help, call 800-827-3338.

+ To talk to the sales staff, use 800-827-6364.

+ TTY users call 800-759-3323.

Parental Controls

Just as you wouldn't send a child into the bad parts of the city (or into the mall alone with your charge card), you don't necessarily want little eyes to command full access to America Online and the Internet. That's where the Parental Controls come in. The Parental Controls are your tools for steering and blocking an impressionable child's access to online content.

Keeping kids safe today is tougher than ever before, particularly when the kids have online access. That's why America Online created the Parental Controls. These tools help parents delimit simple, enforceable boundaries in the freewheeling cyberworld. (See Book III, Chapter 1, for more on Internet safety and security issues.)

Three levels of control are available:

+ **Kids Only:** This one-size-fits-all blanket restriction limits your child's screen name to content in the Kids Only channel within America Online, as well as to Kids Only-approved Internet sites. Child Access accounts have no access to America Online's premium games — the games you pay extra to play. For kids under 12, this level is your best option.

+ **Young Teen:** Older children (those in the 13-through-15 age group) need a bit more flexibility to explore the online environment. Young Teen access balances a child's longing for unrestrained command of the world with a parent's goal of not letting the child out of the front yard. AOL's Young Teen controls govern chat areas, download libraries, games, certain Web sites, and the Internet newsgroups.

✦ **Mature Teen:** This setting, designed for mature teens age 16 through 18, allows almost everything on the system. Certain "mature content" Web sites are blocked from these accounts, and the setting also blocks access to premium games (those games that carry a service charge).

Before applying Parental Controls, create a screen name for your child. The child should use her own screen name for online access. Follow these steps:

1. **Sign on to America Online using your master screen name.**

(You must use a master screen name to access the Parental Controls.)

2. **Use keyword** Parental Controls **or choose Settings⇨Parental Controls from the toolbar.**

The Parental Controls window appears, as shown in Figure 1-6.

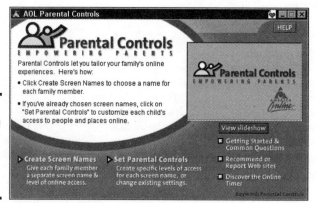

Figure 1-6:
Set Parental Controls to limit access to some sites.

3. **Click the Set Parental Controls button.**

The Set Parental Controls window hops to the screen.

4. **Use the drop-down menu to choose the screen name that's destined for the new controls.**

5. **Choose either Kids Only, Young Teen, or Mature Teen, depending on the child's age or maturity.**

Use the Custom Controls button in the Parental Controls window to set controls on e-mail so that the kids can't send or receive pictures or files. This button also lets you limit Instant Messages for the child's screen name.

Signing Off and Exiting AOL

When you finish visiting America Online, always remember to sign off. After you sign off, you exit the America Online program to free up some memory in your computer for other jobs. Follow these steps:

1. **If you started either a chat log or session log, close the log file before leaving America Online. To close the log file, choose My Files⇨ Log Manager and then click Close Log.**

2. **Choose Sign Off⇨Sign Off, and AOL signs you off.**

The Sign On box reappears with a friendly `Goodbye from America Online!` message along its top bar.

3. **Choose File⇨Exit.**

The software bids you a fond farewell and closes.

Windows 95/98 users can sign off and shut down the software in one motion by clicking the Close box in the upper-right corner of the screen.

Chapter 2: Going Places with AOL

In This Chapter

✔ Moving fast with keywords and shortcut keys

✔ Remembering your Favorite Places

✔ Customizing My Places with your favorite stops

✔ Finding and printing stuff on AOL

✔ Downloading software and uploading files

*W*onderful gems abound on America Online, but you have to know how to find them. This chapter shows you how to locate areas and services on America Online and tells you what to do with a treasure when you find one. For example, you discover tools for nabbing online information and tucking it away on your hard drive or saving a copy on paper.

Using Keywords

Many areas on America Online use their own *keywords*. Think of keywords as shortcuts through a city. Instead of navigating menus and windows, you type a word or short phrase, and the window opens.

To use a keyword, follow these steps:

1. **Press Ctrl+K, choose Favorites⇨Go To Keyword from the toolbar, or click the Keyword button on the navigation bar.**

The Keyword window hops into action.

2. **Type the keyword in the text field.**

3. **Press Enter or click the Go button.**

With AOL 6.0, you have yet another cool way to use keywords:

1. **Click the navigation bar text field at the top of your screen.**

2. **Type the keyword in the navigation bar text field.**

3. **Click Go or press Enter.**

Most main-menu screens and many individual forums sport their own keywords. Look for keywords in the lower-right corner of the window or on the window's top blue bar. (Sometimes the information hides in another corner, but the lower-right corner is standard.) The text is small and says Keyword: (or KW:), with the specific keyword after the colon.

Getting a List of Keywords

Keywords provide shortcuts to different places on America Online. To get a current list of all America Online keywords, follow these steps:

1. **Press Ctrl+K or click the Keyword button on the navigation bar.**

2. **Type** Keyword **in the text field or click the Keyword List button.**

3. **Click the Go button.**

The keyword **Keyword** window appears, as shown in Figure 2-1.

Figure 2-1:
You can
view a list
of AOL's
keywords —
alphabeti-
cally or by
channel.

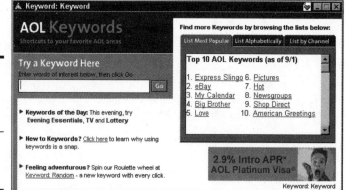

4. **Click the List By Channel tab at the top of the list box on the right side of the window.**

Finding a specific keyword is much easier when you begin with a general topic rather than trying to filter through the alphabetical-by-keyword list.

5. **Choose a channel to explore and double-click it to see a list of that channel's available keywords.**

To copy the keyword list to your hard drive, open each channel's window individually, highlight the text, and copy it to a new text file (using File⇨New). Then save the text file(s) under an appropriate name.

Keywords change all the time as new keywords appear and nonfunctioning ones phase out. Be prepared for the system to tell you that it can't find the keyword you're looking for.

Remembering Your Favorite Online Spots

Returning to neat places becomes half the fun when you cruise AOL. These methods can help you to remember your favorite online spots:

+ Use the Favorite Places list.
+ Set up the My Places feature.
+ Customize your HotKeys list.

If you spend a great deal of time online, you may want to customize the HotKeys list to include the places you visit each time you sign on to America Online. You can reserve Favorite Places for really cool places elsewhere online or on the Web. (See "Building Your Own HotKeys List," later in this chapter.)

Using the Favorite Places List

Favorite Places is the bookmark feature of America Online. Use it to remember an area, window, or chat room that's too good to forget. Put forums, Web pages, chat rooms, or message boards into the Favorite Places list. Any window that contains a Favorite Places icon (that white, dog-eared page with the red heart) in the upper-right corner qualifies as a potential Favorite Place.

Your software comes with several Favorite Places already installed. Open the Favorite Places window and then double-click any folder to open it, revealing Favorite Places to explore.

Adding an item to your Favorite Places list

To add something to your Favorite Places list, follow these steps:

1. **While looking at an online area or Web site, fall deeply in love with it. Convince yourself that you must be able to return there at any time.**

2. **In the upper-right corner of the window, you see an icon that looks like a heart on a white sheet of paper with the edge turned down. That's the Favorite Places icon. Click it.**

   A small dialog box appears, asking whether you want to save this site in your Favorite Places, insert it into an Instant Message, or insert it into an e-mail message.

3. **Click the Add to Favorites button.**

   The area's address and name are now part of your Favorite Places list.

Changing an item in the Favorite Places list

Change is part of the online world's nature. Web-page addresses change from time to time, forums reorganize, or maybe you just thought of a better name for that folder that holds the miscellaneous best of the best.

Update your Favorite Places list by modifying it:

1. **Choose Favorites⇨Favorite Places.**

2. **Highlight the item you want to change.**

3. **Click Edit.**

   If you highlighted a Favorite Place entry, a dialog box appears that contains two text boxes (see Figure 2-2). Alter the place name, the address, or both. If you highlighted a folder, a cursor appears at the end of the highlighted folder name. Use the Backspace key to erase the part of the folder's name that you want to change.

Figure 2-2: You can edit items in your Favorite Places list.

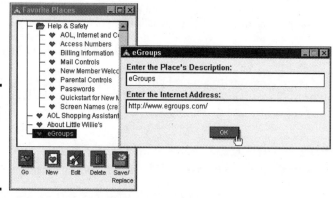

4. **Make the changes to your Favorite Place and click OK. On a folder, change the name and then click the folder icon or anywhere in the Favorite Places window to set your changes.**

Going to a Favorite Place

After you find a really cool area and place it among your Favorite Places, you can return to that area. Here's how:

1. **Choose Favorites➪Favorite Places.**

The Favorite Places window opens.

2. **Double-click the place's heart icon from your Favorite Places list (or highlight the place and click the Go button at the bottom of the window).**

Your Favorite Places fall into line at the bottom of the Favorites pull-down menu. For a quick trip to one of your favorite areas, follow these simple steps:

1. **Click the Favorites toolbar button.**

2. **Click your chosen Favorite Place to open its window.**

Any folders you've created appear in the Favorites menu, too. Rest your cursor over the folder, and its contents pop up in a secondary menu.

Organizing your Favorite Places

If the Favorite Places list becomes overwhelming, organize it by creating folders that contain *categories* of places. Follow these steps:

1. **Choose Favorites➪Favorite Places.**

2. **Click the New button at the bottom of the Favorite Places window.**

3. **Click the New Folder option button, type a folder name into the text field, and click OK.**

The folder appears at the bottom of the Favorite Places list.

4. **Click and drag Favorite Places entries to the folder and drop them in.**

Use the same technique to move the folder itself. Just click and drag it to a new location. (You can even put folders inside other folders!)

Deleting items from the Favorite Places list

When a Favorite Place's luster fades, delete it. Follow these steps:

1. **Choose Favorites➪Favorite Places.**

2. **Highlight the Favorite Place in question.**

3. **Click the Delete button or press the Delete key.**

   A dialog box asks whether you're sure you want to delete the item.

4. **Click Yes to reassure AOL and kiss that Favorite Place goodbye.**

If the item disappears without asking your permission, and that bothers you, then you need to set your Personal Filing Cabinet Preferences to confirm before it deletes single items.

Selecting My Places

Think of AOL's My Places feature as a controlled Favorite Places list. Although you can't select from every keyword on the service, My Places enables you to select from many of the most popular online areas. After you set up your individualized list, you can click one of the buttons in the My Places list to go directly to that area. Look for My Places in the Welcome window.

You can select up to ten favorite online destinations for My Places. Follow these steps to set up My Places:

1. **Click the Customize My Places button on the right side of the Welcome window to open the Change My Places screen.**

2. **Click the top Choose New Place button and highlight a channel from the list that appears.**

3. **Click to select an area from the channel you highlight.**

   That area takes its place in the first My Places slot. (Optional) You can continue until all the slots are filled.

4. **Click Save My Changes to save your changes.**

   A dialog box appears to tell you that AOL saved your selections.

5. **Click OK to close the dialog box.**

You can select each of your ten favorite areas from different channels, or you can choose them from the same channel. To change your selections, click the Set My Places button in the Welcome window and choose new areas.

Flipping between Windows

Sooner or later, the AOL windows pile up on-screen. Somewhere at the bottom lies the window you seek. To locate the lost window, either look in the Window menu or press Ctrl+Tab:

✦ Choose Window⇨# (where # is 1 through 9) to go directly to a window. If more than nine windows lie open on the screen, and none of these nine is the window you want, choose Window⇨More Windows.

✦ Press Ctrl+Tab to cycle through the windows one at a time. Each press of that key combination reveals another window.

Printing

When you want a paper copy of something cool that you find online, print it. Within America Online, you can print text windows and many online graphics, plus most Web pages. You can't print menu lists, though.

To print something, follow these steps:

1. **Open the window that you want to print.**

2. **Choose Print⇨Print.**

The Print dialog box appears.

3. **Make sure that your printer is online; then press Enter or click OK.**

Unless you're in a text-only window, such as a message board posting, you may receive a surprise when you try to print from the screen. Sometimes, the Print button gives you the graphic; other times, you receive the text. Often (especially if the top of the window says something like `Printing Graphic 1 of 2`), you get both.

Finding Almost Anything on AOL

Use the AOL Search feature to locate nearly everything on America Online — channels, window contents, Web links, the Member Directory, and more. (If you want to search for another *person* on AOL, see Book VI, Chapter 6.)

Open the general AOL Search window and begin a search in a jiffy by typing your topic in the text box on the navigation bar and then clicking the Search button. The AOL Search engine returns a list of message boards, AOL areas, and Web sites that meet your search criteria.

Finding Files to Download

America Online offers a marvelously extensive software library. You can locate files in two ways:

✦ **To browse through file lists:** Use keyword **Download Center** to open the main software center screen. Remember that most online areas have their own software libraries, as well.

✦ **To search the online libraries:** Use keyword **Download Center** and then click the Shareware button. The main Software Search window, as shown in Figure 2-3, covers primarily DOS and Windows programs.

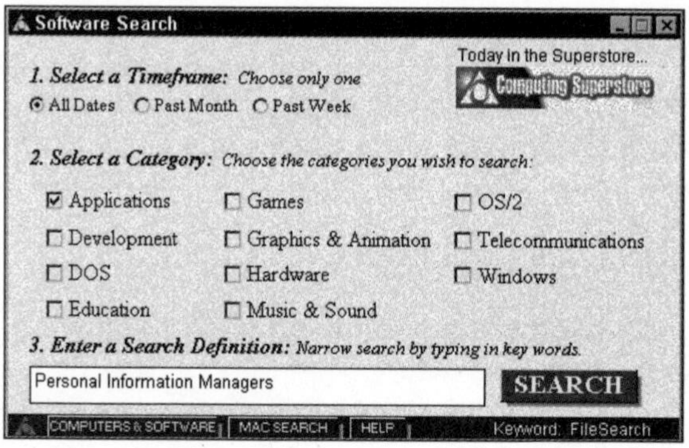

Figure 2-3:
Choose the category of software you want to search.

Downloading Files Right Now

A world of stuff awaits you in the America Online file libraries: programs, information, graphics, and more — they're all just a download away. Just follow these steps:

1. **In your favorite online area, find the file library (almost every area has one).**

   It's often behind a button labeled Software, Files, Cool Stuff, Downloads, or something like that. A window that lists different shareware items appears. (If you're in a very small online area, you may go directly to a list of available files. In that case, skip to Step 3.)

2. **Choose a category that looks interesting and double-click it.**

   A list of available files pops onto the screen, as shown in Figure 2-4. If you're in a particularly large online area, this window may contain another list of categories, like those in Step 1. In that case, repeat this step (Step 2) until you get to a file list.

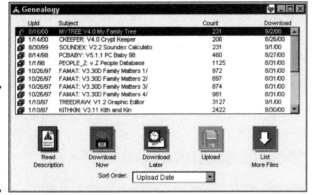

Book VI
Chapter 2

Figure 2-4:
Choose the
actual file
from the list
of available
files.

Going Places
with AOL

3. **Scroll through the list until you find a file that looks interesting. To organize files by popularity or by subject, click the arrow next to Sort Order at the bottom of the file list window. Select your preferred sorting method (Upload Date, Subject, Download Count, or Download Date) and watch the items fall into line. You can click List More Files to reveal more of the files in a particular library.**

4. **At this point, you can look at the file's description, download it, or mark it for downloading later.**

   • **To see a description of the file:** Double-click the file's entry in the list. A window that tells you everything you ever wanted to know about the file hops onto the screen.

   • **To download the file right now:** Click Download Now. When the Download Manager window pops up, select a destination for the file (and change the filename, if you like). When you're ready to go, click Save or press Enter. The file begins to make its way to your computer.

   • **To download the file later:** Click Download Later. America Online notes the filename and location in the Download Manager and presents a dialog box on-screen, telling you that the file was successfully added to your download list.

If you choose Download Later, remember to start the Download Manager sometime (choose My Files⇨Download Manager) and finish transferring the file to your computer. Otherwise, when you sign off, the software displays a dialog box that asks whether you want to download the files you marked earlier.

Downloading Files Later with the Download Manager

The Download Manager tracks files that you mark with the Download Later button, and it remembers the files that you downloaded in the past. To open the Download Manager, choose My Files⇨Download Manager. The Download Manager window lists all files that are waiting to be downloaded (see Figure 2-5). When you click Download Later while looking at a file, the Download Manager stores that file's information in this window.

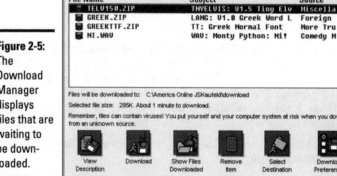

Figure 2-5:
The Download Manager displays files that are waiting to be downloaded.

Downloading files in waiting

To download the waiting files in the Download Manager, click Download. The File Transfer dialog box appears, providing an estimate of the download time. The estimate is frequently wrong, so don't be surprised if downloading takes longer than the estimate. If you're downloading a bunch of stuff, click the Sign Off After Transfer check box and go on with your regularly scheduled day. When the Download Manager finishes, it automatically signs you off the system.

Removing files from the download list

To remove a file from the Download Manager's list of waiting files, click the filename you want to remove and then click Remove Item. A dialog box appears, asking whether you're sure that you want to delete the file. Click Yes, and the entry vanishes without further argument.

Seeing which files you already downloaded

From the Download Manager, you can look at a list of files that you've already downloaded. Just click Show Files Downloaded. The Files You've Downloaded window appears. By default, it shows your last 100 downloads. If you want America Online to remember more (or fewer) than 100 files, click Download Preferences on the Download Manager window and change the Retain Information About My Downloads entry.

Checking file descriptions

To check a description of a file waiting to be downloaded, double-click the file's entry in the Download Manager list. (Sorry, this trick won't work if you're not signed on to America Online.)

Choosing where to store files to download

To tell the Download Manager where to store files waiting for download, click Select Destination. In the Select Path dialog box, use the folders to click your way to the right path. If you decide not to change the storage location, look for all your files in your AOL software's Download folder.

Don't worry if the word path is in the File Name area of the dialog box — that's normal, if somewhat odd, behavior.

Saving Text from a Window

If a news story, information window, e-mail message, or Web site sparks your interest, you can save a copy of the item on your computer. Here's how:

1. **Browse through the system until you find some text that looks interesting enough to keep.**

2. **Choose File⇨Save or press Ctrl+S.**

   The Save File As dialog box pops up. Unless you specify another file location, America Online saves the file to the AOL Download folder.

3. **Type a filename for the text file you're creating in the File Name box.**

4. **After you finish, press Enter or click Save.**

Uploading Files

Submitting a file to America Online gives you a good feeling, like you're contributing to the community. When possible, offer something in return to the online community by uploading your favorite shareware programs or artwork.

Remember that you can only upload freeware or shareware programs, text files that you wrote, or artwork that you created. You can't upload commercial programs. (In fact, America Online can cancel your account if you do, because uploading commercial programs violates federal copyright law.)

To submit a file to America Online, follow these steps:

1. **Use a keyword or menu selection to get into an online area that covers the subject of your file.**

2. **Look for a menu entry labeled Library, File Library, or something similar and double-click it to view the area's Library window.**

3. **Click the Upload button on the File Library window.**

   The Upload dialog box appears. (If you don't see an Upload button, AOL is probably trying to tell you that this particular area doesn't accept files from members. Not every library takes uploads. If you aren't sure whether that particular library accepts uploads, send an e-mail message to the forum leader and ask for information and guidelines for posting.)

4. **Fill out the informational entries in the Upload File window.**

   Pay particular attention to the Needs and Description sections. People who want to download your file rely on you for this information.

5. **Click Select File.**

   The Attach File dialog box pops up.

6. **Find your file among the teeming multitudes in the dialog box list. To include the file in your upload, double-click its entry.**

7. **Click Send, and your file is on its way.**

ZIP Files

In the world of Windows and DOS, ZIP files rule as the undisputed leaders of file compression. Although the AOL software understands ZIP files, keep your own unzipping software handy.

VBRUN files (Visual Basic Runtime Modules)

Many shareware authors use the Microsoft Visual Basic system to write their programs. To execute a program written with Visual Basic, you need a special file called a runtime module on your system. Basically, a runtime module is a collection of instructions that the program uses when it runs. Think of runtime modules as crib notes for your software.

Each runtime module available on America Online corresponds to a different version of Visual Basic; the number in the filename is the version number of Visual Basic that the particular library supports.

Each library supports only its specific version of Visual Basic. The Version 4 runtime library, for example, won't do a thing for a program written to look for the Version 2 file. Because of this, you may need multiple runtime libraries — not just the most recent one — in your WINDOWS/SYSTEM subdirectory. On the other hand, if only one of your programs requires a VBRUN file,

just install that particular file. (After all, there's no sense in wasting hard drive space.)

The following VBRUN files are available through the software library (keyword **Download Center**):

VBRUN100.EXE   Runtime library for Visual Basic Version 1.0

VBRUN200.EXE   Runtime library for Visual Basic Version 2.0

VBRUN300.EXE   Runtime library for Visual Basic Version 3.0

For runtime modules above VBRUN300.exe, go to Download.com (at www.download.com) and search for visual basic runtime. Here you can download modules for Visual Basic versions 4.0, 5.0, and 6.0. As with all the other Visual Basic Runtime Modules, these files are free to download and use.

In a Windows environment, the popular choice is the Niko Mak WinZip program. To download a copy, use keyword **Download Center** and search for WINZIP. (Click the Shareware button to open the Software Search window.) For DOS, use the original PKZIP program. PKZIP is available online, too — use keyword **Download Center** and then search for PKZIP.

Chapter 3: Using AOL E-Mail

In This Chapter

✔ **Creating, formatting, and sending e-mail**

✔ **Addressing e-mail by using the Address Book**

✔ **Saving money by reading and writing e-mail offline**

✔ **Sending and receiving file attachments**

✔ **Automating AOL sessions**

*W*hat would an online service be without e-mail? This chapter tells you how to send electronic mail to AOL members or to others via the Internet. I explain how you can save some connect time by using the Automatic AOL feature to retrieve your messages so that you can read them offline. You also discover how to use the new You've Got Pictures feature in AOL 6.0, which enables you to receive your developed photos online and share them with others.

Creating and Sending E-Mail

Electronic mail makes the Internet go 'round. To put your two cents' worth into the process, you can create and send your own e-mail messages to friends and colleagues. Although you can write messages while online, you shorten your connection time by first writing them offline. If you're feeling creative, you can spice up your e-mail by adding formatting such as bold-face, italics, different text and background colors, or images.

Writing an e-mail message online

Follow these steps to compose a message while online:

1. **Choose Mail➪Write Mail or click the Write toolbar button (or press Ctrl+M).**

The Write Mail window opens.

2. **Type the recipient's e-mail address in the Send To text box on the Write Mail window (see Figure 3-1).**

(See the section "Addressing E-Mail by Using the Address Book," later in this chapter, to find out how to use the Address Book to quickly insert e-mail addresses.)

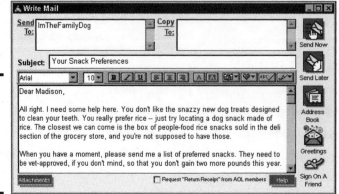

Figure 3-1:
Use the
Write Mail
window to
compose
your e-mail
message.

3. **In the Subject text box below the address, type a few descriptive words that tell the intent of the message.**

   A subject line, such as Lunch Sunday, tells more than Hello.

4. **Press Tab to continue and then write your message in the message text box that takes up most of the Write Mail window.**

5. **(Optional) Dress up your message with some text formatting.**

   Use the buttons at the top of the message box to apply bold, italic, and other highlights to your text. Try clicking the camera icon and inserting an image to spice up your e-mail. Also, you can right-click in the message text box for several new e-mail options. Use the shortcut menu that appears to insert a background image, open and insert a saved text file, insert a regular image, or create a hyperlink to your favorite Web site.

6. **After you finish writing the message, click the Send Now button on the right side of the Write Mail window.**

   America Online immediately sends the e-mail to its destination. If you have second thoughts after you send a message to an America Online member, check out the section "Unsending e-mail," later in this chapter.

Writing an e-mail message offline

If you use one of America Online's measured service options, writing messages offline saves money by shortening your connection time. As you compose e-mail messages offline, you can ponder word choices without watching the America Online clock tick or needing to click the Yes button in the You've Been Idle — Do You Want to Stay Online? dialog box.

To write an e-mail message offline, follow these steps:

1. **With the AOL software running but not connected by modem, choose Mail⇨Write Mail (or click the Write button on the toolbar).**
2. **Type the recipient's e-mail address in the Send To text box.**
3. **In the Subject text box below the address, type a few descriptive words that tell the intent of the message.**
4. **Press Tab and then write your message in the Message text box.**
5. **After the message is complete, click the Send Later button at the right side of the window.**
6. **When you're ready to send the message, sign on to America Online and begin an Automatic AOL session.**

See also the sections "Automating Your AOL Sessions," later in this chapter and "Writing an e-mail message online," earlier in this chapter.

Sending e-mail to an AOL member

To send an electronic mail message to another America Online member, use the member's screen name in the Send To text box of the Write Mail window. E-mail that you send from one AOL account to another requires only the member's screen name and not the @aol.com extension that you need on the Internet.

Sending e-mail to someone on the Internet

An Internet e-mail message requires the entire Internet address. Use the person's entire e-mail address, including the @whatever that comes after the name or account name. E-mail that you send to other online services also needs the Internet extension, as in 710303.3713@cis.com. Type the Internet address into the Send To text box of the Write Mail window.

Sending e-mail to several addresses

You can send electronic mail to several addresses at once instead of retyping the same message to several people. Type the addresses in the Send To text box of the Write Mail window one after another, separating the addresses with commas.

Copying others with CC/BCC

Sending *carbon copies* (CC) or *blind carbon copies* (BCC) of e-mail messages to friends or colleagues is a snap on America Online. Just follow these steps:

1. **To send a carbon copy, type the screen name(s) or Internet address(es) in the Copy To text box on the right side of the Write Mail window (see Figure 3-2).**

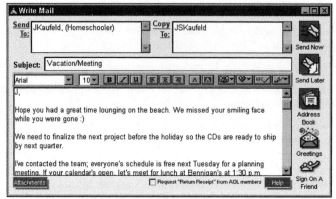

Figure 3-2: You can send carbon copies (CC) as well as blind carbon copies (BCC).

2. **To send a blind carbon copy, type the screen name(s) or address(es) in parentheses ( ) in either the Send To text box or the Copy To text box, as shown in Figure 3-2.**

3. **Fill in the Subject and Message text boxes and click Send Now (or Send Later).**

If you use the BCC option, the original recipient of the e-mail message knows nothing of a carbon copy. A carbon-copied message lists the e-mail address of the additional recipient(s) at the top of the e-mail message, but a message with a blind carbon copy lists nothing.

Expressing yourself in e-mail

Conveying an entire range of feelings, expressions, and other subtleties can prove difficult if you're communicating via e-mail. To solve this problem, creative e-mailers around the world use several methods of adding a touch of humor, class, and personality to the otherwise dry text of electronic mail. Refer to Book III, Chapter 2, for details on e-mail etiquette and a list of abbreviations (such as BTW for "By the way") and emoticons, such as the smiley face :-).

Formatting e-mail

You can use the buttons at the top of the Message text box in the Write Mail window to format your e-mail message. To format existing text in a message, click and drag across the text to highlight it; then click the buttons for the formatting that you want. To mix and match formatting options, just click more than one button. (To make text both bold and italic, for example, click the Bold button and then the Italic button.) To format new text as you type it, first click the format buttons that you want and then enter the text.

Right-clicking in the Message text box opens a shortcut menu. From here, you can add a hyperlink, insert a text file you previously saved, or insert a background image into your message.

Adding a hyperlink to an e-mail message

A *hyperlink* enables you to type the name of a really cool Web site and include a link to it in your message; the recipient can simply click the site's name to open it on-screen. To create a hyperlink, follow these steps:

1. **Right-click in the Message text box.**

2. **Choose Insert a Hyperlink from the shortcut menu that appears.**

   The Edit Hyperlink dialog box appears, awaiting your instructions.

3. **Type the name of the site in the Description text box of the Edit Hyperlink dialog box.**

4. **Type the Internet address in the Internet Address text box and click OK.**

   The name that you type in the Description text box appears in the Message text box.

Checking e-mail status

You can find out what your America Online e-mail correspondents actually do with your messages by using the e-mail status option. This option works only for mail sent to another America Online subscriber. If you try to check the status of an Internet e-mail message, the system reports that you cannot check status of Internet mail.

To check the status of an e-mail message you send, follow these steps:

1. **Choose Mail⇨Sent Mail.**

   The Mailbox window hops into view, displaying the Sent Mail tab.

2. **Click the message that you want to check to select it; then click the Status button at the bottom of the window.**

   A Status window appears, showing the time and date the recipient(s) read the message, as shown in Figure 3-3. If the recipient hasn't read the message yet, the Status window reads Not yet read; if the recipient deletes the message without reading it, the Status window reads Deleted.

**Book VI
Chapter 3**

**Using AOL
E-Mail**

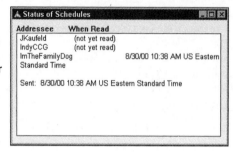

Figure 3-3:
AOL
enables you
to check to
see whether
and when
your recipients read
your e-mail
messages.

Unsending e-mail

If you write a message that makes you think twice after you send it, try unsending it. Follow these steps to unsend an e-mail message:

1. **Choose Mail⇨Read Mail. Then select Sent Mail from the pop-up menu that appears.**

    The Mailbox window appears, open to the Sent Mail tab.

2. **Click the message in question to select it.**

3. **Click the Unsend button at the bottom of the window.**

    A dialog box appears, asking whether you really want to unsend the message.

4. **Click Yes in this dialog box.**

    The message is unsent, and a small dialog box pops onto the screen, displaying a terse `The message has been unsent` notification.

5. **Click OK.**

Think fast — you can only unsend an e-mail up to the point that the recipient opens the mail to read it. (See the section "Checking e-mail status," earlier in this chapter.) After that, you're stuck buying flowers or ice cream for the recipient.

This trick works only for unread messages that you sent to other America Online members. You can't unsend an e-mail message that you send to an Internet address. (Choose your words wisely if they're heading for the Net.)

Setting your e-mail preferences

You can choose from several e-mail preferences. You can set preferences to save copies of incoming and outgoing mail automatically, use AOL style quotes in mail messages, and turn off the annoying Your Mail Has Been Sent dialog box. For information about these settings and many others, see Book VI, Chapter 1.

Addressing E-Mail by Using the Address Book

The *Address Book* remembers the e-mail addresses of your friends and associates. You can use it to create mailing lists, to track names and e-mail addresses, or to do a little of both.

Adding an entry

To create an Address Book entry, follow these steps:

1. **Choose Mail⇨Address Book.**

The Address Book window opens, as shown in Figure 3-4.

Book VI
Chapter 3

Using AOL
E-Mail

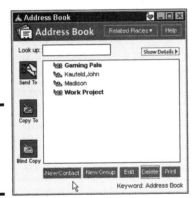

Figure 3-4:
AOL's
Address
Book
window.

2. **Click either the New Contact or New Group button to open the appropriate window.**

New Contact creates an Address Book entry for an individual's screen name. New Group creates a single Address Book entry for a group of screen names or Internet addresses, such as a list of family members who receive the annual Happy Holidays newsletter via e-mail.

3. **Type the appropriate name and address information in the Contact Details or Group Details window.**

- **In the Contact Details window:** Type the person's first name, last name, and screen name or Internet address in the text boxes. Type any information that you want to remember about that person, such as where you met online or any special interests, under the Details tab.

- **In the Group Details window:** Type a name for the group, such as Family, Friends, or Work Associates, in the Group Name text box. Then type the screen names or Internet addresses of the group's members in the large Addresses text box. You can also add entries to the new group from the existing address book members by highlighting the person's screen name and clicking the Add button.

4. **Click Save.**

   The name that you type in the First Name and Last Name text boxes or the Group Name text box appears as an entry in the Address Book.

Changing or deleting an entry

To change or remove an existing Address Book entry, follow these steps:

1. **Choose Mail⇨Address Book.**

   The Address Book opens on-screen.

2. **Click the name in your Address Book that you want to change or delete.**

3. **Click the Edit button to change the entry or click the Delete button to remove it.**

   - **Edit:** Click the Edit button to change the name or e-mail address of an entry. Make any changes you want in the Contact Details dialog box and then click OK to save the changes.

   - **Delete:** Click the Delete button to remove an entry from the Address Book. After a dialog box appears asking whether you're sure, click Yes. The entry is toast.

If the Address Book entry disappears without showing the dialog box, and that bothers you, set your Personal Filing Cabinet Preferences to ask you to confirm before single items are actually deleted. (See Book VI, Chapter 1, for details.)

Printing your Address Book

America Online 6.0 gives you the option to print your Address Book contents. Now you can print your e-mail addresses, hole-punch them, and stick them into your paper-based planner.

To print your Address Book, follow these steps:

1. **Choose Mail⇨Address Book to open the Address Book.**

2. **Click the Print button in the Address Book window.**

The Print dialog box opens.

3. **Click the button next to Print all contacts and then click OK.**

The Windows Print dialog box opens.

4. **Click OK to print the Address Book contents.**

Writing e-mail by using the Address Book

To save time in writing e-mail messages, you can copy the recipient's address directly from the Address Book. Just follow these steps:

1. **Click the Write button on the toolbar.**

The Write Mail window appears.

2. **Click the Address Book button on the right side of the window.**

3. **After the Address Book window appears, select the name of the person or group that you want to contact and click the Send To button — or simply double-click the entry.**

That person's e-mail address appears in the Send To text box of the Write Mail window.

What's your Internet e-mail address?

Your Internet e-mail address is your America Online screen name. Type your AOL screen name in all-lowercase characters (the Internet ignores upper-case in mail addresses) and add **@aol.com** to the end. My screen name, for example, is JSKaufeld, but my e-mail address is jskaufeld@aol.com.

Attaching a File to an E-Mail Message

Use the Attachments button in the Write Mail window to send a file along with the e-mail message itself. The file then downloads to the receiver's computer. (See "Receiving an Attached File in an E-Mail Message," later in this chapter.)

To attach a file to an e-mail message, follow these steps:

1. **Click the Write button to open the Write Mail window.**

2. **Click the Attachments button at the bottom-left of the window.**

The Attachments window opens.

3. **Click the Attach button to open the Attach dialog box (see Figure 3-5).**

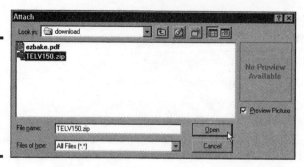

Figure 3-5: Select the file that you want to attach to your e-mail message.

4. **In the File Name text box, type the name of the file that you want to attach to your message and click the Open button. Or you can locate the filename in the list of files and double-click the name.**

   The filename appears in the Attachments window.

5. **If you want to attach only the one file, click OK; if you want to attach more than one file, skip to Step 6.**

   The filename then appears beside the Attachments button in the Write Mail window.

6. **To attach a second (and any subsequent) file, repeat Steps 3, 4, and 5 until your file collection is ready to launch.**

   You can attach multiple files to an e-mail message. After you add a second file, AOL adds a comma to the filename beside Attach. You can view your attached file list by clicking the Attachments button. If you like the attachment list, click OK. If you don't like the attachment list, you can use the Attach or Detach button in the Attachments window to modify the list until it satisfies you and then click OK.

7. **Fill in the e-mail address of the recipient and a subject to describe the e-mail message; then write a note in the message box explaining the attachment and click Send Now (or Send Later).**

Reading and Replying to E-Mail

If your account contains mail and you have a sound card with the speakers turned up, America Online notifies you with a cheery "You've Got Mail!" announcement as you sign on. You can read messages while online or use an Automatic AOL session to download unread mail that you can then read offline.

Reading e-mail online

To read new mail while you're online, follow these steps:

1. **Click the You've Got Mail link on the Welcome screen or click the Read button on the toolbar.**

2. **Use the mouse or arrow keys to navigate to the message that you want to read.**

3. **Double-click the highlighted message or click the Read button at the bottom of the window.**

   The e-mail message opens.

If you read an e-mail message that's too good to lose, click the Save to Filing Cabinet button. Doing so enables you to save the message in the Incoming/Saved Mail folder, the Mail You've Sent folder, or in a folder you name yourself.

Reading e-mail offline

To access your new mail anytime that you want, so that you can read your e-mail offline, just follow these steps:

1. **Use an Automatic AOL session to download unread e-mail.**

   See the section "Automating Your AOL Sessions," earlier in this chapter.

2. **Choose Mail⇨Filing Cabinet and then browse through the Incoming/Saved Mail folder in the window that appears. The Mail tab should be active in the Filing Cabinet window.**

3. **Select the message that you want to read and click Open or double-click the message to open it.**

Click to select the message in the Filing Cabinet window and then click Delete if you no longer need the message. Remember, however, that as soon as you delete a message, it's gone for good.

Replying to an e-mail message

E-mail relationships last only if you write back. Respond to messages by following these steps:

1. **With the original e-mail message open, click the Reply button.**

   A new mail window appears with the address and subject already filled in.

To include text from the original message in your reply, right-click anywhere inside the original message box, choose Select All, and click the Reply button. A new mail window appears with the e-mail address and Subject line (with the addition of Re: at the beginning) already filled in as well as a complete copy of the message. Erase the parts that you don't want to send back. Then type << and > at the beginning and end of paragraphs that you want to keep from the original message to show that those paragraphs are quoted material.

If you want to quote only a small portion of the e-mail message, highlight that sentence or paragraph and then click Reply. The Reply Mail window opens containing a copy of that portion of the message, including the quotation marks.

2. **Type your replies and comments in the Message text box.**

3. **Click Send Now.**

Receiving an Attached File in an E-Mail Message

If you open the listing for new mail and see a message with a small disk icon underneath the message icon in the Online Mailbox window, that message includes an attachment of some kind. Document files, programs, and sound files are some of the possible attachments that you can receive with e-mail.

To download the attached file, follow these steps:

1. **Double-click the message to open it.**

2. **Click one of the two buttons at the bottom of the message —**
   Download Now or Download Later:

   - **Download Now:** This option opens the Download Manager dialog box so that you can select a destination for the attachment and then click Save.

   - **Download Later:** This option places the file in the Download Manager. When you're ready to download, choose File⇨Download Manager to open the Download Manager window. If necessary, click Select Destination to change where the file goes on your hard drive. Finally, click Download.

If you use Automatic AOL to download your mail and you previously selected Automatic AOL's Download files that are attached to unread mail check box, Automatic AOL copies the file to your hard drive during the Automatic AOL session. You still need to locate the file on your hard drive and open it, however. It's waiting for you in the destination file that the Download Manager lists.

Never download any file from someone you don't know. AOL 6.0 enables you to send multiple attachments in e-mail, but only the first attachment's name appears in the recipient's mail message. So the first attachment may be a text file, but a subsequent attachment may be an executable virus.

Deleting an E-Mail Message

Annoyed by unwanted marketing junk mail? No problem — that's why America Online created the Delete button. (For related information, see the section "Unsending e-mail," earlier in this chapter and the following section, "Undeleting an E-Mail Message.")

After you delete a message from your America Online mailbox, it's gone after 24 hours. Nothing can bring it back.

If you're really, really sure that you want to trash that spam or any e-mail message, follow these steps:

1. **Click the You've Got Mail icon in the Welcome screen or click the Read button on the toolbar.**

2. **Use the arrow keys or click the message name to select the message in the New Mail window.**

3. **Click Delete at the bottom of the Online Mailbox window.**

A similar process works for mail that you've previously read:

1. **Use the arrow keys or click the message name to select the message in the Old Mail window.**

2. **Click Delete at the bottom of the Online Mailbox window.**

After you send an e-mail message, a copy remains in your outgoing mailbox. If you don't want the copy hanging around, follow these steps to delete it:

1. **Choose Mail⇨Read Mail and then select Sent Mail from the pop-up menu that appears.**

2. **Use the arrow keys or click the message name to select that message in the Sent Mail window.**

3. **Click Delete at the bottom of the Online Mailbox screen.**

Undeleting an E-Mail Message

On those days that your fingers move faster than your brain and you delete some impressively important e-mail message, you no longer need to panic. Take a deep breath — fix yourself another cup of java if you want — and then undelete the e-mail you mistakenly toasted.

To undelete an e-mail message, follow these steps:

1. **Choose Mail⇨Recently Deleted Mail.**

The Recently Deleted Mail window opens.

2. **Highlight the wayward e-mail message by clicking it.**

3. **Click Keep As New.**

The message takes its rightful place in your New Mail window.

Use the Read button to look at the e-mail contents if you need to know exactly which received message you want to resurrect. If you find one or two you're sure that you don't want, highlight them and click Permanently Delete. They're history.

Automating Your AOL Sessions

Automatic AOL automatically signs on to America Online and downloads your e-mail and files into your computer. You then can read the e-mail offline, which cuts down on connect time and, in turn, saves you money if you subscribe to one of America Online's measured-service options.

Setting up Automatic AOL

Before you can use Automatic AOL, you must tell the America Online software what you want to do with it. Just follow these steps:

1. **Choose Mail⇨Automatic AOL.**

You don't need to be online to set up Automatic AOL. If you select no new options and deselect existing ones, the Automatic AOL session still runs but does nothing.

2. **Click the check boxes for the tasks that you want Automatic AOL to perform.**

You can choose from the following options:

- **Send Mail from the Mail Waiting to Be Sent Folder:** This option sends e-mail that you've written offline and saved to send later.

- **Get Unread Mail and Put It in Incoming Mail Folder:** This option downloads all new, unread e-mail to your computer.

- **Download Files That Are Attached to Unread Mail:** Select this option if you want America Online to download any files attached to e-mail messages at the same time that it downloads the e-mail messages themselves. You can leave this option deselected and download all files manually if you decide that you want them. Doing so minimizes the chance of discovering too late that you downloaded a hacker file.

- **Send Postings from the Postings Waiting to be Sent folder:** This option sends any newsgroup postings you may have written to their respective newsgroups.

- **Get Unread Postings and Put in Incoming Postings folder:** If you select this option, America Online grabs the new postings from any newsgroups to which you subscribe and downloads them to your computer.

- **Download Files Marked to be Downloaded Later:** Selecting this option copies to your computer any files that you found while roaming around AOL and marked with the Download Later button. You find the files in the folder you designated for downloads under Download Preferences (keyword **Preferences**).

3. **Click the Schedule Automatic AOL button to tell AOL when to download your e-mail.**

   The Schedule Automatic AOL window appears.

4. **Specify the days, times, and frequency that Automatic AOL should be run; then select the Enable Scheduler check box to activate the scheduling feature and click OK.**

5. **Click Run Automatic AOL Now to begin an Auto AOL session immediately.**

   A small dialog box appears, asking whether you want the system to sign you off after the Automatic AOL session finishes.

6. **Select the Sign Off When Finished check box if you're ready to leave America Online for awhile and then click Begin.**

   If you click Begin without selecting the check box, the system downloads your e-mail and then awaits your next keyword or mouse click.

7. **Click the Automatic AOL window's Close box to save your changes.**

If you want your computer to sign on to America Online automatically and download your e-mail, you must store the passwords for the screen name(s) on your computer. To do so, click Select Names in the Automatic AOL window. The Select Screen Names dialog box appears. Click the check boxes next to the screen name(s) that you want to use and type the password next to the corresponding screen name(s). Click OK to save your changes or Cancel if you change your mind.

If you type your password in the Select Names section, remember to use the Schedule Automatic AOL button to select the days and times for the Automatic AOL sessions. Select the Enable Scheduler check box in the Schedule Automatic AOL dialog box, or your password entry work is for naught.

Storing your password in the Automatic AOL screen doesn't provide general access to your account. No one can get to your computer and sign on to America Online under your name. The password that you include here enables your computer to download your e-mail from AOL without your physical help.

Using Automatic AOL

After you patiently set up the Automatic AOL information, you can watch Automatic AOL do its stuff. Follow these steps:

1. **Choose Mail⇨Run Automatic AOL.**

The Run Automatic AOL Now dialog box pops up.

2. **Click Begin to start the Automatic AOL session.**

The Status window appears and displays each e-mail message subject as AOL downloads it.

Chapter 4: Browsing the Web with AOL

*W*hen the Internet quietly began to take shape back in the mid-'60s, few people guessed that it would turn into the worldwide power that it is today. What began as a small military experiment grew slowly through the '70s, matured in the '80s, and absolutely exploded in the '90s. Today, this global network of networks offers an incredible array of information through FTP sites and the World Wide Web. Best of all, you can access both of these information services through America Online.

World Wide Web Adventures

Of all the information systems on the Internet, only one truly captured the public's imagination: the *World Wide Web*. With their flashy graphics, point-and-click interfaces, and limitless interlinks, Web sites are easily the Net's most popular destinations.

The America Online access software contains a powerful built-in Web browser. To hop onto the Web through America Online, you simply type the Web address into the navigation bar at the top of your AOL screen and click Go. The Web browser appears, displaying the AOL Web page, as shown in Figure 4-1. From there, you can browse the world's Web pages with ease.

Figure 4-1:
As you first access the Web you see AOL's Web page.

Navigating the Web by clicking *links* in each Web page is easy. Links usually appear as colored, underlined text or as a graphic image on a Web page. As you move the mouse pointer over a link, the arrow changes into a pointing hand, indicating that you can click that link to view that Web page or document. (See Book III, Chapter 3, for more information on Web basics.)

Your other navigational tools are the following buttons across the left side of the navigation bar:

 ✦ **Back:** Takes you to the last window or Web page you viewed.

 ✦ **Forward:** Takes you back where you were before you clicked Back.

 ✦ **Stop:** Stops loading a Web page. This button is helpful if a Web page takes too long to load.

 ✦ **Reload:** Tells your browser to request a new copy of the Web page. This button is useful if something goes wrong while loading a page.

Going to a specific Web site

Use the navigation bar's text box or the Keyword dialog box to quickly access any Web site on the Internet. Just follow these steps:

1. **Click the text box of the navigation bar to highlight the text or choose Favorites⇨Go to Keyword to open the Keyword dialog box (or press Ctrl+K).**

2. **Type the address of the Web site into the text box and then press Enter or click Go.**

   The built-in Web browser comes to life and begins loading the requested page (see Figure 4-2).

Book VI Chapter 4

Browsing the Web with AOL

Figure 4-2: A Web page as it appears in AOL's built-in Web browser.

Remembering a site through Favorite Places

With millions of sites available, you're bound to find a few best-loved locales on the Web. Use the Favorite Places feature to keep your favorite sites organized and easy to find. Just follow these steps:

1. **Go to the Web site that you want to mark.**

2. **Click the Favorite Places icon (the heart on a sheet of paper in the upper-right corner of the window).**

3. **After America Online shows you its questioning dialog box, click Add To Favorites.**

To go back to the page, click the Favorites toolbar button and then click the item's entry in the list. (See Book VI, Chapter 2, for more details on AOL's Favorite Places feature.)

Visiting friends at Hometown AOL

Hometown AOL is what America Online calls its members' Web page area. It's completely free to America Online members. You can upload your Web page to Hometown AOL for other members to see, or you can spend an evening reading through other members' Web pages.

Divided into categories, Hometown AOL features member pages that discuss entertainment, education, health, hobbies, culture, and sports. Hometown AOL even contains a Business Park category for members who want to promote their businesses through a Web page.

Keyword **Hometown** AOL opens the Hometown AOL Welcome screen. Click Add Pages to find out how to add your own Web page to the collection. To browse by general topic and subtopic, click Site Map. If you want to locate a specific topic or Web page, click Find.

Other Internet denizens who want to visit Hometown AOL (and who don't know your exact screen name) can see your page by using the Web address `http://hometown.aol.com`.

Building your own home page

In Internet lingo, a *home page* is your personal spot on the World Wide Web. A home page is a place to showcase your interests, promote your business, or expound the virtues of your particular viewpoint. What sets the Web apart is its worldwide reach — your words are available to anyone with a Web browser and Internet access.

For all the Web's power and reach, building a home page doesn't take a great deal of complex programming. In fact, putting your best foot forward on the Web doesn't take much programming at all. The key to this simplicity is America Online 1-2-3 Publish (keyword **123 Publish**), an interactive tool that handles the technical stuff for you.

To create your own Web page using AOL's 1-2-3 Publish, follow these steps:

1. **Press Ctrl+K and then type keyword** 123 Publish **to open 1-2-3 Publish in the browser window.**

The screen fills with a list of template suggestions. Decide what kind of Web page you have in mind. Do you want a page that showcases your baby's photos? Is this Web site's purpose to advertise your business? Do you want to post your favorite recipes or share your delight over a television show? If ideas such as these interest you, you can find them (and more) in the item list.

2. **Click a page template's link to select it and then progress through the next screen's sections one at a time, a title for your Web page, selecting background colors, and including text.**

If you want to include a photo in your page design, you can do so, too. Click the Browse button to locate the picture or graphic. AOL uploads it automatically.

3. **To see how the page is going to look after you type all the information, click Preview My Page.**

Your page is previewed in the browser window. If you want to change anything in your new page, you can click the Modify button while previewing it.

4. **To upload your page to Hometown AOL, the Web storage space that comes with your screen name, click Save.**

For more advanced information on Web page construction, use the keyword **Hot Dog Express**.

Get more in-depth information about America Online Web page design from *America Online For Dummies,* 7th Edition, by John Kaufeld (published by IDG Books Worldwide, Inc.).

File Transfer Protocol (FTP)

The Internet, being the odd place that it is, uses its own special system for downloading files. *FTP,* short for *file transfer protocol,* is the Internet's file-transfer magician. FTP is also sometimes known as *Anonymous FTP,* because most of the computers that offer files through FTP don't ask you for a special password. Because the computers are open to everyone, the service is deemed *anonymous.*

To access the FTP area, use keyword **FTP**. The FTP window appears on-screen. From there, you can check out some general FTP information, search for FTP sites, or set up a connection to a particular site.

Don't download files through FTP unless you have a virus-checking program running on your computer. Carefully virus-check *absolutely every file* that you get through FTP — don't trust *anything*.

Using a particular FTP site

Getting into a specific site is easy with the America Online FTP system. Just follow these steps:

1. **Press Ctrl+K, type keyword** FTP, **and click OK. From the FTP window, click Go To FTP.**

2. **In the Anonymous FTP window that appears, click Other Site.**

   The Other Site dialog box appears.

3. **Type the address of the FTP site that you want; then either press Enter or click Connect.**

   The addresses for FTP sites usually start with FTP — for example, `ftp.apple.com` or `ftp.microsoft.com`. If the address you have starts with `www`, the address is for a World Wide Web site and not an FTP site.

Downloading from FTP sites

Copying a file from an FTP site isn't hard, but the process is a little more complicated than downloading a file from America Online. Follow these steps:

1. **Press Ctrl+K, type keyword** FTP, **and click OK. From the FTP window, click Go To FTP.**

2. **In the Anonymous FTP window that appears, choose an FTP site from the list or use the address of another site:**

   • **To choose a site from the list in the Anonymous FTP window:** Scroll through the list until you find the site you want; then double-click its entry.

   • **To enter your own special address:** Click Other Site. Type the site address in the Other Site dialog box and then click Connect, as shown in Figure 4-3.

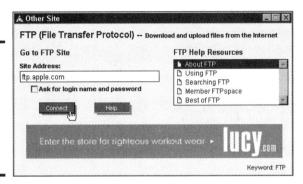

Figure 4-3:
Type a
specific
FTP site
address
in the
Other Site
dialog box.

Either way that you choose to use an FTP site, America Online responds after a moment, either to say that you made the connection or to report that something didn't work. If you connect to the FTP site, a list window appears showing you all the files available in the FTP computer's current directory. If the connection doesn't work, America Online suggests that you check your spelling and try again.

If the FTP window says something about *mirror access,* that's okay. That message means that you connected to a copy (or *mirror*) of the FTP site, which America Online created to give you faster access to the same information.

3. Browse by double-clicking entries on the list.

4. If an entry piques your interest, click it.

If the Download Now button comes to life, that entry's available for downloading. If not, the file isn't available. After you click the button, America Online briefly opens a Retrieving Data dialog box. Behind the scenes, the America Online computers are copying the file at very high speed from wherever it happens to reside on the Internet. After the AOL computers finish receiving the file, the Download Manager window appears on-screen, asking what you want to call the file on your computer.

5. Type a name for the file in the Download Manager window and then press Enter.

Make sure that your new file name keeps the same extension — for example, you can't rename a zip file as a doc file.

The download starts immediately.

6. After the file finishes downloading, America Online beeps and tosses up a simple report announcing that the file arrived safely.

7. To download more files, repeat Steps 4 through 6.

8. After you finish downloading files, click the Close button to close the FTP window.

Closing the FTP window after you finish downloading is very important. America Online keeps a connection to the FTP site until you close the site's window. Because many sites limit the number of people who can download files at once, other people on the Net often can't access the site until you leave by closing the FTP window.

Uploading to FTP sites

Some (but not all) FTP sites accept file uploads from Internet users. If you have software to share, consider uploading it to an FTP site.

Upload *only* files that you write yourself or shareware programs — don't even *think* about uploading a copy of your favorite commercial program or game. (We don't want you to break the copyright laws!)

To upload files to an FTP site, follow these steps:

1. **In the FTP window (keyword:** FTP**), click Go To FTP.**

The Anonymous FTP window appears.

2. **To connect to the site that you want, click Other Site, type the site's address in the text box, and then press Enter or click OK.**

If the connection works, you're in; if it doesn't, check the spelling and try again. The correct name opens the FTP site's window.

3. **In the FTP site's window, click the Upload button.**

A file name dialog box appears. If an upload button doesn't appear on-screen, you can't upload files to this FTP site. Sorry, but that's how it goes.

4. **Type the name of the file in the dialog box as you want it to appear on the FTP server.**

You're not telling America Online where to find the file on your computer yet. Instead, the software wants to know what to call the copy you're uploading to the FTP computer.

5. **If you're uploading a plain-text file or HTML files (Web pages), click the ASCII option button; if the file is anything other than plain text or HTML, click the Binary option button.**

6. **Double-check your entries for accuracy and then click Continue.**

The Upload File dialog box appears.

7. **Click Select File.**

The Attach File dialog box pops up.

8. **Scroll through the dialog box until you find the name of the file that you want to send and then double-click it.**

The file's name and path appear in the Upload File dialog box.

9. **Click Send to start the transfer.**

A File Transfer dialog box updates you on the transfer. Finally, an annoying little dialog box appears telling you that the transfer is complete.

10. **Click OK.**

11. **To send more files, repeat Steps 3 through 10.**

12. **After you finish sending files, click the Close button to close the FTP window.**

If you want to upload files to your private Web space on AOL, press Ctrl+K and type the keyword **My FTP Space** and then click the See My FTP Space button in the My FTP Space window. You go directly to a window by the name of `members.aol.com/screen name`. After you're there, open the Private folder and begin at Step 3.

Winsock Applications and AOL

In the world of Internet software, *Winsock* is a piece of programming that helps Windows applications interact with the Internet. Thanks to America Online's built-in Winsock support, you can use almost any standard Internet program through AOL, including Telnet, Internet Relay Chat (IRC), and World Wide Web client applications.

AOL for Windows 95/98 supports a full 32-bit Winsock, which means that AOL for Windows 95/98 works with just about any Winsock-compatible program out there. For more details about using Winsock programs with AOL, plus a library of downloadable Winsock software, use the keyword **Telnet**.

America Online For Dummies, 7th Edition, by John Kaufeld (published by IDG Books Worldwide, Inc.), gives you more information about using different Web browsers and various Winsock applications with the America Online software.

Chapter 5: Reading Newsgroups with AOL

In This Chapter

- ✔ Finding and subscribing to newsgroups
- ✔ Searching and browsing for particular topics
- ✔ Reading newsgroups online and offline
- ✔ Posting messages to a newsgroup
- ✔ Replying to a posting

Shortly after the Internet started, the researchers who were using it created an electronic bulletin board for online discussions. This bulletin board evolved into the Internet *newsgroups,* a collection of several thousand rollicking conversations covering computers, hard science, industrial music, and almost everything in between. America Online offers a very complete collection of the world's newsgroups. (For much more on newsgroups, see Book III, Chapter 6. This chapter relates specifically to using AOL to access newsgroups.)

Accessing Newsgroups from within AOL

To get into the Newsgroups window, use keyword **Newsgroups**. (The first time you use this command, AOL may display instructions for filtering junk messages in newsgroups.) The Newsgroups window offers useful information about how newsgroups work in general, plus some specifics about using them through America Online. Take a few minutes to read through the documents there.

The Terms of Service rules, which give America Online its family orientation, don't extend to the Internet newsgroups. Free, uncensored speech is often the rule, not the exception. If frank (and sometimes downright rude) language offends your sensibilities, you may want to avoid the newsgroups. (See Book VI, Chapter 1, for information on using Parental Controls.)

Subscribing to a Newsgroup

When a friend tells you about the cool pattern she found in `rec.crafts.textiles.needlework`, subscribe to the newsgroup by using Expert Add and check out the place for yourself. You need to know the exact Internet name of any group you want to subscribe to. If you aren't sure of the name, use the search feature described in the section, "Searching for a Particular Topic."

To subscribe to any newsgroup, follow these steps:

1. **In the Newsgroups window, click Expert Add.**

The Expert Add dialog box appears.

2. **Type the name of the newsgroup you want to join; then press Enter or click Subscribe.**

After a moment, America Online either confirms your subscription or asks you to double-check the newsgroup name and try again.

3. **Click OK to close the dialog box.**

Searching for a Particular Topic

The America Online newsgroup search system covers most of the newsgroup hierarchies. It searches on the newsgroup name or parts of the name. This procedure is useful if you don't know the exact name of the newsgroup you want.

To use the newsgroup search system, follow these steps:

1. **In the Newsgroups window, click Search All Newsgroups.**

The Search All Newsgroups dialog box appears.

2. **Type a word or two describing your interest; then press Enter.**

After a moment, the search system proudly displays its results.

3. **(Optional) If the system says that it can't find anything, click OK and search for a different word.**

To get the best results, search for one word or part of a word (*compu* instead of *computer,* for example). Remember, you're searching newsgroup titles, which are sometimes a little arcane.

4. Browse through the list and look for a newsgroup that interests you. Double-click a newsgroup's name to open the Add or Read Newsgroup window.

This window lets you view a description of the newsgroup and read the newsgroup's postings or subscribe to the newsgroup, as detailed in the following list:

- **To subscribe to a newsgroup:** Click the <u>Subscribe to Newsgroup</u> link. A window opens with a list of unread postings. Double-click any posting title to open it.

- **To read a newsgroup's postings without subscribing:** Click the <u>List Articles in Newsgroup</u> link. A list of the newsgroup's active articles appears in the same window that you see if you click the <u>Subscribe to Newsgroup</u> link. However, this time AOL shows the postings without actually subscribing you to the newsgroup.

5. Close any open newsgroup windows and the Add or Read Newsgroup window when you finish.

**Book VI
Chapter 5**

Reading
Newsgroups
with AOL

Browsing through the Lists

Sometimes, you're just curious about what's out there. When those moments hit, browse through the newsgroup lists. With thousands of newsgroups out there, you better bring your patience along for the trip.

To browse through the newsgroup lists, follow these steps:

1. In the Newsgroups window, click Add Newsgroups.

A list of newsgroup hierarchies appears.

2. Double-click a hierarchy that looks interesting.

A list of newsgroups pops into view.

3. Scroll through the list and look for something that interests you; then do one of the following:

- **See a listing of the newsgroup's articles.** Double-click the newsgroup's name; its window then appears, listing active postings.

- **Subscribe to a newsgroup.** Click the newsgroup name and then click Subscribe. If all goes well, America Online announces that you're subscribed. Click OK to make the dialog box go away.

4. Close the various windows when you finish.

Reading Newsgroups Online

After subscribing to a newsgroup, take time to read the messages. To read the message online, follow these steps:

1. **Use keyword** Newsgroups **to get to the Newsgroups window.**

2. **Click Read My Newsgroups.**

You see your personalized list of newsgroups. AOL starts you out with a handful of groups (including news.announce.newusers, news.answers, and news.groups.reviews) and some AOL help groups.

3. **Double-click the newsgroup that you want to read.**

A list of unread newsgroup messages opens on-screen.

4. **Scroll through the list until you find a message that looks interesting and then double-click the message to read it.**

5. **When you finish with the message, close its window.**

Do likewise when you finish with the newsgroup.

Reading Newsgroups Offline

Newsgroups are fun and interesting, but they're also time-consuming. Keep your phone line free by reading newsgroups offline. Reading the news-groups offline is a two-step process. First, you configure the America Online software to read the newsgroups you want. Then you actually download the newsgroup messages and read and reply to them offline.

To set up the software to read newsgroups offline, follow these steps:

1. **Subscribe to the newsgroups that you want to read offline.**

If the newsgroup is extremely active, you may want to clear the posts by clicking the Read My Newsgroups button, highlighting the newsgroup in question, and clicking the Mark Read button. Then, when you download the newsgroup postings to your hard drive, you don't need to wade through 3,000 unread postings.

2. **In the Newsgroups window, click Read Offline.**

The Choose Newsgroups window displays, as shown in Figure 5-1.

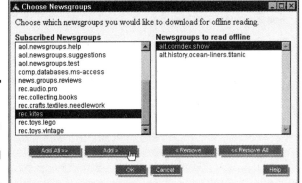

**Book VI
Chapter 5**

Reading
Newsgroups
with AOL

Figure 5-1:
Select the
newsgroups
that you
want to read
offline.

3. **To read a newsgroup offline, double-click its entry in the Subscribed Newsgroups list.**

After a moment, the newsgroup hops to the Newsgroups to Read Offline list. Repeat this step for all the newsgroups that you want to read offline.

If you double-click the wrong newsgroup or want to stop reading a newsgroup offline, double-click its entry in the Newsgroups to Read Offline list. The newsgroup returns to the Subscribed Newsgroups list.

4. **When you finish, click OK.**

America Online returns you to the Newsgroups window.

5. **To finish configuring America Online to retrieve your newsgroup messages for offline reading and replying, choose Mail⇨Automatic AOL. Click the check boxes beside these folders:**

• Get Unread Postings and Put in Incoming Postings Folder

• Send Postings from the Postings Waiting to Be Sent Folder

6. **Close the window when you finish.**

It's a quick and easy process to read newsgroups offline. Just follow these steps:

1. **Download newsgroup messages to your computer. Choose Mail⇨Automatic AOL to open the Automatic AOL window.**

To download newsgroups during an Automatic AOL session, you need to check Get Unread Postings and Put in Incoming Postings folder.

2. **Click the Run Automatic AOL Now button to start an Automatic AOL session, just as you do to download your mail.**

   A small Automatic AOL Status dialog box appears and gives you play-by-play commentary as the Newsgroup messages come down the phone line into the Personal Filing Cabinet. (See Book VI, Chapter 3, to find out more about Automatic AOL.)

   Stop by every now and then to check the Automatic AOL process. If America Online decides that your newsgroups contain too many postings, it shuts down your Automatic AOL session with a terse message: Too many articles — download remaining articles in another Auto AOL (FlashSession). If that happens, begin another Automatic AOL session right away. The system downloads more postings to your computer.

3. **To read and reply to the messages, choose My Files⇨Personal Filing Cabinet.**

4. **Scroll through the Personal Filing Cabinet to find the Newsgroups folder.**

   New messages are in the Incoming/Saved Postings folder and are organized by subject line. Replies and new messages you write offline live in the Postings Waiting to Be Sent folder.

5. **Double-click a message to read it.**

Posting a New Message to a Newsgroup

A newsgroup audience is just waiting to hear what you have to say. Share your thoughts by posting a message. Before posting to a newsgroup, however, take time to read several days' worth of postings. Listen to what the members discuss and how they do it. When you do speak up, make your posting appropriate for the newsgroup, both in topic and in tone.

To post your message, follow these steps:

1. **In the Newsgroups window, click Read My Newsgroups.**

   If you're doing this offline, open the Personal Filing Cabinet instead and go directly to Step 4.

2. **In the Read My Newsgroups window, double-click the name of the newsgroup to which you want to post a message.**

3. **Click the New Message button.**

   The Post New Message window appears.

4. **Type your message, give it a Subject, and then click Send (or Send Later, if you're working offline).**

   After you finish writing messages, use Automatic AOL to post them. (See Book VI, Chapter 3, for more information on Automatic AOL.)

Replying to a Newsgroup Posting

Newsgroups live for discussion. When something in a newsgroup piques your interest (or ire), add your opinion by posting a reply.

To reply to a posting, follow these steps:

1. **View the message to which you're replying.**
2. **Decide what kind of reply you want to send; then click the Reply button at the bottom of the window.**

   The Post Responses window opens, showing the message in the Original Message Text box.
3. **Check the Post to Newsgroup option if you think that everyone out there would find your words interesting; do this only if your reply is part of an ongoing discussion. Check the Send Via E-mail option if you have a specific question or if most of the newsgroup would yawn at the topic.**
4. **Type your reply and click Send.**

**Book VI
Chapter 5**

Reading
Newsgroups
with AOL

Unsubscribing from a Newsgroup

To unsubscribe to a newsgroup, follow these steps:

1. **Use keyword** Newsgroups **to open the Newsgroups window.**
2. **Click Read My Newsgroups.**

   The Read My Newsgroups window appears.
3. **Click the newsgroup that you want to remove from the list.**
4. **Click Remove.**

   A dialog box confirms that you no longer subscribe to that newsgroup.
5. **Click OK to make the dialog box go away; then close the other newsgroup windows.**

(For information on subscribing to newsgroups, see "Subscribing to a Newsgroup," earlier in this chapter.)

Chapter 6: Channels, Chatting, and Discussion Boards

In This Chapter

- ✔ Browsing through AOL's channels
- ✔ Chatting interactively for hours on end
- ✔ Calling for help when chat room conversations get out of hand
- ✔ Tracking friends on the system
- ✔ Carrying on a private conversation with Instant Messages
- ✔ Swapping notes on a discussion board

The heart of America Online beats with interactive discussion and chatter. Wherever people congregate to discuss issues, lifestyles, or interests, cyberspace flutters with activity. Join the fray! This chapter tells you how to locate online friends and engage in live talk in the chat rooms.

And what would an online service be without discussion boards? Sharpen your cyberpencil and share your views on life, politics, hobbies — whatever makes your heart flutter. This chapter also tells you how to find and join a discussion on the message boards.

Browsing through the AOL Channels

Automatically opening on the screen each time you sign on to America Online, the Channels list is your doorway to the online world. Channels cover everything in the service from sports to shopping. Click a channel's button to explore. You can find the channel buttons arranged, in alphabetical order, down the left side of the screen.

Clicking a channel button opens a window dedicated to that overall topic. Looking for an online area dedicated to women? Try the Lifestyles channel. Interested in nutrition? The Health channel provides articles, links, and other resources.

For more information on each channel's contents, check out *America Online For Dummies,* 7th Edition, by John Kaufeld (published by IDG Books Worldwide, Inc.).

Chatting on AOL

Chat rooms are the live-interaction areas of America Online. Most of the online forums use chat rooms for interest-specific chats and presentations; the People Connection consists entirely of chat rooms. People Connection chat rooms are divided into categories, which are further split into public rooms created by America Online and member rooms created by AOL members.

Private chat rooms and event arenas are other options for America Online interaction. Anyone can create a private chat room to meet with friends. Large arenas (such as the Rotunda and the Coliseum) are reserved for scheduled presentations with guest speakers.

General chat room do's and don'ts

As with any place that hosts a gathering of people, chat rooms have their own protocol for what is and isn't proper. Sometimes etiquette differs among chat rooms, and the formality of a presentation alters etiquette, as well.

The following are all-around etiquette guidelines for chat rooms:

✦ **DON'T SHOUT.** Typing in all caps is considered shouting and is generally frowned upon.

✦ **Refrain from vulgarity.** Avoiding the use of vulgarity is a general rule of AOL etiquette and also part of the Terms of Service (TOS). Swearing in a chat room can cause trouble.

✦ **Create a Member Profile for your screen name.** Profiles function as introductions in the online world, and other members like to see who they're talking to. (See "Viewing member profiles," later in this chapter.)

✦ **Stick to the topic at hand.** If you visit a cooking chat room and begin a long, involved discussion about industrial rock music, other members may request that you return to the topic or leave.

✦ **Feel free to question what people say in a chat room** (after all, conflict is the basis of many good discussions), but you can't question their right to say it. The only exception to this is when someone violates the Terms of Service by swearing or being generally obnoxious.

Connecting with people

Communicate with the world through People Connection — the doorway to interactive chats on America Online. To reach the People Connection screen, do one of the following:

+ Click the Chat button at the bottom of the Welcome window.

+ Choose People⇨People Connection.

+ Use keyword **Chat**.

This action takes you to the opening window of the People Connection screen. From there, use the buttons to navigate to the chat room of your choice. Choose from Find a Chat (which gives you a choice of chats by category), Chat Now! (which drops you right into a general chat room), the Live Events (an area that lists various chat rooms and their hosts), or New to Chat? (a tutorial section).

For general help about life in the People Connection, click the Help button in the upper-right corner of the chat room screen. If someone's being obnoxious, click the Notify AOL button in the lower-right corner of the Chat window.

Finding a chat room

You can find a chat room in one of several ways:

+ Click the Chat button in the Welcome window to open the People Connection window; then click Find a Chat and click AOL Chat Schedule. The AOL Chat Schedule window lists systemwide chats for the week. Click a day's button to see what chats fill the schedule. Some of the chats occur in various online areas; others are part of the regular People Connection roster.

+ Choose People⇨Find a Chat. Select a chat category that looks interesting. When you double-click a category, the category's chat rooms appear in the item list box to the right of the category list. Click one of the chat rooms in the list box and then click Go Chat. You land in the chat room.

+ Go through AOL Live (keyword **AOL Live**) to see what's coming up. Click the Coming Soon button or browse through the Live Today list box to view the upcoming presentations. Click an item that looks interesting to find out more about it. If you miss a chat, browse through AOL Live to download the transcript. Click the Transcripts button in the AOL Live window to reach the AOL Live Transcripts window.

If none of the public rooms in the Find a Chat window (get there by choosing People⇨Find a Chat) interest you, click the Created By AOL Members tab in the Find a Chat window to change the item lists. Now, only rooms created by members appear in the lists. Double-click a category to see its rooms. Highlight a room name, click the Go Chat button, and AOL sends you to that room.

Expressing yourself in a chat room

How do you convey emotion and facial expressions in an all-text medium? The Internet pioneers had that same problem — and thus began the character-based symbols known as emoticons or smileys. If you've seen characters in a chat room like :), which stands for a smile, or {{}}, which means virtual hugs, but never really understood what they meant, you can find a list of popular emoticons in Book III, Chapter 2.

Along the same lines, you can't hang out for long in the chat rooms without seeing shorthand, such as AFK or LOL scroll across the screen. These letters are abbreviations for commonly used terms. Away From Keyboard and Laughing Out Loud define only two of the abbreviations developed by busy typists. Because they appeared in e-mail first, you can find more of them listed in Book III, Chapter 2.

Chat room fonts and formatting

Add flash to your chat room conversations with the chat room formatting bar. Perched above the text-entry field, the buttons on this bar let you change fonts. Use the buttons next to the text field to change text color — or to bold, italicize, or underline your text.

Playing sounds in a chat room

Noise livens life, so why not use it to add some spark to a chat room? In a chat room, type {S *soundname*. Replace *soundname* with the name of the sound. (By the way, you must use a capital *S* in the command; otherwise it won't work. Capitalization doesn't matter in the sound name.) Standard America Online sounds include *Welcome, Drop, IM,* and *Goodbye*.

To play any wav file sound in your America Online folder or Windows directory, type the name of the sound file itself. For example, to play a sound called POINK.WAV, type the command {S **poink**.

Playing too many sounds in a chat room gets annoying very fast, so use sounds sparingly.

Chats run by AOL Protocol

Many scheduled presentations use America Online Protocol, which adds a layer of complexity to the chat room but generally keeps things running smoothly. These chats often feature guest presenters, but they're scheduled in a regular service area chat room rather than in one of the large arenas. When participating in a chat that uses protocol, follow these general guidelines:

✦ Type and send **?** (a question mark) to ask a question, but wait until the room host recognizes you before you send the question itself.

✦ Type and send **!** (an exclamation point) to comment; then wait until you're recognized to type the comment itself.

✦ Wait until called upon to ask a question or voice a comment. The room host calls upon members by typing **GA** (for Go Ahead) and your screen name.

Creating a Member Chat Room

You can create a member chat room to discuss a favorite interest — live. To do so, follow these steps:

1. **Choose People⇨Start Your Own Chat.**

The Start Your Own Chat dialog box appears, awaiting your instructions.

2. **Click the Member Chat button.**

The Create a Member Room window jumps to the screen.

3. **Select a category for your chat room; then type in a name for the new room and click Go Chat.**

You land in your newly created chat room.

Creating a Private Chat Room

To talk privately with someone (or a group of someones), follow these steps to create a private chat room:

1. **Choose People⇨Start Your Own Chat.**

2. **Click the Private Chat button.**

The Private Chat dialog box appears.

3. **Type a name for your new private room and click Go Chat.**

You zoom off to the new private domain.

Your chat room name must be unique — the more unique, the better. Don't be surprised if, every now and then, someone drops into your private room because they accidentally thought up the same name. Anyone who wants to join you must know the room's name and the correct spelling. Otherwise, they create another private room and sit there all alone.

Want to meet some new people? Create a private chat room and name it hello or chat and see who shows up! You may be amazed at how little time you spend sitting in an empty private chat room.

Going to a Friend's Chat Room

Friends hide in the most unlikely places, but joining them is easy if they're hanging out in a chat room. You can find a friend who's part of a Buddy List group (see "Creating a Buddy List Group," later in this chapter) by following these steps:

1. **Choose My AOL⇨Buddy List or use keyword Buddy.**

The Buddy Lists window opens.

2. **Click the member's name in your Buddy Lists window.**

3. **Click the Locate button at the bottom of the window.**

America Online looks for your friend and gives you a report in the Locate Screen Name dialog box. If the member is in a chat room, the dialog box gives the name of the chat room, as shown in Figure 6-1.

Figure 6-1:
You can jump directly to the chat room your friend is visiting.

4. **Click Go to leap directly into the chat room.**

If your friend's screen name is mysteriously missing from your Buddy List groups, find her online this way:

1. **Choose People⇨Locate Member Online.**

You see the Locate Member Online dialog box.

2. **Type the member's screen name in the text field and press Enter or click OK.**

If your friend is visiting a chat room, the dialog box tells you where she's hiding.

3. **Click Go to join your friend in the chat room.**

The Locate feature may reveal that your friend is in a private room. In that case, send an Instant Message to find out the name of the room. Of course, your friend may respond that she's in a private room, and you can't come . . . so there! But if she's a true friend, she gives you the name of the private room. After you know the room name, joining her in the private room is easy.

To join your friend in a private chat room, follow these steps:

1. **Choose People⇨Start Your Own Chat.**

2. **Click the Private Chat button.**

The Private Chat dialog box appears.

3. **Type the name of the private chat room in the Private Chat dialog box and click Go Chat to join the private fun.**

Ignoring Someone in a Chat Room

When someone in a chat room gets too obnoxious, ignore him. (It's the best form of revenge.) After you ignore the person, none of his text appears in your Chat window.

To ignore a person in a chat room, follow these steps:

1. **Double-click the obnoxious person's screen name in the People Here list.**

2. **When the dialog box pops up, check the Ignore Member box.**

3. **Close the dialog box.**

Repeat these steps to stop ignoring someone (assuming that he repented of his crime).

Locating Someone on America Online

Looking for someone? Try using the Member Directory to search for the person's name or screen name. If the person created a Profile, then the member's information is indexed in the Member Directory. If the person doesn't have a Profile entry, you can't find the name by searching the Directory. (In fact, you probably can't find the name at all.)

You can search the People Directory to find people who share your interests. To find the Member Directory window, do one of the following:

✦ Choose People⇨People Directory.

✦ Click the Member Directory button in any chat room window.

✦ Use keyword **Member Directory**.

If you're looking for specific answers to individual fields in the Member Profiles (such as single men who have chosen "To be or not to be" as a personal quote), choose the Advanced Search tab and fill in the appropriate fields. If you're just out for a quick search, the aptly named Quick Search tab should suit you fine.

If you're looking for someone with a common name, such as John Smith, include an interest, occupation, or place of residence to narrow the search.

Profiles identify America Online members. The profile is also your listing in the Member Directory. When you meet people in a chat room and want to know a little more about them, take a peek at their profiles. Profiles tell you as much or as little about a member as that person wants you to know. Some profiles are very specific, listing first and last names, occupations, and hobbies. Others are downright silly. (But being silly makes life fun.)

To view another AOL member's profile, follow these steps:

1. **Choose People⇨Get AOL Member Profile or press Ctrl+G.**

The Get A Member's Profile dialog box opens.

2. **Type the screen name of the member in the text box and then click OK or press Enter.**

3. **If the member has a profile, the Member Profile window opens.**

If no profile exists, a dialog box appears that states that no profile is available for a user by that name.

To locate a member online, use the Locate button at the bottom of the Member Profile window. To send an e-mail, click the E-mail button. The Write Mail window displays with the member's screen name entered.

If you happen to be in a chat room when the profile urge strikes, double-click any screen name in the member list to the right of the chat room window. A small Screen Name dialog box appears. Click the Get Profile button, and the profile appears if it's available.

Creating a Buddy List Group

Use a Buddy List group to find your friends as they sign on to America Online (keyword **Buddy**). This list window appears when you sign on to the service, and you can set it to notify you when certain people sign on. You can also set a Buddy List Group preference to keep certain screen names from locating you with their Buddy List Groups.

To create a buddy list group, follow these steps:

1. **Use keyword** Buddy **or click the Setup button in the Buddy List window.**

   The Buddy List Setup window appears, as shown in Figure 6-2.

Book VI
Chapter 6

Channels, Chatting, and Discussion Boards

Figure 6-2:
You can create multiple Buddy List groups.

2. **Click the Add Group button.**

   The Create a Buddy List Group window opens.

3. **Type a catchall name for this Buddy List group, such as** Work Pals **or** Friends; **then click the Save button.**

Changing a Buddy List Group

Sometimes, your Buddy List group needs a little tweaking to stay current. You can alter someone's screen name, Internet e-mail address, or Buddy List name after you create the Buddy List.

To change your Buddy List group, follow these steps:

1. **Click the Setup button in the Buddy List window or use keyword** **Buddy.**

2. **Click to highlight the list entry that you want to change.**

3. **Click the button that corresponds to what you want to do:**

   - **Remove:** Deletes that screen name from the Buddy List.

   - **Rename:** Type a new name in the text box and click the Save button to alter a Buddy List group name.

   - **Add Buddy:** Type the screen name in the text field and then click Save.

4. **When everything looks correct, click the Return to Buddy List button at the bottom of the Buddy List Setup window.**

Deleting a Buddy List group

Follow these steps to delete a Buddy List group:

1. **Open the Buddy List Setup window with keyword** Buddy.

2. **Highlight the group name Buddy List Setup window.**

3. **Click the Remove button.**

4. **A dialog box appears to ask whether you're sure you want to delete the selected item. Click Yes.**

Instant Messages

Communicate privately and individually with online friends through *Instant Messages.* These little windows appear on the top-left side of your screen. Instant Messages enable you to drop someone a quick question or comment if she's online or talk privately with another member while sharing a public chat room.

Sending an Instant Message

To start an Instant Message (IM) session, double-click the person's name on a chat room list and click Send Message. You also can click the People icon on the toolbar, choose Instant Message (or press Ctrl+I), and then type the member's screen name.

Use the buttons in the Instant Message window to make your IMs look like professional documents. Located at the top of the message text box, these nine buttons do almost the same tasks as the e-mail formatting buttons. To use a button to format an IM, click the button before typing text or highlight text after typing and then click the desired button.

To send a friend the name of a really neat place you found on America Online, open the area you want to tell your friend about. Then click the Favorite Places icon and click Insert in Instant Message. An Instant Message window opens with a blue underlined title inserted. That's your link!

Receiving an Instant Message

Sometimes, an Instant Message appears on your computer screen, especially if you're cruising the chat rooms or several people have you in their Buddy List groups. To respond to an Instant Message, follow these steps:

1. **When you receive an Instant Message, a small window pops up in the upper-left corner of the screen. The sender's screen name and message appear in the top window.**

2. **Type your response in the lower window, using the format buttons to spice up the text.**

3. **Click the Send button.**

Your response jumps to the top text box of the Instant Message window so that the original sender can read it.

4. **Continue the conversation by typing in the lower window, clicking Send, and then reading the response in the upper window.**

When you need to step away from the keyboard, let your Instant Message buddies know by setting up an Away message. Click the Away Message button at the bottom of the Buddy List window and select the appropriate message for your absence. Then click OK to activate the Away message. If nothing you see fits your mood, click the New button and create an Away message of your own.

Discussion Boards

Discussion boards resemble electronic bulletin boards. You wander in, read the messages that other folks have posted, and perhaps add a few messages of your own. The process is like a chat in slow motion. The online symbol for a discussion board is often an index card with a little red tack through it. Click anything that has this icon to go to the discussion boards for that area. (Sometimes, a Messages button marks the boards.) Look for discussion boards on every America Online channel.

Book VI
Chapter 6

Channels, Chatting, and Discussion Boards

Reading a discussion board message

To find out what others think about a topic, read the messages posted in a discussion board. Follow these steps:

1. **Open the forum and look for the discussion board icon.**

   You may see a square icon that looks like a note fastened with a pin, or you may find a button cleverly labeled "Messages" or "Boards."

2. **Double-click the icon or click the button to open the messages window.**

3. **Highlight a topic in the Topics list and click List All (or double-click the topic).**

4. **Highlight a Subject and click Read Post (or double-click the subject).**

   A message window opens and shows the first message.

5. **To read all the postings under that subject, click Next Post when you want to move forward. To jump to the next subject, click the Subject button at the right side of the window.**

   When any arrow turns gray, you've reached the end of the messages in that direction.

After you visit a discussion board for the first time, on your next visit you can click List Unread to see the new topics and pick up where you left off.

Checking for new discussion board messages

Flipping through the boards and looking for new messages defines the word *tedious*. Make your life easier by using the Find By drop-down list at the bottom of the discussion board window.

To check for new discussion board messages, follow these steps:

1. **Use the Topics windows to locate the forum of your choice.**

2. **Click the online area's messages icon to enter the discussion board.**

   The discussion board window hops onto the screen, showing you a list of subject folders.

3. **Highlight a folder and click the Find By drop-down list; then select Date to open the Find Since dialog box.**

   You see three option buttons.

4. **Click the option button next to your choice, fill in any requested information, and then click Find.**

   If you select the second or third option, type in the number of days you want to search or the date range. The first option shows you the new postings since your last visit to that discussion board.

Posting a reply to a discussion board

Lively discussion requires two-way conversation. On the America Online discussion boards, posting a reply to someone's comment enables you to add your opinions to the topic at hand. You can either reply publicly to the board itself, or you can reply privately via e-mail.

Replying to the board

When you reply to the board itself, your input is public. Anyone can browse the boards and see what you've written.

To reply to the discussion boards, follow these steps:

1. **Find a message that you want to discuss and click Reply.**

A Reply window opens, with the subject line already entered. In most cases, leave the subject line as it appears so that others can follow the discussion.

2. **Type your response in the Reply Window box. Use the formatting buttons along the top edge of the text box to jazz up your post.**

3. **To include some or all of the previous poster's message in your reply, use the Original Message Text box and highlight the words, sentences, or phrases that you want to include. Then click the Quote button (see Figure 6-3).**

The highlighted text jumps into the Reply window, complete with a message board quote mark.

Book VI Chapter 6

Channels, Chatting, and Discussion Boards

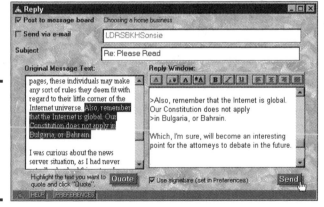

Figure 6-3: You can quote text from the original message in your reply.

4. **Type your name or AOL screen name at the bottom of the message. Or you can check Use Signature at the bottom of the message box.**

5. Check the Send Via E-mail box to send your post to the author of the original message, check the Post to Message Board box to add your thoughts to the message thread, or check both boxes.

6. Click the Send button.

Click the Preferences button at the bottom of any of the colorful message board windows to set your Message Board Preferences. These preferences let you sort messages, show messages posted within so many days, or add a special signature to your message board posts.

Replying via e-mail

Replying to a discussion post via e-mail enables you to voice your opinions privately to the original poster. These messages never reach the discussion boards. Instead, they go directly to the America Online member's mailbox. To post a reply, follow these steps:

1. Click Reply to open the Post a Reply message box.

2. In the Original Message Text box, highlight any material that you want to include from the previous post. Then click the Quote button.

3. Write your response in the Reply Window text box.

4. Type your name.

5. Check the Send Via E-mail box.

6. Uncheck the Post To Message Board box.

7. Click Send.

You can also use the Write Mail window to send your reply, if you like. (See Book VI, Chapter 3, for more on creating and sending e-mail.)

Index

Book VII

Digital Photography

The 5th Wave   By Rich Tennant

"Well, well! Guess who just lost 9 pixels?"

Contents at a Glance

Chapter 1: Deciding on a Digital Camera

In This Chapter

✔ Assessing digital cameras

✔ Choosing an LCD or optical viewfinder

✔ Determining your lens, resolution, and storage needs

✔ Evaluating exposure controls

✔ Thinking about other features

A question like, "What's the best digital camera to buy?" is a lot like asking yourself "What boat should I get?" First, you need to decide whether you actually *need* a boat (or digital camera) and then narrow down the features you must have based on what you want to do with it. Digital cameras are available in models ranging from under-$100 kiddie-cams to professional-quality precision machines costing $5,000 to $30,000 or more. They may have image quality — *resolution* — from 640 x 480 pixels to multi-megapixel (one million total pixels or more). Some digital cameras offer zoom lenses, self-timers, and other helpful features.

Assessing Digital Cameras

While the cost of digital cameras is dropping, an entry-level $75 conventional camera can still produce better images than your average $500 digital model. Ask yourself these questions before going further:

✦ **Do I need my pictures quickly?** Digital cameras beat even the best one-hour photo lab for quick turnaround. If you need pictures fast for your Web site or newsletter (or you're just impatient), digital cameras provide instant gratification.

✦ **Do I take a lot of pictures?** Because you can use digital camera *film* hundreds of times, you can save big bucks on film and processing if you take many pictures.

✦ **Do I want to try many different angles and choose only a few?** You pay for every print you get from conventional film, even if you end up using only a couple pictures per roll. You can delete unwanted digital pictures.

✦ **Do I need very high image quality at a low price?** Conventional cameras still produce the best image quality per buck. Unless you're willing to spend $500 or more, film remains your best choice if you want the ultimate in quality.

✦ **Do I want to make a lot of prints?** Conventional prints can cost a few pennies. Those you make on your own printer may cost you 50 cents to $1 or more each. If you make a lot of prints, particularly when they'll be made from only a few negatives, traditional film can be more economical.

✦ **Do I want to manipulate the images myself?** Photo labs can customize your prints with special cropping and exposure but only to a certain extent. Digital photography gives you complete freedom to manipulate your images.

Photo labs can copy your film images to a Photo CD, floppy disk, or distribute them over the Internet by using a service, such as AOL's You've Got Pictures (see Book VI, Chapter 3). So, you may be able to manipulate traditional camera photos in your computer without investing in a scanner.

For more information comparing digital and conventional cameras, see *Digital Photography For Dummies,* by Julie Adair King (published by IDG Books Worldwide, Inc.).

Choosing a Digital Camera Category

First, choose the category — point-and-shoot, intermediate, or advanced — you'll be considering when selecting your camera. You can narrow your search for the ideal model considerably by deciding which general type of digital camera best suits your needs. Ask yourself these questions:

✦ **Can a point-and-shoot model do the job?** The lowest-priced digital cameras are literally *point-and-shoot models,* with which you frame your subject in the viewfinder and snap off a shot by pressing the shutter button. Point-and-shoot models have few options to confuse you and not many features to give you much flexibility. If you just want to grab quick snapshots and don't need things like high resolution, a zoom lens, low-light capabilities, and scads of storage for large numbers of pictures, a point-and-shoot model may be what you're looking for.

✦ **Is the camera likely to be lost, stolen, or damaged?** Purchasing an expensive digital camera for a child or for use in rigorous conditions rarely makes sense. If you really must have a digital camera instead of a single-use conventional picture-taker, seriously consider the lowest cost point-and-shoot cameras.

✦ **Do I need an intermediate camera?** The next step up is a camera with features that are more convenient to use and that let you take pictures that are difficult to take with basic snap-shooter models. You'll also find that intermediate cameras often produce much better resolutions.

✦ **Is size important?** If you want to slip a camera in your pocket and keep it available, a point-and-shoot model may work best for you. However, fairly compact intermediate models also exist. Cameras that use small storage devices (such as SmartMedia), digital zoom lenses instead of optical zoom, and a small LCD (liquid crystal display) screen can be quite portable.

✦ **Am I looking to photography as a creative outlet?** If you want the most control over your results, intermediate to advanced cameras provide the best combination of automation and manual options for focusing, exposure, framing, and other elements of an image.

✦ **Can a digital camera complement my conventional film camera?** If you're already an active photo hobbyist, you may want your digital camera to closely match and complement the features of your existing equipment. That probably means through-the-lens viewing (like an SLR, or single-lens reflex camera), automatic and manual focus, zoom capabilities, multiple shot options (simulating a traditional camera's motor drive winder), and other features found only in top-of-the-line models.

✦ **Do I have lenses and other accessories I want to use with a digital camera?** If you're willing to spend a significant sum (at least $5,000), you can purchase a digital camera built around a conventional camera body made by Nikon or Canon. These digital cameras can use the lenses, filters, flash units, and other accessories designed for their siblings.

Selecting an LCD Viewfinder

The latest digital cameras generally have both an optical viewfinder, which you can use to quickly frame an image, and an LCD screen on the back of the camera for more precise composition and picture review. Here are some of the additional factors you want to consider when evaluating your camera's LCD viewing system:

✦ **Is the camera's LCD screen visible in daylight and cold temperatures?** The brightness of the LCD screen can vary from camera model to camera model. Some screens may be almost invisible in daylight. Look for a bright screen, especially one with some sort of built-in shading provided by the camera for easier viewing. If you take many photos in cold weather, make sure that the LCD operates under chilly conditions — some do not.

✦ **How large is the LCD screen?** LCD screens are a mass-produced component available from a relatively few number of companies, so you won't find as wide a variation in sizes as you may think. Most measure about two inches diagonally. A larger LCD screen is usually easier to view than a smaller one, particularly if the larger display is also brighter.

✦ **How much power does the LCD screen consume?** You usually won't find any indication of how much power the LCD screen consumes, but rest assured that the LCD screen, especially if it is lit from behind (backlit) is a major drain on your camera's battery. The best option is found in some of the latest digital cameras, which use a TFT (thin-film transistor) active matrix display that provides a bright image, illuminated by the same sunlight that's the bane of backlit displays.

Selecting an Optical Viewfinder

When you want to put your camera up to your eye rather than hold it in front, away from your face, an optical viewfinder is the most convenient option. Here are some questions to take into account:

✦ **Where is the optical viewfinder located?** A traditional window-type viewfinder provides a slightly different view from what the lens sees, which can result in clipping off part of an image. A viewfinder that is located directly above the lens eliminates clipping on either side of the image. Placing the viewfinder as near as possible to the taking lens reduces the tendency to chop off the tops of heads.

✦ **Do I shoot many close-ups?** A single-lens reflex (SLR) camera provides a view of your subject through the same lens used by the sensor, giving you a much more accurate preview (similar to that seen by the LCD screen). If you take many close-ups and want more convenient viewing than a camera-back display, a SLR camera may be your best choice.

✦ **How bright is the view?** Both window-type and SLR optical viewfinders can vary in brightness, depending on the method used to present the view. If you take pictures in low light conditions, you want the brightest view possible.

✦ **Does the viewfinder provide camera-status feedback?** Many cameras include red, green, and yellow LEDs (light-emitting diodes) in the viewfinder to let you know when the camera is ready to take the next picture, whether too little light exists to take a picture without a flash, and other information. If you keep a camera glued to your eye while snapping off shots, a viewfinder display of info is better than having to check the top or back of the camera for this information.

+ **Can the viewfinder be adjusted for eyeglass-wearers?** Some cameras have built-in diopter correction (like that found in binoculars) that you can use to adjust the view for near-and farsightedness. With such an adjustment, you won't need your glasses to see the image clearly.

+ **Is the view clear when wearing glasses?** The physical design of the viewfinder may also limit how well you can see the entire field of view when wearing glasses. A ridge or bezel around the viewport and the amount of magnification provided may prevent someone wearing glasses from seeing the entire subject area.

Choosing a Lens

The lens is the "eye" of your camera, capturing the light used by your sensor to create the picture. Your choice of lens can affect the quality and convenience of your photographic experience. Consider the following:

+ **Do I need to take pictures in dim light?** While the sensitivity of a digital camera's sensor partly determines the light levels required to take a picture, the amount of light the lens admits to the sensor — its *speed* can also be important. Lens speed is measured in f-stops: the smaller the number applied to the lens opening, the more light that can be supplied to the sensor. A f/4 or f/2.8 lens is "slow" while a f/2 or f/1.4 lens is "fast."

Lens speed relationships seem contrary because they are actually the bottom-half (denominator) of a fraction. Converted to such, you can see why f/4 is larger than f/8 (as 1/4 is larger than 1/8). Moreover, each f-stop increment provides twice as much light as the last: f/8 admits twice as much light as f/11; f/5.6 twice as much as f/8; f/4 twice as much as f/5.6, and so on.

+ **Do I want to adjust my lens settings manually?** Virtually all digital camera lenses adjust themselves for the proper exposure automatically (except for the least expensive models with fixed-exposure lenses that you can't adjust at all). Serious photo hobbyists and professionals may also want the option found in higher-end cameras of setting the lens manually to provide special effects or more precise exposure.

+ **Can I move around freely as I take photos?** Can I move closer or farther away to change image size, or do I want to capture several views from one position, as with a zoom lens? A zoom lens is a convenience for enlarging or reducing an image without the need to get closer or farther away. It's an especially useful tool for sports and scenic photography or other situations where your movement is restricted.

+ **Do I need a long zoom range?** Cameras offer small enlargement ratios (say, 2 to 1 or 3 to 1) as well as longer zoom ranges (4 to 1 and up). If you need a long zoom range, look for cameras that provide the ratio you need.

✦ **Is sharpness an important factor while I use my lens to zoom in and out?** Optical zoom lenses move glass or plastic elements internally to provide the best zoom quality. If your needs are less rigorous, a digital zoom lens, which provides enlargement and reduction by manipulating pixels, may be sufficient. Cameras with higher resolutions produce better results with digital zoom, because they have more information to work with.

✦ **Do I plan to shoot many close-up pictures?** If you want to take a lot of tabletop pictures or close-ups, make sure that the cameras you're considering have a close-up (or macro) setting. In addition, an easily viewed LCD display or through-the-lens optical viewing (with a single-lens reflex, or SLR model) can make tight shots easier to produce.

✦ **Is automatic focus important?** Lower cost cameras with fixed-focus lenses may not have focusing capabilities at all. These models provide sufficiently sharp focus at normal shooting distances (a few feet and farther) and, possibly, at a particular close-up distance (typically 18 to 24 inches). More expensive cameras have automatic focus that adjusts for the best setting at any distance.

✦ **What focus ranges should I look for?** Intermediate and advanced cameras may have autofocusing that adjusts automatically from 20 inches to infinity in normal mode and from 8 inches to 20 inches in close-up or macro mode.

✦ **Do I want a manual focusing option?** Manual focusing can let you zero in on a portion of your image by making everything else seem blurry. Single-lens reflex (SLR) models often let you choose the focus setting yourself visually. Other models may have fixed-focus settings at typical distances, such as three feet, eight feet, and infinity.

✦ **Does the lens take attachments?** Serious amateurs and professionals often need to attach accessories to the front of the lens, such as filters, special-effects devices, close-up lenses, or lens hoods. If you need these options, look for a digital camera with a lens equipped to accept them. The ability to use add-ons in standard screw-thread sizes is a plus.

Evaluating Exposure Controls

Digital cameras all have automatic exposure features for both flash and non-flash photography, but some are more flexible than others. For more information on using flash, see Book VII, Chapter 4. Ask yourself these questions when choosing a camera:

✦ **Can I take low-light pictures without flash?** Low-light pictures call for a more sensitive sensor. Camera specs often provide the equivalents to conventional film speeds, measured in ISO (International Standards Organization) ratings such as ISO 100, ISO 200, and ISO 400. The higher the number, the more sensitive the sensor.

✦ **Can I compensate for backlit or frontlit pictures?** Intermediate and advanced cameras may have a simple provision for departing from the standard exposure determined by the camera's sensor. For example, you may be able to vary the exposure to compensate for subjects that are strongly backlit or frontlit so that the exposure is determined by your actual subject, rather than an overall average of the scene.

✦ **Are exposure modes provided?** Cameras may have exposure modes fine-tuned for particular kinds of picture-taking sessions, such as sports, portrait, and landscape photography. You can dial in one of these and improve the quality of your pictures effortlessly.

✦ **Is there a spot meter?** A *spot meter* zeroes in on a particular, small area of the image and determines the exposure from that, ignoring the rest of the picture. This feature can be handy when you take many pictures in difficult lighting conditions and want to specify which area of the picture is used to determine exposure.

✦ **Can I set the exposure manually?** Cameras that let you set the lens f-stop manually may also let you choose either a mechanical shutter (like the one found on a conventional camera) or an electronic shutter or both. The ability to choose a shutter speed gives you creative control when you want to, say, stop fast-moving action under low light levels.

✦ **Can I combine manual and automatic exposure control?** You may want to use a particular shutter speed or lens opening for creative reasons, such as to stop action or to provide selective focus. Intermediate and advanced cameras may let you choose a priority for automatic exposure control. That is, you set either lens opening *or* shutter speed, and the sensor determines the other automatically.

✦ **Can I get the range of flash exposures I need?** Camera vendors typically provide a recommended flash range that offers well-exposed pictures. For example, you may be advised to shoot between 2.5 to 12 feet for pictures at a wide-angle setting but only up to 8 feet in telephoto mode. If you take pictures requiring a particular flash range, check the recommended settings for your camera carefully.

✦ **Can I determine when the flash is triggered?** Most cameras let you choose from modes, such as automatic flash, always-on flash, and always-off flash.

✦ **Can I use an external flash unit?** Built-in flash is fine for snapshots, but if you're shooting portraits and want to use multiple lights or need a high-powered flash for sports photography, being able to couple an external flash to your camera is great. Look for a connector (usually a device called a *hot shoe*) that can mount an external flash or connect to one positioned elsewhere.

**Book VII
Chapter 1**

**Deciding on a
Digital Camera**

Choosing Resolution

Image resolution, the number of pixels your camera can capture, is a chief determiner of how sharp your final images will be. Choosing the resolution that you want is an important first step in narrowing down your choices to one particular camera. Ask yourself these questions early in the process:

✦ **Do I want to make prints or just use my digital images for display on my computer or Web page?** Digital images used with Web pages or in presentations rarely need more than 640 x 480-pixel resolution. If you don't make many prints, you may be happy with an inexpensive model that doesn't boast megapixel resolution.

✦ **Do I want to crop my photos?** If you often need to trim out unwanted portions of your pictures, you probably need a higher-resolution camera (1024 x 768 pixels or more) to provide you with image information to spare.

✦ **Do I need to make large prints?** Most megapixel cameras produce images suitable for 4 x 6-inch prints. If you make many 5 x 7-inch to 8 x 10-inch prints (or larger), look at cameras with resolutions in the 1600 x 1200 pixel (or more) range.

✦ **Is image sharpness my most important concern?** For the ultimate in sharpness, merely looking at the resolution of a camera isn't enough. Consider these factors, as well:

   • **Quality of the lens:** Test several models to compare.

   • **True resolution versus interpolated resolution:** Some cameras use interpolation to simulate a resolution beyond what their sensors can actually capture. Interpolation uses mathematical formulas to simulate the extra resolution. While this technique can work well, interpolated resolution is rarely as good as the real thing.

   • **Storage format:** Digital cameras usually store photos in a compressed format known as JPEG (Joint Photographic Experts Group). JPEG format achieves smaller file sizes by discarding information. Look for a camera that lets you choose the highest-quality JPEG mode when you need it or that has an optional mode for storing in a higher-quality format, such as TIFF.

✦ **Do I want the maximum amount of flexibility in choosing resolution?** Most medium-priced cameras offer a choice of resolutions. You can elect to use 640 x 480-pixel resolution when you want to take a lot of pictures for an application (such as a Web page) that doesn't require the ultimate in sharpness. And then switch to ultra-sharp mode when you snap a picture that you want to print out.

✦ **What resolutions should I look for?** Cameras label their resolution choices with names like Standard, Fine, Superfine, Ultrafine, and so on. A typical range in a multimegapixel model looks like the following:

- **Standard:** 640 x 480 pixels
- **Fine:** 1024 x 768 pixels
- **Superfine:** 600 x 1200 pixels (with medium JPEG compression)
- **Ultrafine:** 1600 x 1200 pixels (with low JPEG compression)
- **Hi-Res:** 1894 x 1488 pixels

Choosing Storage

Your camera's built-in storage determines how many photos you can take at one time at a particular resolution and often determines the method you can use for transferring them to your computer. Here are the questions you should ask:

✦ **How many pictures do I want to take in one session?** The more pictures you take before you download them to your computer, the more storage you need. High-resolution color pictures consume more storage than low-resolution or black-and-white images.

✦ **Do I need removable storage?** Most cameras in the medium price range and above accept removable storage devices, such as CompactFlash or SmartMedia cards. If you take only a few pictures at a time and are willing to link your camera to your computer every time you copy them, a camera with a fixed amount of built-in memory can do the job at a lower price.

✦ **Which removable storage device do I need?** CompactFlash and SmartMedia cards are the most common. Sony's Memory Stick and floppy disk options let you share storage among several devices. Some new devices, such as Iomega Clik! and Imation LS-120 disks, offer especially low-cost, high-density storage.

✦ **What's the easiest way to copy pictures to my computer?** You can insert removable storage devices directly into a PC Card adapter, floppy disk drive, or other compatible device in your computer. You can also attach an external reader. Your camera can also link to your computer through a serial or USB (Universal Serial Bus) cable.

The available storage alternatives are summarized in Table 1-1:

Table 1-1	Storage Devices	
Storage type	*Pros*	*Cons*
Camera's built-in nonremovable storage	Comes with the camera	Can't be expanded
SmartMedia	Smallest removable media; available in 64MB or larger sizes	More expensive than floppy disk; SuperDisk media
CompactFlash	Almost as small as SmartMedia; available in variety of sizes to 128MB or larger	More expensive than floppy disk; SuperDisk media
Floppy disk	Very inexpensive	Large size; relatively low capacity
SuperDisk	Less expensive than SmartMedia or CompactFlash for 120MB of storage	Large size; requires SuperDisk drive in your computer
Tiny hard disk	Largest capacity (340MB and up); very small size	Expensive
Sony Memory Stick	Compact; can be used in other devices, such as MP3 players	Locks you in to Sony components
Iomega Clik	Compact, inexpensive	Still not widely used
PC Card (PCMCIA)	Can be read directly by notebook PCs	Only a few digital cameras use them

Thinking about Other Features

You may want to look at some other cool features found in digital cameras before making your final selection. Here are some of them:

✦ **Can I record sound?** Adding a voice message can be a great way of annotating your images. Some cameras have built-in speakers and can record 3 to 10 seconds of sound in audio formats compatible with PCs.

✦ **Can I output to a TV?** Many digital cameras have NTSC and PAL-format video outputs so that you can view your pictures on a TV screen without transferring them to a computer. This option is great for previews and can turn your camera into a portable slide projector!

✦ **Are high-capacity rechargeable batteries available?** Digital cameras use a lot of juice. A set of alkaline batteries may be good for only a dozen pictures or fewer if you use the LCD screen a lot. The best digital cameras can use or are furnished with rechargeable NiCd (nickel-cadmium). Even better are lithium or NiMH (nickel metal hydride) batteries, good for 20 to 30 or more pictures between charges.

Chapter 2: Digital Camera Basics

Digital photography is a wonderful, convenient blend of two technologies: photography and computers. By combining all the great things about photography (capturing memories, preserving the precious moments of our lives, and providing a vehicle for creative and artistic expression) with the immediate gratification of seeing your pictures as soon as you take them, this techno-marriage offers so many advantages. No more running to the drugstore to buy film or pick up prints. No more negatives to lose, no more mountains of photos to archive, and no more prints that fade. This chapter provides a quick tour through this advancement in photography.

Parts of a Digital Camera

All digital cameras share certain components, such as a lens, viewfinder, and shutter release. Many additional features not found in the most basic cameras are common to a broad range of upscale models, such as a zoom lens and a slot for removable storage. Figure 2-1 shows the various parts of most digital cameras. Your camera may not have all of these features.

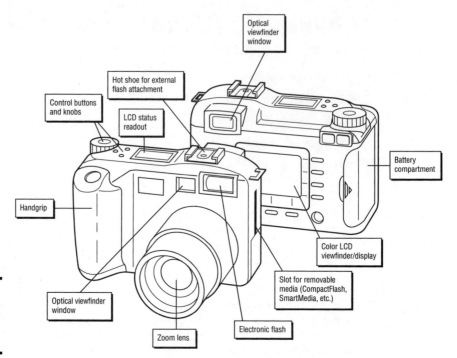

Figure 2-1:
The parts of
a digital
camera.

The following list describes the features shown in Figure 2-1:

+ **Battery compartment:** Cells to power camera functions, LCD screen, electronic flash go here.

+ **Control buttons and knobs:** Adjust camera settings, such as quality level, flash mode, zoom setting, and so on.

+ **Handgrip:** Molded into the camera body to make it easier to hold.

+ **Hot shoe for external flash:** You can attach more powerful flash units here.

+ **Infrared sensor:** Infrared-sensitive device used to calculate distance from the camera to your subject for focusing or, in some cases, adjusting flash settings. Some cameras also have an infrared emitter that you can use to transmit pictures to your computer or printer.

+ **LCD status readout panel:** View the number of exposures taken or remaining, quality level, flash status (on/off/automatic, and so on), and other information.

+ **LCD viewfinder:** View the actual image seen through your lens with this electronic display.

+ **Neck or wrist strap attachment:** An eyelet or loop for attaching a neck or wrist strap.

+ **Optical viewfinder:** Look through the viewfinder to frame your image.

+ **Optical zoom lens:** Adjusts magnification of the image, making it larger or smaller.

+ **Power switch:** Press to make the camera active by turning on the sensor, making the electronic flash ready, and illuminating the LCD viewfinder.

+ **Slot for removable media:** Electronic "film" cards, such as CompactFlash or SmartMedia, go here.

+ **Tripod socket:** Use this screw-thread socket on the underside of the camera to attach tripods, special handgrips, electronic flash attachments, and other equipment.

Taking Your First Pictures

You can be taking and enjoying your first photos within minutes of unpacking your digital camera. All you need to do is prepare your camera, compose a picture, take the photo, and transfer the image to your computer. Some cameras may require that you charge the battery before you begin using the camera, however.

Setting up your camera

The first time you use your camera or each time you replace the batteries, you may need to set up your camera, entering information such as the date, time, and preferred picture-taking modes. You need to make only the camera settings appropriate for your camera, and you don't have to set them in the order shown here:

1. **Use your camera's controls to enter setup mode.**

Consult your camera's provided instructions. Your camera's setup mode consists of a series of menus allocated to each particular type of setting you can make. You use several buttons on your camera to move up or down in the menus, over to different menus, and to select an item.

2. **Adjust the camera to the correct date and time.**

The date and time display on your camera's LCD panel and are included with the image file when the picture is transferred to your computer, so you know exactly when it was taken.

**Book VII
Chapter 2**

**Digital Camera
Basics**

3. **Turn on or off special features available in your camera from the available menus. These features may include:**

   - Audio signals that sound when the camera takes a picture and/or is ready for another picture.

   - An information display of data that you may or may not want to view, such as date and time.

   - The default resolution setting the camera uses unless you specify another mode during a picture-taking session.

   - Whether *playback mode* (the mode that shows you the pictures you've already taken) displays one picture at a time or several of them (for example, two rows of two or three rows of three).

   - The language used for the informational displays of your camera — for example, English, French, German, or Japanese.

Preparing and starting the camera

Make a quick check of your camera each time you begin a snap-shooting session to ensure that it's ready to go:

1. **Turn on the camera.**

2. **Check the LCD panel's battery icon to ensure that the batteries are charged and ready for picture taking. Replace batteries if necessary.**

   Your camera has a series of icons that show the relative amount of power remaining in your batteries.

3. **Examine the camera lens to make sure that no fingerprints, smudges, or other debris are on it that can affect your picture quality.**

   Use only special camera lens-cleaning fluid and lint-free lens-cleaning tissue to clean the lens. At the very least, breathe on the glass surface to add a little moisture before cleaning. Rubbing dust around on a dry lens surface can scratch the glass or plastic.

4. **Check the LCD panel's display to see the number of pictures remaining.**

   Have extra digital "film" memory modules available. Or you may want to erase unwanted photos before you begin your new snapshooting session. (Deleting photos is done differently with different kinds of digital cameras. Refer to your camera's instruction book for more information.)

5. **Check the LCD panel's display to determine the quality level and adjust to the setting you want if necessary. Your camera denotes quality level by using a series of stars or another kind of icon.**

Higher quality levels provide the sharpest results, but the fewest number of pictures with a given amount of storage.

6. **If your camera offers both black-and-white and color mode, double-check the LCD panel's display to view the current mode and adjust if necessary.**

   The icon or message used to represent color or black-and-white mode varies by type of camera. You get more pictures in the available storage with black-and-white mode.

Composing images with an optical viewfinder

When your camera is prepped, view your subject and compose a picture. The optical viewfinder is the fastest way to frame a picture. Most digital cameras have both an optical viewfinder and an LCD viewfinder. To frame a picture, follow these steps:

1. **Place the viewfinder to your eye to view the scene.**

   With a standard optical viewfinder, you see the subject through a window, usually placed on the left side of the camera. With a high end SLR camera, you view the subject through the actual lens that takes the picture.

2. **Zoom in or out by using your camera's zoom controls to adjust the size of the image.**

3. **Change the lens to its Close-Up setting if you want to take a close-up picture.**

4. **Frame your picture within the viewfinder to include only the subject matter you want.**

   Optical viewfinders usually have a pair of lines at the top and sometimes to the left side of the view screen. Keep your subject matter inside these lines to ensure that you won't cut off the top of someone's head or otherwise trim your image without intending to.

5. **If you're using a non-SLR optical viewfinder, adjust the image for parallax.**

   Parallax is the phenomenon that accounts for the difference between what an optical viewfinder sees and what your camera lens, located an inch or two away, actually sees. Parallax is most evident when shooting pictures up close.

Composing images with an LCD screen

Although you use the LCD screen most often to review pictures after you take them, you can also use it to compose a photo. This option, which shows the exact image the camera's sensor sees, works best for close-up pictures, because a traditional optical viewfinder can cause you to cut off part of the image.

To compose an image with the LCD screen, follow these steps:

1. **Turn on your camera's LCD screen if it's not already on.**

2. **If bright light is shining on the LCD screen, use your body to shield the display so that you can view the image clearly.**

3. **Frame the picture using the image you see on the LCD screen.**

4. **Change to your lens's Close-Up setting if you want to take a close-up picture.**

Setting flash mode

You may need to adjust the flash setting of your camera, depending on whether you take the picture indoors, outdoors, or under mixed lighting conditions. Follow these steps:

1. **Choose a flash setting.**

   - Use Auto Flash to let your camera trigger the flash automatically when there isn't enough light.

   - Use Manual Flash/Fill Flash when you want the flash to always go off.

   - No Flash turns the flash off completely, even under low light.

   - External flash lets you use an external electronic flash.

   - Red-eye reduction mode reduces the orange or red pupil effect.

2. **Turn on the flash if necessary.**

3. **Watch for an LED alert, usually located near the viewfinder, that glows red when the flash is not ready to take a picture and turns green when the flash is ready.**

Locking in exposure and focus to take a picture

Just before you take a photo, you want to lock in the exposure and focus settings:

1. **Examine your subject.**

   If you see any very bright or very dark areas in your picture, step in close and reframe your subject temporarily so that only the area you want exposed and focused correctly shows in the viewfinder.

2. **Press the shutter button down halfway and hold it there.**

This action causes the camera to lock in the exposure and focus based on the subject matter in the viewfinder.

3. **With the shutter button still held down, reframe your picture to include only the subject matter you want.**

   If you moved in close to zero in on part of the image, you may have to take a step or two back to reframe the entire composition.

4. **Press down the shutter button the rest of the way to take the picture.**

   Press the button gently rather than punching it to reduce the possibility of blurry images caused by camera shake.

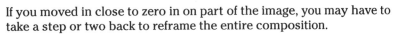

Reviewing Photos

After you take your pictures, you can review them by using your camera's LCD screen. Follow these steps:

1. **If required, change the LCD screen from Preview mode to Review or Playback mode.**

   Many cameras have a switch for changing the LCD screen from a "live" view of what's shown through the viewfinder in real-time, to a review mode that displays the pictures that are in memory.

2. **Review your photos.**

   • If your camera is set in single-picture display mode, review each photo by pressing the forward or backward buttons (usually located next to the LCD screen on the back of the camera).

   • If your camera is set to multiple-picture display mode, review the array of photos.

3. **While reviewing pictures, delete any that you don't want to keep, by using your camera's provision for removing pictures from memory or your removable storage.**

4. **Switch from Review/Playback mode to Preview mode or simply turn off the LCD screen to return to picture-taking mode.**

Transferring Photos

After you finish taking pictures, you'll want to transfer them to your computer for archiving, viewing, editing, or printing. Digital cameras often provide a choice of image transfer methods. These methods include using a serial or USB cable that connects directly to your computer and using a card reader that can copy photos from your CompactFlash, SmartMedia, or other removable storage. (For more on storage options, see Book VII, Chapter 1.)

Book VII
Chapter 2

Digital Camera Basics

While using a serial connection is slower than a Universal Serial Bus (USB) link, this method works with all Windows-based computers because every one has a built-in serial port.

To transfer your images by cable, follow these steps:

1. **Locate the serial cable or USB cable provided with your digital camera.**

2. **Plug the cable into your camera's port, which may be located under a hinged or sliding door.**

3. **Plug the other end into your computer's serial or USB port.**

   When your computer's software connects with the camera, you're offered a choice of actions to take.

4. **Select the transfer option you want to use.**

   You can choose from viewing the pictures in the camera without copying them, copying the pictures and leaving them in place in the camera, or copying all the pictures from your camera and erasing them on the camera.

Follow these steps to transfer pictures via removable media:

1. **Remove the media from your camera.**

2. **Insert the media in your card reader.**

   The software in your computer should connect with the card reader automatically and provide options for downloading or viewing the pictures.

Transferring pictures through infrared connections

Some digital cameras, including several models from Kodak and Hewlett-Packard, have infrared ports that enable them to beam picture information directly to printers and computers. If you have a camera with this feature, follow these steps:

1. **Use your camera's controls to set it for infrared image transfer.**

2. **Place the camera so that its infrared window points toward the infrared sensor of the receiving device.**

The closer that you can position the two devices to each other, the better. Most newer laptop computers and some printers (especially those from Hewlett-Packard) have an IrDA (Infrared Data Association) infrared sensor. You can also purchase an add-on infrared port for desktop computers and laptops that lack this capability.

3. **Start the transfer by using the transfer software for your camera that you previously installed on your computer.**

Chapter 3: Getting the Most from Your Lens

In This Chapter

- ✔ Zooming in and out
- ✔ Changing aperture settings
- ✔ Adjusting the focus and depth of field
- ✔ Taking care of your camera lens

*W*hether your digital camera has a fixed focus, fixed focal-length lens, or versatile zoom optics, you can use the characteristics of your lens creatively. Digital camera lenses have three attributes that you can put to work: the focal length (zoom setting), the aperture (the size of the opening that admits light to the sensor), and the focus. This chapter details techniques for using your lens's zoom settings to change focal length. You find out how to use the aperture settings to change exposure and put selective focus and depth of field to work and how to avoid problems with the distortion that telephoto and wide-angle lenses can cause.

If you want to learn more about getting the most from your digital camera's lens, pick up a copy of *Digital Photography For Dummies*, by Julie Adair King (IDG Books Worldwide, Inc.).

Zooming In and Out

Using a digital camera's zoom lens is a convenient way of framing the exact picture you want without the need to move closer or farther away from your subject. Cameras can magnify or reduce the actual image by either moving the elements of the lens (optical zoom) or cropping the picture so that only the pixels from a smaller area are used to form the image (digital zoom).

Enlarging an image with zoom

Follow these steps to zoom in closer to crop a picture tightly, removing any extra area from the photo:

1. **If your camera offers both optical and digital zoom, use the camera's optical zoom control first — usually a double switch marked W (for wide-angle) and T (for telephoto) to zoom in.**

   Optical zoom provides better quality, so you should use it first. If it provides enough zooming, you can skip the digital zoom entirely.

2. **After using the optical zoom (if any), zoom in further with the digital zoom control.**

3. **If your camera is set on manual focus, recheck focus.**

   Because the lens elements move in an optical zoom, the point of exact focus can change slightly as you zoom in or out; refocus as necessary after changing zoom magnification. (See "Adjusting focus manually," later in this chapter.)

Reducing an image with zoom

Zooming out enlarges your area of view to provide a wider angle. To reduce an image by zooming, follow these steps:

1. **Use either optical or digital zoom controls to zoom out.**

2. **If your camera is set on manual focus, recheck focus.**

   (See "Adjusting focus manually," later in this part.)

3. **If your camera is set for automatic exposure, check to see whether the overall scene is much lighter or darker than when the lens was zoomed in.**

Because the camera's exposure meter may take into account the entire scene, the exposure may change. If you want to lock auto exposure in on the zoomed subject, press the shutter button down part way before zooming out.

Minimizing telephoto distortion

The distortion produced by telephoto and wide-angle lenses is only apparent distortion. It's not caused by the lens but by the distance between the camera and the subject. If you enlarged the center portion of a wide-angle picture to provide the same field of view as a telephoto picture, the enlarged picture would have the same compressed look. A telephoto lens, which magnifies the image, can introduce apparent distortion in two ways:

✦ The distance between subjects appears to be compressed.

✦ Subjects may appear to be wider than they are at normal and wide-angle settings.

Examine your scene and then take one of the following corrective measures:

✦ If objects seem to be compressed together that you want to be shown separated, move them farther apart before shooting.

✦ You also can manually open your lens wider to separate the main subject from others in the foreground and background using selective focus.

✦ Reduce your zoom setting until you achieve the look you want and then enlarge the finished picture.

Minimizing wide-angle distortion

Wide-angle lenses also can provide apparent distortion, actually caused by moving the camera very close to the subject. At close range, objects that are much closer to the camera (such as a human's nose) appear to be much larger than they are in comparison to objects that are farther away (such as ears). Because of this distortion, the telephoto setting can provide more flattering pictures of humans than wide-angle settings. Examine your scene and then take one of the following measures:

✦ If objects, such as buildings, seem to "fall away," it's because you tilted the camera. Try to keep the back of the camera parallel with the subject. If necessary, step back so that you can include the whole subject in the frame without tilting.

✦ If objects very close to the camera look large and out of proportion, step back slightly. Zoom in a little to keep the same image size, if you want.

Aperture Settings

The *aperture* settings of a lens determine how much light is admitted to the sensor during the exposure time and how much of an image is in focus. The larger the lens opening, the more light admitted, but, at the same time, the range in which your subject is its sharpest (in focus) is reduced. Smaller lens openings cut down the amount of light but increase this zone of sharpness, also called depth of field. Most of the time, you can let your digital camera determine the aperture settings. But if you have a camera that lets you make manual adjustments, you can use this lens setting creatively.

Changing apertures to adjust lightness/darkness

Your camera's exposure meter may provide an exposure suitable for the overall average illumination of a scene. You may want to make a picture lighter or darker to change the look or for an artistic effect. (For more information about lighting, check out Book VII, Chapter 4.)

To change the aperture setting, also called the f-stop, follow these steps:

1. **Set your camera to Manual mode or Aperture Priority mode.**

   In Manual mode, you must set both the aperture and shutter speed yourself. In Aperture Priority mode, you set the aperture, and the camera adjusts the shutter speed to provide the correct exposure.

2. **To make a scene brighter, use the aperture control to select a smaller f-stop number.**

   The smallest lens opening is typically f/22 or f/16; the largest may be f/2 or f/1.4. Each number increment admits twice as much light as the last one. A typical array of f-stops from smallest to largest is f/22; f/16; f/11; f/8; f/5.6; f/4; f/2.8; f/2; f/1.4.

3. **To darken a scene, use the aperture control to select a larger f-stop number.**

Bracketing exposures with the lens aperture

Bracketing is taking a series of pictures, each with a slightly different exposure, to see how the different photos vary from a creative standpoint. One easy way to create this effect is to expose each picture using a different f-stop, as described here:

1. **Set your camera to Manual mode.**

   Don't use Aperture Priority mode; if you do, your camera will adjust the shutter speed and the exposures will all be equivalent.

2. **Take a picture at the lens setting you (or your camera's exposure meter) determine to be ideal.**

3. **Open up the lens (use a smaller number) one f-stop and take a second picture.**

   Bracketing with increments smaller than one f-stop often won't produce results that look much different from picture to picture.

4. **Open up one more f-stop and take another picture.**

5. **Move the aperture setting control back to the original ideal setting set in Step 2 and then close down the aperture (choose a larger number) by one f-stop. Now take a picture.**

6. **Move the aperture setting to the next larger number and take the final picture.**

You have exposed five pictures at five different f-stops. Usually this range is enough to produce all the useful exposure variations.

Focus and Depth of Field

Focus is the distance from your camera at which your subject appears sharpest. Anything located significantly in front of or behind the focus point appears to be less sharp. The zone of sharpness is called *depth of field* and varies depending on how far you are from your subject and the size of the lens opening. At any given zoom setting, the larger the lens opening, the smaller the zone of sharpness. You can adjust both the focus and lens opening manually to change a picture's depth of field.

Adjusting focus manually

You can focus your lens manually to select what portions of the image will be sharp. You need one of two objects in order to do so:

+ A through-the-lens viewing single-lens reflex (SLR) camera.

+ The LCD panel on the back of your camera to judge focus.

After you have one of the preceding items, follow these steps:

1. **Set your camera to Manual Focus mode.**

2. **View the subject through your SLR viewfinder or by using your LCD screen.**

3. **Adjust the focus by using your camera's focus control and take the photo.**

Traditional cameras change focus with a ring around the barrel of the lens. Digital cameras (which may not even have a lens barrel as such) may use a knob or sliding control.

Adjusting focus automatically

Even with your camera set on automatic focus, you can still determine what areas of the picture are sharpest by using this technique:

1. **Look through the viewfinder and move close to your subject, so only the portion that you want sharpest is shown.**

2. **Press the shutter release button down halfway and hold it.**

   Doing so locks in the current focus setting.

3. **Move back and then frame the picture you want.**

4. **Press the shutter button the rest of the way to take the picture.**

Adjusting depth of field with the aperture

Focusing the camera determines the position that is sharpest. You can use the aperture to increase or decrease the zone in front of or in back of the focus point to make more or less of your subject sharply focused.

To adjust the depth of field with the aperture:

1. **Set your camera to Manual Aperture mode or Aperture Priority mode.**

2. **To reduce the depth of field (focus zone), open the lens (use a smaller f-stop number).**

   The wider the lens opening is, the less depth of field you have.

3. **To increase the depth of field, close the lens (use a larger f-stop number).**

4. **If you are in manual mode, adjust the shutter speed to compensate for the additional or reduced exposure that results from changing the f-stop.**

Optimizing sharpness

Your lens is only one of several factors that determine how sharp a picture is. If you must have the sharpest picture possible, follow these steps for adjusting your lens, shutter speed, and other controls:

1. **Set your camera to Manual mode.**

   Use the highest resolution setting and lowest compression ratio available for your camera, usually referred to as Fine or UltraFine mode.

2. **Set your lens to its sharpest f-stop.**

Lenses generally provide their sharpest images at two to three f-stops smaller than wide open. The very smallest f-stops provide additional depth of field, but the overall sharpness of the image is reduced.

3. **Use the highest (shortest) shutter speed you can.**

   Obviously, if you want to use a particular f-stop you may not be able to choose the shortest shutter speed. You may instead want to increase the amount of illumination so that you can use the optimal lens opening. Electronic flash units have a built-in, very rapid shutter speed because they fire for a brief instant of time.

4. **If you're not using a very short exposure time, mount the camera on a tripod.**

5. **Focus carefully to make the most of your available depth of field.**

6. **Press the shutter button gently.**

   You may want to use the self-timer to let the camera carry out this step smoothly and vibration-free.

Lens Care

Because your lens is your sensor's "eye," be careful to keep it clean and free of scratches. Most digital cameras have covers that protect the lens when the camera is off, but it's still easy for moisture, dust, or fingerprints to mar the surface.

Avoiding problems

The best way to take care of your lens is to avoid problems in the first place:

+ **Always turn off your camera when not in use.** While most digital models shut themselves off after a few minutes if not in use, the lens cover may not retract.

+ **Keep your fingers away from the lens.** Oily fingerprints are your lens's worst enemy.

+ **Don't let rain or snow fall on your camera's lens.** Moisture blurs your pictures, and even the cleanest precipitation contains dust picked up from the atmosphere.

+ **Avoid smoky environments.** Smoke can coat your lens quicker than dust!

If you must work in a dirty or wet environment, you can mount a plain glass filter, or a so-called *skylight filter,* on the front of your lens to protect it. Many photographers who use expensive cameras leave these on their lenses all the time, as they are easier to clean than the lens itself, and if the filter gets scratched or damaged it can be easily and cheaply replaced. With a digital camera that hides its lens behind a cover between uses, doing this may be unnecessary.

Cleaning your lens

At one time, virtually all lenses were made of optical glass, which was relatively soft, so that it could be ground into the proper shape. However, optical glass is easy to damage. Hardening coatings, plastic lenses, and glass covers over the actual lens have reduced the potential for damage. But you should still be careful when cleaning the inevitable fingerprint smudges and dust spots. To clean your lens properly, follow these steps:

1. **Remove as much dust as possible by blowing on the lens with an air bulb, syringe, or canned air supply. Waft the airflow at an angle to remove the dust from the lens.**

2. **Brush the lens surface lightly to remove stubborn dust that remains.**

   Use a clean lens brush or roll up a piece of lens-cleaning tissue and tear off one end to create an ad-hoc brush. Ordinary facial tissue or cloth may be too hard or contain lint, lotion, or oils that just dirties your lens again.

3. **If you still see dust, breathe on the lens and brush the dust from your lens a little more vigorously. A little moisture can prevent the dust particles from scratching the lens surface.**

4. **If all else fails, you can use special lens cleaning fluid. Place just enough lens fluid on a piece of lens cleaning paper and stroke gently to remove the fingerprint or other stubborn dirt.**

   Don't use window cleaner or other liquids that may leave a residue.

Chapter 4: Composing Great Pictures

In This Chapter
- Conceptualizing your photo
- Positioning your subjects
- Lighting portraits
- Creating advanced compositions

*P*icture composition involves arranging your subject matter by physically moving the subjects around (as you often can with people), changing your point of view, or adjusting the lighting. Although the art of composition has rules, these rules are merely guidelines. Your instincts and creative sense tell you when it's a good time to break those rules and come up with an unusual, eye-catching picture.

Conceptualizing Your Photo

Take some time to visualize your photo before you begin the actual picture-taking process. You don't need to spend hours dwelling over your photo, but you at least need to have a general plan in mind before starting to shoot. Select your subject matter, center of interest, and how the picture will be oriented first.

Planning your picture

Random snap-shooting sometimes yields interesting results, but you end up with more pleasing photos if you stop to think about what kind of picture you want before you put the viewfinder up to your eye. Ask yourself these questions:

✦ **What kind of picture do I want to take?** Do you want your photo to be a portrait, a sports action shot, or a scenic masterpiece? The kind of picture you want to take affects where you stand, how easily you can set up the picture, and other aspects of composition. For example, to shoot a close-up, you may want to use a tripod so that you can frame the picture tightly and lock in your composition. For a sports picture, you may want to get a high angle or one from a particular location to suit the composition you have in mind.

✦ **How do I want to use the photo?** If you plan to print the picture in a publication or enlarge it, you want a tight composition to maximize sharpness. If you want to use the shot on a Web page, you may want to step back and take in a little extra and crop later with your image editor because resolution isn't as critical for Web graphics.

✦ **Who am I shooting the picture for?** You compose a photo created for your family differently from a photo that your colleagues or strangers view. Your family may like a picture better if the composition revolves around that cute new baby. Colleagues may want to see a product highlighted or the CEO shown in a decisive pose.

Choosing your subject matter

Good pictures are simple and uncluttered. To examine your subject for excess busyness, ask yourself these questions:

✦ **Will my photo picture many objects or just a few?** If shooting many objects that are similar, consider singling out a few of them for emphasis.

✦ **Will my photo show something viewers will care about and want to look at?** A pile of sand is boring; a sand dune can be graceful and beautiful. A swarm of ants can be featureless, but a close-up of two soldier ants from opposing anthills may be fascinating.

✦ **Can my photo make a statement about something that goes beyond the picture itself?** Instead of simply photographing a poor child, show how a poverty-stricken youth can still be happy or ambitious. Some of the best photographs take a stand and say something.

Composing through the viewfinder

Most of the time you'll feel most comfortable composing your picture through the optical viewfinder. Follow these steps to line up the shot:

1. **Make sure that you can see the entire viewfinder area.**

   Depending on the magnification of the image in the viewfinder, you may be able to see the whole viewing area with your eye a half-inch or more behind the eyepiece — or you may have to put your eye right up to it.

2. **If necessary, remove your glasses and adjust the viewfinder's diopter setting.**

   If you have to remove your glasses to see the entire viewfinder, it may be difficult to see the subject. Many intermediate and advanced cameras have a viewfinder diopter adjustment, like those found on binoculars, that let you at least partially correct the viewfinder for your vision needs.

3. **Remember that the viewfinder usually shows less than what you get.**

   Even single-lens reflex models often provide an image that is slightly larger than what you see through the viewfinder. If the exact borders of your image are important, you'll have to crop within your image editor, as you can see in the Figure 4-1.

**Book VII
Chapter 4**

**Composing Great
Pictures**

Figure 4-1:
Use an
image editor
to crop a
photo to the
desired
borders.

4. **Allow for parallax when shooting close-ups.**

   Look for lines at the top (and sometimes at the side) that indicate the upper or side limits of the picture area when taking a close-up picture.

Choosing a center of interest

Photographs shouldn't send the person looking at them on a hunting expedition. As interesting as your subject may be to you, you won't want viewers puzzling over what's the most important part of the image. So, every picture should have a single, strong center of interest. Try these techniques:

✦ **Find something in the photograph that the viewer's eye should concentrate on, forming a center of interest.** Usually, your center of interest is a person, group, or the object you're seeking to highlight. You don't want eyes roaming around your photo searching for something to look at. An aspect of the photo should jump out and grab their attention.

✦ **Make sure that your center of interest is the most prominent object in the picture.** Certainly, you may think that your Aunt Mary is a worthy photo subject, but if she's standing next to an outlandish custom-painted automobile, she may not even be noticed.

✦ **See that the center of interest is either the brightest object in the photo or at least is not overpowered by a brighter object.** Gaudy colors or bright shapes in the background distract viewers from your main subject. Eliminate them, move them, or otherwise minimize their impact.

✦ **Make sure that only one center of interest is in your composition.** Other things in a photo can be interesting, but they must be subordinate to the main center of interest.

✦ **Avoid putting the center of interest in the exact center of the photograph.** Move the important subject to either side and a little toward the top or bottom of the frame. Don't take center literally.

Choosing subject distance

As you take pictures, constantly examine your distance from the subject and move closer or farther away if adjusting your position improves the composition. Here's how to choose a subject distance:

✦ **To convey a feeling of space and depth, move back a bit or use a wide-angle lens.** Standing back from your subject does several things. The foreground area becomes more prominent, adding to the feeling of space. You also take in more of the sky and other surrounding area, giving additional depth.

✦ **Make sure that your subjects don't appear too small when you move back; they should still be large enough to be interesting.** Moving too far back is the most common mistake amateur photographers make. If you're showing wide-open spaces in your picture, be certain that it's because you *want* to.

✦ **For photos that emphasize a person, group of people, or a particular object, move in as close as you can.** A close-up viewpoint adds intimacy and shows details and textures of a subject that can't be seen at greater distances. A short telephoto setting is often the best route to getting closer.

✦ **Move so that you fill the frame completely with interesting things.** Whether you're shooting close up to your subject or at a distance, your composition should not include anything that isn't needed to make the picture. Full frames mean less enlargement and sharper pictures, too.

Choosing orientation

You don't see many square pictures; they tend to be static-looking and not very interesting unless a square frame is used cleverly, for example, with subject matter that is also square. Most pictures are composed using a vertical (tall) or horizontal (wide) orientation.

Digital cameras are built with a horizontal layout to better fit into our hands. However, too many photographers never take anything but horizontally composed pictures. By turning your camera 90 degrees in either direction, you can frame a great-looking vertical shot. Use these techniques when choosing between horizontal and vertical formats:

Book VII Chapter 4

✦ **If you're taking pictures for a slide show or, more likely, for a computer presentation, stick with horizontally composed pictures.** Slide show images are seen sequentially and should all have the same frame that is often sized to fill the horizontal screen as much as possible.

✦ **If your subject has dominant horizontal lines, use a horizontally composed image.** Landscapes and seascapes with a prominent horizon, photos of sprawling buildings, many sports photos, and the majority of animal pictures look best in horizontal mode.

✦ **If your subject has strong vertical lines, use a vertical composition.** The Eiffel Tower, trees, tall buildings, pictures of individuals (whether full length or portrait photos), and similar compositions all call for a vertical orientation, as you can see in Figure 4-2.

Composing Great Pictures

Figure 4-2:
Use a vertical composition for subjects with strong vertical lines.

✦ **Use a square composition if vertical and horizontal objects in your picture are equally important and you don't want to emphasize one over the other.** A building that is wide but that has a tall tower at one end, may look good in a square composition.

Positioning Your Subjects

A basic skill in composing great images is finding interesting arrangements within the frame for your subject matter. You need to position your subjects, make sure that they're facing an appropriate way, and ensure that they are well placed in relation to the horizon and other elements of your image.

Positioning your subject matter

The position of your subject matter within a picture is one of the most important decisions that you make. Whether you can move the subject or objects around, change your position, or wait until everything moves to the right spot, you should constantly be aware of how your subject matter is arranged. Use these guidelines:

✦ **Divide the frame into thirds horizontally and vertically.** You want to avoid having your subject matter centered. By imagining the frame in thirds, you automatically think about those ideal, off-center positions.

✦ **Try to place important objects at the four intersections.** Dividing a composition in this way is called the Rule of Thirds. Objects at any of the intersections are naturally arranged in a pleasing way, as you can see in Figure 4-3.

Figure 4-3:
Use the Rule
of Thirds to
help you
position the
subject
matter.

✦ **Avoid having objects at the edge of a picture unless the part that isn't shown isn't important.** If you're taking a picture of a group of people, cropping out part of the building they're standing next to or trimming off half a tree that's not an important part of the composition is okay. But don't cut off heads!

Facing objects into the frame

A photo composition is a whole little world to the viewer. You won't want to destroy the illusion by calling attention to the rest of the universe outside the frame. Here's how to orient people and other objects in a picture:

✦ **If your subjects are people, animals, or statues, make sure that they are looking or facing either the camera or into the frame, rather than out of it.** If a person seems to be looking out of a picture, rather than somewhere within it, viewers may spend more time wondering what the person is looking at than examining the actual person.

✦ **If objects in the frame are moving or pointed in a particular direction, make sure that they are heading into the frame, rather than out of it.** A stationary automobile, a windmill, a palm-tree bent over by a strong wind, anything with a sense of direction to it should be facing into the frame for the same reason that a person should be looking into it.

✦ **Add extra space in front of any fast-moving object (such as a race car) so that the object has somewhere to go, while still remaining in the frame.** It may seem odd, but if an object is moving, having a little more space in the frame in front of it is best so that the viewer doesn't get the impression that it's on its way out of view.

Positioning the horizon

The horizon can be a natural part of many outdoors pictures. Even if it's not the most important element, the horizon is prominent enough that you need to take into account its position when you compose your photos:

1. **Examine the horizon through the viewfinder.**

   Make sure that the horizon is generally parallel with the bottom of the frame. The horizon itself doesn't slope, although it may not be a straight line if mountains, foliage, or other objects delineate its boundaries. In such cases, you still should keep in mind the unseen parts of the horizon when orienting your camera. Otherwise, other elements of your picture tilt.

2. **Point the camera up or down slightly so that the horizon doesn't bisect the picture exactly.**

   You can make your composition seem more interesting if the horizon is closer to the top or bottom of the frame rather than in the middle — another application of the Rule of Thirds.

3. **If you want to accent the "wide open spaces," choose a low angle that emphasizes the part of the picture above the horizon.**

Lighting Portraits

Many common picture-taking situations, such as portraits, can benefit from standard lighting techniques that you can then modify creatively. Here are some of the standard portrait situations you often work with.

Flash settings

Your camera probably has, at least, the first three of these flash settings, and may have the last two. Here's how to choose between them:

+ **Use Auto Flash mode to let the camera set exposure for you.** The camera's exposure meter (or the exposure cell in an accessory flash) examines the scene and triggers the flash if enough light isn't available. Advanced units even measure the amount of light bouncing back from the subject and adjust the level of flash illumination emitted to compensate for the darkness or lightness of your subject.

+ **Use Manual Flash/Fill Flash mode to have the flash always go off.** In this mode, the flash always is triggered, even if plenty of light is available. Use it when you want to brighten dark shadows.

+ **Use No Flash mode to prevent the flash from firing.** You can use No Flash mode even in low illumination. Use this setting to preserve the lighting effect of the original scene. Perhaps your subject is seated next

to a candle, and a moody, dimly lit picture is what you want. Turn off your flash and grab that image!

+ **Use External Flash mode to replace or supplement your internal flash.** Some digital cameras may have a connector to plug in an external electronic flash. You can use this flash instead of your camera's built-in flash or to supplement it.

+ **Use Red-eye Reduction mode when photographing people, particularly in dark areas.** Red eyes, those orange or red pupils caused by light reflecting from a subject's retina back into the camera, can be reduced (but not always eliminated) by a feature in some digital cameras. In this mode, the flash fires twice — once to cause the irises of your subject's eyes to dilate, making them smaller and less prone to producing red-eye when the "real" flash fires a fraction of a second later.

Lighting a portrait with available light

Portraits aren't especially tricky to light, but you want to use flattering illumination to make your subjects look their best. Here are some tips to follow:

+ **Arrange the subject in a comfortable pose.** Have the subject turn slightly to one side or another and look at the camera.

+ **Try to arrange the lights so that three-quarters of the subject's face is fully lit and one-quarter is in shadow.** This technique is called *broad lighting.* You can also use the reverse arrangement for dramatic effect; this technique is called *short lighting.*

+ **Use soft light (reflected light) where possible instead of direct light.**

+ **Arrange to have some light behind the subject shining on the background so that the subject won't blend in.**

Lighting a portrait with electronic flash

Flash is trickier to work with but, when used properly, can make your subject look good. Just use these tips:

+ **If you're using only your camera's built-in flash, you may want to soften it a little by using a handkerchief.**

+ **With a single accessory flash, point the flash at a white umbrella, piece of white cardboard, or other reflective material to soften the light.**

+ **If possible, use several flashes to provide light that gently sculpts the shape of the face (as opposed to flattening it with a single direct flash).**

Lighting a portrait in sunlight

Here are a couple of tips for taking a portrait in sunlight:

+ **Pose your subject out of harsh sunlight: under a tree, in the shadow of a rustic building, or a similar area.** Don't include bright areas in the same picture; your exposure may be wrong or the photo too contrasting.

+ **Pose your subject so that some bright light outside the shadowed area provides some highlights.** You want soft light, not bland light.

Creating Advanced Compositions

After you have the basics out of the way, progressing to the next level and creating even better compositions is easy. All you need to know is when to apply — or to break — some simple rules. Just remember that one of the key elements of good composition is a bit of surprise. Viewers like to see subjects arranged in interesting ways rather than lined up in a row.

Composing with lines

Lines within your image can help your compositions by directing the eye towards the center of interest. The lines don't have to be explicit; subtle shapes can work just as well. Try these techniques:

✦ **Look for straight lines in your image and try to use them to lead the eye to the main subject area.** Some lines are obvious, such as a fence or seashore leading off into the distance.

✦ **Find diagonal lines to direct the attention to the center of interest.** Diagonal lines are better than straight lines, which are static and not particularly interesting.

✦ **Use repetitive lines to create an interesting pattern.** Repetitive lines can be multiple lines within a single object, such as the grout lines in a brick wall or several different parallel or converging objects, such as a road's edges, the centerline of the road, and the fence that runs along the road.

✦ **Curved lines are more graceful than straight lines, and they can lead the viewer gently from one portion of the composition to another.** Curved roads are an example of arcs that can contribute to a composition.

✦ **Look for shapes within your composition to add interest.** Instead of posing groups of people in rows and columns, stack them in interesting arrangements that make shapes the viewer's eye can explore.

Framing an image

Photos are frequently put in frames for a good reason: A border around a picture defines the picture's shape and concentrates our attention on the image within the frame. You can use framing to provide an attractive border around your own pictures by using these tips:

✦ **Look for obvious framing shapes in the foreground that you can place your composition within.** You won't easily miss the most readily apparent frames — doorways, windows, arches, and spaces between buildings. These have the advantage of being a natural part of the scene and not something you contrive in order to create a frame.

✦ **Make your own frames by changing position until foreground objects create a border around your image.** Find a curving tree branch and back up until the scenic view you want to capture is wrapped in its leafy embrace. Climb inside something and use an opening as a frame.

✦ **Place your frame in the foreground.** Shapes in the background that delineate your image don't make an effective frame. You want something that appears to be in front of your subject matter, just as a real frame would be.

✦ **Use a frame to create a feeling of depth.** A flat looking image can jump to life when it's placed in a frame. Usually you want to have the frame and your main subject in focus.

✦ **Use a telephoto lens setting to compress your frame and your subject; use a wide-angle lens setting to add distance between the frame and your main subject.** With a telephoto lens, however, you have to be especially careful to keep the frame in focus.

Balancing an image

If you place every element of interest in a photograph on one side or another, leaving little or nothing to look at on the other side, the picture is imbalanced, like a see-saw with a large child at one end and nothing on the other. The best pictures have an inherent balance that makes them graceful to look at. Use these techniques to balance your image:

✦ **Arrange objects so that anything large on one side is balanced by something of importance on the other side.** A group of people arrayed on one side can be balanced out by having a tree or building on the other. The people are still the center of interest; the other objects simply serve to balance the composition.

✦ **To create a symmetrical balance, the objects on either side of the frame should be of roughly similar size or weight.**

✦ **To create a nonsymmetrical balance, the objects on opposing sides should be of different size or weight.**

Optimizing backgrounds

Unless you're taking a picture in the dead of night or on a featureless sand dune or snowfield, you'll have some sort of background to contend with. A background can be a plus or a minus, depending on how you use it in your composition. To make the most of your background, follow these suggestions:

✦ **Check your background to make sure that it is not gaudy, brightly colored, or busy.** The background should not be more interesting than the subject, nor should it be a distraction.

✦ **For portraits, a plain background, such as a seamless backdrop can be effective.** A plain, featureless background can work for portraits as long as it isn't totally bland. Notice how professional photographers who pose subjects against a seamless background still use lights to create an interesting gradient or series of shadows in the background.

✦ **Outdoors, trees, grass, cloud-studded skies, plain walls, and other textured surfaces can make good backgrounds.** Such backgrounds are interesting, without overpowering your subject.

✦ **Watch for strong lines or shapes in the background that don't lead the eye to your subject.** Straight or curved lines are good for compositions, but not if they distract the viewer from your subject.

Chapter 5: Additional Resources

This chapter provides a quick reference to some additional photography resources you can draw on if you have additional questions or are interested in tasks not described in this book. All these were current when this book was written, but keep in mind that Web site addresses change, books go out of print, and companies go out of business. Most of the material here should remain current for a long time, however.

Image-Editing Add-Ons

You can find some more image-editing tools and add-ons, such as filters and specialized image editing components, from these leading vendors. Filters work within your image editor to give you great special effects; other tools are stand-alone programs you can use to process your images.

✦ **Alien Skin.** Alien Skin's Eye Candy and Xenofex are the absolute best add-on filter sets to use with Photoshop and compatible image editors.

  Alien Skin Software
  1100 Haynes Street, Suite Zero
  Raleigh, NC 27604
  919-832-4124
  www.alienskin.com

✦ **Andromeda.** Andromeda provides a vast line of add-on filters that provide interesting photographic effects right within your image editor.

  Andromeda Software
  699 Hampshire Rd., Suite 109
  Thousand Oaks, CA 91361
  805-379-4109
  www.andromeda.com

+ **Extensis.** Extensis markets a broad range of essential filters, including the Kai's Power Tools plug-ins from MetaCreations and PhotoTools. You can find some free downloads at their Web site.

Extensis Products Group
1800 SW First Avenue, Suite 500
Portland, OR 97201
503-274-2020
www.extensis.com

+ **Nova Design.** Find out about ImageFX and Alladin 4D.

Nova Design, Inc.
1910 Byrd Ave., Suite 204
Richmond, VA 23230
800-IMAGE-69 / 804-282-1157
www.novadesign.com

Photography Instructions

To find out more about photography, books should be your first resource, because you can pull a book from your shelf and refer to it at any time.

General books

The leading publisher of general photography books is Amphoto. You can write to them for a catalog at Amphoto Books, 1515 Broadway, New York, NY 10036-8901, or call 212-536-5103. For other titles, check out your bookstore or online book retailers like Amazon.com and Barnes & Noble for these great books:

+ *Beyond Basic Photography: A Technical Manual,* by Henry Horenstein, Henry Isaacs (Illustrator); Bullfinch Press

+ *Fun With Digital Imaging: The Official Hewlett-Packard Guide,* by Lisa Price, Jonathan Price; IDG Books Worldwide, Inc.

+ *How to Photograph Your Family: Getting Closer with Your Camera and Your Heart,* by Nick Kelsh; Stewart Tabori & Chang, Inc.

+ *National Geographic Photography Field Guide: Secrets to Making Great Pictures,* by Peter K. Burian, Robert Caputo; National Geographic Society

+ *The Lighting Cookbook: Foolproof Recipes for Perfect Glamour, Portrait, Still Life, and Corporate Photographs,* by Jenni Bidner; Amphoto Books

Hungry Minds, Inc.

You can find these books at `www.hungryminds.com`:

✦ *Adobe PhotoDeluxe For Dummies,* by Julie Adair King

✦ *Digital Photography For Dummies,* by Julie Adair King

✦ *Photography For Dummies,* by Russell Hart, Dan Richards

✦ *Photoshop 6 For Dummies,* by Deke McClelland

Schools

Photography schools are a great way to learn photography in-depth and virtually the only way to build the expertise you need to go into photography as a profession (aside from working alongside a photographer as an apprentice). Your local community colleges and vocational schools probably have some photo courses you can take. If you're interested in more professional-level instruction, here are some leading photography schools you may want to investigate:

✦ **Brooks Institute of Photography:** 801 Alston Road, Santa Barbara, CA 93108; 805-966-3888; `www.brooks.edu`

✦ **International Center of Photography:** 1130 Fifth Avenue, New York, NY 10128; 212-860-1777; `www.icp.org`

✦ **New York Institute of Photography:** 211 East 43rd Street, New York, NY 10017; 212-867-8260; `www.nyip.com`

✦ **New York School of Visual Arts:** 209 East 23rd Street, New York, NY 10010-3994; 212-592-2000; `www.schoolofvisualarts.edu`

✦ **Rochester Institute of Technology:** Rochester, NY 14623; 716-475-2411; `www.rit.edu`

✦ **San Francisco Academy of Art College:** 79 New Montgomery Street, San Francisco, CA 94105; 800-544-ARTS/415-274-2200; `www.academyart.edu`

✦ **Santa Fe Workshops:** P.O. Box 9916, Santa Fe, NM 87504; 505-983-1400; `www.sfworkshop.com`

Web Sites

Web sites are your best source of up-to-date information on products and techniques. These sites are a gold mine of useful tricks, tips, and information.

Book VII Chapter 5

Additional Resources

Overviews/reviews

Although the Digital Photography Review shows lots of advertisements, it's a great source of information. You can find reviews on a whole range of digital cameras. All the news about recent product introductions is here, too: `www.dpreview.net/reviews/`

Vendors

Here's the list of the Web sites of key vendors of digital photography equipment, storage devices, and related equipment. You can find lots of information about cameras and other gear, photographic tips, trouble-shooting advice, and much more at many of these:

- **Agfa:** `www.agfa.com`
- **Artec:** `www.artecusa.com`
- **Avision:** `www.avision.com`
- **Caere Corp:** `www.caere.com`
- **Canon Computer Systems:** `www.ccsi.canon.com`
- **Casio:** `www.casio.com`
- **Compeye:** `www.compeye.com`
- **Epson:** `www.epson.com`
- **Ezonics:** `www.ezonics.com`
- **Fujifilm:** `www.fujifilm.com`
- **Fujitsu:** `www.fujitsu.com`
- **Hewlett-Packard:** `www.hp.com`
- **Kensington Technology:** `www.kensington.com`
- **Kodak:** `www.kodak.com`
- **Konica:** `www.konica.com`
- **KYE:** `www.genius-kye.com`
- **Largan:** `www.largan.com`
- **Logitech:** `www.Logitech.com`
- **Memorex:** `www.memorex.com`
- **Microtek:** `www.microtekusa.com`
- **Minolta:** `www.minolta.com`
- **Mustek:** `www.mustek.com`

✦ **NEC:** www.nec-global.com

✦ **Nikon:** www.nikonusa.com

✦ **Olympus:** www.olympus.com

✦ **Panasonic:** www.panasonic.com

✦ **Pentax:** www.pentax.com

✦ **PhaseOne:** www.phaseone.com

✦ **Philips:** www.philips.com

✦ **Plustek:** www.plustekusa.com

✦ **Primax:** www.primax.nl

✦ **Reality Fusion:** www.realityfusion.com

✦ **Ricoh:** www.ricoh-usa.com

✦ **Samsung:** www.simplyamazing.com

✦ **ScanSoft:** www.scansoft.com

✦ **Umax:** www.umax.com/usa

✦ **Visioneer:** www.visioneer.com

✦ **Vista Imaging:** www.vistaimaging.com

✦ **Xerox:** www.xerox.com

Image-editing software

If you need more information about image-editing software, here are some places to look. You can find information about the products themselves, ideas for using them, patches to update software, and much more.

Digital photo albums:

✦ **Flip Album:** www.ebooksys.com

✦ **PhotoImpact Album:** www.ulead.com

Image editors:

✦ **Adobe Photoshop; Adobe PhotoDeluxe:** www.adobe.com

✦ **Corel Photo-Paint and Corel Painter:** www.corel.com

✦ **MGI PhotoSuite:** www.mgi.soft.com

✦ **Ulead PhotoImpact:** www.ulead.com

Photography

You can find a wealth of information available online about photography, information about photographers, graphic design, using digital cameras, tips for selling your photos, and lots of other stuff:

✦ `mavicausers.org/NYIphotoCover.html`: Take a basic photo course in digital photography.

✦ `members.home.net/jonespm/PJDigPhot.htm`: Find other digital photography links in this large, well-researched list.

✦ `www.askme.com`: Ask the experts, for free, about any digital photography topic.

✦ `www.kodak.com`: Kodak has online photography courses that cover everything from composition to lighting.

✦ `www.photo-seminars.com`: Choose from a selection of online classes.

Index

Book VIII

Upgrading and Fixing a PC

The 5th Wave   By Rich Tennant

©RICHTENNANT

"Ronnie made the body from what he learned in Metal Shop, Sissy and Darlene's Home Ec class helped them in fixing up the inside, and then all that anti-gravity stuff we picked up off the Web."

Contents at a Glance

Chapter 1: Upgrade, Repair, or Replace: Examining Your Options

In This Chapter

✔ **Knowing when not to do it yourself**

✔ **Calculating the cost of upgrading**

✔ **Protecting your computer**

✔ **Gathering tools and resources**

*M*aybe you've had your computer for a while now and you're beginning to notice that it's getting a little gray around the edges. Or maybe your computer isn't very old, and you want to protect your investment. In this chapter, we show you how to decide when to add the new components your computer lacks and when to bite the bullet and buy a new computer. We also provide some basic advice for keeping your computer healthy and happy, and safety precautions to take if you decide to upgrade the computer yourself.

If you plan to spend a lot of time on the Internet, also refer to Book III, Chapter 1, for specifics on what components your computer system needs in order to access the Internet effectively.

Deciding to Upgrade, Repair, or Replace Your PC

The bad news is that your computer either is broken or doesn't have the features and components you need, but the good news is that the toughest aspect of fixing computers is deciding whether to repair or upgrade at all. Sometimes replacing the old beast with a newer model just makes the most sense. You should repair or upgrade your system if one or more of the following examples is oh-too familiar to you:

✦ You want to run some new software, but your current computer configuration doesn't support this software.

✦ You don't have enough memory or hard drive space to run new software that you've installed.

✦ Your hard drive has failed, but the other components are in good working order. Buying an inexpensive hard drive probably makes more sense than shelling-out the bucks for a whole new system.

✦ Your computer seems to take forever to perform daily tasks, but investing in a new computer simply isn't in the cards.

✦ A part on your computer no longer works. Perhaps your mouse lost its zip, or your floppy drive refuses to read diskettes.

Of course, sometimes upgrading doesn't pay. Don't perform an upgrade today if:

✦ A computer store runs a special, offering free installation of components that you buy.

✦ It's 10:00 p.m. on a Tuesday, and you need to have that budget forecast for the boss by 8:30 a.m. Wednesday.

✦ Your computer is a 486 or older. You may end up spending more to upgrade this older machine than to buy a new one. Consider purchasing a new computer.

✦ A part of your computer fails while still under warranty. If your computer is under warranty, the manufacturer will fix it free of charge.

✦ A part of your computer fails, and you've been looking for an excuse to buy a new system.

If your computer has a problem that's covered by a warranty and you attempt to upgrade or repair the computer yourself, you could void the warranty. This means that if something goes wrong at any time (during or after you tinker with the PC), the manufacturer could refuse to honor the warranty. If you have the repairs or upgrades performed at the store where you purchased the computer, however, it's possible that the warranty won't be voided. Read your warranty documents carefully so that you understand specifically what is covered and don't hesitate to call the manufacturer if you have any questions.

Figuring Out Your Costs

Before you make a final decision about whether you should upgrade, repair, or replace your computer, figure out your costs. If you are going to perform the repair or upgrade yourself, the cost will be the price of the components and parts, so be sure to shop around to find the best prices possible. If you have access to the Internet, you can quickly compare prices from a variety of vendors by using a shopping guide such as PriceSCAN (www.pricescan.com).

If you are going to have a professional do the upgrade or repair, be sure to obtain a firm price quote. With hourly service fees ranging from $50 to $70 or more, service fees can end up costing more than the components themselves. Make sure that you deal with a reputable shop with trained service technicians who are authorized by the manufacturer of your computer.

If you are going to upgrade or repair several components at one time, add up the cost of the components and service fees, if any. Then consider the cost of buying a new computer. As of this writing, new, name-brand computers range in price from $500 to $2,500.

The most important thing you can do for your computer is narrow down the possible causes for your computer's disgruntled behavior. Look for warning signs that your computer may have a problem that needs to be fixed and think about the actions you want the computer to perform in the future so that you're not suddenly hit with the notion that you have a report to do and your PC has quit on you. You can do a lot to give your PC plenty of TLC so that you can stave off some of the problems that come with a computer's old age.

An Ounce of Prevention . . .

You can do some things to improve your computer's performance that don't require you to take the computer apart. The following few sections offer some pointers for making sure that your computer system stays happy and healthy. You may not be able to avoid upgrading or performing repairs, but following these easy tasks can definitely extend your PC's life.

For more information on how to maintain your computer, refer to Book I, Chapter 7. There, you find procedures for scheduling disk maintenance, deleting temporary files, defragmenting your hard drive, running ScanDisk, scanning for viruses, and backing up your hard drive.

Protecting your computer from power surges

Obviously, your computer needs electrical power to run. The power company obligingly sends the power you need (if you pay the bill), but sometimes you can get too much of a good thing. Every now and then the power company sends just a little too much juice down the line. This doesn't harm most electronics that you plug into a wall outlet, but surges can be deadly to your computer and its components.

You can protect your computer from power surges by plugging your computer into a surge suppressor. Don't confuse a power strip with a surge suppressor. They may look alike, but a standard power strip won't protect your computer from power surges. Also, surge suppressors do wear out over time. Spend a couple of extra dollars to buy a surge suppressor with an indicator that tells you if the surge suppression is working. If the box doesn't actually say "Surge Suppressor," it is probably just a power strip.

Lightning can also be deadly on your computer. Even if you have your computer plugged into a battery backup and surge suppression unit, modems and other peripherals can get fried like scrambled eggs and bacon. The best insurance is to unplug your computer and peripherals when lightning is flashing outside.

Making sure that you have clean power

If you have the opposite problem — drops in power instead of surges — you may want to consider buying an uninterruptible power supply. An uninterruptible power supply or *UPS* — makes sure that your computer receives just the right amount of power, no more, no less. For example, if the voltage drops, or you experience a power outage, your computer resets or turns off, meaning that you lose any unsaved work and possibly damage your files. The UPS prevents these problems because the UPS supplies power from a built-in battery. The battery probably won't last long enough to run your computer until the power comes back on, but the battery does provide enough power for you to shut down the computer in an orderly manner.

Protecting your computer from heat and sunlight

Computers don't have very many moving parts, and computer components rarely suffer from mechanical failure. The computer's biggest enemy is heat build-up.

The easiest way to keep your computer from burning out is to make sure that your computer has adequate ventilation. Here are some easy tips:

✦ Don't place boxes or other items in front of the computer's vents.

✦ Make an effort to keep dust out of your computer. You can take the cover off and blow any dust from the computers innards using a can of compressed air that you can buy at an office supply or computer store.

✦ Avoid placing your computer in direct sunlight. Sunlight can make the monitor difficult to read, and it can heat up the computer. Remember, cooler is better.

Before You Begin

Before you make upgrades to your computer, read the information in this section very carefully. Your computer has several slots — the exact number varies with different computer models — that can accept new hardware. The collection of slots is known as the computer's *expansion bus*. The hardware devices that you install in the slots are known as *expansion cards* — they expand the capabilities of your computer. Expansion cards are often called *adapter cards,* or simply, *adapters.*

Gathering your tools

You are going to need some tools to upgrade your computer. But you don't need to rush out to Sears and buy the 400-piece Craftsman Master Mechanic set. A standard (slot head) screwdriver and a Phillips (cross head) screwdriver usually do the trick. If you have a Compaq computer, a Torx (you know, that funny star-shaped screw head that you only find on old Macintosh and Compaq computers) driver set comes in very handy, as well. If you think you'll be getting into the computer upgrade routine quite often, it may be worth the investment to get a small computer tool kit for around $20 or $30.

Playing the safety game

Most people probably think of the danger of electrocution when they consider making repairs or upgrades. If you unplug the computer before taking the cover off, you run very little risk of zapping yourself.

Computers have a lot of wires and sharp edges. While you need to be careful as you poke around inside your computer, the biggest risk you face is damaging your computer (and the component you're installing) by making a mistake.

Removing a stubborn computer cover

Some computer covers require you to get out the screwdriver and remove a bunch of screws, which is fine — but you need to be careful not to remove the screws that hold the power supply in place. Normally, these are the screws that surround the fan that you can see on the back of your computer. On some systems, especially tower configurations, removing these screws can cause the power supply to fall into the computer and damage some of the internal components. If you have any doubts about how to remove your computer's cover, be sure to check your system documentation.

Chapter 2: Upgrading Memory

*Y*our computer needs memory to get its work done. Think of memory as you would your desk. On your desk, you lay all the paperwork you're working on. As you know (especially if you have a lot of paperwork), the bigger the desk, the more stuff you can put on it. The same applies to your computer — the more memory (*random access memory,* or RAM) you install in your computer, the more room you have to run programs and save your work.

Having a lot of RAM can provide these benefits:

+ **You can do more.** You can run multiple programs, even programs that are large and complicated, at the same time.

+ **You can help your computer run faster.** The more room the computer has to work, the less time it wastes shuffling information between RAM (which is very fast) and your hard drive, which is relatively slow compared to RAM.

Understanding the Different Types of Computer Memory

Memory comes in various shapes and sizes. When you go to the computer store, you may hear the word DRAM, which is short for *dynamic random access memory,* the most common type of RAM used in desktop computers. DRAM comes in two varieties:

+ **SIMMs,** or *single inline memory modules.* A SIMM is a computer card that generally has RAM chips soldered to one side of it. You put it in your computer to increase your RAM. Older computers use SIMMs.

✦ **DIMMs,** or *dual inline memory modules.* A DIMM is a computer card that has RAM chips soldered to both sides of it. DIMMs have a higher capacity to hold RAM than SIMMs and are found in newer computers.

If you have an older computer, it probably uses 30-pin SIMMs, whereas newer computers, like Pentiums, use a 72-pin configuration. *Pin configuration* is simply the number of pins on the SIMM needed to connect the SIMM to your PC's motherboard. (Refer to Book VIII, Chapter 3, for more information on the motherboard.)

If you have the newest and fastest Pentium II and Pentium III computers, your PC uses *synchronous dynamic random access memory,* otherwise known as SDRAM. SDRAM is configured with 168-pin DIMMs.

Knowing How Speed and Size Affect RAM

When you think about RAM, you must also consider the speed of your computer's memory chips. The older your computer, the slower your RAM.

RAM speed in older computers is measured in *nanoseconds* (ns) and in newer computers is measured in *megahertz* (MHz). Just to put things in perspective, a nanosecond is one billionth of a second. Megahertz refers to millions of cycles per second.

Table 2-1 shows you the RAM speeds you find in various computers.

Table 2-1	RAM Configuration, Speed, and Upgrading		
Computer	*# of Pins*	*Speed*	*How to Upgrade*
486	30- or 72-pin SIMMs	60–70 ns	Slow RAM; install 30-pin SIMMs in banks of four; install 72-pin SIMMs individually
Pentium	72-pin SIMMs or 168-pin DIMMs	50–70 ns	Faster RAM; install SIMMs in matched pairs; DIMMs can be installed individually
Pentium II/III	168-pin SDRAM	100 MHz	Very fast RAM; DIMMs can be installed individually

Your computer may run erratically or refuse to function if you install memory that is too slow or too fast. If you put newer, faster memory in an older computer that is designed to use slower memory, the memory may work, but we don't recommend it because the older computer isn't capable of taking advantage of the new memory's full potential — you will have paid more money for the memory you can't really use. The converse is also true. If you put slow memory in a fast computer, it may work, but it will slow down the computer.

Don't mix and match the speed of the memory chips. Your computer probably won't like that very much. Instead, match the correct memory speed to your computer's current memory speed.

Determining How Much Memory Your Computer Has

If you're wondering how much memory your computer has, the answer is simple: probably not enough. Your computer should have a minimum of 32 to 64MB (megabytes) of RAM. One of the easiest ways to find out how much RAM your computer has is to turn on the computer and watch it count its memory. After you turn on the computer, you will see a rapidly changing number in the top-left corner of the screen. After this number stops changing, you have the amount of RAM installed in your computer.

While this method works on most computers, other systems won't give you this visual. You can dig into Windows to find the answer. Right-click the My Computer icon on the Windows desktop and choose Properties. You see the amount of installed RAM listed on the General tab of the System Properties dialog box. Click the Cancel button to close the System Properties dialog box.

Understanding Memory Requirements

The amount of memory that you should have installed in your computer depends on several factors:

+ **The operating system you're running.** If your operating system takes a lot of memory, you may need more RAM to keep it running optimally.

+ **The types of programs that you run.** If you run programs that take up a lot of memory (like graphics programs), you may need more RAM.

+ **The number of programs that you want to run simultaneously.** If you expect your computer to run several different programs at a time, you may need more RAM.

Table 2-2 shows you the minimum amount of RAM required to run your PC effectively.

Table 2-2	**Memory Requirements for Optimum Use**	
If You're Running	*You Need*	*You're Better Off With*
Windows 95	8MB of RAM to run basic applications	A minimum of 12–16MB of RAM to run applications effectively
Windows 98	16–32MB of RAM to run basic applications	48MB to 64MB of RAM if you want to run your Web browser while working on word processing documents or spreadsheets
Windows 2000	32–64MB of RAM to run basic applications	An additional 64MB of RAM if you run memory-intensive applications such as photo editing or multimedia presentations
Windows Me	32–64MB of RAM to run basic applications	An additional 64MB of RAM if you run memory-intensive applications such as photo editing or multimedia presentations

Installing More Memory

Make sure that you buy the correct type of memory for your computer. If you have any doubt about the type of memory that you need to buy, remove one of the old memory chips and take it with you to the computer store. If the friendly folks at your computer store can't tell you what type of memory you need to buy from that sample, you are probably shopping at the wrong computer store.

Many older computers have either four or eight memory card slots. These slots may be divided into pairs or groups of four called *banks*. Newer computers may have only two or three slots that can be filled individually. When you install memory in the older computers, you have to fill in an entire bank.

You cannot install memory cards of differing capacities in the same memory bank. You can, however, install memory cards of differing capacities in different memory banks if your system's motherboard and BIOS support it. If you have any questions about how many banks and slots your PC has, refer to your system documentation.

Memory chips are very sensitive to static electricity. Before you install memory in your computer, consider spending a couple of dollars on a grounding strap. You don't have to shell out big bucks for one — unless you plan on getting into the memory installation business. You should be able to buy a disposable grounding strap for a dollar or two from the store where you purchase the memory. If you don't use a grounding strap, the static electricity from your body or from shuffling on the carpet can ruin your PC's new memory.

Before you decide to install new memory in your computer, consider having a professional install it. Some computer stores offer free installation. If you decide to do it yourself, see Book VIII, Chapter 1, for important safety information.

If you decide to install the memory yourself, follow these steps:

1. **Turn off and unplug the computer.**

2. **Remove the computer's cover.**

   You may have to refer to your computer's documentation for this.

3. **If necessary, remove the old memory.**

   You usually have to pry the metal or plastic tabs from both ends of the memory card and push gently until the card is at an angle. Pay attention to the way the old memory card was installed.

4. **Plug in the new memory.**

   Be careful to plug in the memory cards correctly. The memory cards are notched at one end. Gently place the memory card into the slot at an angle and slowly stand the card up until it clicks into place.

5. **Replace the computer's cover.**

6. **Plug the computer in and turn it on.**

   Your computer should recognize the new memory. If the computer doesn't, you need to run the computer's BIOS setup program. If you aren't sure how to start your computer's BIOS setup program, refer to your system documentation or check out Book VIII, Chapter 3.

**Book VIII
Chapter 2**

Upgrading Memory

Chapter 3: Modernizing Your Motherboard

In This Chapter

✔ **Changing system settings**

✔ **Replacing a dead battery**

✔ **Upgrading the BIOS**

✔ **Upgrading the CPU**

*Y*our computer's motherboard holds all the important components that make your computer run, including the SIMM sockets (discussed in Book VIII, Chapter 2) that hold the PC's random access memory. The motherboard also includes the BIOS, or *Basic Input/Output System,* which houses — among other things — your computer's system settings. In addition, the motherboard is also home to the CPU, or *Central Processing Unit,* otherwise known as the brain of a computer system.

If your motherboard is older than a 486, the CPU may not be able to keep up with any new programs that you add. The most cost-effective solution may be to replace the entire motherboard. See "Upgrading the CPU," later in this chapter, for more information.

Changing Your Computer's System Settings

If you add or remove hardware from your older computer, you must tell your computer what changes you have made. To change the settings stored in your computer's *CMOS chip* (the chip that monitors all of your computer's activities), you must access your system's BIOS (the group of chips that sets up your system's programs and makes sure that they run). Usually you don't have to worry about this on newer Pentium-class computers. They come with a Plug and Play BIOS, which recognizes hardware changes you make and makes adjustments accordingly.

How you start the setup program depends on the make and model of your computer. When you first turn on your computer, look for a message telling you how to start the setup program. You may see a message such as

```
Press F2 to enter Setup
```

Or

```
Press Del Setup
```

Some computers have you press Ctrl+Alt+Esc, Ctrl+Alt+Insert, Ctrl+Alt+Enter, or F1 to enter the setup program. If none of these methods brings the setup screen to life, you need to hit the books. Look in your computer's manual for more information on your PC's BIOS setup.

As soon as you get into the setup program, here are some of the features that you need to set:

+ **Date:** To tell your computer what day it is.

+ **Boot sequence:** To tell your computer where to find the operating system. On most systems, you want to set this to Floppy and then to Hard Drive.

If your computer is capable of booting from the CD-ROM drive, set this drive last so that your computer won't try to boot from the CD-ROM drive if you leave a CD in the drive.

+ **Diskette drives:** To tell the computer what type of floppy disk drives it has.

+ **Hard drive:** To tell the computer what type and size of hard drive is installed. Usually the type is 47, but check the documentation for the hard drive.

+ **Memory:** To tell the computer how much memory it has.

+ **Time:** To tell the computer what time it is.

+ **Video card:** On some systems, you have to tell the computer what type of video card is installed. If you install a video card in a computer that has a built-in video card, you have to tell the computer which card to use.

Getting into the CMOS setup is not for the weak at heart. If you are unsure or nervous of making any changes in the CMOS setup, don't go there. Doing so may cause your computer to not boot properly or cease operation. If you have some good knowledgeable friend or trusted computer consultant to bribe with dinner, this would be a good time to start thawing steaks.

Replacing a Dead Battery

Your computer has a special chip called the CMOS — Complimentary Metal-Oxide Semiconductor — that stores information about the amount of RAM, the number and type of hard drives and floppy drives, and the type of video adapter installed in your system. The CMOS also keeps track of the date and time for your computer. In order to remember all this stuff, especially when the computer is turned off, the CMOS needs a source of electrical power. That's where the battery comes in. If the battery goes dead — most batteries last for three or more years — the CMOS loses all of its settings. After you turn off the computer, the CMOS forgets how much memory the computer has, what type of drives are installed, and so on. Follow these steps to locate the battery on your system board:

1. **Turn off the computer and unplug it.**

2. **Remove the computer's cover.**

3. **Locate the battery on the motherboard.**

   Your computer's battery may look like a circular, flat disk — sort of like an overgrown watch battery. Or it may look more oblong, like two AA batteries wrapped together in plastic.

4. **Remove the existing battery by gently prying the retaining clips apart. If your computer has AA-type batteries, disconnect the cable from the motherboard.**

   Note the connector where you disconnected the cable.

5. **Install the new battery. If your computer uses one of the watch-type batteries, install the battery with the plus sign up. If your computer uses the AA-type battery, connect the cable to the motherboard.**

6. **Replace the computer cover.**

7. **Plug in and turn on the computer.**

After you turn on the computer after installing the battery, don't be surprised that the computer suffers from amnesia. The CMOS won't remember the date and time, or what kind of hardware it has until you run the BIOS setup program. See the preceding section for information on running the setup.

While your computer is still in good working order, it's a good idea to either print the settings that are stored in your computer's CMOS or write them down. You can easily print the information by entering Setup and pressing the Print Screen or PrtSc key. Doing so causes the information displayed on screen to be printed on whatever printer you have on LPT1. If that happens to be a laser printer, you may have to press the form feed button after each screen. When one screen is captured, go to the next setting screen and repeat. File the information away with your manuals.

Upgrading the BIOS

Who is this BIOS guy, and why would you need to upgrade him? The BIOS is a set of computer chips that provide the basic instructions necessary for your computer to function, including the following:

✦ The BIOS allows your computer to *boot,* or start up.

✦ This system is also responsible for performing the computer's *Power-On Self-Test,* or POST, which checks to make sure that your computer's hardware components are functioning.

✦ Probably the most important function of the BIOS is that it acts as the interface between your computer's operating system (for example, Windows Me) and its hardware (for example, your printer).

You may need to upgrade your computer's BIOS so that it can communicate with new hardware devices that weren't available when the BIOS was created. For example, some older BIOS may not be able to cope with dates beyond December 31, 1999 because of the so-called Y2K bug.

Using software to upgrade the BIOS

Most computers have a *flash BIOS.* A flash BIOS is simply a set of BIOS chips that can be upgraded by running a software program. You can usually get the software you need to complete the upgrade from the manufacturer of the computer. If you don't have any luck getting the software from the computer manufacturer, try going directly to the BIOS manufacturer — almost certainly AMI (www.ami.com) or Award (www.award.com).

Upgrading the BIOS the old-fashioned way

If you have an older BIOS that you can't upgrade with software, you are going to have to roll up your sleeves and get under the hood of your computer and perform the upgrade manually. You need some tools to upgrade the BIOS the old-fashioned way, but don't worry, the work isn't difficult. Here's what you need:

✦ A screwdriver to remove your computer's cover.

✦ A chip puller to remove the old BIOS chips. If you have a computer toolkit, you probably already have a chip puller, which is the tool that resembles a pair of tweezers. If you don't have a computer toolkit, you can buy a basic set for about $20. Or you can use a small screwdriver to gently remove the old BIOS chips.

✦ Of course, you also need new BIOS chips. You can purchase these from your computer's manufacturer or from a BIOS manufacturer, such as AMI or Award.

To upgrade your BIOS and manually replace BIOS chips, follow these steps:

1. **Turn off your computer and unplug it.**

2. **Remove the computer's cover.**

3. **Locate the BIOS chips on the motherboard.**

   The BIOS is probably contained on a single chip with the word *BIOS* printed on it. The BIOS may consist of up to five chips, labeled BIOS-1 through BIOS-5.

4. **Make a note of the location and orientation of the BIOS chips.**

   You have to install the new chips in the same place as the old chips.

5. **Gently pry out the old BIOS chips with a chip puller or a small screwdriver.**

6. **Carefully insert the new BIOS chips in the vacated chip sockets. Be sure not to bend the pins on the BIOS chips.**

7. **Replace the computer's cover.**

8. **Plug in the computer and turn it on.**

   The computer displays the new BIOS version on startup.

Upgrading the CPU

The CPU, or *Central Processing Unit,* is your computer's brain. CPUs must be made of very hardy stuff, because the CPU is one of the least likely components in your computer to fail. In fact, your CPU is more likely to outlive its usefulness than it is to die on you.

For example, a day may come when you find some shiny new program that you just have to have, but you realize that your aging computer's CPU isn't up to the task. Should you ditch that faithful computer for a newer, fancier model? Maybe. But if your computer is otherwise healthy, has lots of RAM and hard drive space, you may consider replacing the PC's central processor instead.

Before attempting to install a new processor in your computer, be sure to check with the processor's manufacturer to make sure that the new processor will work in your system.

Currently, if your computer has a 486 or newer CPU, you can probably install a faster processor. Some older computers have a CPU that is permanently attached to the motherboard. These CPUs cannot be easily removed and are not good candidates for an upgrade. If you have any questions about the CPU of a specific computer model, be sure to check with the vendor selling the processor upgrade, or consult the following list of processor upgrade companies.

✦ **Evergreen Technologies:** From 486 to Pentium II upgrades, Evergreen makes around a dozen processor upgrades to rev up older systems. Visit www.evertech.com to research your system's compatibility with Evergreen products.

✦ **Intel:** Offering the OverDrive processor upgrade for many systems, the Intel Upgrade Guide gives you the most current listing of upgrades available for your Intel-based processor. Those having older 486 systems may be out of luck, however, because those processor upgrade products have been discontinued. Consult the Intel Upgrade Guide to see if your system can be boosted at a reasonable price: www.intel.com/overdrive/upgrade/index.htm.

✦ **Kingston Technology:** Third-party processor upgrades can offer an economical way to add some zip to your computer. Kingston Technology (www.kingston.com) offers about half a dozen processor upgrades, depending on the currently installed processor and the motherboard manufacturer. Look for the Processor Upgrade link on the home page of the Kingston site and consult the compatibility listing for each upgrade to find the right product for you.

✦ **PowerLeap:** Also offering about a dozen products to upgrade Intel Pentium and AMD processors, PowerLeap's compatibility section can guide you through shopping for the right product to upgrade your system. A nice addition to the PowerLeap site is a community forum where you can post questions and receive responses from staff and customers. You can get an idea about customer satisfaction, too. The Web address is www.powerleap.com.

Chapter 4: Drives and Adapters

In This Chapter

✔ **Removing and replacing a hard drive**

✔ **Installing a CD-ROM drive**

✔ **Installing a tape backup unit**

✔ **Adding a Zip drive**

✔ **Understanding adapter cards**

✔ **Troubleshooting adapter cards**

C omputers can have a variety of storage devices. Some storage devices are faster than others, and some have a greater capacity to store files than others. No matter what type of storage device your computer has, all storage devices have one thing in common: They don't lose their contents when you turn off the computer — well, hardly ever. This chapter covers how to install or replace storage devices on your computer. For a description of the various types of storage drives that are currently available and how they work, refer to Book I, Chapter 4.

In this chapter, you discover which type of adapter you should use, as well as how to fix any problems you may have with a sound or graphics adapter, and how to install a new adapter card to your PC. See Book VIII, Chapter 1, for important information you need to know before you make any additions to your computer.

Removing and Replacing Your Hard Drive

When you need to replace your computer's hard drive, remember that you should already have a current backup of the information on your old hard drive. If you're replacing a drive because you need more capacity, be sure to make a backup copy of all the files on the drive. A tape backup unit provides the easiest and fastest method of backing up your hard drive. If you don't have a tape backup unit, consider backing up to a CD-RW, to a Zip drive, or to some removable media drive. Back up to floppy disks only as a last resort. Floppy drives are slow and don't hold much information. You need a lot of floppies to back up your hard drive.

If you must back up your hard drive to floppy disks or Zip disks, consider backing up only your data files. You can install your operating system and application programs from the original disks, which saves you a lot of time and gives you a cleaner operating system to begin anew.

Of course, if you're replacing a drive that has failed, you already know that it's too late to worry about creating a backup.

To replace your computer's hard drive, follow these steps:

1. **Turn the computer off and unplug it.**

2. **Remove the computer's cover.**

   You may need to refer to your documentation for this step.

3. **Unplug the old hard drive's ribbon and power cables.**

   The ribbon cable is the flat gray cable with the black or gray connector. The power cable is the cable with the four colored wires.

4. **Remove the mounting screws that hold the drive in place.**

   Some computers have, instead of screws, little tabs that you have to press in order to release the drive.

5. **Remove the drive from the computer.**

   Most hard drives slide out the front of the computer. Other drives slide out toward the back of the computer. Still other drives just lift out.

6. **Insert the new hard drive in the computer.**

   If your drive uses mounting rails, make sure that you install them. You may have to remove the rails from the old drive if your new drive didn't come with rails.

7. **Connect the data cable to the hard drive.**

   Most drives have a notched connector so that you can't accidentally plug the data connector in upside down. If your drive doesn't have this notched connector, make sure that the side of the data cable with the red stripe matches up to the side of the connector marked with a 1.

8. **Connect the power cable to the hard drive.**

   You can't go wrong fitting the power cable because you can fit the cable in one way only.

9. **Secure the drive with the mounting screws.**

10. **Replace the computer's cover.**

    Be sure not to pinch the drive cables when you put the cover back on.

11. **Plug in the computer and turn it on.**

Now you have to make sure that your computer and the new hard drive are properly acquainted. In most cases, you simply place the installation disk that came with your new hard drive into the floppy drive and turn on the computer. The installation program makes the introductions for you and tells your computer's *CMOS chip* (a little computer chip that keeps track of the various components installed in your computer) the type and capacity of the drive you just installed. The program also partitions the drive so that you can format the new drive with the operating system of your choice.

After the drive's installation program finishes, you can install your operating system. The operating system is almost certainly some version or other of Microsoft Windows. Place the Windows boot disk in the floppy drive and restart the computer. Follow the on-screen instructions to install the operating system.

Installing a CD or DVD Drive

If you don't have a CD-ROM, CD-R, CD-RW, or DVD drive, or if your original CD or DVD drive has failed you, you can purchase and install either an internal or external CD or DVD drive to your PC. External drives usually plug into the computer's parallel printer port, but some newer models plug into the USB port.

Installing an external CD or DVD drive is a snap — just follow these directions:

1. **Turn off the computer and unplug it.**
2. **If necessary, unplug the printer cable from the back of the computer.**
3. **Plug one end of the CD or DVD drive's cable into the printer port on the back of the computer. Plug the other end of the cable into the CD or DVD drive.**
4. **Plug the printer cable into the printer pass-through port on the CD or DVD drive.**
5. **Plug in the CD or DVD drive's power cable and turn it on.**
6. **Plug in the computer and turn it on.**
7. **Run the installation program that came with the CD or DVD drive.**

If you're installing a USB external CD or DVD drive, you don't have to shut off the computer. Just plug in the CD or DVD drive and turn it on. Then connect the USB cable to the CD or DVD drive and to the computer. The computer recognizes the fact that a new USB device has been connected and prompts you for the installation disk. Installing an internal CD or DVD drive is a little more complicated, but not greatly so. Follow these steps:

1. **Turn off the computer and unplug it.**

2. **Remove the computer's cover.**

3. **Slide the CD or DVD drive into an empty drive bay.**

   On some systems, you must remove a piece of plastic that covers the empty drive bay. The empty drive bay is the slot at the front of the computer that's just a little bigger than the CD or DVD drive. If you're unsure where to install the CD or DVD drive, check your computer's documentation.

4. **Connect one of the IDE/EIDE controller cable connections to the CD or DVD drive.**

   In some cases, the controller ribbon cable attaches to a sound card or into the same interface as the hard drive. If you are unsure, consult the instructions that came with the drive that you're installing for the proper connection procedure.

5. **Attach the sound wire to the back of the CD or DVD drive and to the appropriate spot on the sound card or motherboard.**

   Depending on the configuration of your computer, some sound connections are found on the motherboard. Others use a separate sound card. Consult the documentation that came with your computer to be sure. If you are replacing an existing CD or DVD drive, use the same connection as before.

6. **Connect a power cable to the CD or DVD drive.**

7. **Secure the CD or DVD drive in the drive bay with screws.**

8. **Replace the computer's cover. Be sure not to snag the cover on any cables.**

9. **Plug the computer in and turn it on.**

   Windows recognizes the new CD or DVD drive and prompts you for the installation disk that came with the drive. If Windows doesn't prompt you, put the installation disk in the floppy drive and run the installation program.

Installing a Tape Backup Unit

Tape backup units are great devices for making copies of important information. If something happens to the original files on your hard drive — the drive may fail or the files may be inadvertently erased — you can restore the files from the copy you stored on tape. Installing a tape backup unit is very similar to installing a hard drive or CD-ROM drive. If you have a USB drive, just plug it in and feed the computer the installation disk when asked for it.

Follow these steps to install an external parallel printer port tape backup unit:

1. **Turn off the computer and unplug it.**

2. **If necessary, unplug the printer cable from the back of the computer.**

3. **Plug one end of the tape backup unit's cable into the printer port on the back of the computer. Plug the other end of the cable into the tape backup unit.**

4. **Plug the printer cable into the printer pass-through port on the tape backup unit.**

5. **Plug in the tape backup unit's power cable and turn it on.**

6. **Plug in the computer and turn it on. Run the installation program that came with the tape backup unit.**

Installing an internal tape backup unit is very similar to installing an internal CD-ROM drive. Follow these steps:

1. **Turn off the computer and unplug it.**

2. **Remove the computer's cover.**

3. **Slide the tape backup unit into an empty drive bay.**

   On some systems, you must remove a piece of plastic that covers the empty drive bay.

4. **Connect one of the IDE/EIDE controller cable connections to the tape backup unit.**

   Some tape units come with a replacement controller cable that enables you to plug the ribbon cable from the tape drive into the connector in the new controller cable. Other tape units simply use one of the IDE/EIDE drive controller cables. Make sure that the red stripe on the cable matches up with pin 1 on the connector.

5. **Connect a power cable to the tape backup unit.**

6. **Secure the tape backup unit in the drive bay with screws.**

7. **Replace the computer's cover. Be sure not to snag the cover on any cables.**

**Book VIII
Chapter 4**

Drives and Adapters

8. **Plug the computer in and turn it on.**

   Windows recognizes the new tape backup unit and prompts you to feed it the installation disk that came with the drive. If Windows doesn't prompt you for the installation disk, put the installation disk in the floppy drive and run the installation program.

Installing a Zip Drive

If you have a lot of information (up to 250MB) that you want to back up or move from one computer to another, a Zip drive can be a very useful tool. Most Zip drives are external and connect to either the parallel printer port or the USB port.

To install the USB version, just plug in the Zip drive's power cord and connect the USB cable to both the Zip drive and the computer. The computer recognizes that a USB device has been connected and prompts for the installation disk. Insert the disk and follow the on-screen prompts. Follow these steps to install an external Zip drive with the parallel printer port version:

1. **Turn off the computer and unplug it.**

2. **If necessary, unplug the printer cable from the back of the computer.**

3. **Plug one end of the Zip drive's cable into the printer port on the back of the computer. Plug the other end of the cable into the Zip drive.**

4. **Plug the printer cable into the printer pass-through port on the Zip drive.**

5. **Plug in the Zip drive's power cable and turn it on.**

6. **Plug in the computer and turn it on.**

7. **Run the installation program that came with the Zip drive.**

Follow these steps to install an internal Zip drive:

1. **Turn off the computer and unplug it.**

2. **Remove the computer's cover.**

3. **Slide the Zip drive into an empty drive bay.**

   On some systems, you must remove a piece of plastic that covers the empty drive bay.

4. **Connect one of the IDE/EIDE controller cable connections to the Zip drive.**

Make sure that the red stripe on the cable matches up with pin 1 on the connector.

5. **Connect a power cable to the Zip drive.**

6. **Secure the Zip drive in the drive bay with screws.**

7. **Replace the computer's cover. Be sure not to snag the cover on any cables.**

8. **Plug the computer in and turn it on.**

Windows may recognize the new Zip drive and prompt for the installation disk that came with the drive. If it doesn't, put the installation disk in the floppy drive and run the installation program.

Some of the newer, affordable drives and media that are on the market today may provide you with more economical data storage. Check into the products from OnStream (www.onstream.com) and Castlewood (www.castlewood.com) for more choices.

Understanding the Different Kinds of Adapters

All adapters are not created equal. Adapters come in various shapes and sizes with varying features and functions. This section helps you sort them out.

Adapters are often called *adapter cards,* or just plain *cards.* Some people even refer to them as *expansion cards.* These terms all refer to the same thing: a piece of hardware that plugs into the computer's innards and adds to the computer's capabilities.

Video adapters

Video adapters take the 0s and 1s that your computer likes to sling around and translate them into text and pictures that can be displayed on your monitor. Most computers come with either a built-in *video adapter* — a set of computer chips soldered onto the motherboard — or a video adapter installed in one of the computer's expansion bus slots. Prices for video adapters start at about $50.

Sound adapters

Most computers built in the last few years include a sound card, which allows your computer to play sounds and music. You also need a pair of speakers to plug into the sound card. If your computer didn't come with a sound card or if your computer has a sound problem, you can add a new sound card. You can purchase a bottom-of-the-barrel sound card for as little as $20.

Knowing which type of adapter to use

Before you buy a video adapter or sound adapter, make sure that the card will work with your computer by matching the card to the type of connector that your computer has.

You need to have one of these three types of connectors to add a graphics or sound adapter to your computer:

✦ If you bought your computer in the last couple of years, the computer probably has a mixture of *Peripheral Component Interface* (PCI) bus connectors and *Industry Standard Architecture* (ISA) bus connectors. You can use these connectors for both sound and graphics cards.

✦ Some new computers have a special graphics card port called an *Accelerated Graphics Port* (AGP) slot. This connector only accepts an AGP video card.

✦ If you have an older computer, it may not have a PCI or AGP connector. You will probably have to install an ISA-type video or sound card.

Sounds cards are available with either ISA- or PCI-type connectors. Make sure that you buy the correct type for your computer. If you're unsure of the type of sound card that you need, check your computer's documentation. If that doesn't provide the information you need, you may have to contact the computer's manufacturer.

If you're unsure about this connector business, check your computer's documentation.

Troubleshooting Your Sound or Video Adapter

Here are some things to check if your sound adapter isn't working the way you expect it to:

✦ Check all the cables. Make sure that the speaker cables are plugged into the proper port on the back of the sound adapter.

✦ Turn up the volume on the speakers if they have an external volume control. Also, turn up the volume with the on-screen control located in the lower-right corner of the screen.

✦ Double-click the volume control in the lower-right corner of your screen and drag the CD volume slider up. If your sound adapter won't play your music CDs but otherwise seems to function, you probably have the CD volume turned down.

✦ If none of these solutions solves your problem, reinstall the software that came with the sound adapter.

Here are some things to check if your video adapter isn't working the way you expect it to:

✦ Make sure that the monitor cable is securely attached to the video adapter. A loose cable can cause distorted video.

✦ Try adjusting the brightness and contrast controls on the monitor.

✦ Check the settings in the Display Properties dialog box. You may have set the display incorrectly. Right-click the Windows desktop and choose Properties. Look in the Settings tab and be sure that the Colors setting is compatible with your video card and the Screen Area settings are within the limits of your video adapter and monitor.

✦ Reinstall the software that came with the video adapter.

Installing a New Adapter

As soon as you have the correct new video or sound card, you can install it. If your computer already has a video adapter or sound adapter built in to the motherboard, you have to disable the old adapter before installing the new one. Refer to the documentation that came with your computer for instructions on disabling the built-in adapter.

To install a new video or sound adapter, follow these steps:

1. **Turn off the computer. Disconnect the monitor from the back of the computer. Unplug the power cable and remove the computer's cover.**

2. **Find and remove the old video or sound adapter. Remove the retaining screw that holds the adapter card in place and gently pull the adapter card from the slot.**

3. **If the adapter card that you're installing is the same type as the one you just removed, insert it into the same connector. Otherwise, find an empty connector that matches the connector tabs on your new adapter card and remove the retaining screw and slot cover. Insert the adapter card into the slot.**

**Book VIII
Chapter 4**

Drives and Adapters

4. **Install the retaining screw to secure the adapter card to the computer's case.**

5. **Replace the computer's cover and plug in the computer's power cord.**

6. **Connect the monitor's signal cable to the connector on the video adapter.**

7. **Turn on the monitor and the computer.**

With a little luck, Windows recognizes the new adapter card and sets up the card for you. If it doesn't, you need to properly introduce your new adapter card to Windows. Follow these steps:

1. **Choose Start⇨Settings⇨Control Panel, and double-click the Add New Hardware icon.**

   The first screen of the Add New Hardware Wizard informs you that you should close all programs before continuing.

2. **Save your work and close any open programs and then click Next.**

   The Add New Hardware Wizard politely informs you that it will search for new devices.

3. **Click Next.**

   Windows displays a list of new devices that it finds.

4. **Click the name of the device that you just installed and then click Next.**

   If you don't see your video or sound adapter card listed, skip to Step 6.

5. **Click the Finish button.**

   You're done! Windows sets up your new adapter card. You will probably have to restart your computer after it is finished.

6. **If you didn't see your video or sound adapter card listed under Devices, select the No, the Device Isn't in the List option button and click Next.**

   Windows offers to search for new hardware that isn't Plug and Play–compatible or that it could not find an appropriate driver for.

7. **Make sure that the Yes (Recommended) option button is selected and click Next.**

8. **Click Next again to begin the search.**

   If Windows finds the new video or sound adapter card, you're done.

9. **If it doesn't find the card, Windows tells you so and instructs you to click Next to manually install the device. Click Next.**

The Add New Hardware Wizard displays a list of hardware types for you to choose from, as shown in Figure 4-1.

Figure 4-1:
Types of
hardware to
install.

10. **Select Display Adapters or scroll down to Sound, Video and Game Controllers if you are installing a sound card and click Next.**

11. **Select the manufacturer and model of your new video adapter card and click Next.**

12. **Click Next again to install the software for your new video adapter card.**

13. **If your manufacturer or model is not listed, click the Have Disk button.**

14. **Insert the floppy or CD-ROM that came with your video adapter card. If you insert a disk, click OK to install the software. If you insert a CD-ROM, you must type the name of the CD-ROM drive (usually D:) and click OK.**

15. **Be prepared to restart your system after Windows finishes installing the software for your video adapter card.**

**Book VIII
Chapter 4**

Drives and Adapters

Chapter 5: Monitors, Mice, and Keyboards

In This Chapter
- Maintaining your monitor
- Choosing and installing a new monitor
- Adding a mouse, trackball, or touchpad
- Adding a new keyboard

You spend the great majority of your computer time looking at the monitor, so keeping your monitor properly adjusted pays dividends. The same goes for your computer's other essential components — if your mouse doesn't seem to be able to keep up with you or your keyboard is goofed up — you may discover that instead of replacing your computer entirely, all you need are the right accessories. This chapter can help you add some of those bells and whistles to your system.

Maintaining Your Monitor

Many monitor problems can easily be solved with the right adjustments. The hardest part is making the correct diagnosis. You can make several small changes to your display without spending a ton of money, but if you do discover that your monitor is shot, we show you how to replace it later in the chapter.

Adjusting your monitor's display settings

If you have a small computer screen, you may be surprised to find out that you can change the amount of information that your screen displays. No, you can't make the screen bigger — without replacing it, that is. But you can make everything on the screen a bit smaller so that you can fit more on-screen.

All you have to do is adjust the monitor's resolution. *Resolution* is the term for the number of dots of color (called *pixels*) that your monitor displays. Resolution is displayed in the following format: 640 x 480. The first number refers to the number of pixels displayed horizontally across the screen, and the second refers to the number of pixels displayed vertically down the screen. The higher the numbers, the more information that's displayed on your computer screen. And the more information that's displayed on your computer screen, the smaller the information has to be. Refer to Table 5-1 to see how resolution affects your computer's display.

Table 5-1	Monitor Resolutions	
Number of Pixels	*Relative Size of Information*	*Readability*
640 x 480	Large	Less information, but easy on the eyes
800 x 600	Medium	A compromise between amount of information and size
1,024 x 768	Small	More information but can be tough on the eyes
1,280 x 1,024 (or more)	Tiny	Suitable for 19-inch or larger screens

How attractive a resolution looks on your computer depends a lot on the size of your screen. Unless you have eagle eyes, any setting higher than the ones listed in Table 5-2 are too small to read comfortably.

Table 5-2	Screen Size and Resolution Settings
Screen Size	*Suggested Resolution Setting*
14-inch	640 x 480
15-inch	800 x 600
17-inch	1,024 x 768
19-inch or larger	1,280 x 1,024 (or 1,600 x 1,200)

To change your screen's resolution, follow these steps:

1. **Right-click a blank area of the desktop and choose Properties from the shortcut menu that appears.**

   The Display Properties dialog box appears.

2. **Click the Settings tab.**

3. **In the Screen Area box, drag the slider control to the left or right to decrease or increase the resolution, respectively (see Figure 5-1).**

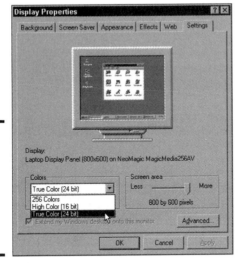

Figure 5-1:
Use the Display Properties dialog box to adjust colors and resolution.

4. **Click OK.**

5. **If you see a dialog box informing you that you must restart your computer, close any open applications and click Yes.**

   Your computer restarts with the new resolution setting.

Depending on your video adapter card, you may have the option of changing the settings without restarting. If you see an option labeled Apply Setting without Restarting, you can select it to change your display setting without having to shutdown and restart the computer.

Adjusting your monitor's colors

In addition to the resolution, you can adjust the number of colors that the screen displays. The number of colors ranges from 16 to over 4 billion depending on your video card and monitor. So if your monitor's reds aren't so red and its blues aren't so blue, try making some minor adjustments before you replace it.

Here is how to change the number of colors that your screen can display:

1. **Right-click a blank area of the desktop and choose Properties from the shortcut menu.**

   The Display Properties dialog box appears (refer to Figure 5-1).

2. **Click the Settings tab.**

3. **Select the desired setting from the Colors drop-down list and then click OK.**

   Remember, the colors that you can see on your computer depend on your video card and monitor; Table 5-3 shows you how many colors you get with each option. Unless you're working on photo-realistic images, the 16-bit setting works just fine.

4. **If you see a dialog box informing you that you must restart your computer, close any open applications and click Yes.**

   Your computer restarts with the new color setting.

Table 5-3	Number of Color Options
Setting	*Number of Colors*
16-bit	65,000
24-bit	16 million
32-bit	4 billion

When Your Monitor Needs to Be Replaced

Maybe your monitor is too small and your colors look terrible. Maybe your monitor clashes with your office décor. If you decide to replace your monitor for any reason, you have a lot of choices on what kind of monitor to get. The good news is that the technology is great, and your colors and graphics will look good. Also, getting rid of your old monitor and replacing it with a new one is one of the simplest upgrades you can do.

Deciding on a new monitor

If you're thinking about buying a new computer monitor, you have these choices:

✦ The traditional CRT monitor runs about $125 for the cheapest 14-inch models to around a thousand dollars or more for 21-inch and larger models.

✦ The newer flat panel LCD monitors start off at about $1,000 for a 15-inch model and go up from there.

✦ A short-depth or short-neck monitor (recently introduced) works just like a regular CRT monitor, but it takes up significantly less desk space. Expect to pay a premium for this feature.

Buy the best-looking monitor you can afford. LCD technology is improving all the time, and these screens are becoming popular because they provide crisp, clear, and distortion-free images, while taking up very little desktop real estate. LCD screens also consume less than half the energy of their CRT counterparts.

Replacing your monitor

Your old monitor has passed on to a better place, and you've just purchased your new one. Here's how to get the old one disconnected and install the new one.

To disconnect an old monitor, follow these steps:

1. **Turn off your computer and monitor.**

2. **Unplug the power cord and disconnect the monitor cable from the back of the computer.**

3. **Remove the old monitor from your work area.**

To install a new monitor, make sure that your computer is off and then follow these steps:

1. **Place the new monitor where the old one has been.**

2. **Connect the new monitor's signal cable to the video port on the back of the computer, using the 15-pin D-connector shown in Figure 5-2.**

Figure 5-2:
A 15-pin
D-connector
plug.

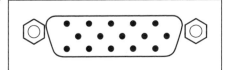

3. **Plug in the monitor's power cord.**

4. **Turn on the monitor and computer.**

If your new monitor comes with any special features, make sure that you install the software. Follow these steps to install the new monitor's software:

1. **Right-click a blank area of the desktop and choose Properties from the shortcut menu.**

2. **Click the Settings tab and then click the Advanced button.**

**Book VIII
Chapter 5**

Monitors, Mice, and
Keyboards

3. **In the dialog box that appears, click the Monitor tab and then click the Change button.**

4. **Select the manufacturer of your monitor from the Manufacturers list of the Select Device dialog box.**

   You may get the Update Device Driver Wizard (shown in Figure 5-3), which will search for new drivers for the monitor. If the monitor you purchased came with a CD or diskette, insert it and choose Specify the Location of the Driver (Advanced) option. If no software came with the monitor, choose the Automatic Search for a Better Driver (Recommended) option and be prepared to insert your Windows CD. Click Next and follow the instructions.

Figure 5-3:
Choose the manufac-
turer and model from this dialog box.

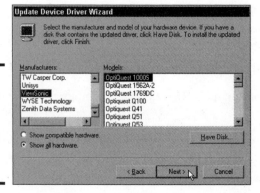

5. **Select the model of your monitor from the Models list.**

6. **Click OK twice to close both dialog boxes.**

Adding a Mouse, a Trackball, or a Touchpad

Your mouse probably takes more abuse than just about any other part of your computer. After your mouse finally gives up the ghost, just go to your favorite computer store and buy a mouse of the same type. Prices can vary widely for a mouse — anywhere from about $5 to $100. Before you spend that money, make sure that your mouse is truly dead. Sometimes, it is just a matter of the mouse cord coming loose from the back of the computer. Other times you just need to remove the ball from the underbelly of the mouse and clean out the cat hair.

You have several available options if you're interested in replacing your machine's pointing device. You can purchase the following:

✦ **A traditional mouse,** which is about the size of the palm of your hand. Laptop users should look for some of the newer, smaller mice that fit easily into their carrying case. If you don't like your mouse being tethered to the box, check into wireless mouse options.

✦ **A trackball,** which is essentially an upside down mouse (see Figure 5-4). The trackball device remains stationary while you manipulate the ball to move the pointer. Trackballs, like traditional mice, can come with either a serial- or PS/2-type connector. Many trackballs also come with the equivalent of a scroll button.

✦ **A touchpad,** which is a device with a square of pressure-sensitive material and two buttons. You slide your finger around on the pad to move the pointer. You most commonly find touchpads on laptop computers, but touchpads are also available for desktop computers and may come embedded in some keyboards (see Figure 5-4).

✦ **Digitizing tablets** are gaining popularity, especially among the artsy-types. By using a pen stylus on top of a tablet, you move the mouse as if you were drawing with a pen. You can pay anywhere from $50 to several hundred dollars for high-end tablets used by engineers who use computers for drafting.

✦ **The Renaissance mouse** is a joystick-type pointing device from 3M that moves on the desktop like a traditional mouse, but is more ergonomical because your wrist remains upright. The rocker button on the top of the joystick handle enables you to right and left click.

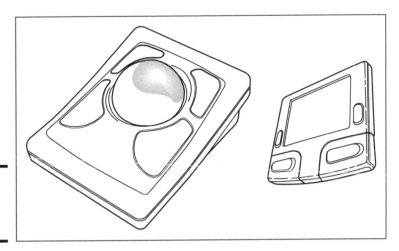

Figure 5-4:
A trackball and touch-pad.

Trackballs, touchpads, and digitizing tablets tend to cost a bit more than mere mice. Some computer stores put these items on display so that you can try them out before you buy. If your local computer store doesn't, ask to try the model in which you're interested.

Before you replace your pointing device, you need to know which of the basic varieties of plugs your current mouse has — PS/2, serial type, or USB. Keep the following in mind:

✦ Serial mouse plugs are trapezoidal in shape and have nine little pins. They plug in to your computer through a *serial port* (or socket).

✦ PS/2 mouse plugs are easy to spot because they are small and round and they plug into a circular mouse port.

✦ If you're replacing one of the preceding with another just like it, buy a device with the same kind of connector (serial or PS/2).

✦ If you have a mouse port, buy a device with a PS/2 type connector.

✦ If you have only a serial connector on the back of your computer, get a serial type.

✦ If you have other needs for your serial port, you can opt for the new USB pointing devices. You can save the serial port for other devices like personal label printers.

Here's how to add or replace a mouse, trackball, or touchpad:

1. **Turn off your computer to avoid damaging it when you plug in the device.**

   Get in the habit of turning off your computer whenever you connect or disconnect components. The exception is with USB devices. Most of the time, Windows should be running for the device to be recognized automatically.

2. **Plug the device's connector into the USB port, mouse port, or serial port on the back of the computer.**

3. **Turn the computer on if you are adding a device that goes into the mouse port or serial port.**

If you're replacing a pointing device with another, different type of device (for example, you're replacing a mouse with a trackball or a trackball with a mouse) and the new device doesn't work, you may have to install some software for it.

You know instantly that you need to install software because the software comes with the package. Just locate and run the device's installation program and follow the directions. You will probably have to reboot your computer after running the installation program before the device will work.

Upgrading Your Keyboard

Sometimes keyboards develop sticky keys or may cause your wrists pain when you type. If so, you may want to upgrade to a new keyboard. Keyboards come with either a large, round, AT-style connector (for older computers) or a small, round, PS/2-style connector (for newer computers). When you shop for a replacement keyboard, make sure that you buy one with the same type of connector as your current keyboard or at least one that comes with a small adapter for the connection on your computer.

 Be sure to try out any keyboard before you buy it. Each keyboard has a different feel. On some keyboards, you have to press firmly to type. On others, you barely have to touch the keys. Find one that is comfortable for you. Here is how to install a new keyboard:

1. **Turn off your computer to avoid damaging it and then unplug the old keyboard.**

2. **Plug in the new keyboard.**

   Be sure that you don't plug the keyboard into the mouse port by mistake. It won't cause any damage, but the keyboard won't work.

3. **Turn the computer on.**

   If you're replacing your keyboard with the same type of keyboard, you're finished. If you're installing a new type of keyboard — one that has additional functionality — proceed to the next step.

4. **Put the keyboard's floppy disk or CD into the drive and run the installation program.**

   You may need to restart your computer after you perform this step.

Chapter 6: Upgrading and Troubleshooting Modems

In This Chapter

✔ **Troubleshooting modems**

✔ **Installing an internal modem**

✔ **Installing an external modem**

✔ **Installing the modem's software drivers**

*I*n this chapter, we show you how to handle modem malfunctions and walk you through the process of installing the hardware devices you need to get your modem running. Refer to Book III, Chapter 1, for detailed information on the types of modems available, as well as additional high-speed alternatives such as ISDN, DSL, cable, and wireless.

Troubleshooting Modem Problems

Here are some things to check if your modem doesn't work the way you expect it to:

✦ Check all the cables. Make sure that the telephone cord is plugged into the phone jack on the wall and the line jack on the modem.

✦ For internal modems, be sure that the line coming from the wall is plugged into the line port and the line that goes to the optional attached phone is plugged into the phone port. It does make a difference on most modems.

✦ For external modems, ensure that the serial or USB cable is securely connected to both the modem and the computer. Also, make sure that the modem has power and is turned on.

✦ Verify that the phone line is working. Plug a telephone into the line and dial a number.

✦ Try using a different telephone cord. The one you are using may be damaged even if you can't tell by looking at it.

✦ Be sure that you are dialing the correct number. If you are calling the wrong number, having a perfectly working modem won't do you any good.

+ Disable call waiting by dialing *70 before the number. Don't worry. As soon as you disconnect, call waiting is reactivated.

+ Make sure that no one picks up an extension phone while your modem is in use.

Installing a New Modem

If you can't get your modem to do what it should be doing or if your PC doesn't have a modem and you want one, all the information you need about installing one is right here.

Installing a new modem involves two separate procedures:

+ First, you must physically install the internal modem or connect the external modem.

+ Second, you have to introduce the modem to Windows by installing the appropriate software.

Installing or replacing an internal modem

To install an internal modem, follow these steps:

1. **Turn off and unplug your computer.**

2. **Remove your computer's cover.**

3. **Remove the cover from the expansion slot where you intend to install the modem or remove the old modem.**

4. **Insert the modem into the expansion slot.**

5. **Replace the computer's cover.**

6. **Attach the telephone cord from the telephone jack to the line port on the modem.**

7. **Plug in and turn on the computer.**

Installing an external serial-port modem

Follow these steps to install an external serial-port modem:

1. **Turn off your computer.**

2. **Connect the serial cable to the modem and to the serial port on the back of the computer.**

Some inexpensive modems have the serial cable permanently attached to the back of the modem.

3. **Connect the phone cord from the phone jack on the wall to the line jack on the modem.**

4. **Connect the modem's power cord.**

5. **Turn on the modem and computer.**

Installing an external USB-port modem

Use the following steps to install an external USB-port modem:

1. **With the computer on, plug in the modem's power cord and turn on the modem.**

2. **Connect the USB cable to the modem.**

3. **Connect the other end of the USB cable to the USB port on the computer.**

   Most computers have the USB port located on the back of the computer, but a few have the USB port located on the front.

Installing the software drivers

After you have installed and/or connected your modem, you have to tell Windows what you have done:

1. **Choose Start⇨Settings⇨Control Panel and double-click the Add New Hardware icon.**

   The first screen of the Add New Hardware Wizard informs you that you should close all programs before continuing. If you are installing a modem through the USB port, Windows recognizes the hardware addition automatically.

2. **Save your work, close any open programs, and click Next.**

   The Add New Hardware Wizard informs you that it will search for new devices.

3. **Click Next.**

   Windows displays a list of new devices that it found.

4. **Click the name of the device that you just installed and then click Next.**

   Skip to Step 6 if you don't see your modem listed.

5. **Click the Finish button, and Windows sets up your new modem.**

   You're done! You will probably have to restart your computer.

6. **If you didn't see your modem listed, select the No, the Device Isn't in the List option button and click Next.**

   Windows offers to search for new hardware that isn't Plug and Play or for which a driver is not found.

7. **Make sure that the Yes (Recommended) option button is selected and click Next. Then click Next again to begin the search.**

   If your modem came with a CD or diskette, insert it so that Windows can find the appropriate drivers provided by the manufacturer. Otherwise, put the Windows CD in so that the driver may be found.

8. **If Windows finds the new modem, you're finished. If it doesn't find it, Windows tells you so and instructs you to click Next to install the device manually. Click Next.**

   The Add New Hardware Wizard displays a list of hardware types for you to choose from.

9. **Select Modem and click Next.**

10. **Select the manufacturer and model of your modem and click Next.**

11. **Click Next again to install the software for your modem.**

12. **If your manufacturer or model is not listed, click the Have Disk button.**

13. **Insert the floppy or CD that came with your modem. If you inserted a floppy, click OK to install the software. If you inserted a CD, you must type the name of the CD-ROM drive (usually D:) and click OK.**

   Be prepared to restart your system after Windows finishes installing the software for your modem.

Chapter 7: Printers and Scanners

In This Chapter
✔ Connecting a printer

✔ Installing printer software

✔ Troubleshooting printers

✔ Installing a scanner

Although the Internet is now a very popular means of sharing information, there seems to be no replacement for the convenience of the printed page. This chapter helps you install your printer and provides troubleshooting information for when you encounter printing difficulties. (For information on selecting a printer for your specific needs, refer to Book I, Chapter 5.) This chapter also provides information on adding a digital scanner to your computer. A digital scanner is a great, inexpensive tool for getting pictures into your computer without having to spend hundreds of dollars on a digital camera.

Connecting a Printer to Your Computer

Back in the Dark Ages of personal computing, connecting printers to the computer's serial port was common. Today, printers almost invariably connect to the computer's parallel printer port. The parallel printer port is the 25-pin D-shaped connector on the back of your computer. Some new printers connect to the computer's USB — Universal Serial Bus port, however. To install a printer that has a parallel port

1. **Turn off the computer and existing printer if you have one.**

2. **Disconnect the printer cable from the back of the printer and remove the existing printer.**

3. **Connect the cable to the centronics printer port on the back or side of the new printer.**

   The *centronics printer port* found on the back of the printer is about the same size as the printer port on the back of the computer. However, instead of having 25 holes, it has little gold teeth that look sort of like a zipper.

4. **Plug in the printer's power cable.**

5. **Turn on the printer and computer.**

After you connect the printer and turn on the printer and computer, you must tell Windows about your new printer. Refer to the following section on adding and removing printer drivers.

If you have a scanner connected to the computer's parallel port, plug the printer cable into the scanner's pass-through printer port. A *pass-through port* is simply a printer port on the back of the scanner. You can plug the printer into the scanner and plug the scanner into the back of the computer. This setup enables you to use both your scanner and printer without having to disconnect/reconnect cables. If your scanner doesn't have a pass-through printer port, you must disconnect your scanner before connecting your printer.

Installing a USB printer is easier yet. No need to turn off the computer — just connect the USB cable to the printer and to the computer's USB port. Windows usually recognizes the printer and attempts to install the software for the printer automatically.

If you already have devices connected to all of your USB ports — many computers have two USB ports — you can purchase a USB hub that lets you connect additional USB devices.

Adding and Removing a Printer Driver

Before you can use a printer that you connect to your computer, the printer and computer must be properly introduced. You accomplish this feat by installing a bit of software, known as a *printer driver,* that tells Windows how to control the printer. Make sure that you have handy your Windows installation CD-ROM, along with any other disks or CD-ROMs that came with your printer.

Follow these steps to install a new printer driver:

1. **Choose Start⇨Settings⇨Printers and double-click the Add Printer icon.**

The Add Printer Wizard displays.

2. **Click Next.**

The Add Printer Wizard wants to know if the printer is attached to your computer or some other computer on the network.

3. **Select the Local Printer option and click Next.**

4. **Select the manufacturer and model of your printer from the Manufacturers and Printers lists (see Figure 7-1) and then click Next.**

Windows asks where the printer is connected.

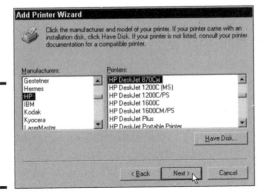

Figure 7-1:
The
Manufac-
turers and
Printers
lists.

5. **Make sure that you select the LPT1 Port option and click Next.**

6. **Accept the suggested name for your printer or type a new name.**

7. **Click the Yes (Recommended) option to set the printer as the default and click Next.**

   Setting the printer as the default printer lets Windows know that this is the printer you will always print to unless you tell Windows otherwise.

8. **Accept the default option to print a test page and click Finish.**

9. **Windows may ask for your Windows CD-ROM. If so, insert your Windows CD-ROM and click OK.**

   Windows installs the printer driver and prints a test page.

10. **If the test page prints properly, click Yes in the dialog box that appears.**

    That's it — you're finished!

    If the test page doesn't print as expected, click No to start the Print Troubleshooter. Printer problems are discussed in the next section.

Fixing Common Printer Problems

If you have a printer, sooner or later you'll experience some type of printer problem. These problems generally fall into two categories. Either the printer doesn't print anything, or the printer prints nonsensical garbage.

If your printer won't print

If you see an error window, or if the printer just plain refuses to print anything:

   ✦ Ensure that the printer is plugged in and turned on (sounds obvious, but you never know).

✦ Check the connections between the printer and the computer. Sometimes they work loose just enough to prevent the computer from talking to the printer.

✦ If your printer has an Online button, make sure that it is on.

✦ Check to see if the printer has paper. If the printer has paper, but still won't print, the printer may be jammed. Open the cover and remove any paper stuck inside.

✦ Make sure that you haven't run out of ink or laser toner. Many printers refuse to print if something is empty.

✦ Make sure that you have told your application the correct printer to print to. If you are on a network, you may be merrily printing away to a printer in another location.

If your printer won't stop printing

Occasionally, printers have just the opposite problem. They print plenty, but everything that comes out looks like hieroglyphics. Here are some things to try:

✦ Verify that you have selected the correct brand of printer in your application's Print dialog box. If you tell your program that you have a Stoneprinter III but you really have a PaperEater Deluxe connected to your computer, the program won't know how to communicate with the printer.

✦ Try printing from another program, such as WordPad. If that works, you probably have a problem with your software. Check your printer setup in the software that won't print. You may have to dig out your software documentation for this one.

If these hints don't solve your problem, you can try the Windows troubleshooter for help. Here is how to get started with the Print Troubleshooter:

1. **Choose Start⇨Help.**

Windows 98 users should click the Contents tab.

2. **Click Troubleshooting.**

3. **Click Hardware and System Device Problems from the list on the left.**

Windows 98 users click Windows 98 Troubleshooters to expand the topics.

4. **Click Hardware, Memory & Others.**

In the Windows 98 Troubleshooters topic, click the word Print to start the Windows 98 Print Troubleshooter. Follow the steps provided by the Print Troubleshooter.

5. **From the listing on the left, choose Printing Troubleshooter.**

In the window on the right, begin the troubleshooting process by clicking the option that resembles your problem.

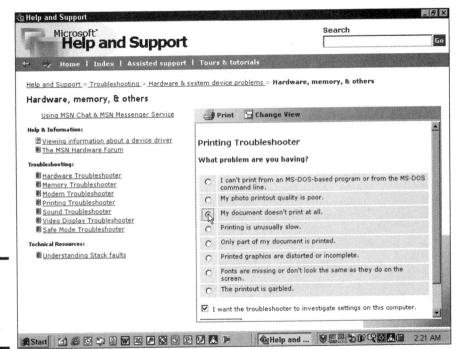

Figure 7-2:
Specific
printing
problem
options.

If you're using Windows 95, choose Start⇨Help and click the Index tab. Then type **printer problems** and press Enter. The print troubleshooter jumps into action and guides you through the process of diagnosing and fixing printer problems.

Adding a Digital Scanner

A scanner is a device that captures images of pictures, documents, or any fairly flat object — and saves those images in electronic format. Additionally, *Optical Character Recognition* (OCR) software is available or may have come with your scanner to convert images of text documents into editable text files.

Most scanners built for home use connect to your computer's printer port. You may also want to make sure that your scanner has a *printer pass-through port,* which enables you to connect both the scanner and the printer at the same time.

Some new scanners connect to your computer's *Universal Serial Bus* (USB) port. USB ports can support up to 127 devices, whereas your parallel port can support only one or two. USB ports can transfer information at a faster rate than parallel ports. If your computer has a USB port, consider buying one of these devices. Also, some printers don't like having something between them and the parallel port. That includes switch boxes, Zip drives, and scanners. Check the documentation of the device that will be connected to the scanner to be sure that everything will work as you want. Installing a USB scanner is straightforward — no need to turn off the computer or disconnect the printer. Plug in the power cord to the scanner and power outlet, and then connect the USB cable to the scanner and to the computer's USB port. Install the software that comes with the scanner. Here is how to connect your new parallel scanner:

1. **Turn off the computer.**

2. **If you have a printer, turn it off and disconnect the printer cable from the back of the computer.**

3. **Connect the scanner's data cable to the back of the scanner and to the printer port on the computer.**

4. **Plug in the scanner's power cable.**

5. **Plug the printer into the scanner's printer pass-through port.**

   This method enables you to print to your printer without having to disconnect the scanner and reconnect the printer.

6. **Turn on the printer, scanner, and computer.**

7. **Install your scanner's software.**

Refer to the scanner's documentation for instructions on installing the software. Most scanners include software to tell the computer how to communicate with the scanner as well as some software for manipulating the scanned images. Be prepared to restart your computer after installing the software.

Index

Book IX

Home Networking

The 5th Wave —By Rich Tennant

WIRED HOME OF THE FUTURE

@RICHTENNANT

"I'm setting preferences – do you want Oriental or Persian carpets in the living room?"

Contents at a Glance

Chapter 1: Understanding and Planning a Home Network

In This Chapter

✔ **Finding out about computer networks**

✔ **Defining your networking goals**

✔ **Planning your network**

✔ **Considering computer contents**

*Y*ou may be wondering why anyone would be interested in setting up his or her own home computer network. If you have two or more computers in your home, you can *network,* or connect, the computers together so that you can share files, disk space, Internet access, and more with any number of other individuals in your family. Imagine being able to print using the printer connected to the computer a couple of bedrooms down without leaving your desk, or using one computer to send e-mail via the Internet while your teenager is surfing the Web on another computer, all the while using the same modem, Internet connection, and Internet account. An efficient home network can save you money by letting you share expensive equipment like printers and CD-ROM drives with other members of your family.

The benefits seem pretty obvious, but you may be concerned that setting up a home computer network can end up being a rather complicated affair. The sections in this chapter show you that setting up a home network is not at all as complicated as it sounds, after you understand some of the basics of computer networking.

Peer-to-Peer Networking

Usually when people speak of a home computer network, they are referring to a *peer-to-peer network,* the most common type of home computer network. So-called *client/server networks,* where one powerful computer provides resources to other less-powerful computers, do offer an alternative networking method, but they are typically found in business situations where more than ten computers are networked. For the purposes of home computer networking, then, peer-to-peer networks are the more practical solution.

In a peer-to-peer network, all computers are on a level playing field in terms of their participation in the network. Each computer can still work alone — run its own programs, save files, print (if it has a printer attached), run a CD-ROM (if it has a CD-ROM drive) — but, with the help of a bit of cable, some software, and a few connections, each computer now has access to the other computers on the peer-to-peer network and can share its resources with the others. These resources include files, folders, hard drives, CD-ROM drives, and printers.

Figure 1-1 illustrates an example of a peer-to-peer network. The Windows computers are connected to each other. The laser printer is connected to one computer, but everyone on the network can use it.

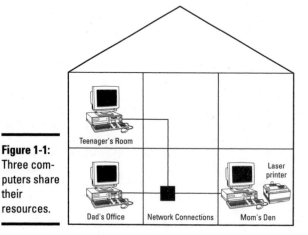

Figure 1-1:
Three computers share their resources.

Defining Your Goals

You need to set network goals to help determine what networking hardware and software you'll use to build your system. You must consider equipment expense, network speed, the layout of the network, and your family's use of the network. Take an inventory of your current hardware and determine what equipment is viable for network use and what equipment you may want to replace.

Consider the following when planning your networking goals:

✦ **Find out the programs each person wants to run.** Check the minimum requirements of these programs and make sure that each computer has the power, memory, hard drive space, and other necessities to run the programs needed. Also, ask what types of programs the users will want for the future.

✦ **Decide which tasks you want to perform on the network.** For example, these tasks may include sharing files and folders, sharing a printer or Internet access, playing network games, transferring music files, and so on.

✦ **Think about how much money you want to spend on the network.** With the available networking equipment and software, you can spend anywhere between $25 and $15,000 on a home network. The amount of money you spend depends on several things: how important the network is in your family's life, how much you will use the network each day, and what results you want from the network.

✦ **Consider all the nice extras you have attached to your computer.** These extras (technically referred to as *peripherals*) can include printers, CD-ROM drives, Iomega Zip drives, modems, and so on. You can share all of this equipment over the network, but you have to make sure that each piece can handle the extra use that comes with being on a network.

Planning Your Network

In planning your network, make sure that each individual computer is in good shape before putting it on a network. You may even consider upgrading some of the features of your computers by adding memory or an extra hard drive or by changing operating systems. Next, decide which *resources* (printers, CD-ROM drives, hard drives, and so on) need to stay on which computer. Finally, decide where to locate each computer and each piece of peripheral equipment before continuing to plan your network.

You may also want to keep a summary sheet, or a needs list, of hardware and software. As you decide the type of networking hardware and software you'll be using, keep a list of what you need. Check each computer to make sure it meets the minimum hardware and software requirements for each software application or networking extra you add. The packaging on most software applications or hardware extras you buy usually lists the minimum system requirements to use them effectively. Remember that "minimum" often means "bare minimum." If you really want your software applications and hardware extras to run properly, make sure that your computer has more than just the bare minimum.

Think about how the network will be laid out in your home. Decide where you will place the fastest computer, where the printer(s) will be located, whether two or more computers can be placed in the same room, and so on. Draw a *network map,* or a sketch of where in the home each computer and peripheral will be located. As you build your network, you can add information about the cabling and networking hardware and other information that will help you add to the network, make repairs, and troubleshoot problems later. List the specifications and programs for each computer.

Looking at Networking Hardware

After you have your networking plan in place, your next step involves purchasing the right kind of networking equipment. In general, you need the following:

✦ **A network interface card (NIC) for each computer on the network.** A *NIC* (pronounced "nick") is a card that plugs into the computer and works to control the flow of information over the network. Each NIC connects to networking cable, which in turn connects to the other NICs on the network to create paths of communication.

✦ *Cables* — **wires that connect the network cards and computers.** You can choose from various types of cables; you can even make network connections using radio frequencies instead of cabling. See Book IX, Chapter 2, for more information on cables.

✦ **Depending on the type of network, you need either a network hub, your house's phone jacks, or a set of transmitters and receivers.** A *network hub* is a centrally located device into which you plug all network cables, a kind of central meeting place for connecting and enabling communication over the network. You use the phone jacks in your home with a different type of network, where your house's phone lines act as the cables for your network. Transmitters and receivers represent yet another network type where radio frequencies, rather than cables, are used to communicate between computers. See Book IX, Chapter 2, for more information.

Putting Your Computer's House in Order

Before you set up a network, consider how each computer uses Windows to keep track of its resources and how each tracking method may affect the other network users. Each network user on a peer-to-peer network can view and use resources from computers other than his or her own. You want to make it easy for the users to find files, folders, printers, and other resources on the network. Be sure that all users are familiar with the My Computer, Windows Explorer, and My Network Places features in Windows. They are invaluable for keeping track of your resources on the network.

In Windows Me, you can browse network connections using the My Network Places icon that's on your Windows desktop. In Windows 95/98, this icon is labeled Network Neighborhood, but they do the same thing.

Network users can view and use shared folders and files on other network computers, so you want to create a system for naming files and folders that makes sense to everyone concerned and makes it easy for people to find what they need. Although certain folders already exist on each computer, you can always add folders that represent specific files, users, and so on. You can create any number of folders to hold your own data, games, and backup files. When creating folders, make sure that you name the folders so that they are easily recognizable.

Leave folders that already exist — such as the Windows folder, Program Files folder, other application folders, and so on — exactly as they are. Never change the name or location of these folders. If you change the name of the Windows folder, for example, the operating system will no longer work.

Consider the following naming guidelines when adding folders to your network:

✦ Long folder names can be difficult to read when viewed in certain windows, such as in the Find Files and Folders dialog box. You end up losing half the folder name.

✦ Keep filenames and folder names consistent. Consider prefacing each folder name or filename with the name of the person who created it.

✦ The My Computer, Windows Explorer, and My Network Places features of Windows list filenames and folder names alphabetically. Keep this in mind when trying to find a file or folder.

✦ Folder names that begin with a number are listed before the alphabetized folder names, and folder names that begin with a symbol are listed before numbered names in this order: #, $, %, &, @.

You can place files in folders named after individual users or specific document types (letters, reports, and so on) or place one user folder inside of another folder (called *nesting*). For example, C:\My Documents\Sue is an example of nested folders where the Sue folder is nested within the My Documents folder.

With filenames, you also have the added luxury of identifying files by using *extensions* (the .doc, .xls, .bmp, or .tif that is automatically added to the filenames of the Word documents, Excel spreadsheets, or image files you create). File extensions make it easier to sort filenames and find the file you want.

By default, Windows hides file extensions of data files that are able to be opened by the programs installed on the system. To view all file extensions, double-click the My Computer icon, then select Tools⇨Folder Options. Select the View tab and look in the list of options in the Advanced Settings window. Uncheck the Hide File Extensions for Known File Types. Click the Reset All Folders button to ensure that every folder you open from now on will have the file extensions showing in their listing.

Windows 98 users will find the Folder Options listed under the View menu. Otherwise, the rest of the procedure above is the same.

Understanding Networked Programs

When planning how best to use your various computer programs across your network, ask yourself these questions:

✦ What are the system requirements for each program?

✦ What are the legal issues involved in using multiple copies of a program?

✦ Which computer on the network is best suited to store all the shared data from multiple users?

Using networked programs

When working on a peer-to-peer network, you still need to install your programs on each computer. By now, you know that a network allows you to share files, but it's important to remember that accessing a shared file from another computer on the network does you no good if you don't have the program necessary to read that file on your own computer. This limitation is why making sure that all the computers on your network can meet the system requirements for a particular program is important. If you can't install a program on one of your computers on the network because the computer doesn't meet the minimum system requirements, you're out of luck. The computer can't "borrow" memory or hard drive space for installing a program from another computer on the network.

Using a program on a network comes with its own special quirks. Users can share the files created from any program (as long as the user's computer has the necessary program installed), but no two users can open the same file at the same time unless the program allows for network file sharing. Normally, if one person is using a file — a word processing, a spreadsheet, an accounting, or other file — and someone else tries to open that same file, a warning dialog box appears. The dialog box states that the file is already in use and asks if the user wants to make a copy of the file. This safeguard ensures that two users don't unwittingly try to edit the same file at the same time.

Certain networkable programs — games, for example — are specifically designed to let two or more people play the game at the same time. Other networkable applications — databases and accounting programs, for example — also try to protect open files, but they take a different approach. These types of programs let two or more people open the same file, but only the person who opened the file first is actually allowed to make any changes to the file. The second person is locked out from making any changes and can only read the file. True network programs, which can be a costly investment, will allow multiple people to access the same file and track changes that both users make.

Understanding licensing

Word processors, spreadsheets, drawing programs, and many games are licensed to one user only. You install these applications on your computer, and only you are licensed to use them. Licensing agreements are issued by the manufacturer and state the legal uses of programs.

Some manufacturers produce network versions of their applications. You can install these programs on multiple machines, depending on the number of licenses you own. Network versions of applications have built-in features that make them efficient and effective over the network. They also contain features that protect the data when in use by more than one person.

You may network a calendar or scheduling program, for example, or an accounting program, a database, or a multi-user game. When purchasing an application, make sure that you check to see if it's a network version and find out about the licensing as well.

Storing shared files

Determine where you will store the data that network users use. Store the data on the most powerful computer you have — the one with the most powerful processor, the largest hard drive, and the most memory — so it can efficiently handle the increased demands that will necessarily come with more people trying to access the same resources. Also, choose a computer that will be turned on most of the time, because people need access to the computer to retrieve data.

Chapter 2: Choosing Equipment and Connecting the Network

In This Chapter

✔ Choosing a networking kit

✔ Buying and installing network cards

✔ Buying and installing a hub

✔ Connecting only two computers

✔ Using traditional cabling to connect

✔ Using phone lines to connect

✔ Using wireless connections

Choosing your network hardware may seem like a daunting task, but it's easier than you think. Many manufacturers make kits for home networking, complete with instructions and all the equipment you need. Alternatively, you can buy network cards and other equipment separately to put together your own networking configuration.

After you've chosen your network hardware, you're ready to tie everything together. This chapter also covers the different ways you can link your network together. You can choose from various types of cabling, the network speed you want, and the ease of installation. The most affordable and common cabling types for home networking are traditional cabling (Ethernet), phone line, and wireless.

Choosing a Networking Kit

You can hire a computer technician or consultant to install your networking equipment, or you can do it yourself. The easiest way to buy and install networking equipment is to buy a networking kit. Starter kits usually contain everything you need to connect the first two computers, and then you can buy any additional equipment you need for connecting more computers to the network. Make sure that you buy your kit from a reputable company. Some companies that make networking kits include Linksys, 3Com, NetGear, and D-Link.

Networking kits include the following:

+ **Network cards** (also called network interface cards or network adapter cards), which are similar to other cards in your computer — such as sound or video cards. A printed electronic circuit board that snaps into an empty slot inside of the computer, the network card connects to a network cable from the back of the computer.

+ **Network cabling,** which connects one computer to another in the network. Cabling also connects printers to the network.

+ **Networking hardware,** which includes the different kinds of equipment you use to complete a network. Depending on the kind of network you choose, you may need different kinds of hardware.

When you buy additional equipment to add to your existing network, you must buy the same type of cards and cabling.

Different networking kits are designed for different types of networks. The type of network you choose depends on how much money you want to spend and how fast you want the network to transfer data between computers. The three types of network kits suitable for home and small business networks are phone line kits, traditional cabling kits, and wireless kits.

Phone line kits

You may want to explore using your telephone wiring for networking your computers together. When you use phone lines, you don't have to install any extra cabling. Phone line kits include networking cards and extra phone cable for connecting each computer to a wall jack.

Phone line networks do run slowly, however. The standard speed for moving data around on a phone line network is 1 megabit per second (or 1 Mbps). If you consider that 1 Mbps is 20 times faster than a 56 kilobits per second (Kbps) modem, it sounds pretty fast. But remember how slowly even a 56 Kbps modem downloads files. Phone line networks are, however, fast enough for general networking, such as sharing small files or printers. If you want to use large graphic files or perform complex calculations regularly over the network, consider a faster networking technology. See also "Using Phone Lines to Connect," later in this chapter.

Following are some other facts to consider about phone line networks:

+ An organization called the HomePNA (Home Phoneline Networking Alliance) works to ensure that all phone line products adhere to certain standards so you're sure to get good quality and reliable service from phone line networking products.

✦ A phone line network can withstand high levels of atmospheric interference (lightning strikes) as well as signal noise from appliances, heaters, and other devices in the home (such as when your refrigerator or furnace kicks on).

✦ You don't need any other networking hardware when you use a phone line network.

Traditional cabling kits

Traditional cabling is called Ethernet. With Ethernet networking, speeds run at either 10 or 100 Mbps. If a network card or cabling is labeled simply *Ethernet,* you can be pretty sure that it will run at only 10 Mbps. To earn the label *Fast Ethernet,* a piece of equipment must be able to run at 100 Mbps. Fast Ethernet isn't something you need for most home networking. Because it's more expensive to install and purchase, Fast Ethernet is better suited to businesses.

Ethernet cabling comes in various types for various sizes of networks. If you're putting in a home or small business network, be sure to use Category 5 UTP (Unshielded Twisted Pair) cabling. This type of cable provides a good quality network cable that is protected from interference and noise, is reliable, and is fairly inexpensive. See also "Connecting with Traditional Cabling," later in this chapter.

Following are some other facts to consider about Ethernet cabling networks:

✦ If you connect more than two computers with Ethernet cabling, you must use a *hub* (a special piece of networking hardware) as a central connecting device.

✦ The Ethernet kit includes the cable you need, plus the connectors for attaching the cable to a network card and to the hub.

✦ When you buy equipment for adding your third, fourth, or fifth computer to the network, you can buy cable in pre-made segments of 6-, 10-, 15-, 50-, and 100-foot sections. You need to buy a network cable and Ethernet card for each new computer.

✦ Hubs include four, six, eight, or more ports (plugs in which to connect the cables from each computer). Make sure that your hub has enough ports for the number of computers you plan to network. Plan for the future, as well. You may decide to add a computer or two to your network later, so buy a hub with the number of ports you need plus one or two extra.

✦ Ethernet cabling doesn't pick up atmospheric or other interference or noise.

✦ Ethernet kits cost more than phone line kits, but the speed difference may be worth the increased cost.

Wireless kits

Wireless connections use radio signals or infrared beams to connect computers in a network rather than traditional cabling or phone lines. Wireless connections vary from speeds of 1 Mbps to 10 Mbps, depending on the wireless method.

Manufacturers have created wireless network cards, printer connections, and more for use with both desktop computers and portable (notebook or laptop) computers. Wireless kits are a bit more expensive than traditional cabling or phone line kits, but they can be used in your home safely and successfully. You may want to use wireless connections in your home if, for example, your walls are concrete. You cannot easily penetrate concrete walls to run cabling, but wireless works well in this situation. See also "Using Wireless Connections," later in this chapter.

Consider the following facts when thinking about using wireless networking:

✦ Wireless methods are easy to install and use. All you need is a network card and wireless port for each computer. The port enables the transmissions to move from one computer to another.

✦ Wireless provides more mobility for portable computers and users.

✦ The reliability of the connection is always questionable. Atmospheric conditions and obstacles, such as walls or ceilings, can cause the network connection to be less predictable than other networking technologies.

✦ Currently, wireless networks do run slower than most networks with traditional cabling (although some wireless networks are faster than phone line networks).

✦ Wireless is more expensive than traditional wiring methods.

 Wireless connection methods are commonly used in combination with traditional cabling methods. You may want to use traditional cabling for the majority of your network and add a few wireless connections where appropriate, such as for someone using a laptop computer.

Buying and Installing Network Cards

A network card must match the slots for adapter cards in your computer. In addition to choosing the right card for your expansion slots, you want to think about price, brand, warranty, and the type of connectors on the card. When you purchase a networking kit, the network card and cabling come with it, so you're sure you have the right connectors.

Buying a network card

The network card needs to fit the available expansion slots in your computer. Expansion slots are located inside your computer, near the back. These slots let you plug in cards or other devices to expand the usefulness of your computer. Every computer has a limited number of expansion slots. Often, when you buy a computer, most or all of these slots are already in use. Look to make sure that you have a slot open for a network card and to find out what type of slots you have.

The two most common slots for network cards are known as *ISA* (short for Industry Standard Architecture) and *PCI* (short for Peripheral Component Interface). Many computers have both types of slots. If you have a choice, choose a PCI for better communications, greater speed, and more efficiency in your network connections.

 If you're using a portable computer, you need a different kind of card — a PCMCIA (Personal Computer Memory Card International Association) card — to fit the available slot in the smaller computer. The three types of PCMCIA cards are about the size of a credit card. Read your documentation to find out the type of card you can use with your computer.

In addition, consider the following information when buying a network card:

+ Match the type of cabling you're using: phone line, Ethernet, or wireless. The card must specifically name the networking technology to work.

+ Match the end connectors on your cabling to the connector on the network card. For example, if your cabling is phone line, make sure that the network card has a plug that works with a phone jack.

+ Most network cards cost about the same, but avoid any cards that are considerably cheaper than others; these may be obsolete or damaged.

+ Warranties range from a few months to a lifetime warranty. Because it's a buyer's market (so many cards are available, and competition is fierce), always get a card with a lifetime warranty.

+ Use a known company with a good reputation for products and support, such as 3Com, Adaptec, Inc., Digital Equipment Corp., Linksys, Xircom (portables), or IBM.

Installing a network card

Before you install a network card, read your computer's documentation. Become familiar with the installation directions for your network card, as well. When you install a NIC, you must go through two steps. First, you physically install the card to the computer, and second, you install software that runs the network card. When you install that software, you also install and configure other networking software. I tell you more about the other networking software in Book IX, Chapter 3.

If you're installing a network card to a portable computer, you do not remove the case from the computer. Portable computers have a door or slot for network cards that you can reach from the outside. Check your computer's documentation for more information.

Follow these steps to install a network card:

1. **Make sure that you turn the computer off and unplug it before opening the case.**

   Unplug all plugs to your computer's case, including the keyboard, mouse, monitor, and so on.

2. **Remove the case.**

   You may need to remove a few screws or simply push a button or lever. Check your computer's documentation.

3. **Inside of the computer, look for a row of slots along the back edge.**

   Some slots may have cards in them already. You need one open slot for your network card.

4. **Remove the screw that secures the cover for the slot to the frame (it's a metal strip that keeps dust out when no card is installed).**

   Keep the screw (and the strip, too, in case you have to remove the network card in the future and you need the strip to cover up the slot again).

5. **The back of the card is the end into which you can plug a cable. This end must point toward the outside of the computer, through the slot. Holding the card only along the edges, carefully position it over the slot and gently push it straight down. When you're sure the card is in place, seat the card by firmly pushing the card down into the slot.**

   (You may have to push fairly hard.) You'll feel it snap into place.

6. **Insert the screw to hold the card in place, but be careful not to tighten the screw too tight.**

   The screw head needs to be flush with the metal tab of the card and the tab of the card should be flush to the rail of the case.

7. **Check that you didn't accidentally disconnect any wires or cables in the case. Remove all tools from the case.**

   Do not touch the exposed parts of the computer during the next step.

8. **Plug in the computer and turn it on.**

   Make sure that the computer boots. If the card isn't seated properly, the computer won't boot; you won't even get video. If you detect any of these problems, turn off the computer immediately, reset the card, and try turning the computer on again.

9. **If you turned the computer on and everything seems okay, you can continue. Turn the computer off again and unplug the power cord. Replace the case and secure it with screws, if applicable. Reinstall all cables.**

The next step is to connect the cabling to your network card. Again, the computer needs to be off for this process. To be safe, you may want to unplug the power cord, too. The cable you purchased should have the correct connector on the end — Ethernet, phone jack, or other connector. All you have to do is plug the connector into the computer slot containing the card you just inserted.

Buying and Installing a Hub

A hub receives signals from the connected computers and repeats the signals to other computers on the network. You use a hub to extend the network. You need a hub only if your network uses Ethernet and connects three or more computers together. You do not need a hub if you're using telephone line or wireless connections on your network.

If you've connected two computers together using Ethernet technology, cabling, and network cards, you can do without a hub; however, you will have a faster, more efficient connection if you use a hub.

Consider the following before buying a hub:

✦ The first step to using a hub is to determine the technology of the cable and network card and match that technology and speed. For example, if your network cards are 10 Mbps Ethernet, your hub must be 10 Mbps Ethernet.

✦ The next step is to figure out how many computers you need to connect to the network. Choose a hub with at least that number of ports.

✦ Be sure to get a hub with a lifetime warranty. Look for other benefits like cross-shipping of replacement parts and products, and technical support.

When installing the hub, keep the following in mind:

✦ Place the hub in a central area where it will be convenient. After plugging the network cable into the network card, you can run the cable to the hub and plug it into any open port.

✦ Label each cable on the hub with a number or name so you know where it leads, in case you have trouble with that computer's connection.

Connecting Only Two Computers

Using a feature in Windows called *Direct Cable Connection* (DCC), you can easily share files and folders between two computers without using network cards. The connection is slow (slower than a 1 Mbps connection), but it's also inexpensive (between $15 and $25, depending on the type of cable you buy). All you have to do is attach the cable between the two computers and set up Windows to use the connection. You cannot share a printer using this method; however, you can get around this inconvenience by transferring a file from one computer (without a printer) to another computer (with a printer).

If you're using computers that have different versions of Windows on them, you should designate the computer with the latest version of Windows as the host. DCC is a feature that began with Windows 95 and is included in Windows 98 and Windows Me.

The two computers you're connecting must be close together — at least in the same room and perhaps even on the same desk or table. The cable imposes this limit; direct cables are generally no longer than 50 feet.

To connect two computers, you can use a parallel file-transfer cable (also called a high-speed direct parallel cable) or a serial cable. The parallel file transfer cable costs around $25 and connects to the parallel ports (LPT) on each computer. A serial cable connects to the serial ports on each computer and costs only about $10, but it transfers data at a slower rate than a parallel cable.

Installing DCC

To determine whether DCC is installed on your computers, choose Start⇨ Programs⇨Accessories⇨Communications⇨Direct Cable Connection. If Direct Cable Connection isn't listed on the menu, you must install it. If it is listed on the menu, skip to the next section.

To install DCC, follow these steps:

1. **Choose Start⇨Settings⇨Control Panel and double-click the Add/Remove Programs icon.**

   The Add/Remove Programs Properties dialog box appears.

2. **Click the Windows Setup tab.**

3. **Choose Communications and then click the Details button.**

4. **If Dial-Up Networking is not installed, choose it as well by selecting the check box to the left of the option.**

   Dial-Up Networking contains features required by the direct cable connection.

5. **Choose Direct Cable Connection, and click OK.**

   You return to the Add/Remove Programs Properties dialog box.

6. **Click OK again to install the feature(s). Insert the Windows CD-ROM if prompted to. Close the Control Panel when you're finished.**

Configuring Windows

Before you can share files and folders, you must check the network configurations in Windows. Book IX, Chapter 3, explains how to set up the network, but here are the basic steps you need to take to set up network configurations for using DCC:

1. **Locate the My Network Places icon on the desktop.**

2. **Right-click the My Network Places icon and choose Properties from the shortcut menu that appears.**

   The Network dialog box appears.

3. **On the Configuration tab, click the File and Print Sharing button.**

   The File and Print Sharing dialog box appears.

4. **Make sure that both the I Want to Be Able to Give Others Access to My Files and the I Want to Be Able to Allow Others to Print to My Printer check boxes are selected.**

5. **Click OK to close the dialog box.**

6. **Click the Identification tab and check your computer name and the workgroup name. Give the host and guest computers different computer names.**

   The workgroup name must be the same on all computers in the network.

7. **Go back to the Configuration tab and check to see whether a network protocol, such as TCP/IP or NetBEUI, is showing.**

   Both computers must use the same protocol to be able to communicate over the network. When you install the adapter, a protocol for the adapter is installed at the same time.

8. **Click OK to close the Network dialog box. If Windows prompts you to restart your computer, do so now.**

Next, you must share the drive(s) or folder(s) you want to give others access to. For this procedure, you need to use either the Windows Explorer or My Computer features of Windows. For information about sharing resources, see Book IX, Chapter 4.

Configuring DCC and connecting DCC cable

Configuring the direct cable connection and connecting the cable is relatively simple, because Windows supplies a wizard to help. In order to connect the two computers, you must designate one computer as the host and
one as the guest. The *host* computer provides the resources (files and folders), and the *guest* uses the resources. After you set up the host computer,
you need to go through these steps again to set up the guest computer.

To set up DCC and connect your cables, follow these steps:

1. **Choose Start⇨Programs⇨Accessories⇨Communications⇨Direct
Cable Connection.**

The Direct Cable Connection Wizard dialog box appears (see Figure 2-1).

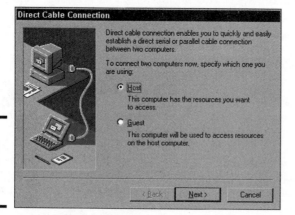

Figure 2-1:
The wizard
guides you
through
setup.

2. **Select the Host option to set up the first computer as the host computer. Then click the Next button.**

The next dialog box lists the available ports on the computer.

3. **Choose the port that corresponds with the direct cable you're using.**

Note that you must use the same type of port on both computers; that
is, if you use a parallel port on one computer, you must use a parallel
port on the other computer.

4. **Plug the cable into the ports and click the Next button.**

The last wizard box appears, telling you that the setup was successful.
If you want, you can set a password for the guest computer. Setting a
password means that only users who know the password can access
your computer from the other one.

After you install the host, the host computer displays a dialog box that states it is waiting for the guest computer to attach, as shown in Figure 2-2. You can now set up the guest computer. Follow the preceding steps, selecting the Guest option (instead of Host) in Step 2. After you complete the guest setup, the two computers are ready to communicate with one another.

Figure 2-2:
The host
looks for
the guest
computer.

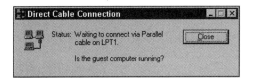

Running the direct cable connection

Anytime you want to connect two computers with DCC, you must first start the host and then start the guest. You can use the My Network Places feature of Windows to view the two computers and to share files and printers.

To establish a connection between the two computers, follow these steps:

1. **On the host computer, choose Start⇨Programs⇨Accessories⇨ Communications⇨Direct Cable Connection.**

The Direct Cable Connection dialog box appears.

2. **Click the Listen button.**

The Status dialog box appears.

3. **Move to the guest computer and repeat Step 1. In the Direct Cable Connection dialog box, click the Connect button.**

The connection is established between the two computers.

After the two computers are connected, you can view the host from the guest anytime by clicking the View Host button in the Direct Cable Connection dialog box. When you view the host, you see the desktop as if you were sitting at that computer. You can open My Network Places and open files or folders you need to access. See Book IX, Chapter 5, for more on using My Network Places.

Let the Home Networking Wizard get you connected

If running through a lot of dialog boxes, making a lot of setting changes, and rebooting your computer a couple of times isn't your idea of a good time, you're in luck. Windows Me comes with a Home Networking Wizard that steps you through your computer-sharing experience. And, because this is a new feature of Windows Me, it's best to begin your network configuration with a computer running Windows Me. Relax, though, those other computers that are still running Windows 98 or 95 will still be easy to setup with Windows Me's help.

To access the Home Networking Wizard, open up My Network Places from the desktop and double-click the Wizard's icon. After the opening splash screen welcomes you to this Windows feature, click the Next button to begin.

First on your list (and the Wizard's) to consider and decide upon is whether you will be sharing an Internet connection. Regardless of whether you have a dial-up connection, DSL line, or cable Internet access, home networking not only makes a lot of sense, it can save you some money and time getting every other computer wired into these high-speed Internet connections. No more waiting until the dial-up phone line is free or claiming sqatter's rights on the one computer connected to the cable modem. By making the correct selections in the Wizard, sharing Internet access becomes a reality. You even have the option of allowing multiple users to access the Internet at the same time, using the same connection.

For those worried about their children's interaction on the Internet in chat rooms and such, passwords can be assigned to users to protect unauthorized Internet access. Conversely, imagine the convenience of not having to double-click icons, enter logins and passwords, or wait any longer.

After the Internet connection preferences are determined, you begin building your network by providing a workgroup and user name, followed by choosing the printers, folders, and drives that are going to be shared.

After all the questions are answered, you can create a diskette that, when run on another Windows Me/98/95 computer wired to the network, will run the same Wizard to set that computer up on the network. Reboot your computer, and then you can start testing and using your own network.

Using Phone Lines to Connect

Using your phone lines to network your computers is an option that you may want to explore. You can use the telephone cabling already in place at your home without rewiring or installing traditional Ethernet cabling. You can also use the RJ-11 modular phone jacks that are already in place in your home as a port for your computers.

Most phone line network kits include complete written instructions for both installing the hardware and software and configuring the computers on the network. You definitely need to install a phone line network card into each computer on your network, but the cabling itself is a snap. Simply plug one end of the telephone cable provided with the kit into the card's telephone port and plug the other end of the telephone cable into a wall phone jack. That's it. The cabling is done, but you still have to install your network card driver (see Book IX, Chapter 3).

Connecting with Traditional Cabling

Direct cable connection is certainly inexpensive, but in certain respects, you get what you pay for. If you want to share printers, applications, games, modems, CD-ROM drives, and other peripherals in addition to sharing files and folders (and you want to do it all at higher rates of speed), you need to invest in traditional cabling for your network.

Examining the cable

You can choose from various types of traditional cabling for your home network. The most common, efficient, and fastest cabling for home networking, however, is *twisted-pair cable*. As its name suggests, twisted-pair cable consists of two or more pairs of insulated wires twisted together and then enclosed within a plastic casing. Twisted-pair is similar to common phone wire, but twisted-pair is a higher grade of cabling that allows high-speed data to travel over it. Twisted-pair is relatively inexpensive.

Twisted-pair uses Ethernet 10BaseT standards. 10BaseT allows your network to run at 10 Mbps. Each computer in the network connects to a central hub. The maximum cable-segment length for twisted-pair is 100 meters, or 330 feet. If you use the Ethernet 10BaseT cabling scheme, you have to buy network cards that accept Ethernet 10BaseT cabling. You also need to buy an Ethernet 10BaseT hub, one with jacks for twisted-pair connectors.

Twisted-pair cabling uses a specific connector known as an RJ-45 for attaching the cable to the network card and/or hub. An RJ-45 connector looks like an RJ-11 connector — the modular telephone jack you've seen around your house. But if you look closely, you'll see that an RJ-11 connector has only four to six pins, whereas an RJ-45 has eight pins.

There are categories, or levels, of twisted-pair cabling. Each level describes the performance characteristics of wiring standards. Of the levels of twisted-pair cabling, Category 3 (Cat 3) and Category 5 (Cat 5) are the most common. Cat 3 is less expensive than Cat 5, but its transfer rate isn't as fast. Use Cat 5 for your home network whenever possible.

Installing the cable

Installing cable can be as easy or as difficult as you want to make it. You can run the cable through walls like telephone wire or under the carpet to hide it. You can run the cable under the house or behind bookcases and around window frames. You may want to purchase *raceway,* a plastic casing that covers the cable and attaches it to the wall.

If you don't want to install the cable yourself, you can hire someone to do it. Check the yellow pages for telecommunications or telephone services, network consultants, or network technicians.

You must decide how and where you want to place the cables and where to locate the hub. The hub is best placed in a central location, easily reachable from the other rooms. Use your network map to sketch out your plan (see Book IX, Chapter 1).

When you're ready to actually lay the cable, label both ends of each cable with a number or name. For example, number the first cable as 1 on each end. That way, it is easier to find the cable at the hub when you're looking for a specific computer's cabling.

If you plan to go behind walls or under the floors of your house, use an electrician to help you pull the wire. For one thing, you want to avoid drilling through any power lines. If you're not sure where the power lines are, do not drill or pull cabling until you find out for sure. You can get a nasty electrical shock, cut the power to your home, or cause some other catastrophe.

Be very careful when installing network cabling in the walls of your house. Going through walls and under floors requires special equipment — snakes and fancy drill bits — and takes two people to pull the wire. You may need to go through cinder block walls or walls full of insulation. Watch that you don't drill through the studs in a framed wall.

Following are some more precautions for installing your cable:

✦ Don't kink the cable. Kinks in the cable can cause connection problems as well as ruin the cable.

✦ Don't use a staple gun or staples of any type to install cabling. You can nick the cable, which ruins it.

✦ If you use a plastic or metal tie to hold several cables together, don't pull the tie too tightly. You can kink a cable and stop the connection.

✦ Don't install cabling so that it runs beside AC power lines of any sort. The power can interfere with the data traveling over the network cable.

✦ Don't install cabling within two feet of fluorescent lighting. Fluorescent lights interfere with the network signal.

✦ If you must cross a power line, cross it at a right angle to get the least interference.

✦ Don't coil excess cabling when the cabling is in use. If, for example, you install the cable and have several feet left over, don't coil it up. Instead, lay the cable out as straight as possible. Coiling the cable can cause interference in the data transmissions.

Using Wireless Connections

You really don't need to do much to "connect" a wireless network together. Not having any wires to connect goes without saying. Any wireless kit you buy will have instructions for setting up your network. You need to install the special NIC, which enables you to transmit your data via infrared or radio frequencies. You also need to install a wireless port on each computer on your network. The wireless ports allow the computers to send and receive data across your network. Depending on the type of wireless technology you use, you may need to position the computers close to one another or in a line-of-sight configuration (where, from one computer, you have an unobstructed view of the other computer).

Chapter 3: Setting Up the Computers

In This Chapter

- ✔ Installing the NIC software
- ✔ Choosing the network client
- ✔ Defining protocols
- ✔ Setting services
- ✔ Identifying the computer
- ✔ Exploring access control

Connecting all your networking hardware — cables, cards, and so on — is only half the job in setting up a home computer network. In order to get all your computers to actually talk to one another, you also have to install and set up networking software on your computers. In Windows, this process involves four different kinds of networking software: *client software, adapter software, service software,* and *protocol software.* Finally, you must also set your computer's identification before you can get down to the business of networking.

Installing and Configuring the Network Interface Card Software

In Windows networking, an *adapter* refers to a piece of software (known as a software *driver*) that enables your computer to work together with the network interface card you installed. Windows does come with a number of software drivers for NICs, listed by manufacturer and network card name, but often these drivers are not the most recent versions. The drivers contained on the floppy disks or CD-ROM that came with your network card tend to be more recent, so using them may make sense.

 If at all possible, install the latest version of a NIC driver to ensure that the card works efficiently with Windows; you can usually download the most recent driver from a NIC manufacturer's Web site. Almost all manufacturers now include a Web address as part of their product documentation.

The adapter driver you install on Windows must match up with the actual physical card you installed on your computer. See Book IX, Chapter 2 for more information about installing a NIC.

Installing the NIC software

During the past few years, NIC manufacturers and Microsoft have both tried to make the bothersome task of installing NIC software easier. Newer network cards are often presented to the public as Plug and Play cards, implying that all you have to do is plug them in and your operating system immediately begins to "play" them without you having to change any settings. If you've installed a Plug and Play network card and you're willing to use the card's driver that came with Windows, installing the software ought to go pretty easily.

The first time you start up your computer after plugging in your Plug and Play network card, Windows detects the card, matches it with the appropriate driver, and guides you through the installation process. Here's what you can expect:

1. **When the NIC software Installation Wizard appears, click Next.**

Windows asks if you want to locate the NIC manually or if you want Windows to do it automatically.

2. **Choose to let Windows detect your NIC automatically and click Next. If Windows prompts you to insert your Windows Setup CD, do so.**

3. **Windows locates the NIC and installs the drivers automatically. Click Finish when Windows displays the Installation Completed Successfully dialog box.**

If Windows didn't automatically detect the network card driver when you turned your computer on, or you plan to install a newer version of the driver (either downloaded from the Internet or included as part of your network card package), you can add the driver yourself by following these steps:

If you download a driver for your NIC from the Internet, copy the driver to a floppy disk so you can easily install it during the steps that follow.

1. **Choose Start⇨Settings⇨Control Panel and double-click the Add New Hardware icon.**

The Add New Hardware Wizard dialog box appears and instructs you to close any programs that are currently running.

2. **Click Next.**

Windows tells you that it will search for any new Plug and Play devices. With a little luck, and as long as you purchased a Plug and Play NIC, Windows will find the card.

3. **Click Next.**

4. **If your NIC is found, it will be listed in the Devices list. Select your NIC and click Next to install the drivers. Once the drivers are installed, click Finish. Restart your computer, if asked to do so.**

   If your card is not in the list, click the No, the Device Isn't in the List option, click Next, and proceed to Step 5.

5. **Choose No, I Want to Select the Hardware from a List and click Next.**

6. **In the list of Hardware Types, choose Network Adapters and click Next.**

7. **When presented with the list of manufacturers and models, you have two options:**

   - Choose the name of the manufacturer of your network card in the Manufacturers list and the type of adapter in the Models list as shown in Figure 3-1. Click OK. Windows installs its version of the driver for you.

   - If you want to use a newer version of the driver that you have on disk, insert the disk containing the driver in the disk drive and click the Have Disk button. Choose the appropriate drive and click OK. Windows installs your version of the driver for you. If the disk has multiple drivers on it for the different cards available from the manufacturer, you may have to choose yours from a list. Be sure to check the box or documentation that came with your card to know which model to choose.

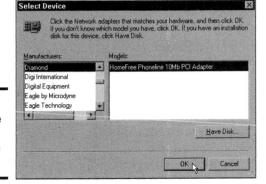

Figure 3-1:
Choose the manufacturer of the card.

If you downloaded your driver from the manufacturer's Web site, go to the drive and folder where the file was saved to. If the file was zipped or compressed, be sure to unzip it first.

Windows 98 users should install the network adapter through the Network option in Control Panel. Choose Start⇨Settings⇨Control Panel⇨Network. Click the Add button and choose Adapter, then click the Add button. In the Select Network Adapters dialog box, choose the manufacturer and model from the list or click the Have Disk button to install more recent drivers from the manufacturer and browse to the file's location. Click OK.

When Windows finishes installing the network adapter, it lists the new adapter in the Network dialog box. Luckily for you, while Windows was installing your adapter, it also installed a client software program (known as Client for Microsoft Networks) as well as TCP/IP as your default protocol program (*TCP/IP* is short for Transmission Control Protocol/Internet Protocol). If you'd rather use a different protocol program, you can remove TCP/IP by selecting it in the components list of the Network dialog box and clicking the Remove button. For more information on your options involving networking protocols, see the "Network Protocols" section, later in this chapter.

Don't close the Network dialog box yet, because you still need it to make a few more settings changes. If you close the Network dialog box now, Windows asks you to restart your computer. Save yourself the trouble of having to start and restart your computer over and over again by changing all of your settings first and then closing the Network dialog box.

Configuring the NIC software

Configuring your NIC software involves setting up a kind of pathway between the network card and your computer's processor. Unfortunately, most computers have only 16 such pathways (known technically as *IRQs,* short for interrupt requests), and the IRQs are reserved for specific pieces of hardware attached to your computer, such as printers, modems, disk drives, and more. If you have a network card assigned to the same IRQ as another piece of hardware, you're going to end up with a *hardware conflict,* another way of saying that either your computer won't run or one or more of your peripherals won't work.

The Plug and Play feature of Windows is supposed to automatically assign an IRQ number to your network card that doesn't conflict with other devices in your computer. That sounds like a good fix to the problem, but it tends to work only 50 percent of the time. If you are part of the lucky 50 percent, you can skip to the next section. If it's not your lucky day, read on.

If you need to change the IRQ number of your network card, you can do so in the System Properties dialog box. Be very careful, however; changing settings can cause conflicts with other cards in your system. Keep a record of the original numbers and the changes you make so that you can backtrack and start over at square one again if conflicts arise. To change IRQ settings, follow these steps:

1. **Choose Start⇨Settings⇨Control Panel and double-click the System icon.**

   The System Properties dialog box appears.

2. **Click the Device Manager tab.**

3. **Click the plus (+) sign to the left of Network Adapters to display your network card.**

4. **Double-click the network card.**

   The NIC's Properties dialog box appears.

5. **Choose the Resources tab, and remove the check mark from the Use Automatic Settings check box if it is present.**

6. **Choose Interrupt Request and then click the Change Settings button.**

7. **In the resulting dialog box, enter the new IRQ number.**

   The most likely number for your purposes is one between 9 and 13.

8. **Click OK, and then click OK twice more to get back to the Control Panel. Windows prompts you to restart your computer. Do so.**

To find an unused IRQ number, double-click Computer at the top of the list of devices in the Device Manager tab to open the Computer Properties window. Select the Interrupt Request (IRQ) options and scan the list of IRQ settings that are already taken. Choose one that is not already assigned.

Windows' Built-In Client Software

The *network client* is the software that enables your computer to become a member of a network. Microsoft supplies client software you can use for a Windows peer-to-peer network called Client for Microsoft Networks. It's automatically installed and configured when you install your network-interface-card adapter software. Nice touch, right?

Network Protocols

Protocols are software programs that define the ways that computers in general can transmit and receive data. In computer networks, protocols also lay down the ground rules for how computers on the network talk with one another. Windows comes with about eight different network protocols to choose from. There are three that you should really concern yourself about. They are

✦ **NetBEUI:** The Microsoft protocol designed to work with Windows. NetBEUI (short for Network Basic Input/Output System Extended User Interface) is perfect for small peer-to-peer networks; it's easy to set up, it provides good performance, and it's a fast protocol. NetBEUI uses very little memory. If you're setting up your first network and you want an easy job of it, use NetBEUI as your networking protocol.

✦ **TCP/IP:** The protocol of the Internet, TCP/IP can also be used on your home network. TCP/IP is versatile, is fast, and provides a wide variety of options for configuration. Because TCP/IP is difficult to configure, however, you probably don't want to use it in your home network if you're just learning about protocols and networking.

✦ **IPX/SPX:** A protocol frequently used with Novell NetWare networks, although you can also use it with Microsoft networks. Unless you have a specific reason for using IPX/SPX (short for Internet Package Exchange/Sequenced Package Exchange — such as integration with a NetWare network — stick with NetBEUI. IPX/SPX doesn't offer as much for Microsoft networks as the NetBEUI or TCP/IP protocols do.

Installing a protocol

Installing protocols is actually a piece of cake. You may remember that Windows even installs TCP/IP for you as the default protocol. Having TCP/IP as your default protocol requires you to assign a unique address (known as an *IP address*) to each computer on your network. I show you how to do that in the following section, "Configuring TCP/IP."

Because you must use the same protocol for all computers on the network, you must install the same protocol on each computer. To do so, complete the following steps for each computer:

1. **Choose Start⇨Settings⇨Control Panel and double-click the Network icon.**

The Network dialog box appears.

2. **In the Network dialog box, click the Add button.**

The Select Network Component Type dialog box appears.

3. **Choose Protocol in the network component list.**

4. **Click the Add button.**

The Select Network Protocol dialog box appears.

5. **In the Manufacturers list, choose Microsoft.**

6. **Choose a protocol from the list, as shown in Figure 3-2.**

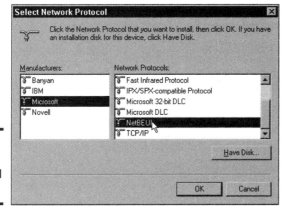

Figure 3-2:
Installing
the NetBEUI
protocol.

7. **Click OK to add the protocol. Windows returns to the Network dialog box when it is done. Restart the computer when prompted.**

Configuring TCP/IP

Because TCP/IP uses a special system of binary numbers for identifying computers on the network, you must configure each computer with a unique IP address using this numbering system in order for TCP/IP to work. Or, you can opt to have Windows assign the IP address automatically.

If you're a Windows Me or 98 user, you're in luck: Windows Me and 98 include LINKLOCAL, a method of assigning unique IP addresses that makes assigning IP addresses a whole lot easier. As you configure each computer on the network, LINKLOCAL keeps track of the addresses used and ensures that each computer receives a unique address. *Note:* Windows 95 does not include LINKLOCAL. Also, LINKLOCAL network addresses are only good for private networks. It won't work with host computers that are linked into the Internet.

To enable LINKLOCAL, follow these steps:

1. **Choose Start⇨Settings⇨Control Panel and double-click the Network icon.**

The Network dialog box appears.

2. **Choose the TCP/IP Ethernet adapter and click the Properties button.**

   The TCP/IP Properties dialog box appears.

3. **In the IP Address tab, select the Obtain an IP Address Automatically option, if it is not already selected.**

4. **Click OK to close the TCP/IP Properties dialog box.**

5. **Click OK again to close the Network dialog box. Windows prompts you to restart the computer. Go ahead and do so.**

   When you start the computer again, it automatically assigns itself an IP address.

You must repeat these steps with each computer on the network to complete the process. When you're finished, your network is up and running using the TCP/IP protocol.

Setting Your Network Services

Part of the whole rationale for having a computer network is based on your desire to share certain resources (such as files, folders, and printers) over the network. You have to make your wishes clear to Windows, however, by first laying down some ground rules. You do so by defining your *network services*. For example, you can choose to share your files but not your printer, or your printer but not your files. You lay down the ground rules by adding the network services you want in the Network dialog box and specifying your options. Follow these steps:

1. **Choose Start⇨Settings⇨Control Panel and double-click the Network icon.**

   The Network dialog box appears.

2. **In the Network dialog box, click the Add button.**

   The Select Network Component Type dialog box appears.

3. **Choose Service.**

4. **Click the Add button.**

   The Select Network Service dialog box appears.

5. **Choose Microsoft from the manufacturers listed in the left column and choose File and Printer Sharing for Microsoft Networks from the network services listed in the right column.**

6. **Click OK.**

   Windows adds the service to the network components column.

7. **If you want to share your files but not your printer, or your printer but not your files, go back to the Network dialog box and click the File and Print Sharing button.**

   The File and Print Sharing dialog box appears.

8. **Deselect the appropriate check box if you want to pick and choose between sharing your files or your printer with others on the network. Then click OK.**

Identifying the Computer to the Network

Even if you're not bothering with TCP/IP and its system of IP addresses, you still must identify your computer to the network. Otherwise, computers on the network won't be able to find each other. Windows makes it easy for you by letting you identify each computer in the Network dialog box.

To identify the computer to the network, follow these steps:

1. **Choose Start⇨Settings⇨Control Panel and double-click the Network icon.**

   The Network dialog box appears.

2. **Click the Identification tab.**

3. **In the Computer Name text box, enter a unique name for the computer.**

   It can be the name of a family member, the name of a famous artist, or even the name of a constellation. Just be sure that the name makes sense to all individuals using the network.

4. **In the Workgroup text box, enter the name of your workgroup.**

   You can simply use your family's last name. The workgroup name must be the same on all computers on the network.

5. **If you want, you can enter a brief description of the computer (brand name, type of processor, built-in memory, and so on).**

6. **Click OK. When Windows prompts you to restart your computer, click Yes to restart.**

You need to repeat all of the preceding steps with each computer on the network. If you add one kind of client, protocol, and service software to a computer, you must add the same kind to all computers. Also be sure that you install the adapter software designed to work with your network interface card. Finally, don't forget that although each computer has its own unique computer name, you must have a common workgroup name on all computers for them to be able to talk to one another across the network.

Exploring Access Control

The Access Control tab of the Network dialog box offers two options for controlling the access to shared resources: Share-level and User-level. Use Share-level access for a peer-to-peer network. User-level works best with a client/server network, such as Windows NT Server or Novell NetWare. The default option is Share-level, so you don't have to make any changes to this tab.

Share-level access control lets you supply a password for each shared resource. If you want to be particular about who gets to share a folder or printer, you can use Access Control to assign a password to that resource. Only people who know the password may then access that resource. Of course, you don't have to use passwords for sharing resources; but it's nice to know that you have the capability to do so if you want to.

User-level access control works by assigning specific users (or groups of users) access to resources on the computer. Because of their larger size, client/server networks often use groups for authentication and permissions purposes. User-level access works better in that kind of environment, but isn't normally something you need to worry about on a smaller home network.

Chapter 4: Sharing Folders, Drives, Files, and Internet Access

In This Chapter

- ✔ Taking a look at limits and permissions
- ✔ Sharing folders, drives, and files
- ✔ Sharing Internet access

One major reason you connect your computer to a network is so that you can share resources with others. Resources refer to files, folders, drives, printers, CD-ROM drives, Iomega Zip or Jaz drives (handy hardware for backing up a large number of files), and so on. You probably want to share most of your computer resources with your spouse and children, or you and your spouse may want to share files containing letters, household accounting information, or genealogy data. Older children in your home may want to share their homework files with you so that you can review them before they print them out. Of course, you likely want to share printers, CD-ROM drives, and other hardware as well.

Understanding Sharing and Access Limits

You may not want to share everything on your computer, however. Networks are designed so that you can also *limit* the access to shared resources in case you have confidential information to protect or equipment that's too expensive for children to use.

Access types

Windows lets you limit the access to any file, folder, drive, or other resource by assigning them *access types*. Following are the access types from which you can choose:

- ✦ **Read-only.** Allows others either to open and view folders, or to open, view, and copy files; however, read-only access doesn't allow others to change a file or delete anything.
- ✦ **Full.** Lets anyone open, change, add, or remove files and folders.

✦ **Depends on Password.** You can set a password on any resource so that only the people who know the password have access to that resource. You can give your spouse password access, for example, but limit the access of your children to a specific resource. Using password limits, you can also choose read-only or full access.

Share designation

Windows gives you another option for sharing resources. In addition to setting access limits to individual files or folders, you can also set up entire sections of your computer for a kind of blanket sharing. You might, for example, share an entire hard drive, or an entire drive on your hard disk if the drive has been partitioned (split into multiple drives). For example, a hard drive with 12GB of space may be separated into four equal partitions of 3GB each. Each partition would have its own drive letter assigned, such as C, D, E, and F.

Sharing Folders, Drives, and Files

In a perfect world, sharing your entire hard drive would be the simplest way to set up a share. The world is far from perfect, however, and if you're concerned that sharing your entire hard drive is asking for trouble, you may want to take the time to choose specific folders for sharing. As always, plan ahead. For your network to work properly, you have to have a clear idea of which folders you want to share.

Before you can share any resource on the network, you must first install the networking software and hardware. When installing the networking software, you must enable file- and print-sharing services. See Book IX, Chapter 3, for more information.

Identifying folders to share

By now you know that you share your folders to provide documents and files to others on the network. You may not know that you don't need to (and shouldn't) share many of your folders at all.

Following are just a few of the folders not to share:

✦ **You don't need to share your Windows folder.** The Windows folder holds all the files that make Windows work, including fonts, configuration files, programming files, help files, and so on. Changes to this folder can cause real problems.

✦ **You may not want to share your Program Files folder.** Each Program Files folder may contain a number of software application folders, including folders for Internet Explorer, Microsoft Office, Outlook,

NetMeeting, and so on. Each application folder contains the files that make a specific program run. More than likely, the other network computers contain these applications and, therefore, don't need to share yours.

✦ **Don't share any folders that contain *device drivers*.** (Device drivers are the software programs that run your computer hardware and peripherals — your CD-ROM drive, network card, tape backup, and so on). Because these folders contain data specific to your computer, no one else needs them. If someone were to accidentally delete a device driver folder, your system may stop functioning properly.

Following are the folders you do want to share:

✦ **A specific program file folder.** Say you use Quicken for your personal accounting program. If you store your account data in the Quicken folder (`C:\Program Files\QuickenW\My Data`, for example), you may want to share this folder so that your spouse can access the data, too.

✦ **Folders that contain data that others may want or need.** For example, you may want to share your My Documents folder or other folders you've created to contain documents.

✦ **Application folders that others can copy.** For example, if you download application files like WinZip (a file compression program) or Netscape from the Internet, you can store all these setup programs in one folder or several folders on the hard drive. If your spouse reformats a drive and wants to copy your WinZip or Netscape setup program to install to the new drive, copying it from your hard drive over the network is the quickest and easiest method.

Designating a shared folder

In order to share folders, you first need a convenient way of locating the folders on your computer. Both the Windows Explorer and My Computer features of Windows allow you to conveniently locate folders by letting you navigate quickly through your various directories until you find the folder you want. After you locate the folder, you can then designate any folder as shared.

When you share a folder nested beneath other folders, only the files within that folder will be available on the network. Files and folders above the shared one cannot be accessed.

To designate a folder as shared, follow these steps:

1. **Double-click the My Computer icon on your desktop.**

The My Computer window appears.

2. **Navigate down through the directories until you find the folder you want, and then select the folder (see Figure 4-1).**

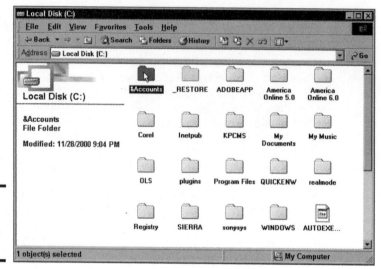

Figure 4-1:
Select the
folder to be
shared.

3. **Right-click the selected folder and choose Sharing from the menu that appears.**

   The folder's Properties dialog box appears with the Sharing tab displayed.

4. **On the Sharing tab, select the Shared As option (see Figure 4-2).**

   The share name for your folder is displayed in the Share Name text box. (The *share name* is the name that others see when they want to access the folder over the network.) The share name is exactly the same as the original name of the folder. If you want to change the folder name, simply delete the text in the Share Name text box and type a new name.

   Putting an ampersand (&) in front of the folder's name forces the folder to display at the top of the folder list in Windows Explorer and My Computer.

5. **If you want, you can enter text in the Comment text box.**

   Comments can describe the documents within a folder, for example.

6. **In the Access Type area, select one of the following:**

   - **Read-Only.** You can apply the limit with or without a password. If you want to add a password, enter it in the Read-Only Password text box.

   - **Full.** If you want to assign a password to a folder with full access, enter that word in the Full Access Password text box.

   - **Depends on Password.** Select this option if you want to apply passwords to both a read-only and a full access. Enter different passwords in the appropriate text box in the Passwords section.

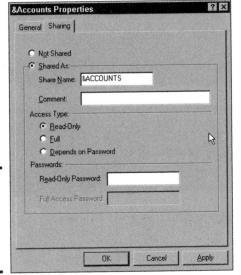

Figure 4-2:
Accept the
default
name or
enter a new
name.

7. **Click OK to accept the changes and close the dialog box.**

When you share a folder (or a drive, or a file) from your computer, an out-stretched hand icon appears on that object in both the Windows Explorer and My Computer windows.

Shared folders from other computers on the network do not display the out-stretched hand by the folder or drive icon. Only your own folders display that shared symbol.

Designating a shared drive

Sharing a drive may not be the safest way to share resources over the network, but it's certainly the easiest. After installing the appropriate software and hardware, you simply designate drives as shared the same way you would designate folders as shared: Locate the drive by using Windows Explorer or My Computer, right-click the drive to access the Properties dialog box, and choose the Shared As option on the Sharing tab. You have the same access options that you have with folders, and when you're done, the same hand icon appears on your drive icon. Everyone on your network now has access to everything on the shared drive.

Designating a file as shared

Sharing files by using the networking features of Windows is simple: When you share a folder or a drive, all files in that folder or drive are automatically shared. However, no easy way exists to set up a situation so that only certain files within a folder or drive can be shared.

If you want to keep a file within a shared folder yet still control access to the file, you may be able to do so by using the built-in password option of the program you use to create the file, but this option is possible only with certain programs. Microsoft Word, for example, allows you to save a file as password-protected, meaning that an individual would need to know a password in order to open or change a file.

If this method seems like too much trouble or your software program doesn't offer a built-in password feature, simply store the files you want to keep private in a separate folder that doesn't offer any share access at all. When it comes to privacy issues, the best policy is always to refrain from sharing anything you don't want others to see.

Sharing Internet Access

Many people use their home computers for Internet access. Surfing the Web, e-mailing family and friends, and joining discussion groups can provide every member of the family with hours of fun and learning. You can set up your Windows network so that everyone connected can access the Internet through one user account quickly and easily. Windows Me comes with all the necessary software to accomplish this using an easy-to-follow wizard.

If you are a Windows 98 user, you can upgrade to Windows 98 Second Edition by ordering the Windows 98 Second Edition Updates CD for around $20 directly from Microsoft. This CD offers several programs you can use with Windows, including an Internet-sharing application. If you already have Windows 98 Second Edition installed, you already have the files necessary for Internet Connection Sharing (ICS).

The basics of using a modem and setting up an Internet account with an Internet service provider (or ISP) are the same whether you are on a computer network or not (see Book III for more information). If you are already set up for the Internet and want to find out how you can share Internet access, read on.

Using third-party applications

A *modem* (the piece of hardware that uses your phone line to connect to the Internet) is not usually set up to allow sharing over a computer network. However, if you use your modem in combination with some additional software (known as *third-party applications,* because they are provided neither by the manufacturer of your computer nor by the modem's manufacturer), you can surf the Net and send and receive e-mail at the same time that others on the network use the Internet connection. Various programs exist that allow you to turn one phone line into multiple Internet connections.

Many ISPs do not allow you to share one Internet account in this manner. Check to see if yours does.

Most of these software applications require you to use TCP/IP as your network protocol. See Book IX, Chapter 3, for more information about network protocols. You install the modem-sharing software to a host machine first; this is the computer that's attached directly to the modem. Then you install the software to the other computers, or guests. The host computer runs the service all the time and is prepared to dial up the Internet account when a guest requests the service.

Software options

Many products exist that enable you to share a connection to the Internet. Following are a few of those programs:

+ **WinGate (Obik New Zealand, Ltd.):** Lets you simultaneously connect multiple users to the Internet using one Internet account and one modem. Installation and configuration are easy. Three versions of the program exist: WinGate Standard, WinGate Home, and WinGate Pro. Each version offers different features. Prices are based on the number of users and the version. See www.wingate.com for more information.

+ **Rideway (ITServ):** Lets you assign each computer on the network an internal IP address. The IP address means you have to use the TCP/IP protocol on your network. If you plan to use TCP/IP anyway, Rideway might be the choice for you. Check out the latest features at www.itserv.com.

+ **WinProxy (Ositis Internet Sharing Software):** Easy and inexpensive to use. Install the host software to a computer attached to the modem, and other computers on the network can get e-mail, join newsgroups, download files, and use the Internet connection through one machine. The Ositis Web site gives the details at www.ositis.com.

Chapter 5: Getting on (And Around) the Network

In This Chapter

- ✔ Logging on and off the network
- ✔ Using network paths to find folders and files
- ✔ Mapping a drive
- ✔ Finding computers on the network
- ✔ Browsing My Network Places
- ✔ Working with files and folders in My Network Places

*A*fter you have set up your various files, folders, and drives for sharing, you still have to find out how to use the networking capabilities of Windows to your best advantage. Working on the network is a bit different than working on a non-networked computer. You need to understand not only how to access the network but also what the best way is to get to the computers and files you need. Windows offers several shortcuts for finding the files and folders you need on the network, including network paths, mapped drives, and the Find Computer feature.

Although you can use Windows Explorer or My Computer to browse the network, My Network Places is built specifically for viewing and using network computers and files. You can view networked computers' files and folders as well as copy, move, rename, or delete them.

In Windows 95/98, My Network Places is called Network Neighborhood.

Logging On and Off

When you log on to a Windows non-networked computer, you enter your Windows user name and password. Logging on to Windows identifies you to the operating system, which can then display your personal settings for your programs, your passwords to the Internet, and so on. Logging on allows multiple users to access one computer and keep their preferences and desktop settings.

Logging on to the network is similar. When you log on to the network by entering your user name and password, Windows immediately identifies you as a valid member of the network group and enables you to access files, folders, printers, and other resources made available to you. For more information on access privileges, see Book IX, Chapter 4.

Looking at user names

Your *user name* is the name by which you're known to the network. You can use your first name or a nickname, for example. You can use any combination of letters (upper- or lowercase) and numbers. If you want, you can even include spaces within a name, so you can use your first and last name the way you're used to writing it. Passwords are case-sensitive; you must use the same upper- and/or lowercase letters each time you enter the password.

Considering passwords

A *password* is normally an identifier for an authorized user to gain access to the network. You can use passwords for security purposes on a client/server network, but on a peer-to-peer Windows network, the password doesn't really keep anyone from accessing the network. On a peer-to-peer network, anyone can log on to any computer at any time. For example, one of your teenager's friends can turn on a networked computer and enter his or her name and any password he or she chooses. If you have not been strict about setting access types, that person can then open My Network Places and access the shared folders and drives on your computer. If that prospect scares you, you may consider toughening up your access limits by relying more on share passwords. For more information on using passwords, see Book IX, Chapter 4.

Logging off the network

You can log off the network if you have two or more people sharing your computer and you want to give someone else time on the network. You log off so that the other person can access his or her network resources. If you don't share your computer with someone else, you don't need to log off in a peer-to-peer situation. You can stay logged in all day if you like.

When you shut down your computer, you're automatically logged off, and your resources are no longer available.

To log off the network, follow these steps:

1. **Save all open files and close all programs.**

   You must do this before logging off so that you don't lose any data.

2. **Choose Start⇨Log Off . . . (your user name).**

   You don't have to enter your user name — Windows already knows it's you that's logging off. After clicking this command, Windows displays the Log Off Windows dialog box, which asks if you're sure you want to log off.

3. **Click Yes to log off. (If you change your mind, click No to cancel and return to the desktop.)**

   After you click Yes, Windows displays a new Enter Network Password dialog box.

4. **The new user should enter a user name and password to log back on to the network.**

Using Network Paths to Find Folders and Files

A *pathname* defines the route through the various directories and folders your computer must take to reach a folder or file. If you know the pathname for a certain file or folder, you can use that information to quickly jump to that file or folder. Determining the pathname of a file or folder on your own computer isn't that difficult. You simply start the pathname with the appropriate drive and then list the folders, with the outermost folder first. For example, if you stored your Pictures folder within your My Documents folder on your C drive, then the pathname would be C:\My Documents\ Pictures.

When you need to determine a pathname for a drive found on a computer somewhere else on the network, you must first list the computer and then the shared folders. Such a *network path* always begins with two backslashes (\\) to indicate that the drive is on another computer on the network.

If you're good at remembering pathnames, you can use them to jump immediately to the file or folder you want on your network. The Windows Explorer, My Computer, and My Network Places windows all have an Address bar near the top, where you can enter the pathname, press Enter, and end up where you wanted to go.

If you want, you can also get where you want to go on your computer network by using the Run dialog box, shown in Figure 5-1. Choose Start⇨Run, type the pathname in the text box, and press Enter. Windows then takes you immediately to the file or folder you want. For all this to work without a hitch, however, the other computer must be turned on, the folder you want must be a shared folder, and you have to have permission to access the folder.

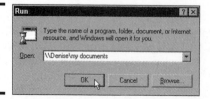

Figure 5-1:
Use a path
to access
another
computer.

Figure 5-2 shows the results of entering the path in the Run dialog box. The My Documents folder on Denise's computer opens for your use.

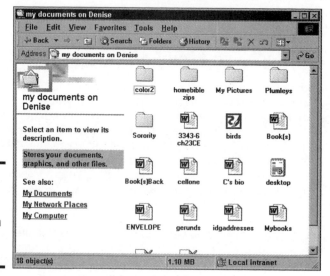

Figure 5-2:
Quickly
access a
folder if you
know the
path.

Mapping Drives

If you connect to a specific drive and folder on one of your networked computers every day (or even several times a day), you may find yourself wanting a shortcut. One option that may work for you involves *mapping drives,* where you assign a new drive letter (such as J, K, L, M, N or any other letter not currently in use) to the drive you're interested in.

Unfortunately, you can map only to one folder level. For example, you cannot map to \\Denise\my documents\My Pictures; you can only map to \\Denise\my documents. Every little bit helps, however, and you'll find that mapping drives can make your networking life easier.

To map a drive, follow these steps:

1. **Right-click the My Computer icon, and choose Map Network Drive.**

   The Map Network Drive dialog box appears, as shown in Figure 5-3.

Figure 5-3:
Use the
Map
Network
Drive dialog
box to map
a drive.

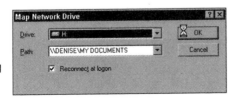

2. **In the Drive drop-down list box, choose a drive letter to represent the folder you're going to map.**

   Only available drive letters appear; you won't see drive letters already used for other drives (CD-ROM or hard drives, for example).

3. **In the Path text box, enter the network path to the folder or choose it from the drop-down list of available network resources.**

4. **Select the Reconnect at Logon check box if you want the mapped drive to connect automatically when you log on to the network.**

5. **Click OK.**

   The mapped drive is now stored with the other drives in My Computer.

If the folder to which you are mapping a drive has an assigned password, the Enter Network Password dialog box appears. The first time you connect to the drive, you can save the password in your password list (PWL file) by selecting the Save This Password in Your Password List option. From then on, Windows remembers the password and enters it for you when you log on.

Accessing a mapped drive

Accessing a mapped drive is as easy as mapping it. To access a folder on a mapped drive, follow these steps:

1. **On the desktop, double-click My Computer.**

   The My Computer window appears, as shown in Figure 5-4.

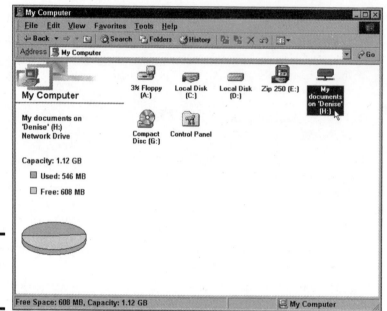

Figure 5-4:
Access the mapped drive.

2. **Double-click the mapped drive to display the contents of the mapped folder.**

3. **Open any file by double-clicking the appropriate file icon.**

Disconnecting a mapped drive

If you find that you are no longer using a mapped drive with any real frequency, you can easily delete it from your drives listing. In Windows terminology, this is known as *disconnecting* a mapped drive.

To disconnect a mapped drive, follow these steps:

1. **Right-click the My Computer icon on your desktop, and choose Disconnect Network Drive from the menu that appears.**

   The Disconnect Network Drive dialog box appears.

2. **In the list of drives, choose the drive you want to disconnect from.**

3. **Click OK to disconnect the network connection.**

Applying Quick Logon

As long as you always select the Reconnect at Logon check box in the Map Network Drive dialog box, your computer reconnects to any drives you have mapped whenever you log on to the network.

Reconnecting network drives takes time, however, and the more mapped drives you have, the longer it takes. Moreover, if a computer you're trying to connect to isn't turned on, Windows notifies you that it cannot map the drive and offers the option of reconnecting to the networked computer the next time you log on. Getting your computer started takes even longer when this complication happens.

You do have an option, however, of logging on more quickly. A *quick logon* ignores any network drive connections you may have set so that you can get on the network and start working immediately. Don't worry. You can restore these connections easily when you need them. All you have to do is double-click the mapped drive icon to connect the drive.

To set your computer for quick logon, follow these steps:

1. **Choose Start⇨Settings⇨Control Panel and double-click the Network icon.**

2. **On the Configuration tab, choose Client for Microsoft Networks from the network components list.**

3. **Click the Properties button.**

   The Client for Microsoft Networks Properties dialog box appears.

4. **In the Network Logon options box, choose Quick Logon.**

5. **Click OK twice to close both dialog boxes.**

It's best to choose a quick logon if the other computers in your network are not always going to be on. If you choose to restore network connections and a network computer isn't turned on, your computer will search for a long time before asking you to cancel the connection.

Browsing My Network Places

My Network Places is the Windows mini-program designed specifically for working with networked computers, folders, and other resources. When you first open My Network Places, all shared folders and drives appear on-screen, as shown in Figure 5-5. In addition, you have a couple other icons that help make your way through the network and all its resources. You don't have to enter a long pathname to get where you want to go.

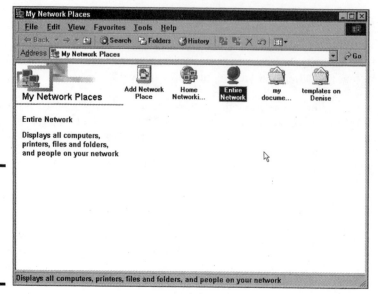

Figure 5-5:
Use My
Network
Places to
view
network
computers.

The Entire Network icon represents additional network printers and folders that are available to your computer. Double-click the icon to display additional resources.

To open My Network Places, double-click the icon on the desktop. To view any computer's contents, simply double-click the Entire Network icon, the workgroup name, and then the icon associated with that computer. All shared resources on the computer appear in My Network Places, as shown in Figure 5-6. If you like, you can change the view from large icons to small icons, list, or details by choosing the View menu and selecting the view you want.

Use the following methods to navigate through the My Network Places window and browse the networked computers:

✦ To open a folder, double-click the folder or select the folder and choose File➪Open.

✦ To move back to the previous window, click the Back button on the toolbar.

✦ To go forward again to the next window, click the Forward button.

✦ To move back to the entire network view, use the Address bar dropdown list.

✦ You can also use the Address bar to enter a path to a computer and folder(s).

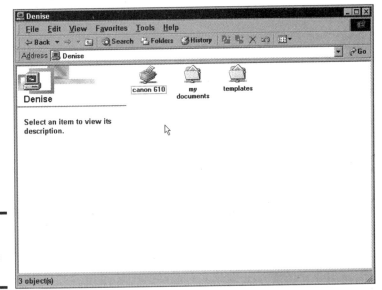

Figure 5-6:
View a
computer's
contents.

Working with Files and Folders in My Network Places

In addition to making it easier to keep an eye on all aspects of your network, My Network Places includes all the features and tools you're used to seeing in My Computer and Windows Explorer. You can rename or delete files and folders that you view in My Network Places, as well as create shortcuts from your desktop to the file or folder you're interested in anywhere on the network. You can cut or copy files and folders from one networked computer and paste them to another. If you want, you can also use the Search button on the toolbar of My Network Places to find files.

The files and folders must be shared, and the networked computer with which you're working must be turned on for you to be able to work with a networked computer's files and folders. If a password is required to access the folders, you must know that password.

Make sure that you ask or at least notify the owner of the files or folders before you delete, rename, or otherwise change the files and folders on a networked computer.

Finding files

Although you can use the Search command to find a networked folder, you do have to remember the folder's pathname. Sometimes a folder's pathname will escape you. You could browse the network searching for a file, but you can also quickly locate a file on another computer by using the Search feature in My Network Places.

To quickly locate a file on another computer using My Network Places, follow these steps:

1. **Double-click the My Network Places icon on your desktop.**

The My Network Places window appears.

2. **Double-click the Entire Network icon.**

3. **Double-click the workgroup icon.**

4. **Double-click the icon of the computer you're interested in.**

The computer's folders are displayed in a new window.

5. **Select the folder containing the file.**

6. **Click the Search button on the toolbar.**

The Search pane opens on the left side of the window.

7. **Click the Files or Folders link at the bottom of the Search pane.**

8. **Enter the name of the file or a word or phrase contained within the file in the Search For Files of Folders Named text box.**

9. **Click the down arrow on the Look In drop-down listing and browse to the folder on the network you want to search.**

You may have to use the Browse option at the bottom of the list to use an Explorer-like dialog box to maneuver to the networked computer and folder where the file may be located. In the list, you will find My Network Places, which will give the shared folders on the network.

10. **Click the Search Now button.**

Windows locates the file in the folder, as shown in Figure 5-7. You can open, print, copy, or otherwise work with the file in the Find All Files dialog box.

Creating a shortcut

If you often use a file or folder on another computer, you're not limited to mapping a drive to access that folder. You can also use My Network Places to create a *shortcut* on your desktop. The shortcut makes accessing the folder or file quick and easy.

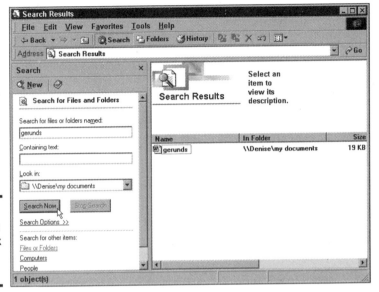

Figure 5-7:
You can use
My Network
Places to
find a file.

To create a shortcut, follow these steps:

1. **Open the networked computer in the My Network Places window.**

2. **Locate the folder or file you want to create a shortcut for.**

3. **Right-click the folder and choose Send To⇨Desktop (Create Shortcut) from the shortcut menu.**

Windows places the shortcut on your desktop.

The shortcut you create doesn't indicate that it's a shortcut to a network computer. For example, the shortcut name may be *Shortcut to My Documents.* You can, however, change the name of the shortcut to better identify it, such as *Denise's Documents.* To change the name of a shortcut, right-click the shortcut on your desktop and choose Rename. Then enter the name you want.

Creating, deleting, and renaming files and folders

My Network Places offers great opportunities to put your networking house in order. When you're inside My Network Places, you can create new folders, delete and rename files and folders, and do other housekeeping chores for any of your networked computers by using the same commands you used for your non-networked Windows computer. Using the familiar options under the File command (File⇨New⇨Folder, File⇨Rename, and File⇨Delete), you can now range far and wide over your network and clean house to your heart's content. Simply double-click the computer you want in the workgroup that you find after clicking the Entire Network icon in My Network Places list to access the computer, and then put your organizational talents to use.

Copying and moving files and folders

Another great housekeeping task involves copying, cutting, and pasting files between networked computers. My Network Places makes this job easy by relying on familiar commands from the standard Edit menu.

To copy or move a file or folder from a networked computer to your hard drive, follow these steps:

1. **Open the networked computer in the My Network Places window.**

2. **Locate and select the file or folder you want to copy or move.**

3. **Choose Edit⇨Copy, or Edit⇨Cut.**

4. **Click the down arrow beside the text box in the Address bar, as shown in Figure 5-8, to access a list of available computers on the network.**

5. **Locate and choose your computer in the My Network Places's computer listing. Select the folder you've chosen as the new home for your file and choose Edit⇨Paste.**

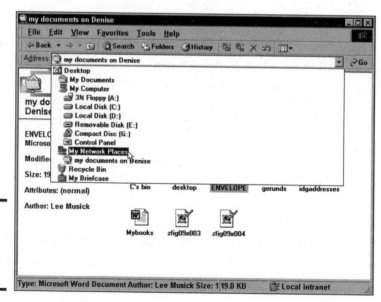

Figure 5-8:
Open
your own
computer's
hard drive.

Chapter 6: Printing on the Network

In This Chapter

✔ Sharing a printer

✔ Installing a network printer

✔ Managing the printer

✔ Getting the most out of your printer

In Windows, you can share any printer attached to a computer on the network as easily as you share a drive or folder. You simply designate the printer as shared (with the access type you feel is appropriate) and assign it a share name, and your local printer is now a network printer available to anyone on the network. As you may expect, you can also set a password on the shared device so that only someone who knows the password can use the printer.

In addition to designating a printer as shared, you must make sure that you have installed your printer's driver on all other networked computers. The printer's *driver* is the software program that enables the computer to communicate with the printer. Without it, computers on the network are blocked from using the network printer. Windows makes it easy for you to install drivers over the network, so don't worry about that for now.

Sharing a Printer

Somewhere on your network, you probably have at least one computer with a local printer physically connected to it. Your mission (should you choose to accept it) is to designate that local printer for network use. Here's how:

1. **On the computer with the local printer, choose Start⇨Settings⇨Printers.**

The Printers dialog box appears.

2. **Right-click the printer's icon and choose Sharing from the shortcut menu.**

The printer's Properties dialog box appears with the Sharing tab displayed.

3. **Choose the Shared As option to display the share options.**

4. **If Windows suggests a share name, you can either accept that name or enter a new one.**

   The share name is the name that displays in the My Network Places window.

5. **If you want, you can enter information about the printer in the Comment text box.**

   Listing the brand name or whether it's a color printer may be helpful. The comment also appears on the left side of the window in the My Network Places window when the printer is selected.

6. **If you want to control the use of the printer, enter a password in the Password text box.**

7. **Click OK to accept the changes and close the Printers dialog box.**

You can view a printer on the network via My Network Places, Windows Explorer, or My Computer.

Installing and Configuring a Network Printer

The one printer physically attached to your computer always acts as that computer's local printer. The trick now is to get this local printer to act as the printer for all other computers on the network. Designating a printer as shared is the first step, but you still have to install the network printer on each of your networked computers that will use it. Luckily, managing this feat isn't so tricky after all, if you let Windows do the work for you.

Installing a network printer

You use the same Add Printer Setup Wizard to install a network printer that you use to install a local printer. When you add a network printer to a printer-less computer on the network, however, the wizard copies the driver already installed on the computer with a printer and installs the driver to the printer-less computer for you. What's more, because you don't actually have a physical printer connected directly to the networked computer, you no longer have to bother selecting a port for the printer to use.

To install a network printer, follow these steps:

1. **Choose Start⇨Settings⇨Printers, and double-click the Add Printer icon.**

   The first Add Printer Wizard dialog box appears, telling you that the wizard will help you install a printer.

2. **Click the Next button to continue.**

The second Add Printer Wizard dialog box appears.

3. Choose Network Printer and click the Next button.

The next wizard dialog box appears.

4. Enter the pathname for the network printer.

If you don't know the pathname, you can use the Browse button to locate the computer for the network printer. If you then double-click the computer to which the printer is attached, you see a listing of attached printers that are designated as Shared. You may have to drill down through the workgroup name and then to the computer where the printer is installed to get to the printer name.

Figure 6-1 shows the Browse for Printer dialog box.

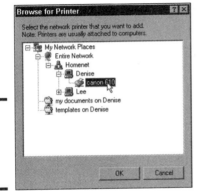

Figure 6-1:
Select the
printer you
want to
install.

5. Choose the printer and click OK. Then click Next.

6. You can enter a new name for the printer or accept the default. Also, choose whether to make the printer the default for your computer. Then click Next.

The wizard asks if you want to print a test page. You should always test the connection. The wizard sends a test page to the printer and asks if the page printed correctly.

7. If the page printed correctly, click Yes; if the page didn't print or had trouble printing, click No.

If you click No, the wizard displays the Print Troubleshooter to help you solve the problem.

After you install the network printer, the printer's icon appears in the Printers window.

Configuring the printer

You can configure any network printer any way you want; those settings apply only to that printer on your computer. Changes you make to the networked printer's properties on your computer don't affect the printer's properties on any other computer. You can configure the following options for a network printer by right-clicking the printer's icon in the Printers window. The shortcut menu that appears has these seven options:

✦ **Open:** Use this option to open the print queue. See the "Managing the Print Queue" section, later in this chapter, for more information.

✦ **Set As Default:** The most basic option you can set is whether the printer is your default printer or not. If you choose to make the printer your default, all applications on your computer automatically print to the default printer unless you specify a different printer with each job. If the Set As Default option is checked, the printer is set as the default printer. Clicking the option toggles this feature on or off.

✦ **Use Printer Offline:** Use this option if it makes sense to set up a number of print jobs without actually being connected (or *on-line*) with the printer. Maybe the computer attached to the printer isn't currently on, for example, but you still want to get your print jobs ready. You can then send them to the printer later, when the computer and printer are turned on.

✦ **Create Shortcut:** Use this option to create a printer shortcut. When you create the shortcut, the network printer appears on your desktop so you can print to it quickly and easily.

✦ **Delete:** Choose Delete if you want to remove the printer driver from your computer.

✦ **Rename:** Choose Rename to change the name of the printer on your computer. This option won't affect other computers on the network.

✦ **Properties:** Printer properties vary from printer to printer. Usually, you can change the paper size and orientation, set the resolution for graphics, or determine the type of fonts you want to use. If you're using a color printer, you may be able to set color options in the Properties dialog box (depending on the type of printer you own).

Managing the Print Queue

When you have a local printer attached to your computer, you are the master. You control all aspects of your printing. You can pause printing, you can rearrange the order in which the documents print, or, if you like, you can even cancel printing a document on a whim. When you print to a network printer not physically attached to your computer, all that power is taken away from you. All you can do is send your job to the printer and hope for the best. By using a network printer, you relinquish all control to the computer physically attached to the printer. To see what kind of control is involved here, look at the role of print queues in a networking environment.

The *print queue* is an area in which all print jobs to a specific printer wait to be printed. The print queue holds the jobs so that you can get on with your work in Windows while the network printer takes care of the printing chores. As the printer becomes available to print a job, the queue sends the jobs to the printer, one by one.

Usually, the print queue passes documents quickly to the printer. If several jobs are waiting in the queue or if the printer experiences a problem (out of paper, paper jam, or some similar catastrophe), the jobs wait in the queue until they can print. Depending on whether your computer controls the network printer or not, you may be able to use the print queue to manage some aspects of your printing jobs. Everyone, however, should be able to use the print queue to pause one of their printing jobs. This feature can be useful when you need to use special paper (such as a letterhead) for a printing job.

To open the print queue, choose Start⇨Settings⇨Printers to open the Printers window, and either double-click the Print icon or right-click the icon and then choose Open.

Following are the things you can do (or manipulate) when you control the network printer:

✦ **You can pause jobs in the queue.** You may want to change the printer's toner cartridge or insert special paper. To pause all print jobs, open the queue and choose Printer⇨Pause Printing. A check mark appears beside the command on the menu. To release the paused print jobs, choose Printer⇨Pause Printing again to remove the check mark.

✦ **You can delete jobs from the print queue.** You may want to delete the jobs in the queue to reset the printer. To delete all the print jobs from the queue, open the queue. Choose Printer⇨Purge Print Documents. All jobs are erased from the queue.

✦ **You can pause the printing of one document.** Suppose you really need that report to print immediately. Unless your job is first in the print queue, you have to wait. By using the power of the print queue, you can pause the printing of any document ahead of you in the queue and take your job to the head of the line. Simply open the queue and select the job you want to pause. Choose Document⇨Pause Printing. A check mark appears beside the job and the word Paused appears in the Status area of the queue. You can pause any job ahead of yours in the queue. When your job is finished, you can continue printing any paused job by choosing Document⇨Pause Printing again to remove the check mark.

✦ **You can cancel one print job.** If you want to cancel just one print job but let the others continue to print, you can select that job in the queue. Choose Document⇨Cancel Printing. Don't abuse this power, because canceling other people's print jobs tends to annoy them.

Although you can pause the current document that is printing, it's not a good idea. The printer may be in the middle of printing a page. If so, that page may stay there until you tell the printer to resume printing or someone manually form feeds the printer to eject the paper. Plus, many printers have a small amount of memory that could be holding some of the information to be printed. Be on the safe side. Pause any document that hasn't started printing, but let the current document finish.

You have much less control over your documents when you send them across the network to another printer, and you have no control over other users' documents on a network printer that isn't attached to your computer. To see how weak you actually are in these situations, consider the following:

✦ You cannot change the order of the jobs in the print queue. You can't even change the order of your print jobs in the queue.

✦ You cannot restart a printer that has been paused.

✦ You cannot cancel all print jobs in the queue.

However, you can control a few small things when printing to a network printer that is not connected to your computer:

✦ **You can pause the printing of one of your own print jobs.** Simply select the job in the queue and choose Document⇨Pause Printing. A check mark appears beside the command. To start printing the job again, select it in the queue and choose Document⇨Pause Printing to remove the check mark from the command.

✦ **You can cancel any of your own print jobs.** To do so, select the job in the queue and choose Document⇨Cancel Printing.

Optimizing Print Resources

You can do several things to optimize your printers and print services, whether the printer is a local or a network printer. These include the following:

✦ **Consider the speed of the printer before you purchase it.** For a home network, speed may not be a big concern; however, a network printer is used more often than a local printer, and a slow printer slows down your network considerably.

✦ **Make sure that you have the correct printer driver for your printer.**
Using a substitute driver or a driver close to but not quite the driver
you need may slow your printer. Use the manufacturer's driver if you
can't find the right one in Windows. Also, if you have a new printer, consider downloading an updated driver version from the Internet for your
printer.

✦ **Network connections affect printing over the network.** If your network
is slow — 1 Mbps or less, for example — printing over the network will
be slow, too.

✦ **Parallel port speeds are two to four times faster than serial ports.** If
possible, use parallel ports to attach printers to your computers.
Depending on the printer, using the USB port can also cause the computer hosting the printer to run slowly.

✦ **Keep your printer clean.** Be careful when cleaning inside the printer;
some parts are delicate. Maintain a cool and consistent temperature
around the printers as well; some components are sensitive to environ-
mental changes.

✦ **Watch how you store your printer paper.** For example, damp or wrin-
kled paper can damage your printer and cause frequent paper jams. Old
paper, heavier paper than your printer can manage, and cheap paper or
envelopes can also cause printer problems.

Chapter 7: Managing the Network

*M*anaging your network should be an easy job with a peer-to-peer network. All you really need to do is make sure everyone on the network can access their files and all other network resources they need in order to do what they want to do.

Of course, you are likely to run into problems from time to time. Keeping a notebook log about your network makes managing the network easier. Include network maps, a list of each computer's resources, configuration settings, and other details that help you quickly and easily find any information about your network as you need it.

Understanding Network Management

Following is a partial list of information you should log about your computers and your network:

+ For every computer on the network, list hardware and software; the operating system; the computer's manufacturer, model, and serial number; the monitor brand and specifications: keyboard type; mouse type; processor speed; RAM amount and type; size and type of hard drives; and so on. This information is useful when you want to upgrade or locate problems with your computers.

+ List protocols, IP address(es) if applicable, and other networking software information.

+ List networking hardware — network cards, cabling, connectors, hubs, and so on. Include brands, types, identification numbers, and any other information you need. List other information, such as IRQs of network cards, and note each user's name and password for the network.

+ List all drives, including sizes, brands, manufacturers, speeds, model, drivers, and so on — CD-ROM, Iomega Zip or Jaz drives, tape drives, and their shares (resources shared).

+ List all peripherals: printers, modems, scanners, and other equipment. Give the manufacturer, model, and any specifications on memory, ports, and cables for each peripheral.

+ List all applications on each computer, plus the licensing and sharing designations.

Keep all documentation in one area and keep a list of contact names and numbers for help, tech support lines, and so on. Keeping this information handy and up-to-date helps you with optimizing your network and troubleshooting problem areas.

Next, add to that log any problems you have and how you've fixed them. If you run into a problem with your network once, you'll likely run into it again at a later date. Having a log of those problems and solutions can help you later if the problem recurs.

Using NetWatcher

NetWatcher is a Windows application you can use on a network to monitor shared resources. You can view each user attached to a computer and the folders and files they're using. You can also disconnect a user, close a file, add a shared folder, view the shares on your own computer and on other computers (if you have the password), and more. You can also perform tasks on a remote computer after you open it in NetWatcher.

Configuring the computer for NetWatcher

To use NetWatcher, you must first allow remote administration on all computers on the network. Allowing *remote administration* on a computer means that any user is able to create, change, and monitor shared resources on that computer. However, Windows lets you assign a password to this process so that only a person who knows the password can perform the task. The person who knows the password can then monitor all other computers from any computer on the network.

To allow remote administration, follow these steps:

1. **Choose Start**➪**Settings**➪**Control Panel, and double-click the Passwords icon in the Control Panel.**

2. **Click the Remote Administration tab.**

3. **Select the Enable Remote Administration of This Server check box.**

4. **Enter the password and then enter it again to confirm it.**

5. **Click OK. Repeat these steps on any other computers on the network you want to allow remote administration on.**

In addition to allowing remote administration, you must allow file and print sharing, if you have not already done so. Open the Network icon in the Control Panel and click the File and Print Sharing button. Make sure that both check boxes are selected. For more information, see Book IX, Chapter 3.

Starting and quitting NetWatcher

When you start NetWatcher, any connections to your computer appear in the window. As additional users or connections are made, the window displays those connections as well. You can also update the view at any time to make sure that all connections are showing. To open NetWatcher, choose Start⇨Programs⇨Accessories⇨System Tools⇨NetWatcher.

If NetWatcher is not installed on your computer, open Control Panel and click Add/Remove Programs. Select the Windows Setup tab and select System Tools. Click the Details button and put a check mark in the box next to System Tools. Click OK twice. Have your Windows CD handy, just in case.

Figure 7-1 shows NetWatcher monitoring a user on the network. The program lists the folders that are shared: the C drive, the color printer, and the Zip drive; it also shows two documents the other user has opened.

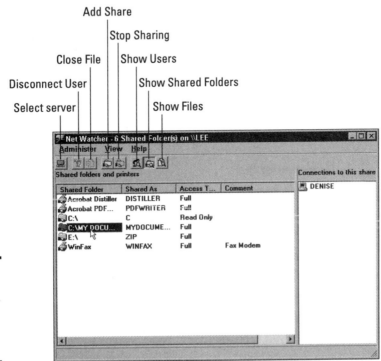

Figure 7-1:
Use
NetWatcher
to view
shared
resources.

NetWatcher includes various tool buttons you can use to control it. Table 7-1 explains the tool buttons.

Table 7-1	NetWatcher Tool Buttons
Tool Button	*Description*
Select Server	Choose the computer you want to monitor. You must know the remote administration password.
Disconnect User	Disconnect any user from the selected share. The user loses all unsaved data.
Close File	Close any shared file, even when the user is connected. The user loses all unsaved data.
Add Share	Designate a folder or resource as shared.
Stop Sharing	Designate a folder or other resource as no longer shared.
Show Users	Displays a view of connected users, their computers, the number of open shares and open files, the amount of time they've been connected, and the names of the shared folders.
Show Shared Folders	Lists the shared folders' paths, names, and access types. You can also view which computer is attached to each shared folder.
Show Files	Lists the open files, the share used, and the user connected to the file. You can also see the access type of the open file.

Selecting a server

NetWatcher refers to all computers on the network as servers, even in a peer-to-peer network. The server, in this case, is the NetWatcher server software. You can view your own shared resources as well as other computers on the network, as long as you know the password set in the Remote Administration dialog box.

To select a server, follow these steps:

1. **Open NetWatcher.**

2. **Choose Administer⇨Select Server.**

   The Select Server dialog box appears.

3. **Enter the server's name or use the Browse button to locate the computer.**

4. **Click OK.**

   The Enter Network Password dialog box appears.

5. **Click OK.**

   The selected server's shares appear in the NetWatcher window.

After you've accessed a server using the password, Windows adds it to your password list. You only have to enter the password once to access each server.

Disconnecting a user

You can disconnect a user from the server you're monitoring at any time. When you disconnect the user, however, you should make sure that the user has closed all open files from that computer. You disconnect a user in Show Users view.

To disconnect a user, click the Disconnect User button. A warning dialog box appears. Click Yes to continue. NetWatcher doesn't warn the user when you disconnect him or her.

Closing a file

As with disconnecting a user, you must be careful when closing a file in use. You should warn a user before you close the file so the user can save changes. If the user doesn't save changes, he or she loses any unsaved data.

To close a file, select the Show Files view. Select the open file and click the Close File button. A warning dialog box appears. Choose Yes to close the file. Again, NetWatcher doesn't warn the user.

Working with shared folders

You can share folders on any server computer to which you're attached with NetWatcher. You can open any drive and share any folder; the remote administration password gives you the permission you need to perform these tasks. To share a folder, follow these steps:

1. **Open NetWatcher and the computer you want to monitor.**

2. **Change to the Shared Folders view.**

3. **Choose Administer⇨Add Shared Folder.**

   The Enter Path dialog box appears.

4. **Enter the path or use the Browse button to locate the desired folder on the server computer.**

5. **Click OK.**

   The Share dialog box appears.

6. **Choose Shared As and enter the share name and access type.**

7. **Click OK to close the Share dialog box.**

You can stop sharing a folder by selecting the folder and then clicking the Stop Sharing Folder button. You can view a shared folder's properties by selecting the folder and choosing Administer⇨Shared Folder Properties.

Using WinPopup

WinPopup is a Windows program that enables you to chat with others on the network. You can send messages to one person or to all network users. You can also set options to play sounds or otherwise notify you when someone sends a message. WinPopup is a simple program you can use to notify the others on the network, for example, that you have to disconnect someone from your computer or that the printer is turned off.

Locating WinPopup

No icon or program listing exists for WinPopup, but you can create a shortcut for the program in Windows Explorer. WinPopup is located in the Windows directory. Locate the program icon (WinPopup), right-click it, and choose Send To⇨Desktop (Create Shortcut) from the shortcut menu that appears. You may also want to place WinPopup in your StartUp folder so that it starts automatically when you start your computer.

Sending messages

To use WinPopup, you must start the program and leave it running. For you to contact anyone on the network, that person must also be running WinPopup. You can send a message to one user by entering the user's name or the computer name. You also can send a message to all users by entering the workgroup name.

To send a message, follow these steps:

1. **Open the WinPopup window.**

2. **Click the Send button (the envelope).**

   The Send Message dialog box appears.

3. **In the To area, choose either the User or Computer option or the Workgroup option and then enter the appropriate user or workgroup name in the text box below the options.**

   Choose multiple names to send the message to more than one person.

4. **Enter text in the Message area, and click OK.**

   WinPopup sends the message and displays a dialog box telling you the message was sent successfully.

5. **Click OK. You can minimize the WinPopup window if you want.**

Receiving messages

When you receive a message, the WinPopup window pops up on your screen, as shown in Figure 7-2. Notice that the sender sent the message to everyone on the network; the name of the workgroup is HOMENET. When you receive a message, you can choose to discard it by clicking the Delete button.

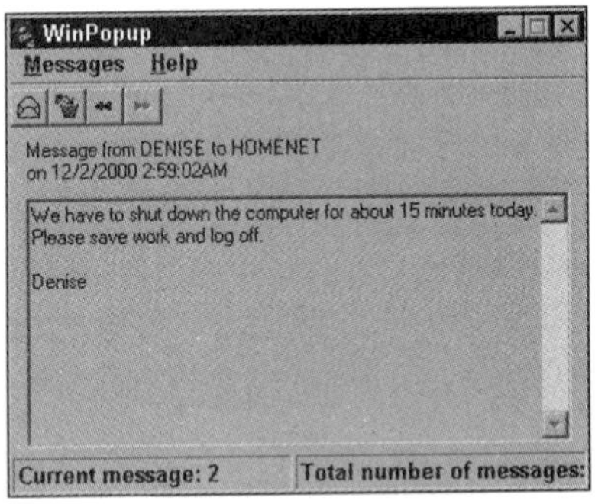

Figure 7-2:
You can send a message to everyone on the network.

Changing options

You can change a few options in WinPopup. For example, you can change whether or not to play a sound when a new message arrives, whether to always display the WinPopup window on top of all other windows, and whether to pop up the window when you receive a new message.

To change options, choose Messages➪Options or press Ctrl+O. Select (or deselect) as many options in the Options dialog box as you like, and then click OK.

Index

Index

1

Notes

Notes